P9-CDX-850

HOLLYWOOD ON THE COUCH

HOLLYWOOD ON THE COUCH

A CANDID LOOK AT THE OVERHEATED LOVE AFFAIR BETWEEN PSYCHIATRISTS AND MOVIEMAKERS

STEPHEN FARBER AND MARC GREEN

William Morrow and Company, Inc. • New York

Copyright © 1993 by Stephen Farber and Marc Green

All rights reserved. No part of this book may be reproduced or utilized in any form or by any means, electronic or mechanical, including photocopying, recording, or by any information storage or retrieval system, without permission in writing from the Publisher. Inquiries should be addressed to Permissions Department, William Morrow and Company, Inc., 1350 Avenue of the Americas, New York, N.Y. 10019.

It is the policy of William Morrow and Company, Inc., and its imprints and affiliates, recognizing the importance of preserving what has been written, to print the books we publish on acid-free paper, and we exert our best efforts to that end.

Library of Congress Cataloging-in-Publication Data

Farber, Stephen.
   Hollywood on the couch : a candid look at the overheated love affair between psychiatrists and moviemakers / Stephen Farber and Marc Green.
      p.   cm.
   ISBN 0-87795-998-6
   1. Psychoanalysis and motion pictures. 2. Motion picture actors and actresses—California—Los Angeles—Mental Health.
   3. Psychotherapists—California—Los Angeles—Professional ethics.
   I. Green, Marc, 1943–   . II. Title.
   PN1995.9.P783F37   1993   93-18992
   791.43'019—dc20   CIP

Printed in the United States of America

First Edition

1 2 3 4 5 6 7 8 9 10

BOOK DESIGN BY LINEY LI

In memory of my mother, Zelda Hantman Farber
—S.F.

For Ellen, Alec, and Matthew
—M.G.

PREFACE

When we let it be known that we were writing a book about the symbiotic relationship between psychiatry and the movies, we were met with a few raised eyebrows and many knowing chuckles. The mutual infatuation that exists between movie people and the psychiatric community is no secret to Hollywood insiders. A few wags wondered how we would be able to limit ourselves to a single volume.

Certainly we are not the first to see a link between the two worlds. Freudian interpretations of various films abound, and whole treatises have been written about the image of the psychiatrist in cinema. While we, too, are concerned with the influence of psychoanalysis on filmmaking and with the portrayal of the psychiatric profession in movies, our primary interest in this book is to illuminate the off-screen relationships that have galvanized those on-screen dramas.

In the course of writing an earlier book about family dynamics in Hollywood, *Hollywood Dynasties* (1984), we were struck by the central role psychiatrists had played in the lives of so many prominent moviemakers. Actors, producers, directors—and their spouses and children as well—had all spent time on the analyst's couch. Psychotherapy was one of the shared rituals that distinguished households in Hollywood from those in other prosperous American communities. As they evangelized for psychoanalysis, the Hollywood elite led the way in making the Freudian science—with all its contemporary offshoots—an integral part of American life.

It was not simply through stories told on-screen that Hollywood promoted psychiatry. Anyone who reads popular magazines or watches television talk shows knows how common it is for movie stars to gush about their life-altering experiences on the couch. Such candid revelations by America's idols have helped give legitimacy to psychotherapy, making it not just acceptable but chic.

Despite the intimacy of these public confessions, we knew that the matter of patient-doctor confidentiality could present impediments. It's one thing for patients to gab about their analysis, but what would the therapists disclose? We soon discovered that many (though by no means all) doctors who deal with movie folk are not above a little boasting. In a town where success is measured by the company one keeps, even psychiatrists who conscientiously avoid hobnobbing with their patients sometimes reveal more than they should about their celebrity clientele.

One interview we conducted with an eminent psychoanalyst is especially telling in this regard. The doctor, an orthodox Freudian with a massive curriculum vitae and an international reputation, spent much of the afternoon railing against his Los Angeles confreres for the sins of social climbing, publicity seeking, "parading their patients in public."

"That is anathema to some of us," he scoffed. "You will *never* hear that so-and-so was a patient of mine, not from the patient and certainly not from me!"

An hour or so into our conversation, during a less heated discussion of old movies, the son of a legendary producer was mentioned in passing. "Oh, yes," the doctor mused, turning to his wife, who happened to be seated beside him on the sofa. "Isn't he the one I saw?"

The wife, not so oblivious to the cloud of irony now hanging over the room, tittered nervously and tried to change the subject. But the doctor, still wrestling with his faltering memory, abruptly cut her off.

"Yes," he said, "he came to me when he was in trouble. I saw him briefly."

An equally amusing incident illustrates another fact that we soon came to appreciate: While psychiatrists may be prohibited from talking about their patients, they are often quite eager to talk about each other.

A prominent TV producer suggested that we contact his former analyst, a man apparently notorious for his social connections. We called the doctor, explained the nature of our book, and set up an interview. "I have many hilarious stories to tell you about my colleagues," he assured us.

Shortly before the scheduled meeting, he called to make sure that the "terms" were understood.

"My regular fee is one hundred fifty dollars per hour," he said.

We replied, somewhat sheepishly, that authors do not generally pay for interviews.

"Well," he grumbled, "that's my rate."

Whether for reasons of ethics or economy, the doctor's "terms" were declined.

Most of those whom we approached were neither so ridiculous nor so venal. They generously shared ideas, reminiscences, information, and insights. For assistance and cooperation of various sorts, we gratefully acknowledge the contributions of Jane Attias, Jay Presson Allen, Nancy Allen, Woody Allen, Julie Andrews, Gerald Ayres, Dr. Leon Balter, Dr. Samoan Barish, Thomas Baum, Ann Bayer, Robert Benton, Tony Berlant, Dr. Toni Bernay, Julian Blaustein, Dr. Jacqueline Bouhoutsos, Marshall Brickman, Cyril Carlson, Saul Chaplin, Ruth Charney, Dr. Dorothy Colodny, Glenn Close, Martha Coolidge, Frank Corsaro, Mart Crowley, Eudice Daly, Michael Dempsey, Bruce Dern, Dr. Michael Diamond, Faye Dunaway, Dr. S. Mark Doran, Blake Edwards, Jill Eikenberry, William Fadiman, Peter Feibleman, Karl Fleming, Dr. Susan Forward, Dr. Erika Freeman, Lelda Gelman, Dr. Margaret Brenman Gibson, Dr. Arnold Gilberg, the late Edith Mayer Goetz, Dr. Roderic Gorney, Hildi Greenson, the late Dr. Martin Grotjahn, Nancy Hardin, Valerie Harper, Goldie Hawn, Bill Hayward, Brooke Hayward, Dr. Melvin Heller, the late Audrey Hepburn, Dr. Joshua Hoffs, Tamar Simon Hoffs, Celeste Holm, Harry Horner, Dr. Christine Hradesky, the late Charles Kaufman, Dr. Lorraine Kaufman, Dr. David Kessler, the late James Kirkwood, Dr. Samuel Klagsbrun, John Kohn, Larry Kramer, Jonathan Krane, Julie Kurlander, the late Dr. William Laczek, Sherry Lansing, Arthur Laurents, Frances Lear, Ernest Lehman, Dr. Norman Levy, Dr. Peter Loewenberg, Sidney Lumet, Dr. Melvin Mandel, Christopher Mankiewicz, the late Joseph L. Mankiewicz, Tom Mankiewicz, Janet Margolin, Dr. Judd Marmor, Paul Mazursky, Daniel Melnick, Jeff Melnick, Nicholas Meyer, Dudley Moore, Hunter Murtaugh, Pat Newcomb, Walt Odets, Sonya Schulberg O'Sullivan, Linda Palmer, Gail Parent, Arthur Penn, the late Anthony Perkins, Abraham Polonsky, Michael Pressman, Ju-

dith Balaban Quine, Marcella Rabwin, Ann Rabinowitz, Dr. Leo
Rangell, Robert Redford, Mort Reed, Gottfried Reinhardt, Susan
Rice, Dr. Arnold Richards, Jason Robards, the late Dr. Alexander
Rogawski, Dr. Steven Roos, Winifred Rosen, Dr. Leonard Rosen-
garten, Howard Rosenman, Leo Rosten, Dr. Theodore Rubin, Dr.
Janice Rule, Theresa Russell, Dr. Penelope Russianoff, Sara Rykoff,
Barry Sandler, Dr. Andrea Schalman, Julian Schlossberg, Budd
Schulberg, Joel Schumacher, David Seltzer, Daniel Selznick, Artie
Shaw, Dr. Lee Shershow, Evelyn Silvers, Stephen Sondheim, Dr.
Philip Solomon, Susan Strasberg, Kim Townsend, Marty Gwinn
Townsend, Jack Valenti, Trish Van Devere, Dr. Milton Viederman,
Judy Walker, Robert Walker, Jr., Dr. Martin Wasserman, Henry
Weinstein, Dr. Harvey Weintraub, Dr. Louis Jolyon West, Dr. Mil-
ton Wexler, and Dr. Christopher Zois.

In doing research for the book, we relied on articles, documents, and archival materials contained in numerous special libraries, including the Margaret Herrick Library of the Academy of
Motion Picture Arts and Sciences; the Biomedical and University
Research Libraries of the University of California at Los Angeles;
the Oral History Collection of Columbia University; and the libraries of the New York Psychoanalytic Association, the Los Angeles
Psychoanalytic Institute, and the Southern California Psychoanalytic Institute.

Our agent, Candace Lake, has been a steady source of sound
advice. Deborah Weaver provided expert legal counsel. We are especially grateful to our editor, Liza Dawson, who spurred us on with
patience and good humor. She and Mercer Warriner assisted
greatly in focusing our thoughts. To Ellen Wilson Green, thanks for
her continuing encouragement, and for much more.

CONTENTS

PROLOGUE: UNDER THE BIG TOP

"A LOT OF PROFESSIONALS ARE CRACKPOTS," proclaims the neon sign that greets the arriving guests at the industrial-chic offices of Chiat-Day, Los Angeles' trendiest ad agency. For tonight only, the vaulted plywood-and-sheet-metal interior of the cavernous structure has been adorned with helium balloons, crepe-paper parasols, and gaudy gimcracks evocative of Main Street at Disneyland. But the crowd attending this particular gala is far more elite than the collection of also-rans who might show up for the Magic Kingdom's Night of 1,000 Stars.

Internationally renowned architect Frank Gehry, who planned the striking redesign of the converted drapery factory for his pal Jay Chiat, pauses at one of the hot-dog carts to chat with some of the local artists—Ed Moses, Tony Berlant, and Robert Graham—whose canvases and sculptures command top prices at the galleries on Melrose Avenue. Off in a corner activist-rocker Jackson Browne engages in an intense tête-à-tête with First Daughter Patti Davis. Peter Falk slouches against the Reebok advertising display, shooting the breeze with a pair of composers, Henry Mancini and Quincy Jones. Directors Sydney Pollack and Mark Rydell are comparing notes by the popcorn stand as a couple of Creative Artists agents hover nearby. Another leather-jacketed filmmaker, Blake Edwards, and his wife, Julie Andrews, trade pleasantries with political moneybags Max Palevsky. They all turn to gaze as the ageless star Jennifer Jones sweeps into the room with her son, Robert Walker, Jr.

After distributing a few dry kisses, Jones approaches the evening's honoree, a tall, silver-haired gentleman in a white cardigan sweater, white slacks, and a bright red tie. Who is this *éminence grise?* A recently knighted thespian, a studio potentate, or perhaps a visiting dignitary from Washington? No, Dr. Milton Wexler is a psychoanalyst, and his friends and patients are here to celebrate the double occasion of his eightieth birthday and the twentieth anniversary of the scientific research organization he created, the Hereditary Disease Foundation.

If not certifiable crackpots, most of the high-powered professionals in the room have at least undergone a few rounds of psychotherapy with Dr. Wexler. Frank Gehry and his artist friends venerate the analyst as a creative muse. Patti Davis credits Wexler with empowering her to tell the dirty truth about her parents, Ronald and Nancy Reagan, in a blistering memoir that exposed her father's aloofness and her mother's cruelty. Jennifer Jones, a fifty-year devotee of psychoanalysis, found her way to Wexler's couch following a dramatic suicide attempt. She was rescued after throwing herself into the surf north of Malibu; Wexler guided her through her recovery and into her third marriage to billionaire industrialist and art collector Norton Simon. The Simons have been active in bankrolling numerous philanthropic causes, including Wexler's own foundation.

Wexler and his patients tour the extensive photo exhibit set up to commemorate his long career—a lifetime of mingling with artists and writers, movers and shakers. One snapshot that particularly tickles the guests shows Lillian Hellman plopped in the analyst's lap.

Finally the partygoers head toward the giant birthday cake at the rear of the room, where Elaine May is about to make the formal presentations. Like many of the other guests, May is something of an analytic junkie. Known for the satiric salvos that she and Mike Nichols aimed at psychoanalysis in their innovative comedy act in the late 1950s, May was also at the center of one of the biggest scandals in New York psychoanalytic circles. In 1963 she married her own psychiatrist, Dr. David Rubinfine. Immediately afterward Rubinfine was stripped of his position as training analyst at the New York Psychoanalytic Institute. He hightailed it to Los Angeles, where he linked up with Milton Wexler and a group of other maverick shrinks. The reclusive May almost never entertains at glitzy Hollywood parties, but because of her affection for Wexler, she agreed to act as his M.C. on circus night.

"Some of you may not know that Milton is not only a respected screenwriter but also an analyst," May begins joshingly, going on to tweak Wexler about the poor reviews he received for *The Man Who Loved Women* and the box office failure of his subsequent feature film *That's Life!* (Both screenplays were cowritten by Wexler and his patient, Blake Edwards.) When the laughter subsides, May continues, "Maybe there are one or two people here who are not Milton's patients. But everyone who's known him has come away a little better."

Wexler ambles to the podium on the arms of his two daughters. He thanks the throng of generous donors and remarks that from this benefit alone, his foundation will net $1.5 million. When Wexler announces the take, Sydney Pollack leads the group in thunderous applause.

Then Julie Andrews, Carol Burnett, and Sally Kellerman come up to croon "Happy Birthday" to Milton, and the beaming octogenarian cuts into his cake—an oversized profiterole designed especially for the occasion by Claes Oldenburg. Munching their slices of the Oldenburg original, the show-biz nabobs return to their schmoozing.

The idea of a roomful of celebrity patients feting their analyst might seem like the quintessence of California kookiness, something out of a comedy by Paul Mazursky—or Blake Edwards. And indeed, most traditional Freudian analysts sternly disapprove of the jumble of professional and social contacts between Dr. Wexler and his star patients, as well as their financial involvement in his charitable foundation. But the strictly clinical relationship between patient and analyst considered obligatory elsewhere has seldom prevailed in the movie colony. Treating the Hollywood aristocracy, psychiatrists have often overstepped the conventional boundaries, insinuating themselves into all aspects of their patients' lives.

Of course those boundaries were never so firmly entrenched as the purists pretend. Freud himself was more than a little star-struck. Although he wrote papers advocating a formal distance between doctor and patient, he was not above socializing with his favorite analysands. For example, Princess Marie Bonaparte, the descendant of several of Europe's royal families, became not only one of Freud's pet patients (he gave her two hours a day) but a friend and acolyte who contributed vast sums of money to his research and publishing ventures.

Several of Freud's most distinguished disciples also basked in the celebrity of their patients. When Otto Rank was practicing in Paris, he established a salon of writers and artists that included Henry Miller and Anaïs Nin. Rank psychoanalyzed Nin and also enlisted her to work as his private secretary and to rewrite his books in more sparkling prose.

Prominent psychoanalysts have long chafed at the cloak of secrecy demanded of their work; they have yearned for the same premiums available to successful professionals in other fields—not just financial perks but public recognition and choice social contacts. And as a number of recent contretemps indicate, psychiatrists continue to be compromised by their desire to reap personal rewards from their intimate associations with the wealthy and the well connected.

In 1986 a lawsuit was filed against one of Chicago's most illustrious analysts, George Pollock, who was at the time president of both the Chicago Institute for Psychoanalysis and the American Psychiatric Association. Pollock was sued by the son of one of his deceased patients, Anne P. Lederer, who left the bulk of her five-million-dollar estate to a psychiatric research institute administered by Dr. Pollock. Mrs. Lederer had also established a fat personal trust for Pollock, which paid him fifty thousand dollars a year, and another trust that paid thirty thousand dollars a year to members of his family. Anne Lederer's son charged that the crafty analyst had brainwashed his mother and robbed him of his inheritance.

Mrs. Lederer, the widow of a Chicago physician, initially came to see Pollock in 1969 because she was suffering from depression. He put her on antidepressants and advised her on many personal matters, including the revision of her will. Dr. Larry Strassburger, a psychiatrist at Harvard Medical School, reviewed Mrs. Lederer's medical records on behalf of her son and concluded that Pollock had prescribed enough drugs to make his patient "psychologically habituated and physically dependent." Her son's attorney summed up the patient-doctor relationship with a melodramatic flourish: "She gave him her mind and he took her pocketbook." Ultimately Pollock agreed to settle the lawsuit out of court and forked over a reported one million dollars to his patient's son.

Equally discomfiting to the psychiatric establishment was the case of Dr. Robert Willis, who pleaded guilty to securities and mail fraud for using inside information derived from therapy sessions with Joan Weill, the wife of Wall Street financier Sanford Weill. In

1981, when Weill arranged for the acquisition of Shearson Lehman Hutton by American Express, Weill's wife mentioned the impending merger to Willis during one of her analytical sessions. Willis quickly bought 2,100 shares of Shearson stock before the news was made public; he bagged $43,700 within three weeks. Five years later Mrs. Weill confided to Willis her anxiety at the prospect of moving to San Francisco, where her husband had been offered the presidency of the troubled BankAmerica Corporation. Dr. Willis promptly called his broker and bought more than 10,000 shares of BankAmerica stock. Once again the psychiatrist profited handsomely, netting more than $27,000. Not only was he fined $150,000 and sentenced to 600 hours of community service for his crime, but his ex-patient Joan Weill slapped him with a $5 million lawsuit, claiming that she had suffered "great personal distress and anguish" as a result of her doctor's betrayal.

The most highly publicized scandal involved a lust for glory rather than money. In the summer of 1991, *The New York Times* reported in a front-page article that a new biography of the poet Anne Sexton, who committed suicide in 1974, drew heavily on information provided by Sexton's psychiatrist, Dr. Martin T. Orne. Dr. Orne not only granted an interview to the author, Diane Wood Middlebrook, but gave her the tapes of his private sessions with Sexton. (Sexton was also alleged to have had sexual relations with another of her psychiatrists, Dr. Frederick J. Duhl.) Orne defended himself in an op-ed piece for the *Times,* claiming that he was only fulfilling his patient's unspoken wish. "In the judgment of all who knew her well," Orne wrote, "Anne definitely would have wanted the tapes released exactly as was done. . . . Sharing her most intimate thoughts and feelings for the benefit of others was not only her expressed and enacted desire, but the purpose for which she lived. Privacy was of no concern to her."

Of course Sexton was not around to dispute the good doctor. But other psychiatrists lashed out at Orne's self-serving claims. "A patient's right to confidentiality survives death," Dr. Jeremy A. Lazarus, the chairman of the ethics committee of the American Psychiatric Association, declared bluntly. Leonore Tiefer, clinical associate professor of psychiatry at Montefiore Medical Center in New York, offered her own evaluation of why Orne shared the tapes with Sexton's biographer: "Therapists have needs, like everyone else, and unfortunately, sometimes their needs for recognition or accomplishment are not satisfied unless people know all about the famous people they are treating."

Despite the rigorous self-scrutiny that is supposed to render psychiatrists above temptation, these secular priests are far from infallible—as the cases of Pollock, Willis, and Orne make clear. But tendencies toward self-enrichment and self-aggrandizement that may have always been inherent in the practice of psychiatry were magnified under the blinding lights of Hollywood.

Nowhere else was psychiatry embraced with such giddy enthusiasm. It has been suggested that actors are prime candidates for psychotherapy because of their massive insecurities, unstable sense of identity, and hunger for applause. Some authorities contend that creative artists in general display a greater tendency toward depression, manic depression, hysteria, and other psychological disorders than the population as a whole. Whether or not performers and filmmakers are more emotionally distraught than other individuals, the pressures of their careers would certainly intensify whatever anxieties they might already have.

Given the tremendous instability of the film business, where fortunes rise or fall with every hit or flop, it is not surprising to find movie people flocking to psychiatrists for solace. And perhaps it would have been unreasonable to expect their therapists to resist the chance to cozy up to the world's most seductive and glamorous profession. Dr. Charles Wahl, a practicing analyst for over forty years, has written a definitive essay, "Analysis of the Rich, the Famous and the Influential," in which he recalled one patient, a leading actor, who told him that he had made little progress with his two previous psychiatrists because they "were more like friends than doctors. They fawned on me, seemed to want to know me as a friend and one of them even asked me for an autograph for his daughter."

Many stars, on the other hand, welcomed such truckling behavior. Accustomed to having battalions of lackeys indulge their every whim, they invited their analysts to join the entourage. Before long the shrinks were acting as agents without portfolio, meddling in studio politics to cut deals for their patients. A few doctors even used their contacts to pursue a second career of their own—as actors, screenwriters, or producers. The strict proprieties of what Freud called an impossible profession proved to be even more impossible to maintain in Hollywood, a place where analysts and artists swoon in mutual adoration and cavort under the big top together.

1. O PIONEERS!

In 1909, the greatest of the pioneer filmmakers, D. W. Griffith, arrived in southern California, enticed by the promise of eternal sunshine that had already drawn a cluster of fledgling movie companies to a sleepy suburb called Hollywood. That same year, on the other side of the American continent, an equally enterprising visionary was doing his best to promote another of the new century's most promising inventions.

G. Stanley Hall was an exuberant intellectual with a taste for novelty and a flair for showmanship. A psychologist by training, Hall had gained prominence (and some notoriety) as the author of primers introducing Americans to the avant-garde ideas about childhood sexuality and adolescent development then percolating in Europe. As the first president of Clark University in Worcester, Massachusetts, Hall had embarked on an ambitious campaign to bring distinction to his young institution. He wanted to make Clark the rival of Harvard as a center for the study of psychology in the United States, and he had already invited a number of illustrious European authorities to Worcester to deliver lectures.

To celebrate the twentieth anniversary of Clark's founding, Hall decided to present an honorary degree to the most brilliant of the maverick European doctors whose works he had come to champion. By 1909 Sigmund Freud's controversial theories of psychoanalysis had won a small but zealous following that extended well beyond his native Vienna. Within the psychiatric establishment, however, Freud was still dismissed as a charlatan. His revolutionary treatises were branded "pornographic stories" and his therapeutic methods derided as "mental masturbation."

But to G. Stanley Hall, Freud was an unsung hero. By publicly heralding his idol's genius, Hall shrewdly determined that he could also seize the international spotlight for his budding university. Nor was the auspiciousness of the moment lost on his fifty-three-year-old visitor from Vienna. Accepting an honorary Doctor of Laws degree from Clark, Freud described the accolade as "the first official recognition of our endeavors." The five lectures he delivered for the occasion, an elegant distillation of his scientific theories, were warmly received by audiences that included the anarchist firebrand Emma Goldman, as well as America's most distinguished psychologist-philosopher, William James, who had made the trip out from Harvard to pay his respects to the father of psychoanalysis. The entire experience was, Freud would later write, "a great success."

That this triumph should come in "prudish America" was at once exhilarating and ironic. Freud had long considered the United States a puritanical backwater, wholly inhospitable to any serious reevaluation of human sexuality and hopelessly fixated on the almighty dollar. He referred to America as Dollaria, and he regularly disparaged its inhabitants for their preoccupation with amassing wealth (the primary sin of anal-retentive adults). Nonetheless he was clearly moved by his enthusiastic reception at Clark. "In Europe I felt like someone excommunicated; here I saw myself received by the best as an equal," Freud wrote in his autobiographical notes. "It was like the realization of an incredible daydream, as I stepped to the lectern at Worcester."

In the ensuing decades psychoanalysis developed a vogue in the United States that was never matched in Europe. "The number of people who would read, let alone fully grasp, esoteric texts like *Beyond the Pleasure Principle* or *The Ego and the Id* was bound to remain small," Freud's biographer Peter Gay has pointed out. "Yet his name, and his photograph showing a stern, carefully dressed elderly gentleman with penetrating eyes and the inevitable cigar, became known to millions."

American press lords turned Dr. Freud into a household name by associating him with all things darkly "abnormal" or shockingly sexual. They may have reduced his complex theories to a string of catchy slogans, but they realized that even the crudest summaries of his scandalous views could titillate readers—and sell papers. The frenzy reached an apogee of sorts in 1924, when the flamboyant publisher of the *Chicago Tribune*, Colonel Robert McCormick, offered to pay Freud $25,000 if he would come to Chicago and "psychoanalyze" Nathan Leopold and Richard Loeb on the eve of their murder trial. The sensational story of precocious youths bent on committing the perfect crime had tabloids across the nation vying for new angles. Cold-blooded homicide, performed by a couple of well-to-do young Jews, motivated only by some ill-defined compulsion to prove themselves superior to ordinary mortals, and shrouded in a veil of homoerotic intrigue—here was an ideal puzzle for the Viennese mind doctor to unravel. The *Tribune* printed McCormick's proposal with much fanfare, but Freud declined the invitation without comment.

Yellow journalists weren't the only ones attempting to exploit Freud's growing fame in America. The same year that Colonel McCormick invited Freud to Chicago to probe the criminal psyche, one of Hollywood's top producers asked him to illuminate the mysteries of romance. Samuel Goldwyn, an itinerant glove salesman who had struck it rich as the premier impresario of high-toned entertainment, epitomized the parvenus who had taken over the motion picture industry. Most of the early moguls sought to aggrandize themselves and the new movie medium by snaring prestigious writers and intellectuals as scenarists. Goldwyn had already gone to England in an effort to hire H. G. Wells (who turned him down) and George Bernard Shaw (who had him for tea, but also said no). Undaunted by these rejections, the insatiable culture vulture aimed his talons toward Vienna. As he set sail for Europe in the fall of 1924, Goldwyn informed a reporter for *The New York Times* that he intended to offer the famous Dr. Freud $100,000 to assist in devising "a really great love story." According to the reporter, "Love and laughter are the two ideas uppermost in Samuel Goldwyn's mind in producing pictures," and so he would ask "the expert in psychoanalysis to commercialize his study and write a story for the screen, or come to America and help in a 'drive' on the hearts of this nation."

A later story in a Viennese paper quoted Freud's terse reply to the producer's request for a meeting: "I do not intend to see Mr. Goldwyn."

Goldwyn and his fellow moguls may have tried to capitalize on Freud's racy ideas, but they were initially wary of psychoanalysis itself, a practice as alien and inscrutable to them as voodoo. Introspection was certainly not their strong suit, and Freud's candid emphasis on sexuality was hard to reconcile with their own deep-seated puritanism. "To the patriarchs of Hollywood, psychoanalysis seemed to be quite radical, and they were extremely conservative, in the tradition of the pre-Israel Jews who succeeded in business," says Sonya Schulberg O'Sullivan, who grew up in one of the town's more freethinking households. "The women, on the other hand, were always more sympathetic."

None of these women was more receptive than O'Sullivan's mother, Adeline Jaffe Schulberg, the sister of the powerful agent Sam Jaffe, and the wife of pioneer producer B. P. Schulberg. B.P.'s production of *Wings* was honored with the first Academy Award as best picture of 1928, and among the early moguls—a band of rag peddlers, junk dealers, and song pluggers—he stood out as an erudite man of letters. Among the moguls' wives, Ad Schulberg was the intellectual trendsetter, determined to elevate the cultural level of her nouveau-riche neighbors. A voracious reader with a vast library that contained five shelves devoted to virtually every volume written by Freud and his followers, Ad drew on the theories of child development spawned by Freud and advanced by John Dewey to spearhead the city's first "progressive school." She also organized a women's group called the Friday Morning Club, which sponsored lectures by visiting scholars, including the famous psychoanalyst A. A. Brill and the slightly infamous sexologist Havelock Ellis. Inside her stately Hancock Park mansion, moviemakers and analysts would regularly rub elbows at lavish dinner parties and intimate soirees.

"Ad was responsible, if anyone was, for introducing the whole subject of psychoanalysis to Hollywood," says her son, novelist and screenwriter Budd Schulberg. "She was into everything very early— psychoanalysis, suffragettes, birth control." His sister, Sonya Schulberg O'Sullivan, notes that in sounding the trumpet for Freud, their mother was not just thumbing her nose at the Hollywood patriarchs but transcending her own humble roots. "It's interesting that in that group of women involved in studying and promoting psychoanalysis, Mother was the only one who hadn't 'graduated college,' as she still sometimes said," O'Sullivan observes. "What she had, though, she shared with many immigrant Russian Jews: an almost violent desire to learn, improve, progress. She was so excited, so exhilarated, by the idea of the unconscious, the idea that people could be changed, *improved*, that children could grow up with free minds, undamaged personalities, that women could admit their sexuality, control their lives. It didn't matter that she got it all mixed up— Coué mixed with Freud mixed with Adler mixed with Watson mixed with Dewey. It was a new continent, and she was simply an explorer who couldn't tell the tribes apart."

In the 1920s the movie capital was fast becoming a magnet for other men and women on the cutting edge—scintillating wits and innovative artists who were genuinely excited by the possibilities of the brand-new film medium and who were also intrigued by the boldest ideas and social programs of the time. But there was an even larger contingent of dabblers and hangers-on, who would jump aboard any bandwagon without having the foggiest idea of where they were headed. Eager to sample every heralded new prescription for self-improvement, the denizens of Tinseltown embraced profound ideas and nutty rantings with equal fervor.

Indeed, at the same time that Ad Schulberg and her cultural cohorts were discovering Freud, signs plastered on storefronts in Hollywood or along the boardwalk in Santa Monica advertised PSYCHOANALYSIS, READINGS for three dollars or five dollars—from qualified astrologers. Los Angeles was already turning into a fabled haven for pseudosciences and oddball sects. "This lovely place, cuckoo land, is corrupted with an odd community giddiness," wrote the editors of *Life* in 1930. "Nowhere else do eccentrics flourish in such close abundance. Nowhere do spiritual and economic panaceas grow so lushly. Nowhere is undisciplined gullibility so widespread." Five years later the journalist Bruce Bliven visited Los Angeles and told his readers back east, "Here is the world's prize collection of cranks, semi-cranks, placid creatures whose bovine expression shows that each of them is studying, without much hope of success, to be a high-grade moron, angry or ecstatic exponents of food fads, sun-bathing, ancient Greek costumes, diaphragm breathing and the imminent second coming of Christ."

If psychoanalysis appeared to be little more than another of these crackpot creeds, that may have had something to do with its less than auspicious origins in "cuckoo land." Mary Wilshire, the wife of a millionaire land developer for whom one of the city's main arteries is named, is credited with introducing the natives to the pastime back in 1914, shortly after she returned from Zurich and an encounter with Carl Jung. Mrs. Wilshire was never known for her piercing insights into the libido or the collective unconscious, but she did gain a reputation for her habit of seeing clients while dressed in white Grecian robes and floral diadems. Virtually indistinguishable from the assorted swamis, mind readers, graphologists, and masseurs sprouting up in the environs, she gave credence to Ernest Jones's early admonition to Freud that America's infatuation with psychoanalysis was based largely on its newness and was "absurdly superficial."

It wasn't until 1927 that the first trained Freudians, Thomas and Margrit Libbin, arrived on the scene. But they, too, were lightweights. Thomas Libbin had gone to Vienna to study with Freud and, according to his wife, "somehow along the way got lost and ended up with Adler." Eventually he did receive a certificate from the Freudian institute, though he always seemed to his colleagues to be something of a scatterbrained dilettante. (As one of his fellow analysts caustically summed him up, "I had the impression this is a man who has a great future behind him.") Libbin's wife, Margrit, was not even certified as a lay analyst, although she did manage to build a more substantial practice than her husband—mainly through patient referrals from a friend who worked in Los Angeles Juvenile Court.

The Libbins were soon joined by David Brunswick, the scion of a wealthy New York family who had the distinction of having been analyzed by Freud in Vienna. David's older brother, Mark, and sister-in-law, Ruth Mack Brunswick, were among Freud's tiny handful of American pets, but the younger Brunswick never enjoyed the same privileged status. In fact, Freud treated David Brunswick with an attitude bordering on contempt. "What have you and Ruth done to me?" he groaned to Mark, about a month into David's analysis. "Your brother is the most boring person!" David had dropped out of medical school before coming to Vienna and, at Freud's urging, resumed his medical studies while living there. But he disappointed his mentor by quitting once again and heading for Los Angeles, where he hung out his shingle as a lay analyst in 1930. Although he capitalized on his connection to Papa Freud, his ties to the master were shaky at best.

Freud had long supported lay analysis as a way of spreading his theories beyond the world of medicine to the brightest minds in the humanities and social sciences. The "laymen" who had been attracted to psychoanalysis in Vienna and Berlin were almost invariably distinguished scholars, highly accomplished in some non-medical discipline. Hanns Sachs, for example, was a brilliant lawyer, and Ernst Kris a renowned art historian. The same could not be said of most lay practitioners in the United States, and especially not in Los Angeles, which was already developing a reputation as a mecca for fake healers of various stripes.

By the mid-1930s many of the illustrious analysts who had studied with Freud were presiding over thriving fiefdoms in America: A. A. Brill in New York, Hanns Sachs in Boston, and Franz Alexander in Chicago. The Los Angeles group felt they needed a leader of similar stature, so they asked Sachs and Alexander for recommendations. After sifting through the list of available candidates, the two graybeards nominated Ernst Simmel. A former president of the Berlin Psychoanalytic Society, an internationally recognized authority on war neuroses, a political activist who served as chairman of the Society of Independent Socialist Physicians, a personal friend and confidant of Freud and recipient of one of the prized signet rings reserved for his inner circle, Dr. Simmel would add luster to a town groping desperately for respectability in the competitive world of American psychoanalysis.

Unfortunately, Simmel was as much a naïf as he was a sage. The psychoanalytic clinic he had created in the Berlin suburb of Schloss-Tegel went bankrupt under his inept management. A devout socialist, Simmel had insisted that everyone who worked at the place—including the nurses and janitors—be psychoanalyzed, leaving little time to treat the wealthy *Burgermeisters* who might have been able to subsidize the enterprise.

Dr. Martin Grotjahn recalled a telling incident that occurred while he was being analyzed by Simmel in Berlin. The two men were in the study of Simmel's home when their analytic session was interrupted by an urgent telephone message: "Bring the chart of the sanitarium," the voice on the phone implored. That was a previously agreed-upon code from an informer within the Gestapo. "Please get up, we have to run," Simmel told his young patient. "He was five foot two, and I towered over him by four inches," Grotjahn remembered. "We couldn't go out the front door because that is where the Nazis were coming in. So we escaped through the backyard—I, helping my little analyst out the kitchen window and over a fence.

"But," Grotjahn added, "Simmel didn't believe the Nazis meant it, so he came back."

By the time he received the invitation to come to Los Angeles in 1934, the reality of the Nazi threat had finally sunk in. But it soon became clear to his new colleagues that Herr Doktor was still dangerously naive. As the designated dean of the southern California analysts, it was Simmel's job to welcome newcomers to the fold. One day a gentleman by the name of Louis Montgomery turned up at Simmel's door. He declared that he had letters of introduction from the revered A. A. Brill, and Simmel graciously received the fellow. Montgomery proceeded to build a practice and deliver lectures to the newly formed psychoanalytic study group, throwing around terms like *transference* and *resistance* with convincing authority. He even contributed a paper to a psychoanalytic journal on the relationship between neurosis and acne. When Montgomery applied to become a training analyst, however, his pedagogic methods proved to be somewhat unorthodox. He wanted his students to hide in a closet and eavesdrop on the sessions he conducted with his patients. When word of this technique got back to Simmel, he called up A. A. Brill in New York to make some discreet inquiries. Brill, it turned out, had never heard of Louis Montgomery. He was an impostor, without a smidgen of training. In fact, his true vocation was hairdresser. A posse of other analysts was promptly assigned to run the ringer out of town (though he did return years later and opened up a beauty salon).

Tales like that one did not exactly enhance the prestige of the Los Angeles analytic contingent. Despite the erratic manner in which it was practiced, however, psychoanalysis struck a chord with the Hollywood elite. Writers were particularly enthralled by the new science, and not simply because it was faddish. Many of them had actually read Freud, and they appreciated his trenchant insights into the hidden motives of human behavior. Freud himself had noted the affinity he felt with great novelists such as Dickens and Dostoyevski, and for screenwriters intent on unlocking the secrets of character, psychoanalysis offered a precious key. Not only could it relieve their personal anxieties, it could give them a framework for creating more psychologically penetrating stories.

Contemplative and verbal by nature, writers were ideal candidates for the "talking cure." Although analysis was a protracted, rigorous, sometimes painful process, it could seem like a welcome relief to the scribes who toiled in Hollywood. Lying on the couch, recounting their dreams, free-associating about their sexual hangups and career crises, they savored the experience as a mix of intensive self-examination and luxurious self-indulgence. After a day of knuckling under to ignoramuses on the studio lot, beleaguered writers like Clifford Odets and Ben Hecht could retreat to their analyst's chamber and—for one precious hour—become the center of the universe.

Among the very first to partake of the ritual were two remarkable brothers, Herman and Joseph Mankiewicz. Unlike the crass moguls who sprang from the ghettos of Eastern Europe, the Mankiewiczes came from the same cultivated German-Jewish stock that had produced so many of the lions of the psychoanalytic movement. Their father, Franz Mankiewicz, was a professor of linguistics at New York's City College. He served as editor of the *Modern Language Quarterly* and founded a luncheon round table for German-born intellectuals that included Albert Einstein. Through their father the Mankiewicz children had been exposed at an early age to artists, academicians, scientists, and political thinkers.

Both Herman Mankiewicz and his younger brother, Joseph, had lived in Berlin after graduating from Columbia; they were familiar with the currents of psychoanalytic thought swirling about the German capital in the 1920s. When he returned to New York after stints as a foreign correspondent in Germany and as a publicist for Isadora Duncan, Herman worked as a theater critic for *The New York Times* and *The New Yorker*. But the excitement of writing for the screen and the promise of big money drew him west.

In 1926 he arrived in Hollywood and embarked on a career as one of the industry's wittiest and highest-paid writers. He was also one of its most inveterate boozers and gamblers. It was not hard to grasp the source of his problems. Growing up with a highly critical, demanding father, Herman was always made to feel inadequate. He despised himself for his Hollywood hackwork, but was unwilling to sacrifice the monetary rewards that supported his extravagant lifestyle. Many of his best screenplays—including his most famous, the one he wrote with Orson Welles for *Citizen Kane*—reflected his ambivalent feelings about talent and intellect squandered in the chase for wealth and fame.

Herman Mankiewicz was the archetypal example of a gifted writer ruined by Hollywood, though he certainly abetted his own downfall. Even the act of writing *Citizen Kane* was self-destructive—and patricidal as well. Mankiewicz had been a frequent guest of William Randolph Hearst and Marion Davies at San Simeon, and when Mankiewicz drew on that personal relationship to skewer them ruthlessly in his cinematic *roman à clef*, Hearst's sense of betrayal intensified his wrath. The vindictive press baron attempted to block the release of *Citizen Kane*, and failing that, he lambasted Mankiewicz repeatedly in his newspapers after the inebriated writer had the misfortune to smash his roadster into another car directly in front of Marion Davies's Beverly Hills Mansion.

Herman's growing bitterness was exacerbated by his professional rivalry with his younger brother, Joseph, whose fortunes rose while his own declined. Over time Herman's drinking grew more excessive, and the once irrepressible bon vivant sank into a debilitating depression. According to his biographer, Richard Meryman, he originally believed that his alcoholism was bound up with some neurotic condition, and that led him to seek relief in psychoanalysis. At first Herman rather enjoyed his visits to the eminent Dr. Ernst Simmel, calling him "my caretaker" and "the *Obermacher.*" His drinking abated for a while, and he was delighted with the progress he was making. When he noticed friends slinking in or out of Simmel's office, he would taunt them with an embarrassingly loud greeting—and once suggested that they all honor their mahatma by wearing sweatshirts emblazoned with the letter *S.*

Simmel was an expert on addictive behaviors, and he firmly believed in the therapeutic benefit of confining alcoholics to sanitariums, like the one that he had established in Schloss-Tegel. Since there was nothing quite so elaborate as that in Los Angeles, the doctor recommended that Mankiewicz check into a small psychiatric rest home on the outskirts of Pasadena. Herman promptly phoned his wife and reported that he was being carted off to the loony bin. When she asked him what she should pack, he replied, "Just my cocked hat and a little birdseed."

Clearly Herman Mankiewicz was too irreverent to surrender unconditionally to the ministrations of his little *Obermacher* from Berlin. After two years of pouring out all his tortured feelings about his overbearing father and his upstart brother, he was the same neurotic, self-destructive alcoholic he had been when he started. According to his nephew, Tom Mankiewicz, Herman finally went to Simmel and announced that he was quitting.

"You're a quack," he cheerfully told the analyst. Then he could not resist a final jab. "Oh, and by the way," he called back, just as he was walking out the door, "I never mentioned that I have a sister, and I hate her too!"

Another of Dr. Simmel's celebrity patients was the composer George Gershwin, but his brief treatment came to a far more tragic end. In 1937 Gershwin found himself in the employ of Samuel Goldwyn, who was still trying to combine high art and lowbrow schmaltz, just as he had when he invited Sigmund Freud to create a delirious love story for the crowd at the Roxy. *The Goldwyn Follies* was to be the producer's *pièce de résistance,* mixing jubilant vaudeville, arias by Helen Jepson of the Metropolitan Opera, choreography by George Balanchine, and a score of haunting melodies by the great Gershwin.

Working for Goldwyn was a living hell. Despite the producer's utter ignorance of musicology, he brashly offered his critiques of Gershwin's compositions. "I had to live for this," Gershwin moaned to his friend S. N. Behrman, "that Sam Goldwyn should say to me: 'Why don't you write hits like Irving Berlin?' "

The composer soon fell victim to acute nausea and pounding headaches. Knowing the pressure he was under, his friends dismissed the disorder as "Goldwyn phobia." At last a team of physicians was summoned to examine him at home, but they failed to discover any abnormalities. One neurologist did later note that Gershwin was suffering from photophobia, an extreme sensitivity to light, though he could offer no explanation. As the composer's condition deteriorated, he would sit by himself for hours, with the curtains drawn to block out the painful sunlight.

The specialists concluded that Gershwin's problems were psychosomatic and recommended that he see a psychiatrist. Finally, at the urging of his New York analyst, Gregory Zilboorg, he sought a consultation with Ernst Simmel. Gottfried Reinhardt, a producer and the son of the legendary theatrical director Max Reinhardt, knew both Simmel and Gershwin. He remembers visiting the composer in the darkened living room of his palatial home in Beverly Hills. "Gershwin had gone for years to psychoanalysts in New York and also in Los Angeles," Reinhardt remarks. "Simmel was the only one who recognized what was wrong. He knew it was not depression but a brain tumor."

By the time Simmel's diagnosis was confirmed, however, the malignancy was inoperable. Given the nature of Gershwin's cancer and its location deep inside the brain, it is doubtful that the tumor could ever have been removed. But many of Gershwin's friends and associates were bitter that the psychoanalyst brought in to treat his "nervous" condition had not been consulted earlier.

Simmel's medical expertise was unassailable. But under his desultory leadership, Los Angeles analysts were still too disorganized to establish a fully accredited training institute of their own. Their activities had to be supervised by Karl Menninger, who operated a famed clinic and training center in Topeka, Kansas. Already recognized by the American Psychoanalytic Association, the Topekans could "colonize" in such outbacks as California, and Dr. Menninger was more than happy with the arrangement. Not only did it give him added prestige within the ruling councils of the psychoanalytic movement, it allowed him to make regular visits to Los Angeles, where he loved to frequent Hollywood parties. He was even introduced to his second wife, Jeanetta Lyle, a lay analyst who had worked briefly in the film business, during one of these trips to the Coast.

Menninger was well known for courting movie people, especially those who could come up with hefty donations to support his clinic and research foundation. While he liked to contrast the "innate modesty" of his own Kansas kin to the "flamboyant, bombastic egotism of Californians," he took an almost voyeuristic interest in ogling glamorous stars. In 1937 he wrote a letter to his father describing his lunch at the swank Vendôme restaurant, "which is quite a popular movie star retreat." Menninger noted that "we saw quite a few of them at close range. . . . Trying to see these movie stars in the flesh is a game here and seems to be related to the impulse to see Mama getting out of the bathtub in the nude. Anyway they all do it and we follow suit." Menninger also enjoyed mixing it up with producers and moguls, who generated a lot of business for his clinic. Studio heads who had met the jovial doctor at Vendôme or the Brown Derby were soon shipping their mentally unbalanced performers off to Topeka for treatment.

Los Angeles shrinks were generally fond of "Dr. Karl," but most of them bristled at the bush-league status that his supervision perpetuated. Their prospects for independence improved with the arrival in 1938 of Otto Fenichel, a German analyst of impeccable credentials. Unlike Simmel, whose personal quirks overshadowed his scientific achievements and whose dictatorial manner irked his colleagues, Fenichel combined erudition with charisma. As the author of *The Outline of Clinical Psychoanalysis*, the definitive textbook in the field, Fenichel had a sterling reputation, and his presence quickly turned Los Angeles into a magnet for aspiring analysts eager to sit at his feet. His analysands, who included Herman Mankiewicz's brother, Joseph, were among the most talented members of the creative circle, and his leadership promised to give the Los Angeles analytic community a respectability it had never quite attained under Simmel. But Fenichel's career was abruptly cut short, ending on a poignantly ironic note that rivaled the teary melodramas his

Hollywood patients were creating for the screen.

Because so many lay analysts with questionable qualifications were also entering California at the time, the State Board of Medical Examiners began to call for more stringent sanctions. Earl Warren, then the state attorney general, issued a ruling that psychoanalysis was a medical profession, which meant that analysts lacking a medical license could not practice without supervision. The decree had a chilling effect, not just on less reputable lay analysts, but also on medically trained analysts like Fenichel and Simmel whose European medical degrees were not recognized in the United States.

Faced with this predicament, Fenichel could find only one solution. Although he was a world-renowned physician, he decided to go back to work as an intern in order to meet the qualifications set down for an American M.D. degree. Ralph Greenson, the most celebrated of his disciples—a cadre that came to be known as "the Fenichel boys"—has described the irony of the situation. "The idea seemed preposterous," Greenson said. "Otto Fenichel, the famous psychoanalyst and teacher, was going to give up his practice and his teaching and spend a year as an intern. Not only did he seem too big a man for so menial a task; he was almost forty-eight years old, big and heavy, and in no physical condition for night duty and emergency calls."

Fenichel's travails were typical of the indignities inflicted on many European analysts who fled to America in the 1930s. Men who had been revered in Berlin or Vienna were summarily cut down to size by the xenophobic, self-protective American medical establishment. Through sheer determination and innate talent, most of these refugees eventually managed to recoup their standing and rise to the top of the heap in their adopted land. The tragedy of Fenichel's life is that his struggle never bore fruit. In January 1946, at the age of forty-eight, he died of a ruptured aneurysm, probably brought on by the stress of his grueling internship.

Within a year Ernst Simmel was also dead, and the Los Angeles analysts were left without their two most influential leaders. Dr. Martin Grotjahn, who had come to Los Angeles at those two men's behest and who, like most of the other new recruits, had been enchanted by the city's ideal weather, described his sense of shock: "My God, I thought, maybe southern California is not such a happy climate after all."

Before they died, Simmel and Fenichel did manage to lay the groundwork for the formation of the Los Angeles Psychoanalytic

Institute, which finally opened its doors in 1946. But almost immediately, internal dissensions within the new organization tore it apart. American-born analysts chafed at the arrogance and rigidity of their European colleagues, who saw themselves as Freud's true disciples. The Freudian hard-liners resented the younger analysts, many of them trained by the humanist Franz Alexander in Chicago, who wanted to experiment with less formal, more empathic forms of therapy. Alexander advocated a more "spontaneous" relationship between analyst and patient than the strict Freudians endorsed.

At meetings of the new institute the members got into furious arguments over fine points of psychoanalytic theory. But they also engaged in petty personal attacks, tossing out vicious bits of gossip about their rivals. Simmel became so agitated during some of these acrimonious debates that he suffered attacks of angina. "If anything killed him, it was those fights," Ralph Greenson noted.

Following Simmel's death in 1947, a power vacuum developed within the new institute, and two pugnacious women rushed in to wrestle for the crown. One of them was the lone surviving member of the Berlin-bred triumvirate who had dominated the scruffy group of Los Angeles shrinks in the late 1930s and early 1940s. Her name was Frances Deri, and it was she who intended to carry on as defender of the Freudian faith, holding the line against the upstarts.

Madame Deri, as she was called, was an imposing dragon. She emigrated to Los Angeles in 1936, two years after Simmel, whom she had assisted at Schloss-Tegel. The wife of an art historian, she had been analyzed by the eminent Hanns Sachs as well as by Karl Abraham, the first physician to practice psychoanalysis in Germany. Her own background, however, was somewhat less august. Before becoming an analyst, she had been a practical nurse.

From her haughty demeanor one would never have guessed that her early years had been spent in so humble an occupation. Armed with a quick mind and a sharp tongue, she had risen quickly through the analytic ranks; though she had never earned an M.D. degree, she served as head training analyst at the Prague Institute before coming to the United States. Of her decision to settle in California she once recalled, "I wanted to go to the United States and I wrote that to Hanns Sachs who was then in Boston. And he wrote back and said, 'I can give you the names of two cities. One is very ugly but you can earn, very quickly, very much money. That is Detroit. The other is very beautiful. You can't earn so much money so quickly, but you'd live in a beautiful spot.' So I chose. I chose Los Angeles, of course, and I've never regretted it."

If Los Angeles failed to provide Mme. Deri with immediate monetary rewards, it did at least offer her the opportunity to become an instant doyenne. Her ties to the old guard ensured plenty of referrals, and even without a medical degree she was clearly a force to be reckoned with. One of those upon whom she made an indelible impression was a young actress from New York named Celeste Holm, who met her in the late 1940s. Holm was a friend of Dr. Lawrence Kubie, an influential New York analyst with many patients among the Broadway theatrical set. When she came to Hollywood, Kubie recommended that Holm—who was depressed about a series of failed love affairs—consult Mme. Deri. "She looked just like a Buddha," Holm recalls. "She had that German hairdo that's really a Marine cut—straight across the top. She smoked cigarettes with a long wire holder in that German way. I came in to see her and her first words were, 'You don't need to be entertaining here.' "

Within the newly formed psychoanalytic institute, however, Mme. Frances Deri soon found herself at loggerheads with an American-trained M.D. named May Romm. Dr. Romm had attracted attention from the day she arrived in Los Angeles in 1938. To the young Budd Schulberg this feisty little newcomer from New York had much in common with his own redoubtable mother: "They were both warm Jewish mothers on the one hand, and pretty sharp, practical people on the other." Schulberg's sister Sonya also has a vivid recollection of Dr. Romm: "I have the clearest impression of how she looked, smiling a tough smile, neatly but dowdily dressed— ambitious. Ambition is something that anyone who grew up in the picture business easily recognizes."

The enmity that developed between May Romm and Frances Deri was palpable. When Ernst Simmel died, Deri even tried to bar Romm from attending his funeral. Romm, who made sure everyone knew of her own medical training, took to calling her adversary *Madame* Deri (with special emphasis on the title, in order to stress both Deri's nonmedical status and her hoity-toitiness). For her part the regal Deri scoffed at Romm for failing to grasp Freud's theories of childhood sexuality, and she dubbed Romm's allies the May Company, after a less-than-elegant local department store.

After several years of infighting, it became clear that a single institute could not contain two such powerful, contentious women, and so the Los Angeles Institute split into two hostile factions. One by one the analysts-in-training had to declare their allegiance, with the traditionalists falling into line behind Mme. Deri and the so-called reformers following Dr. Romm into the wilderness.

The final candidate to announce his decision was Alexander Rogawski, a cultured Vienna-born physician who had given up a thriving medical practice in Connecticut to become a psychoanalyst in California. "I kept delaying the decision," he recalls. "I hoped that maybe the parents wouldn't have a divorce."

But the differences proved irreconcilable. The feuding lady analysts could not coexist. As Dr. Rogawski wryly puts it, "In no beehive is there space for two queens."

In 1950, twenty-three years after Freudian analysis arrived in Los Angeles and a scant four years after it was legitimized with an institute, a second institute had to be formed to accommodate the disaffected. People whose vocation was to mend other people's lives seemed hopelessly incapable of mending the rifts in their own. Spiteful and suspicious toward one another, many of them began looking for approbation and friendship from others—including those star patients who might make their own reputations shine more brightly.

2. THE QUEEN OF COUCH CANYON

As psychoanalysis began to win converts in Hollywood, it was only a matter of time before the latest passion among the movie folk would be enshrined on the silver screen. Infatuated with the Freudian cure, those in the vanguard wanted to spread the gospel, and what better way than through the movies themselves?

In the 1940s dozens of psychiatric melodramas tumbled off the assembly line. But it was not simply a desire to proselytize for analysis that sparked the craze. The character of the psychiatrist added a novel twist to a durable movie genre: While unraveling a conventional whodunit, the screen analyst could also elucidate *why*. Freudian analysis was not unlike detective work. The analyst helped the patient dissect his dreams and unlock buried secrets in order to discover why he might be paralyzed by phobias or enslaved by powerful compulsions. Couldn't this inherently dramatic process be combined with the thrills and chills that movies had provided since the days of Pearl White? Of course the drawn-out process of analysis would have to be radically simplified for the masses, but filmmakers had no trouble convincing themselves that a breezy synthesis of Freudian concepts could make for dynamic entertainment with an *au courant* edge.

Of all these analytically inspired films of the forties, none made a stronger impression than *Spellbound*. It was also the one with the most sophisticated array of talent, both behind and before the camera. The producer was a two-time Oscar-winner, David O. Selznick, the megalomaniacal showman who was the driving force behind the most popular film of all time, *Gone With the Wind*. To direct, Selznick selected Alfred Hitchcock, who had made *Rebecca* for him and was already cementing his reputation as the Master of Suspense. The screenwriter was the brilliant and versatile Ben Hecht, who was himself a devoted analysand. To create dream sequences that would be both psychologically astute and visually mesmerizing, Selznick hired the surrealist painter Salvador Dali, who was known for utilizing bold, sexually charged imagery in his work. All in all, *Spellbound* was going to be as classy a production as Hollywood had ever seen.

By the time *Spellbound* began shooting in late 1944, several movies—including *Now, Voyager, Blind Alley,* and *Kings Row*—had already had psychiatrists as important characters; even Fred Astaire played a tap-dancing shrink in *Carefree.* Usually the movie psychiatrist was an omniscient father figure like the sage played by Claude Rains in *Now, Voyager.* The novelty of *Spellbound* was that its protagonist was a female analyst, to be played by one of Selznick's discoveries, the radiant Ingrid Bergman. In many ways *Spellbound* was a standard woman-in-jeopardy thriller, but it revitalized a hoary genre by presenting Bergman's character as a brilliant sleuth, who sorted through the psychological clues presented by her disturbed patient, Gregory Peck. She interpreted his dreams—replete with phallic ski poles and Cyclopean eyes—and solved the mystery of his neurosis with the aplomb of Sherlock Holmes.

Centering the story on a female psychiatrist may have seemed like a clever gimmick, but to David O. Selznick, it was more than that. He had actually been treated by a woman analyst, and he hired her to work on *Spellbound.* Among the technical credits for the movie, one finds an unusual title: "Psychiatric Advisor, May E. Romm, M.D." Physically there was little resemblance between Bergman's Dr. Constance Peterson and the real Dr. Romm. Bergman was statuesque, blond, and beautiful, whereas Romm was short, dark, and plain. But Selznick knew that there were also powerful similarities between the Bergman character and the real-life psychiatrist who was serving as his consultant.

Like the trailblazing heroine of *Spellbound,* Dr. May Romm, who was fifty-four at the time the movie was released, was a woman who had triumphed in a man's world. Romm was not the first analyst to make an impact on Hollywood. But she was unquestionably its first real power player; in a career that spanned almost forty years, her influence sometimes rivaled that of the actors, directors, and producers she was treating.

In two crucial respects Romm set the pattern for other popular Hollywood shrinks. As the first psychiatric consultant to a major motion picture, she directly influenced what audiences saw on screen. And she was also the first analyst to be embraced as a crony by the Tinseltown rajahs. She partied with her patients, and in the process became a role model for the star-struck analysts who hoped to follow in her footsteps.

If May Ginsburg Romm relished her life among the smart set in Beverly Hills, perhaps that is because it was such a long distance from the humble place she started out. She was born in 1891 in the Russian village of Vitebsk, the same town where the painter Marc Chagall was born. Her full Russian name was Minyetta Belyoshi Ichi Minya M'Alke, and she sometimes liked to present herself as a poor, simple immigrant. She may have been poor, but she was never simple. Fierce determination was the hallmark of her character. At the age of twelve she arrived in America—at a painful disadvantage. On the ocean crossing she contracted typhoid fever, which made her temporarily deaf. "Can you imagine being in a strange country and not being able to hear the language?" asks her daughter, Dr. Dorothy Colodny. "She used to tell me what she remembered seeing was people sticking their tongues out at each other. At first I didn't understand that, but then I remembered that there is no 'th' sound in Russian. What she was seeing was people saying 'the.' " When she recovered her hearing, Colodny reports, "my mother learned the language in a flash. Pretty soon she was giving English lessons."

It was but the first of many victories. When it came time for her to attend college, May decided she would become a doctor. It was possible then to earn a medical degree without an undergraduate diploma, and in 1915 she completed a four-year program at the Women's Medical College of Pennsylvania. Many of the other students were missionaries who intended to put their medical training to use in the jungles of Africa or South America. "They were a tough bunch," says Dorothy Colodny. "Most of her generation of women doctors were energetic, courageous, and terribly aggressive. They had to be. Their attitude was 'Out of my way, here I come.' " Romm fit right in: This Yiddishe Mama from a Russian shtetl displayed the same missionary zeal as her Christian classmates. A tiny, steely woman, she spoke in a booming voice, slightly singsong, and punctuated with a hearty laugh that was always her most endearing trait.

After earning her medical degree, Romm became a general practitioner in suburban Mount Vernon, New York. She quickly became a familiar figure, traipsing around town with her little black bag, making house calls and cheerfully dispensing her own brand of folk wisdom along with the most up-to-date medications. "She wanted to fix everything," her daughter says. "That was always her style."

What she had trouble fixing was her own personal life. Her first marriage, to Lee Colodny, a handsome but rather aimless young man, ended in divorce when their daughter, Dorothy, was still a toddler. They remarried briefly and then divorced again. May subsequently threw herself into a love affair with a married doctor, but he refused to leave his wife. He did, however, pull some strings and secure a baby boy for her to adopt; she wanted a son and wasn't going to leave matters to chance. But as soon as the boy was old enough, May shipped him and Dorothy off to boarding school. Though she would one day be known for her maternal solicitousness as a therapist, Romm never had much appetite for nurturing her own two children.

Mount Vernon eventually proved too provincial to contain this fiercely independent divorcee, so she decided to move to Manhattan. She married again, but her husband, a building contractor named Alexis Romm, died in 1929. Still, that move to the city changed her life. Through a friend she was introduced to A. A. Brill, the dean of Freud's apostles in America, and he encouraged her to become a psychoanalyst. She was fired up by the idea of conquering this avant-garde science, which appealed to her nonconformist nature. Psychiatry was not yet a glamorous or a lucrative specialty, and analysts were looking for new recruits. "Brill was delighted that somebody would sit at his feet," Colodny says.

Romm completed a one-year residency in psychiatry—all that was required then—at the New York State Psychiatric Institute and then took an apartment right next door to the New York Psychoanalytic Institute on West Eighty-sixth Street. As part of her analytic training she was psychoanalyzed by Sandor Rado, the Hungarian-born analyst who had been close to Freud but was later expelled from the inner circle after quarreling with Freud's daughter, Anna. Dorothy Colodny remembers her mother dashing out in the snow and heading next door for her daily analytic sessions. Romm spent most of the time, she laughingly told her daughter, teaching English to Rado. As Colodny explains it, Romm "was analyzed by Rado, who, I gather, never did speak English, so no harm was done to anybody."

After beginning an analytic practice in New York, Romm married her third husband, a lawyer named Samuel Golding; he was also an amateur playwright, and he awakened her interest in the arts. But that marriage ended in divorce after just a few years. "She wasn't a lady who could stay married long," says Colodny, who suggests that her mother was too domineering to play the role of devoted helpmate to any man.

Romm was enthralled with her new vocation, but her career was stymied by the paternalism of the psychoanalytic elders in New York. She once recalled the dinner parties at A. A. Brill's Manhattan brownstone. After supper the men would sit around the dining-room table smoking cigars, sipping brandy, and debating psychoanalytic theory. The women would all follow Mrs. Brill to an upstairs sitting room "full of caged birds, where the conversation took a less exciting form."

At last Romm decided to break out of this stifling milieu. Like many disaffected New Yorkers, she set her sights on freewheeling Los Angeles. Brill provided her with introductions to the analysts he knew there, including Ernst Simmel, Otto Fenichel, and Frances Deri. Upon her arrival in 1938 these haughty Europeans greeted the interloper coolly, and she was far too arrogant herself to win them over. At one meeting of the Psychoanalytic Society, Fenichel rudely cut Romm off when she tried to ask a question. "If you had paid attention," Fenichel snapped, "you could never come out with such a question."

Romm refused to cower. She may have deferred to A. A. Brill, but she was not about to kowtow to the self-appointed rulers of a provincial outback like Los Angeles. "My mother was a very emphatic lady, very tactless at times," her daughter explains. "She arrived in California and was very proud of her medical degree. She looked down on the lay analysts, some of whom were very cultivated in other areas, but that didn't impress her."

Romm may have reserved special contempt for lay practitioners like Madame Deri, but she could be just as rivalrous toward the lions of the analytic movement. On one occasion Karl Menninger gave a caustic critique of a paper Romm presented to the Beverly Hills Women's Club. Afterward he felt guilty and sent her a large box of chocolates as a peace offering. Romm viewed the gift as a distinctly hostile gesture. "He knows I'm diabetic!" she told a friend.

While she sparred with her colleagues, Romm ingratiated herself with Hollywood insiders. She struck up friendships with powerful women like Ad Schulberg, socialite Anna Bing, and screenwriter Sonya Levien (whose credits stretched back to the silent days and included such popular fare as *Rebecca of Sunnybrook Farm* and *The Hunchback of Notre Dame*). They helped to introduce her around. Levien's Sunday brunches in Malibu drew the crème de la crème—not just major stars like Chaplin and Garbo, but distinguished European emigrés like Aldous Huxley and Arnold Schönberg. Building on these crucial contacts, Romm soon had a thriving practice.

May Romm's greatest coup was landing David O. Selznick as a patient. Not long after delivering the enormously successful *Gone With the Wind*, Selznick experienced post-partum depression. He had always been unstable, and in the 1930s he started taking Benzedrine, a highly touted new drug, which increased his energy but left him hopelessly addicted and subject to extreme mood swings. During a black period in the early 1940s he and his wife, Irene (the daughter of MGM boss Louis B. Mayer), decided to try a change of scenery; they moved to New York and settled into a lavish suite at the Waldorf-Astoria. But David was still immobilized with anxiety and spent most of the time in bed. A friend of Irene's finally suggested that he consult the eminent psychoanalyst Dr. Sandor Rado, who urged the producer to return to California and enter treatment at once. Rado recommended his former protégée, May Romm.

It was the luckiest referral a Hollywood shrink could get. Selznick was known to be critical of everyone and everything, and the fact that this notorious perfectionist had selected Dr. Romm did wonders for her image. On returning to California, Selznick immediately began daily treatments with Romm. After several weeks he had emerged from his depression. The analyst wanted him to stick to his regimen, but the impatient Selznick decided he was cured and no longer needed Dr. Romm. "He confided to me that he knew more than she did; *he* could analyze *her*," Irene Selznick would later comment. Selznick began showing up late to his analytic hour or canceling appointments at the last minute. Eventually he stopped coming altogether.

Selznick's professional relationship with Dr. Romm was not yet over; he returned to her for therapy occasionally, and in 1944 he asked her to serve as his consultant on *Spellbound*. In the meantime Romm also took on the role of mother confessor to the rest of the Selznick clan. Irene had been impressed with Romm when she first met her. Because of the emotional roller coaster she was riding with David—who was notorious not just for his gambling and his drug dependency but for his philandering as well—Irene was experiencing psychological emotional problems of her own. She had been a stutterer since childhood, and now she suffered from a nagging sense of insecurity that manifested itself in a host of psychosomatic ailments. So she entered analysis with Dr. Romm and, in contrast to her restive husband, remained a steadfast patient for several years.

Irene also delivered her sister, Edith Goetz, to Dr. Romm's couch. Edith, who was married to producer William Goetz, was a giddy social butterfly, regarded as Hollywood's premier hostess, and the more serious-minded Irene had always had an uneasy relationship with her. Irene hoped that Dr. Romm could help allay some of the tensions of their lifelong sibling rivalry. But in her view Edie's analysis did not "take." In her autobiography Irene indicated that Dr. Romm casually broke the rules of confidentiality and discussed her sister's problems with her. "Romm told me she was not a good candidate," Irene wrote. "Edie preferred not to separate reality from wishful thinking, therefore Romm was willing to give her only supportive therapy, and briefly at that. Edie, unaware, soon announced that she was fully analyzed."

For her part Edith remembered her "analysis" with Dr. Romm as little more than pleasant chitchat. At one of their very first sessions Romm asked her genially, "What are you doing here? You like your husband, you love your babies. And you're so well dressed!" Nevertheless, goaded by her sister and anxious to partake of a modish new activity favored by wealthy Hollywood wives, Edie continued to see Dr. Romm on and off for a few more years. But she never forgot that early conversation. "I waited two years," Edie recalled, "but I finally had to ask her— 'What's well dressed got to do with it?' "

"When I see someone wearing stripes and dots and plaids," the analyst replied, "I know they're disturbed!"

Irene Selznick sought more profound revelations from her analysis. Romm was instrumental in helping her to relinquish her crippling dependency on her family. With the psychoanalyst's encouragement Irene divorced David Selznick, moved to New York, and established her own career as a successful theatrical producer. Her first Broadway production was Arthur Laurents's *Heartsong*, and shortly after the opening, Irene introduced the outspoken playwright to Dr. Romm. He was struck by the cozy familiarity between the two women. "May Romm was a small woman, and Irene picked her up in her arms and whirled her around," Laurents recalls. "That was not my idea of doctor-patient relations."

Indeed May Romm became Irene's constant companion. "Dr. Romm was always around the house," says Daniel Selznick, David and Irene's son. "At the time I didn't realize how unusual that was. I assumed all psychiatrists were like a part of the family."

Romm's daughter was less tolerant of this intimate connection. "The Selznicks were underfoot terribly," Dorothy Colodny complains. "Irene's dog was always chasing my cat." Colodny recalls that when she was living in northern California after finishing college, her mother came up to see her. "She was on the phone with Irene Selznick all the time," Colodny says. "Finally I said, 'Hey, you either visit me or you go home.' " Years later Romm named her ex-patient and dearest friend, Irene Selznick, the executor of her will.

With the Selznicks as trophies, Romm quickly established herself as the preeminent shrink to the stars. Hers was the first psychoanalytic practice located in the city of Beverly Hills, and countless actors—including Robert Taylor, Ava Gardner, Edward G. Robinson, and even Jennifer Jones, David Selznick's second wife—spent time on her couch.

According to her daughter, however, Romm's favorite patients were never the movie stars. "She told me she got very bored with actors," Dorothy Colodny says. "I don't think she quite appreciated the good actors, or maybe she had the starry ones who were all hysterical. Anyhow she much preferred to deal with high-powered producers, directors, even financial people in the industry. The patients who impressed her were much more important than the stars. She was really a power person."

"My grandmother liked to drop names," Colodny's daughter, Julie Kurlander, adds. "She loved to tell me that so-and-so was a millionaire."

At one point Romm even set out to snare a millionaire of her own. She had been introduced to Louis B. Mayer (who was then the highest-paid executive in America) by his daughter, Irene Selznick, and the titan of MGM occasionally called on the analyst for informal

advice. When Mayer left his wife, Margaret, in 1944, after she suffered a mental breakdown, Romm decided to see if she could lure
him back to the altar. Unfortunately, according to her daughter, she
faced stiff competition from another Russian-born doctor—Jessie
Marmorston, who was Mayer's personal physician. Romm and Marmorston were close friends, but when Louis B. Mayer suddenly became the most eligible middle-aged bachelor in Hollywood, they
vied fiercely for his affections. In the end Mayer married Lorena
Danker, a pretty Gentile widow not nearly as aggressive as the two
distaff doctors.

Romm and Marmorston never spoke to each other again. "Dr.
Jessie," as she was called, at least took a consolation prize when she
married Lawrence Weingarten, one of Mayer's studio lieutenants.
Romm remained single.

Mayer was never officially a patient of Romm's, but for a brief
period in the 1940s his ex-partner and bitter rival, Samuel Goldwyn,
did decide to seek her counsel. Goldwyn had just scored his biggest
success; his production of *The Best Years of Our Lives* swept the
Academy Awards presentations of 1946. But like David Selznick,
who fell into a major depression after the triumph of *Gone With the
Wind,* Goldwyn felt a profound letdown after all the hoopla surrounding *Best Years* had died down. The usually irrepressible producer turned moody and suffered from insomnia. "Anyone who
goes to a psychiatrist should have his head examined," Goldwyn had
once remarked. But now his depression was so severe that he decided to bite the bullet and consult Dr. Romm. Almost immediately,
however, his wife, Frances, made him quit. She blamed Romm for
breaking up the Selznicks' marriage, and she feared that Sam might
walk out on her if he went through intensive analysis. So, at his
wife's insistence, Goldwyn turned instead to a graphologist named
Hilde Berl to relieve his emotional turmoil.

Another of Romm's "power person" analysands was Leland
Hayward, the celebrated agent-turned-producer. Like David O.
Selznick, Hayward was a notorious egomaniac. He was also the
patriarch of one of Hollywood's most dysfunctional families; his
wife, Margaret Sullavan, and two of their children spent time in
mental hospitals. But Hayward's own destructive influence on his
family does not seem to have been an issue he confronted during
his analysis. He later told his children that after a few sessions,
Romm advised him, "Leland, there is no question that you are crazy,
but you also happen to function better than anyone I've ever seen,

and what more can you ask out of life? There's . o point in my treating you; it would be a waste of your money and would probably throw the whole mechanism out of whack. Stay the way you are."

"I think he probably didn't want to get any conflicting opinions," says Leland Hayward's son, Bill, "and I don't think my father ever went to another analyst, though he sent the rest of us."

"Treatments" like that led to a certain disparagement of Romm among the Los Angeles intelligentsia. "She was the greatest Band-Aid psychiatrist," scoffed director Joseph L. Mankiewicz. Romm's fellow analysts were similarly contumelious. One of them, Ralph Greenson, remembered a seminar on "technique" she gave that set his teeth on edge. "Don't have an hour end unpleasantly," Romm told the trainees. "I always like to say a nice thing at the end of an hour or give the patient a friendly pat."

Another prominent analyst, Dr. Judd Marmor, was more approving of Romm's maternal methods. "She was looked on with disdain by the classical group," Marmor acknowledges. "I think they felt she just gave her patients chicken soup, which wasn't true. But she did feed them jokes, and very appropriate ones. She was the George Jessel of the psychoanalytic field. She and I had adjoining offices, with my couch on one side of the wall and hers on the other side of the wall. But the offices weren't as soundproof as they could be, so it was very disconcerting when one of my patients was weeping on the couch to have gales of laughter coming from the other side of the wall."

Romm and Marmor and many of the other early analysts set up offices in the block known as Couch Canyon on Bedford Drive in Beverly Hills. Romm, like other Jewish refugees who became psychiatrists, abandoned her religion in favor of the exhilarating rationalism of Freud's new science. But Romm's daughter feels that the band of psychoanalysts on Bedford Drive was not unlike a conclave of elders in the villages they had left behind in Eastern Europe. "My mother had grown up in an Orthodox home," Dorothy Colodny says. "And then she became very antireligion, as most of the analysts were. But I took a good look and suddenly realized that the repressed had returned. Bedford Drive was the new shtetl."

For a while Romm lived in a plush home on Roxbury Drive in Beverly Hills, not far from her office. But the house was too big for her, and she moved into a string of modest apartments. "She wasn't good with money," Colodny says. "She didn't handle it well and wouldn't take advice, so she didn't end up as rich as her colleagues."

But then, the perks that Romm enjoyed were not the ostentatious emblems of success. Her clothes were dowdy and unpretentious; she never drove a fancy car. She coveted power, not wealth, and she savored her role as the confidante to Hollywood's elite. Romm was especially fond of mixing it up with celebrities at parties. "Everybody knew Karl Menninger liked to meet movie stars," says Dorothy Colodny, "so he would come to her house and she would invite actors and actresses. Claudette Colbert used to be there. I had a wonderful talk with Ava Gardner once. I remember one evening with Menninger and Hedy Lamarr. Menninger was hard of hearing, and Hedy Lamarr never could talk much, so it was an absurd conversation. The little boys from the neighborhood all popped into the house to get a look at Hedy."

Romm may have derived a feeling of satisfaction from knowing that Hollywood luminaries depended on her, but her daughter questions who was really controlling whom. "I don't know where we stood in the scheme of things," says Colodny, who later became a psychiatrist herself, "but it was somewhere beneath the tennis coach, I thought. You have this retinue, and the psychiatrist becomes part of the retinue. And it seemed to me my poor mama didn't realize how she was being used. They'd call her up at all hours, and she was lonesome, and she'd love to rush out into the night. She would pull them out of the surf or go to their houses and sit up and hold their hands all night. I think my mother very much wanted to please them. I also think she had a great need to be needed. Her patients were totally dependent on her, and we are all taught you mustn't do that. But it was her need and their need, and after a while I realized that it was their need maybe more than hers. They wouldn't have tolerated what other therapists demanded."

Classical Freudian analysts argued that it was imperative to maintain a formal distance between doctor and patient. In their view the concept of "transference" depended on the patient's ability to project his own fantasies onto the unknowable analyst; the delicate process could become infected if doctor and patient grew too close to each other. A psychiatrist who becomes chummy with patients is less likely to preserve the strict objectivity that allows for an accurate diagnosis of their problems. Moreover, such a symbiotic relationship may undermine the spirit of independence that analysis is meant to foster.

But some analysts, such as May Romm, were incapable of

maintaining a rigorous detachment from the people they treated, especially if those patients were celebrities. Colodny remembers once treating an actress who was married to a man from a very high-powered Hollywood family. At the same time, her mother was treating the actress's husband. One evening the actress called Colodny and asked to see her immediately. "She marched in with a whiskey glass in her pocket," says Colodny, "and she said, 'You know, I'm supposed to come in here and complain about *my* mother. But the one who's driving me to drink is *your* mother.' My mother was behaving like an accessory mother-in-law to her and just wouldn't stay out of her life and was telling her husband everything they should do."

If Romm meddled in her patients' lives like a nosy yenta, she intruded just as forcefully into her daughter's life. When Dorothy married her first husband, an assistant director from the Netherlands, Romm got him a job at RKO through one of her industry connections. Later, when Dorothy and her husband separated, Romm took Dorothy along to a Christmas party given by one of her famous patients, the bandleader Artie Shaw. He asked Dorothy out, and for a brief period he dated his analyst's daughter.

Along with David Selznick, Artie Shaw was one of Romm's most intriguing cases. He was a national celebrity in the 1940s, partly because of his sold-out concerts and hit records, and partly because of his marriages to glamorous movie stars Lana Turner and Ava Gardner.

Shaw had always been ambivalent about fame; he never felt comfortable with the adulation of bobby-soxers. Nonetheless, he relished his sexual conquests, even when they were sure to cause him grief. "I'd walk into a room of fifty women and unerringly pick the one who would make me the most miserable partner on earth," Shaw notes. "What was I doing with those women I was living with? I was thinking with my groin, that's all. I had no connection with those people. Lana Turner might as well have been a Martian."

Shaw was a sullen man, subject to severe depressions. When he returned to Hollywood after serving in World War II, he felt deeply disillusioned. "When I got out of the navy," Shaw says, "I was barely ambulatory. I couldn't get out of bed. I was so disgusted with the world I lived in that I saw no point in getting up."

Shaw knew he needed help, and a friend recommended that he consult May Romm. Shaw went to meet with her. Romm told him, "Yes, I think you could benefit from psychoanalysis. You're very articulate about your problems, you seem to be ready to pour everything out. When do you want to start?"

Shaw asked her if she could recommend an analyst. "I thought you came here to see me," Romm responded.

Shaw hesitated, mentioning that from what he knew about analysis, it required extremely intimate revelations. "I don't know how difficult it would be to talk to a woman about all that," he said nervously.

"You may have given me the best reason why you *should* see a female analyst," Romm replied shrewdly. "You must have a very strange view of women."

"And so we started," Shaw remembers. "I must say it took a while to break through that discomfort about talking to a woman." He recalls the turning point. He was explaining to her what he perceived as the central dilemma of his life—that his professional success depended on his performing for adoring hordes, and yet he loathed crowds of people. Trying to illustrate the hopeless paradox of his position, he told Romm, "It's as if I were an archaeologist and had to go digging around in caves and ran into spiders all the time, and yet had this neurotic fear of spiders."

Romm stopped him and asked why he used that particular analogy. Shaw dismissed her question as typical psychiatric mumbo jumbo, but Romm persisted, probing his fear of spiders. Shaw recalled a few times when he had encountered spiders, but Romm insisted that he dig deeper and go back to earlier episodes from childhood. Finally he remembered an incident when he was about eight years old. He was standing on the front porch of his new home in New Haven, Connecticut, listening to a violent quarrel between his parents. His father, whom he feared and disliked, came outside. Searching for something to say, young Artie pointed to a conical spider web and questioned his father about it. "I was raised on the Lower East Side," Shaw explains, "and cockroaches were the only animal life we knew. I honestly had never seen a spider web and asked my father what it was. For an answer—he was a very deft man—he caught a fly and threw it into the web. And out came this monster spider and grabbed the fly. I was transfixed and absolutely horrified. When Romm heard that story, she said,

'That's it, you got it. You were watching a primal drama, and you identified with the fly.' It was a classic oedipal scene."

Shaw saw Romm five days a week for a year and a half. She got him back on his feet and working again. "Going to her, I did develop the idea that you can respect a woman," Shaw says. "Up to then I'd been told that women are sex objects. I still have certain things May threw at me running through my mind. She used Yiddish expressions. I tend to be an impulsive person, and May would say, '*Chop nicht.*' It's a marvelously effective way of saying, 'Don't grab. Slow down.' "

Shaw had only one major conflict with May Romm during his analysis, and it concerned her involvement with the movie *Spellbound*. When the picture opened in 1945, Shaw went to see it. Always extremely opinionated, he was rankled by what he felt was a crude distortion of the psychoanalytic experience, and he was disturbed that Romm had lent her name and her authority to a Hollywood potboiler. "I felt she was being neurotically drawn into helping somebody do a piece of shit," Shaw says. Although Ingrid Bergman's neat explication of seminal childhood traumas was not so different from what May Romm had done in analyzing Shaw's fear of spiders, these Freudian epiphanies seemed to him more ludicrous on screen than in his own analytic sessions.

Shaw did not know how to deal with what he felt was a serious lapse of judgment on Romm's part. He simply ended his analysis without explanation. In retrospect, however, Shaw believes that his anger over *Spellbound* was probably a pretext for getting out from under the analyst's thumb. At that time he was falling in love with Ava Gardner, and he sensed that if he continued his analysis, Dr. Romm might question his attraction to yet another of those seductive, inappropriate women he was compulsively drawn to marrying. "I knew if I stayed with May, I would not be able to do what I wanted to do, which I knew I shouldn't do," Shaw says. "So I found an excuse to quit. And I married Ava."

He also consulted another analyst, Charles Tidd, who listened to Shaw's complaints about Romm but refused to take him on as a patient. Tidd insisted that Shaw would never make any progress in his analysis if he did not confront May Romm directly.

With apprehension Shaw made an appointment to see Romm. "I kept your hour open," she said. "I knew you'd be back."

Shaw paced for a moment, then blurted out that he felt she had allowed herself to be exploited for the sake of a piece of claptrap.

Romm listened to him rant for a while, and then she said, "Did I ever tell you I wasn't neurotic? What do you want to do, spend an hour talking about my neurosis, or do you want to talk about yours? Why do you think I became an analyst? I'm as screwed up as anybody you've ever known."

Then Romm cut to the quick. She asked about his marriage to Ava Gardner. "How is it going?" she inquired.

"If I'd been here, I wouldn't have married her," Shaw responded.

"That's right," Romm said. "That's why you got out."

And at that point, Shaw says, "We sat down and started again."

Artie Shaw was not alone in his disdain for *Spellbound*. But if some Freudian purists found the film foolish and superficial, most of America found it enthralling. As Ingrid Bergman analyzed the dreams and delusions of her lover and patient, Gregory Peck, the entire country was transfixed by the romance of psychoanalysis. In his glowing review in *The New York Times*, Bosley Crowther first took pains to assure his readers that he personally had had "little traffic with practitioners of psychiatry or with the twilight abstractions of their science." But then he burbled, "This we can say with due authority: if all psychiatrists are as charming as [Ingrid Bergman]—and if their attentions to their patients are as fruitful as hers are to Gregory Peck . . . then psychiatry deserves such popularity as this picture most certainly will enjoy."

Very freely adapted by Ben Hecht from an obscure English novel called *The House of Dr. Edwardes, Spellbound* is set in an exclusive psychiatric clinic called Green Manors. At the beginning of the film a new director, Dr. Edwardes (Peck), arrives at Green Manors and immediately falls head over heels in love with one of the staff psychiatrists (Bergman). Before long, however, it is revealed that Peck is an impostor—a madman, suffering from amnesia, who may have murdered the real Dr. Edwardes and taken his place. Eventually, with the help of her avuncular Viennese training analyst (Michael Chekhov), Bergman penetrates Peck's tortured psyche, decodes the symbolism of his dreams, exonerates him of the murder of Dr. Edwardes, and unmasks the true culprit.

May Romm was paid $1,500 for her consulting services. One of her principal duties was to serve as an unofficial censor, making sure that the script didn't contain any embarrassing Freudian slips.

She warned Selznick that a dream involving Peck and Bergman dancing was "a symbol of sexual intercourse," and Selznick promptly ordered it eliminated. Romm also objected to another element in Dali's dream sequence—a closeup of a large pair of pliers; she thought that such a blatant symbol of castration could agitate audiences. Selznick agreed to cut that image too.

Romm was concerned about another hidden message not so easy to excise. While *Spellbound* is a testimonial to the power of psychoanalysis to overcome "the evils of unreason," as an opening title card proclaims, its portrait of the analytic profession is not entirely adulatory. For if the heroine is a clever analyst, so is the villain. Leo G. Carroll, as the deposed head of Green Manors, is the embodiment of megalomania and silky duplicity, driven to murder by secret envy and a lust for power.

It was probably this acknowledgment of professional jealousy and infighting that so discomfited some of Romm's colleagues. Writer-director Joseph L. Mankiewicz, an almost religious believer in psychoanalysis, had gotten hold of an advance copy of the script and wrote to Karl Menninger, warning him of the damage to psychiatry that such an unflattering cinematic portrayal could inflict. Menninger fired off a missive to Selznick, voicing strong objections, particularly to the story's denouement. He also contacted May Romm directly and upbraided her.

Romm wrote a long letter to Menninger, who was at the time supervising the Los Angeles analytic colony, attempting to exonerate herself:

> *I spent a considerable time with Ben Hecht trying to modify or eliminate some of the unscientific viewpoints. It was no easy task, but a great deal was altered on the script for the better. However, it was impossible, according to Mr. Hecht, to eliminate the part, or to alter it, so as not to have the head of this private sanitarium commit murder. In order to do that, Mr. Hecht would have had to write a new story at a new fee. Both Mr. Hecht and Mr. Selznick are psychiatrically minded and sympathetic to psychoanalysis, but when it comes to throwing away what to us would be a big fortune, granted to them a small fortune, then resistances set in . . .*
>
> *Naturally the question arises, why should I have had anything to do with a picture which many have interpreted as casting aspersions on psychiatry. Simply because had I*

*not done so it would have been produced in a much more
undesirable form than it is now.*

Despite her disclaimer, many of her fellow analysts excoriated
Romm for compromising herself and the image of her profession.
She was even criticized by the American Medical Association,
whose leaders considered it unethical for a doctor to have her name
on the credits of a film, lest it be construed as a form of "advertisement" for services. "There was a lot of envy of May," says her
friend Judd Marmor. "I thought she did a very good job on that
movie, but a lot of other analysts were very hostile to her, and they
were dismayed when she became very rapidly successful."

Actually, the vicious backbiting within the Los Angeles psychoanalytic community lent credence to *Spellbound*'s melodramatic
plot. Most of the founders of the Los Angeles Psychoanalytic Institute had disliked Romm from the day she arrived, and some of them
even started rumors that she was sleeping with her famous patients.
In 1950 Romm, Marmor, and several of their associates broke away
from the Los Angeles Institute to form a new training center, the
Institute for Psychoanalytic Medicine of Southern California. (They
chose that title in order to emphasize their medical background and
their rejection of lay analysis.)

But before long the members of Romm's new institute were
also feuding with one another. Romm fell out with a former ally,
Martin Grotjahn, when he opposed the admission of her daughter,
Dorothy Colodny, to the Southern California Institute. Grotjahn argued that any hint of nepotism would undermine the credibility of
the organization. "If we had done that as a young and recently recognized institute," Grotjahn said, "we would have lost our standing.
And so May Romm became a deadly enemy of mine."

The irony of Romm's fighting for Dorothy's appointment was
that she was always as testy and adversarial with her daughter as
she was with her colleagues. Colodny felt she missed the attention
that her mother showered on her famous patients. Besides, she resented her mother's condescending attitude. Romm would refer patients to her daughter, but she could not resist taking a little dig: "I
told them if you were too young or if they didn't like you, they could
come back to me."

Colodny eventually ceased practicing psychiatry; she now
spends her time writing poetry, publishing slim volumes from time
to time. The idea of such a genteel retirement would have been

unthinkable to her mother. During the 1960s, when she was already seventy-five, May Romm decided to move back to New York and start a practice there. According to Colodny, the reason for the sudden move was that Romm fell madly in love with a Manhattan-based child psychiatrist named David Levy. "She just picked herself up and started this campaign to win the love of her life," Colodny says. "Unfortunately she didn't know how to do it. She didn't succeed, and she was very angry for the rest of her life." (Romm had apparently forgotten the advice that the elderly Michael Chekhov gave Ingrid Bergman in *Spellbound:* "Women make the best psychoanalysts, until they fall in love—and then they make the best patients.")

While she was in New York, Romm set up an office in the residential hotel where she lived. One of her patients was Mart Crowley, whose 1968 play, *The Boys in the Band,* created a sensation with its candid treatment of homosexuality. Crowley's sudden success disoriented him, and he sought out Dr. Romm. "I went to her place in the East Seventies," Crowley recalls, "and I'd lie down on the hotel couch. As a therapist she was like the good mom. But she bitterly complained about the New York weather, and she eventually moved back to Los Angeles."

When she returned to California, Romm resumed her practice, and she was also active on the lecture circuit, delivering watered-down versions of scientific theory at civic luncheons. In 1974, when she was eighty-three, she gave a jaunty talk to the ladies' auxiliary of the Southern California Psychoanalytic Institute on the sweeping topic of "Neurosis: Yesterday, Today, and Tomorrow." She was as vigorous and ebullient as she had been when she was trekking through the snow with her little black bag in Mount Vernon, New York, sixty years earlier. She had kept up with all the latest psychological literature, and she was very aware of the recent feminist criticisms of Freud. "What Freud knew about women you could put in your eye," she told the women's group, which consisted mainly of her colleagues' wives. "It wouldn't have been so bad if he had only kept quiet about it, but he did us a lot of damage. Freud did an injustice to women in two ways. In the first place, he felt unless a woman gave up sensations in the clitoris, she wasn't feminine. And he also said women did not develop a proper conscience. What a bunch of nonsense! Of course I'm a little old-fashioned because I do think there are differences between men and women. Why do women want to be stevedores? Let the men get the hernias!" And she roared with laughter.

Was Romm a feminist ahead of her time? Her granddaughter, a lawyer living in Berkeley, does not quite see it that way. "She'd tell me about life and sex," Julie Kurlander recalls, "and she had very definite ideas. She always said women are better than men because they can have sex anytime. But she also said women should get married and have kids and not worry about a career. She gave my brother money for graduate school, but she didn't give me any money when I went to law school. She bought into the traditional Freudian view of women but didn't feel it applied to her because she didn't really think of herself as a woman. She was very masculine."

Like so many of her early Freudian colleagues, Romm exalted the principles of marriage and family—even though she had failed to find fulfillment as a wife and mother. The fact that she was so power-hungry herself did not stop her from preaching a different message to her pliable female patients.

No one considered Romm a brilliant scholar. Although she wrote a couple of articles on female sexuality, her contributions to published psychoanalytic literature were skimpy at best. There are even some who doubt her effectiveness as a practitioner. "I don't think my grandmother was particularly talented as a psychiatrist," Julie Kurlander suggests. "She was *politically* talented. She was bright and driven. But she wasn't sensitive or compassionate or intuitive. It's hard for me to imagine her *listening* to anybody."

But those gifts of empathy and compassion were not what made an analyst popular in Hollywood. The stars and moguls were often drawn to someone who radiated the kind of power that they themselves exuded and worshiped. "I know some very good psychiatrists who were marvelous with patients," Dorothy Colodny says. "And you'd never hear their names. They worked in quiet little rooms and did a lot of good in the world. The big wheels who treated famous people were usually not the good therapists. It takes a different quality. I think that is why so many of the important Hollywood people didn't get good care, which is very sad because a lot of them needed it."

Star psychiatrists were cut from the same cloth as the people who succeeded in Hollywood generally; they were not necessarily the most gifted, but rather the most hard-driving, the most adept at self-promotion and manipulation. May Romm had what it took to rise to the top—chutzpah and inexhaustible energy.

Julie Kurlander remembers taking walks with her grandmother when Romm was in her eighties. "I couldn't keep up with her," Kurlander recalls. Even after she was diagnosed with cancer, Romm went on seeing her patients, conducting seminars with her colleagues, kibitzing with her old Hollywood friends—the few whom she hadn't outlived.

"She never retired," Dorothy Colodny says. "And her hair never turned gray. It was always jet black. I know because I used to check the roots. She worked right up until three weeks before she died in 1977. She died on her eighty-sixth birthday. By choice. She said, 'I'm going to live until my birthday.' And she did. This was a lady who had always decided exactly what she was going to do."

3. THE BELIEVERS

The patient is reluctant at first, but prodded by the kindly psycho-analyst, she lies down on the oversized couch and closes her eyes. Urged to "speak any of the thoughts that come into your mind," she begins to free-associate about the fragments of a song she recalls from childhood. As the music rises, the lights start to dim, and the heroine drifts into a dreamlike state; soon she has shed her stern business suit for a gossamer blue gown and is waltzing across the stage with a troupe of chorines. Accompanied by a forty-piece orchestra, psychoanalysis has come to the Great White Way.

Lady in the Dark opened on Broadway on January 23, 1941, and caused an immediate sensation. This "play with music" brought together an exceptional company of artists. Writer-director Moss Hart had already racked up a string of comedy smashes written in partnership with George S. Kaufman. Kurt Weill, renowned for his work with Bertolt Brecht in Germany, composed the music; Ira Gershwin collaborated on the lyrics. The British leading lady Gertrude Lawrence headed an all-star cast, which included the matinee idol Victor Mature and an exuberant young comedian named Danny Kaye. The production design by Harry Horner—five revolving turntables that allowed the play to flow uninterrupted between the protagonist's waking life and her dreams—was an innovative marvel.

Horner's imaginative set gave visual embodiment to the central idea of *Lady in the Dark,* which was just as novel as its striking production. For this was the first important work of popular entertainment to dramatize the process of psychoanalysis for a large audience. Incorporating the character's dreams into the action, the play illustrated Freud's ideas about the primacy of the unconscious in determining human behavior.

The play's heroine, Liza Elliott, is a successful magazine editor who suffers symptoms of a nervous breakdown that she can neither comprehend nor control. In desperation she seeks treatment from a psychoanalyst, Dr. Brooks, who helps her to decipher her dreams and come to terms with the internal conflicts that threaten to disrupt her life. She slowly realizes that she has blocked her feminine nature and sexual desires, a repression rooted in the classic oedipal drama of childhood, when her father mocked her physical appearance and compared her unfavorably to her mother. Once Liza apprehends the source of her anxiety, she is able to snare Mr. Right and finally find tranquility.

Lady in the Dark ran for 467 performances on Broadway, and if the Freudian underpinnings seem simplistic today, at the time they struck audiences like a thunderclap. Paramount Pictures paid almost $300,000 for the movie rights, a colossal sum in those days. The film version was released in 1944, in a somewhat diluted form, with Ginger Rogers as Liza and Ray Milland as the cocky advertising manager whose masculine charms eventually melt her resistance. The studio marketing department feared that the picture's theme might be too recondite for the hoi polloi; according to a *New York Times* story at the time, Paramount would not allow "any reference to psychiatry in the advertising and publicity." The Broadway play had opened with Liza in her psychiatrist's office, but the studio brass believed they needed the endorsement of a regular M.D. in order to persuade audiences, as the press release put it, that psychiatric treatment "is not quackery but a science accepted by the medical profession." So they added a rather fatuous prologue, in which Liza visits her family physician, and he advises her to consult a psychoanalyst.

Despite such hedging on the filmmakers' part, *Lady in the Dark* emerged on screen, as it had on stage, as a glowing tribute to the psychiatric profession. It signaled the start of a trend. Over the next two decades, dozens of plays and movies delivered psychoanalytic theory to the masses. Many of these works were devised by artists who were not just long-term habitués of the couch but evangelical crusaders for the Freudian cause.

Moss Hart, the creator of *Lady in the Dark,* was one of the first converts among the show-business set. He was also one of the first celebrities to talk openly with the press about his psychiatric treatment. A profile of the playwright that appeared in the *Saturday Evening Post* in 1944 noted that even though he and George S. Kaufman had won prizes galore for such plays as *You Can't Take It with You* and *The Man Who Came to Dinner,* Hart "found himself beset with the fear that the most he could hope from the future was to be known as a prominent collaborator-about-town." As a result, he told the interviewer, he "took himself to a psychiatrist."

That psychiatrist was Dr. Lawrence Kubie. Under Kubie's tutelage Hart mustered the confidence to strike out on his own and write *Lady in the Dark.* When he went to see his patient's show, Kubie was delighted with its idealized portrait of psychoanalysis and of the all-knowing therapist, Dr. Brooks. "He enjoyed it enormously," recalls Kubie's daughter, Ann Rabinowitz. "He thought Moss Hart did an excellent job, even though he was often critical of popularized stuff about psychiatry."

One of Kubie's specialties as an analyst was "curing" homosexuals and introducing them to the joys of matrimony. Moss Hart was his most celebrated success story. "Moss was a homosexual and he didn't want to be," says Hart's friend Celeste Holm. "And when he was through with Dr. Kubie, he wasn't. He fathered two children and became a hell of a husband. So what he wanted, Kubie was able to achieve. Moss still was a terrible manic-depressive, had terrible sessions of gloom. But I think he was totally faithful to Kitty Carlisle after their marriage."

Lady in the Dark was not simply a paean to psychoanalysis but also a hymn to the blessed estate of marriage. In a final session with Dr. Brooks, after Liza Elliott relives the traumatic childhood incidents that produced her deep fear of love and sexuality, the psychiatrist summarizes her current dilemma: "What you are facing now is rebellion—rebellion at your unfulfillment as a woman." In order to achieve true satisfaction, she must stop wearing the pants and yield to the hard-driving man who was her subordinate at the magazine. As the curtain falls, Liza and her lover sing Kurt Weill's haunting song, "My Ship," the song she has suppressed since childhood. It is a melody that tells of the magnificent vessel that will bring "My own true love to me." Liza's fulfillment will come not in sublimating her sexual desires through her career but in embracing the traditional female roles of loving wife and helpmate.

Like the androgynous Liza Elliott, Moss Hart longed for the romantic union that he hoped would rescue him from a numbing isolation. Five years after the premiere of *Lady in the Dark,* when

Hart was forty-one, he married the effervescent actress Kitty Carlisle and arrived at the happy ending he had imagined. In the world beyond the proscenium, however, life proved to be more complicated. Alan Jay Lerner, who worked with Hart on *My Fair Lady* and *Camelot* (both of which Hart directed on Broadway), said after his death, "Moss had his secret suffering and unspoken torments. Those close to him knew they were there without knowing what they were. But they were deep and they were painful."

In her autobiography Kitty Carlisle Hart, too, wrote of her husband's agonizing periods of despair before he died of a heart attack at the age of fifty-seven. "In her book Kitty Carlisle says Moss was depressed," playwright Arthur Laurents comments, "but she leaves out the reason for his depression. They supposedly had this wonderful marriage. Something was awry."

In the view of several of his friends, Hart's denial of his homosexuality fostered an internal conflict that eventually tore him apart. "Moss Hart had grown up in poverty," Laurents points out, "and he wanted to be rich and famous and glamorous. By his standards he succeeded. He was mad about gold and even bought gold garters. And I guess his marriage to Kitty Carlisle was a gold marriage. She was somebody most acceptable. His whole world knew her. So this is a man who got what he wanted—to a point. I think the real goal of analysis should be to accept yourself."

Nonetheless, Hart's miraculous "conversion" and his tremendous professional success enhanced Lawrence Kubie's reputation. The playwright was not shy about telling people that he had been treated by Kubie, and his endorsement helped make Kubie the analyst of choice for others in the New York theatrical set. Another of his celebrity patients, director Joshua Logan, called Kubie "the dean of psychiatrists and psychoanalysts."

Kubie's ability to charm the literati had something to do with his pedigree. As his colleague Sandor Rado drily noted, Kubie was "a well-to-do Jewish boy, in contradistinction to the ones who came from the Lower East Side." But Kubie's childhood was troubled; his mother died when he was three, and his German-Jewish father, who prospered in the rubber business, was stern and remote. Kubie's daughter, Ann Rabinowitz, calls her grandfather "very much the Victorian of the family, who had no gift toward his own children."

One thing the senior Kubie did give his son was the best education money could buy; the brilliant young student attended Harvard and Johns Hopkins Medical School, then studied neurology in

London. He became not just an eminent psychoanalyst but a highly visible spokesman for the movement. In the 1930s Kubie was a chief sponsor of the analysts from Europe—such as Heinz Hartmann, Rudolph Loewenstein, and Ernst Kris—who were fleeing Hitler's terror.

Kubie's motives in this campaign were not purely magnanimous. Kubie recognized that by ingratiating himself with these prestigious European analysts, many of whom had close ties to Freud himself, he could boost his own standing in the American psychoanalytic establishment. "He wanted to make himself king and use all these refugees as his devoted supporters," sneered Sandor Rado. But the Europeans were too strong-willed to remain beholden to anyone. Soon they were jousting with Kubie for control of psychoanalysis in America.

Kubie was a prickly personality, and eventually he found himself in conflict not merely with the emigré analysts but with most of his American colleagues as well. "Larry knew he tended to irritate others and even referred to himself as a gadfly," wrote one of his friends, Dr. Leo H. Bartemeier. Another friend, Dr. Louis Jolyon West, observes that Kubie was a curious mixture of generosity and asperity. "He was always finding fault," West notes. "He was usually right, but that didn't make it easier for people to take." After Kubie's death in 1973 the novelist John Hersey delivered a eulogy in which he said that "you always felt the push of words with Larry, and sometimes they would come out like weapons. He had a very sharp tongue, but he also had an almost maternal quality of caring about people."

Words did indeed count for a great deal with Kubie, and he prided himself on being not just a celebrated psychoanalyst but a litterateur. He wrote elegant treatises about the connection between psychoanalysis and the arts. In his book *Neurotic Distortion of the Creative Process*, published in 1958, Kubie set out to explode what he called "the culturally noxious assumption, devoid as far as I can see of the least fragment of truth, that one must be sick to be creative." He argued that artists could only fulfill their creative potential if they confronted the repressed fears and desires that were locked in their unconscious. In other words, he believed that they could benefit enormously from psychoanalysis.

While Kubie was renowned for his penetrating insights into the artistic temperament, his brand of Freudian detective work was sometimes suspect. In 1934 Kubie wrote an exegesis of Hemingway's fiction called "Cyrano and the Matador" for the *Saturday Review*. But when he read the article, the magazine's editor, Henry Canby, refused to publish it. Canby feared that Hemingway would be outraged by the essay, which speculated on the macho writer's oedipal fixation as well as his fears of women and of homosexuality. Kubie was irked that his effort had come to nought. "How would it be if we simply killed Hemingway and then published?" he quipped to Canby. Finally the analyst sent the article directly to Hemingway and asked his permission to publish it. Hemingway responded by threatening Kubie with a libel suit, and the article was not published until 1984, long after both men were dead. By that time it was known that Kubie had not simply relied on the author's texts to draw his conclusions. In 1933, the year before he composed his essay, Kubie was treating Jane Mason, a wealthy adventuress who was Hemingway's mistress at the time. (She was also the reputed model for the castrating Margot Macomber in Hemingway's classic story, "The Short Happy Life of Francis Macomber.") The confidential revelations about her lover that Mason poured out on the couch significantly influenced Kubie's diagnosis of the author's work and personality.

Kubie's confident pronouncements on other matters were also open to question. An orthodox Freudian who advocated marriage and close family ties as signs of mature adjustment, Kubie was, paradoxically, far from a model of stability in his own personal life. He was married and divorced three times. "He was too irritable to stay married," Louis Jolyon West suggests. Ann Rabinowitz, concurs. "Dad had a hard time with marriage," she says. "He had a short fuse. He once said, 'I ask a lot of my family because I consider my family to be an extension of myself, and I ask a lot of myself.' That's absolutely accurate, but it doesn't make you easy to live with."

Celeste Holm, who socialized with Kubie in New York, puts it more bluntly: "He was a rotten husband and a total male chauvinist pig." She also notes that his wives looked exactly alike. Holm once took a friend to consult Kubie. "He practically attacked her," Holm recalls. "He said, 'How dare you come in with this stupid, childish behavior?' She said, 'I don't have to listen to this. I came here for your help. You're not being helpful. Good-bye.' She was in better shape than I thought."

Kubie's imperious manner was not simply reserved for his female patients. Comedian Sid Caesar consulted Kubie in the 1950s;

he wanted to cure his alcoholism and ease the rages associated with his drinking. Kubie felt that analysis could not begin until Caesar stopped drinking, so he instructed the comedian to go cold turkey over the Christmas season. When Caesar returned to Kubie, he reported proudly that he had consumed only three drinks during the entire holiday period. Without hesitating, Dr. Kubie flicked on his intercom and barked at his secretary, "Case of S.C. will be closed and the file put away. Mark it 'incorrigible.' " Then the doctor turned to his astonished patient and announced, "You are dismissed, Mr. Caesar."

Caesar protested, but Kubie refused to relent. Years later Caesar reflected that in a sense Kubie was right; by that time he had learned that "the only way you stop drinking is by stopping drinking." But he added that the doctor might have made more headway "if he had only tried to get it across to me with less authoritarianism, more sensitivity." A pronouncement from Dr. Kubie, Caesar noted acerbically, "was like the Gestapo talking."

Kubie was particularly fascistic in dealing with homosexual patients—especially those who put up more resistance than Moss Hart did. Kubie labored to purge pianist Vladimir Horowitz of his homosexual impulses. In his biography of Horowitz, Glenn Plaskin wrote that after Horowitz consulted Kubie in 1940, "Kubie's unenlightened treatment only made [Horowitz] feel increasingly depressed." Lowell Benedict, who accompanied Horowitz on one of his tours in the early 1940s, told Plaskin that Kubie "was trying to change him from homosexual to heterosexual, and Horowitz's response was to cut himself off from the world entirely, from his own feelings as well." According to Erika Freeman, a New York therapist who knew both Kubie and Horowitz, Kubie advised Horowitz to lock himself in his room whenever he felt homosexual urges coming on. "It was a problem of psychiatrists of that generation who had a sense of what's normal and what isn't," Freeman says.

Ann Rabinowitz contends that her father did at least help Horowitz to overcome his stage fright. Several years later Kubie set out to perform another service for Horowitz—and for his own brother-in-law. Carl Erpf, who was separated from Kubie's sister, was an alcoholic with serious financial problems. At Kubie's instigation Horowitz hired Erpf as his private secretary and valet.

Kubie also treated Tennessee Williams for a time and tried to convince the playwright to adopt a heterosexual life. Williams knew that was impossible, but he did break off with his lover Frank Merlo at Kubie's urging. "Frank was the best influence in Tennessee's life," Arthur Laurents says, "and Kubie broke up their relationship. Tennessee threw Frank out, and Frank really loved Tennessee. Then Frank got cancer, and Tennessee was terribly guilty. It was too late. Frank died. And I don't think Tennessee ever got over the guilt of having abandoned him." Williams himself summed up his treatment by the rigid Freudian analyst as "a case of miscasting."

Among New York analysts Lawrence Kubie's principal rival for the most glittering show-business clientele was Gregory Zilboorg. The two doctors projected opposite images. The patrician Kubie cultivated the posture of a studious, discreet doctor, whereas Zilboorg was a flamboyant showman who wore a black cape and sported an enormous handlebar mustache (which Hollywood wit Carleton Alsop once dubbed the "lunatic fringe"). Their colleague Sandor Rado described the enmity between Kubie and Zilboorg as "just enormous."

Gregory Zilboorg was a leader of the New York Psychoanalytic Association, but he was also one of the first analysts whose treatment of celebrity patients raised serious ethical questions. The eminent psychoanalyst and anthropologist Dr. Abram Kardiner described Zilboorg as "a first-class phony" and voiced the opinion of many New York analysts when he said, "I didn't like [Zilboorg], but I was fascinated by him. I knew that he couldn't be trusted an inch, insofar as loyalty, consideration, friendship or anything like that was concerned, and I knew that he was a dazzler, but he was a mighty convincing dazzler."

Born into an Orthodox Jewish family in Russia, Zilboorg had served in the socialist Kerensky government; when Lenin and Trotsky, with their more radical brand of Bolshevism, ousted Kerensky, Zilboorg fled to New York, where he worked as a translator to put himself through Columbia Medical School. After being certified as a psychoanalyst, he assiduously courted the rich and famous and soon was charging the highest fees of any Park Avenue analyst—an amazing one hundred dollars an hour in the years before World War II. He also spoke eight languages and flaunted his status as a Cordon Bleu chef. Still, Zilboorg remained a committed socialist who advocated left-wing causes to many of his wealthy patients. He even persuaded one of them, department-store magnate Marshall Field, to bankroll the radical newspaper *PM*, which was edited by another of Zilboorg's patients, Ralph Ingersoll.

When he was living in New York, George Gershwin went to see Zilboorg at the recommendation of a composer friend, Kay Swift. According to Swift, Zilboorg discussed Gershwin's personal problems with her and could not suppress his own envy of the popular composer. In November 1935 Zilboorg planned a four-week vacation to Mexico with Gershwin and another of his patients, Edward Warburg, the director of the American Ballet School and the son of banker Felix Warburg. The trip soured the relationship between Gershwin and his analyst. The multilingual Zilboorg was so intent on outshining his celebrated patient that he constantly spoke in Spanish, despite Gershwin's protestations, in order to keep the composer at a disadvantage.

In 1941, one of Zilboorg's other patients, a writer for *PM* (whose identity was never publicly revealed), brought accusations of unethical conduct against him before the New York Psychoanalytic Association. The writer claimed that in addition to his regular fee, Zilboorg asked for a cash stipend of one thousand dollars a month to advise him on job-related matters. "I think that Zilboorg gave him two kinds of sessions," Sandor Rado said. "One was an analytic session, and the other he was making himself the manager of his patient's business." This kind of dual relationship for the purpose of fattening the analyst's bank account was clearly suspect. At the hearings before the board of directors of the New York Psychoanalytic Association, it was also disclosed that Zilboorg had accepted expensive gifts from his patients, and his extracurricular activities with Gershwin came under scrutiny.

A twelve-member panel investigated all the charges. Zilboorg's own training analyst, Franz Alexander, testified against him, an act that Zilboorg melodramatically compared to Abraham's sacrifice of Isaac. With plaintive self-righteousness Zilboorg wrote to one of his supporters, Karl Menninger, "Somehow it is not possible for me to rid myself of a sense of being disquieted by the awareness of how predatory man is and how jungle-like the intertwining of personal animosities." Such vicious infighting was understandable, he conceded, "but also so revolting to one's sense of brotherhood and friendship among men."

After weighing the charges, nine of the twelve members of the board voted to censure Zilboorg. When the matter was raised before the full membership, however, Zilboorg threatened to sue every member of the association who voted against him. The charges were quickly dropped. It was not just that financial threat that saved Zilboorg's neck. The possibility that other patients might be emboldened to sit in judgment of their analysts was a chilling prospect. Karl Menninger, then president of the American Psychoanalytic Association, complained, "The bringing of a patient to a scientific organization to give evidence against a physician is one of the most dangerous and vicious precedents that I can think of." When Ernest Jones—the author of a cautionary essay about the hubris of analysts, "The God Complex"—wrote to Menninger questioning Zilboorg's behavior, Menninger responded tersely, "All of this was based on the sworn declaration of a very sick patient of Dr. Zilboorg's."

There is little doubt that the powers-that-be were more concerned with protecting the image of their profession than with evaluating the case against Zilboorg. As Abram Kardiner noted, "It wouldn't have meant very much to have one of the small fry accused of having abused the confidence of a patient, but to have one of the Brahmins of the psychoanalytic movement in America accused of the same charge would have given it a black eye for many years to come and would have created a scandal of the first order." Even Zilboorg's bitter rival, Lawrence Kubie, was so concerned about the movement's good name that he made a motion to have all mention of the accusations expunged from the record. Kardiner was outraged by the whitewash. "That was the last time that I set foot into the New York Psychoanalytic Society," Kardiner later said. "This was no place for me, for the simple reason that it was obviously being operated as a racket."

Despite the controversies that swirled around Zilboorg, many of his celebrity patients remained fiercely loyal to him. Lillian Hellman, for one, adored the eccentric doctor, whom she believed had cured her alcoholism. The playwright even named her pet poodle Gregory in his honor.

A few years before his death in 1959, Zilboorg was baptized by the celebrated radio priest Bishop Fulton J. Sheen. "When Zilboorg converted, everybody thought that he finally went off the wall," says Dr. Theodore Rubin, who had trained under Zilboorg. The devout socialist and Freudian ended his days in the comforting arms of Mother Church. In one of her volumes of memoirs Hellman made a cryptic reference to her analyst's curious metamorphosis: "Zilboorg ended odd," she wrote, "but the story is too long, too complicated and too American."

*   *   *

Hellman's reluctance to abandon her idol, even when he was shown to have feet of clay, typified the stubborn fervor of the analytic believers. Of all these camp followers, none was more loyal to the cause than the gifted writer-director Joseph L. Mankiewicz. One of the most literate men ever to work in Hollywood, Mankiewicz maintained a sharp skepticism toward almost all shibboleths except those surrounding psychoanalysis. His own three-year analysis with Otto Fenichel in the early 1940s strengthened his commitment to the Freudian faith, but even before then Mankiewicz had devoured virtually every psychoanalytic text.

"My father believed passionately in Freud and in psychiatry," says Joseph's son, Christopher Mankiewicz. "He once confessed to me that he actually wanted to be a psychiatrist but couldn't pass the premed courses at Columbia. So he became a director instead, which was the next best thing. He was a great believer and a major pusher of creative people into psychiatry. In those days he was an atheist. Psychiatry was his only religion. He used to say to my mother, who was Catholic, 'Sigmund Freud is infinitely more important than the Pope.'"

In 1944 Mankiewicz secured a copy of the script of *Spellbound* and was outraged by its simplifications of the analytic process. He contacted Karl Menninger, provided him with a plot synopsis, and urged Dr. Karl to intercede with the filmmakers. Mankiewicz noted deferentially that his own analyst, Dr. Fenichel, "did not object" to his writing the letter and in fact had recommended Menninger as the appropriate overlord with whom to lodge a protest.

In this astonishing missive Mankiewicz—a proud civil libertarian on every other issue—pleaded for censorious restraints on artistic freedom. "I suggest to you," he wrote to Menninger, "that both the American Psychiatric Association and the American Psychoanalytic Association consider *now* what can be done, in some way, to control—or at least temper—the presentation of their respective sciences that will be sent out to the far corners of the globe on millions of feet of film—and to prevent, if possible, the resultant disrespect and distrust that may be generated in the minds of millions of people."

In conclusion Mankiewicz offered to become a foot soldier in this momentous campaign. "It goes without saying that I will do anything you ask," he told Menninger, "and serve in any capacity you indicate." Menninger, who promptly contacted *Spellbound*'s producer, David O. Selznick, gave Mankiewicz a gold star for his efforts. "I think you have done psychoanalysis a great service in having called it to our attention," Menninger wrote to his dutiful informer.

All his adult life Mankiewicz loved discussing psychoanalytic theory with the brightest lights in the field. But the benefits he derived from analysis were not always so cerebral. Mankiewicz was an incurable philanderer, and his own son suggests that he used psychoanalytic techniques to seduce women. He acted as their understanding father confessor, and this approach drew many insecure starlets to him. Christopher Mankiewicz says, "He had great success with women, particularly movie stars, by dealing with them on a psychological level. Rather than saying, 'You have great tits, my dear,' like everybody else was saying, he found a new tactic."

Joseph also urged many of these vulnerable actresses to enter analysis themselves. His most prominent acolyte was Judy Garland, with whom he had an affair in the early 1940s. First Mankiewicz gave Judy several books by Freud to read. Then he arranged for her to meet Dr. Karl Menninger during one of Menninger's regular visits to Los Angeles. At last Judy decided she was ready to be psychoanalyzed, and Dr. Karl recommended the venerable Ernst Simmel, the leader of the budding Los Angeles analytic community.

In 1943 Garland began daily sessions with Dr. Simmel. She would either stop by in the morning on her way to the MGM lot or in the early evening, after her work was completed. But according to her biographer Gerold Frank, "even in analysis Judy found herself performing. . . . She made up stories—wild stories of her treatment as a child." Despite his fabled gullibility, Simmel was not as credulous as Garland had hoped, and she soon began skipping her appointments. She usually had a studio flunky call to cancel. On one occasion Simmel grabbed the phone from his secretary and barked, "Will you tell Judy that I cannot help her if she does not keep appointments. And I cannot help her if she continues to lie to me when she does keep appointments. Give her that message."

Garland soon tired of Simmel. She was hooked on analysis, however, and she visited several other prominent doctors. Eventually she ended up with a promising newcomer, Dr. Herbert Kupper. Simmel had refused to make house calls, even for a star of Garland's stature, but Kupper was not so fastidious. On one occasion he rushed over to a weekend tennis party at the home of Lee and Ira

Gershwin after Garland phoned him complaining of an anxiety attack.

When Garland's emotional condition deteriorated in 1947, Dr. Kupper recommended that she seek treatment at the Austen Riggs Center in Stockbridge, Massachusetts. Judy agreed, but she was afraid to travel by herself. She persuaded Dr. Kupper to accompany her to the sanitarium and stay with her until her treatment was under way. Analyst and patient checked into the Red Lion Inn in Stockbridge, and Judy holed up in a suite of rooms, with Kupper right next door. Judy was to be treated by Dr. Robert Knight, who was dismayed by the unorthodox relationship between Garland and Kupper. He accused Kupper of allowing himself to be at Judy's "beck and call" and demanded that Kupper leave Stockbridge so that treatment could commence. Kupper did agree to return to Los Angeles, but he stayed in touch with Judy by phone.

Judy's sessions with Dr. Knight did not go well. "I can't stand it here in Stockbridge. It's too quiet," she told him. This complaint was repeated again and again, until Knight finally offered his own explanation: "When you don't have a lot of noise around you, the noise inside you becomes overwhelming."

"Judy left the next day," says Dr. Margaret Gibson, a staff psychoanalyst at Riggs who discussed the Garland case with Knight afterward. Having spent a few frustrating weeks in Massachusetts, Garland came home to Dr. Kupper.

Back in Hollywood Garland was about to star in a major new musical film, *Easter Parade,* to be directed by her husband, Vincente Minnelli. (They had previously worked together on *Meet Me in St. Louis, The Clock,* and *The Pirate.*) But just a few days before shooting was to begin, Dr. Kupper called the film's producer, Arthur Freed, and asked him to fire Minnelli. From his sessions with Garland, Dr. Kupper had decided that Judy's insecurities were aggravated when Minnelli directed her; she felt inadequate when she compared herself with her husband, and that was why she behaved so erratically. In effect Kupper gave Freed an ultimatum: Fire Minnelli, or Judy might not be able to complete the picture. Flustered by this unusual demand from a most unlikely source, Freed consulted with his boss, Louis B. Mayer, and then decided that he had no choice but to accede to Dr. Kupper's request. According to Minnelli, Freed called him and told him, "Judy's psychiatrist thinks it would be better all around if you didn't direct the picture—that you symbolize all her troubles with the studio."

Garland and Minnelli never discussed the matter, but Minnelli was crushed by the decision. In fact, he began seeing an analyst himself after Freed fired him. And Judy behaved just as badly on *Easter Parade* (directed by Charles Walters) as she had while working with Minnelli.

"Analysis didn't really do Judy any good," her friend Artie Shaw observes, blaming the failure on her unresolved drug dependency. Another friend, producer and composer Saul Chaplin, reports that when he knew her, Judy was taking five sleeping pills and six Benzedrines every day. Substance abuse, like alcoholism, was a problem that psychoanalysis was notoriously ineffectual at treating. And some analysts aggravated the problem by freely prescribing sedatives and tranquilizers to patients already addicted.

In later years Garland would regale her friends with hilarious stories about her failed analysis. "She even joked about being institutionalized," says writer Peter Feibleman. "When her psychiatrist took her to one hospital outside Los Angeles, they got lost, and Judy claimed he got so anxious, *he* had to take a tranquilizer. Then as they were walking across the lawn of the institution, Judy fell down, and he said to her, 'Judy, you know you have to go in. It's silly for you to fall down. That won't work.' She got up, walked a little bit farther, then fell down again. She did this about eight times, and each time he said, 'Judy, this is not worthy of you. We've discussed this for days, and you know you need the treatment.' Anyway she went inside and checked herself in, and woke up the next morning and looked through the bars of the window at the lawn she had crossed. And there were eight or ten croquet wickets lying on the grass."

Judy Garland's early infatuation with the talking cure reflected the rage for analysis that swept through Hollywood in the forties. A story is told of one prominent screenwriter who walked into a party positively weeping with joy. "My analyst has agreed to see me on Sunday!" the writer exclaimed.

Vincente Minnelli described the vogue of analysis as part of a "status game" in which "one fashionable analyst offering current theory was supplanted by another with even later concepts, later to give way to another . . . and another." The most *au courant* analysts were coveted guests at chic Hollywood gatherings. At one party hosted by Ira and Lee Gershwin, Dr. Gregory Zilboorg was the guest of honor. According to Gerold Frank, "The Gershwins' home was set with eight tables of people playing cards, after dinner, with a psychiatrist at each table."

When Dore Schary ran MGM during the 1950s, he regularly hosted Sunday-night screenings that started out with an informal dinner of hot dogs, bagels, and sauerkraut. Then the guests would retire to the twenty-foot-long sofa to watch previews of the studio's latest offerings. Directors, writers, and actors were among the invitees every week. "The rest of the group," his daughter, Jill Schary, would later comment, "were doctors, which in Hollywood often means psychoanalysts. They were interesting mainly because they could tell great case histories, anonymous, of course. They were also interested in everyone else there, as possible clients. . . . Analysts considered themselves indispensable to the Hollywood scene."

Artie Shaw tells of another Hollywood party, when John Garfield asked Shaw about his experiences in analysis and wondered whether he might benefit from a similar sojourn on the couch. Shaw began to offer his own psychoanalytic profile of Garfield, when Stella Adler came over and dragged Garfield off. Actor Robert Sterling, who was hovering nearby, asked Shaw to continue his disquisition. "I was going to say," Shaw told Sterling, "that Garfield's central problem is exemplified by the fact that he tells you to call him Julie. He wants you to know that he's Julie Garfinkel and he hasn't forgotten that, but he loves being John Garfield because of all the pussy and all the perks. He's trying to straddle two different worlds, and they're moving farther and farther apart."

"I got that far," Shaw recalls, "when, from across the room, Julie called out, 'That's not true!' I said, 'How the hell did you hear that?' Bob Sterling asked me to go on. And I said, 'Bob, this is ridiculous. Why am I talking to you about this? For Christ's sake, you're a nice healthy Gentile boy.' Bob drew himself up and said, 'What are you talking about? I'm as sick as anybody in this room!' I was insulting the poor man! That's a perfect example of what we thought in those days. We equated sick with interesting. If you weren't psychoanalyzed, you were dumb."

The popularity of analysis was solidified during World War II. Psychoanalytic methods were being used to treat shell-shocked soldiers, and the results proved dazzling. After intensive and usually brief treatments with drugs, hypnosis, individual analysis, and group therapy, the soldiers often experienced dramatic recoveries. Of course the wartime situation was unique in that the patients were traumatized by a specific crisis permitting a relatively direct treatment and cure. Nevertheless, therapists came out of the war exhilarated with the possibilities of analysis and with their own ability to alleviate suffering.

"Suddenly psychoanalysis was no longer seen as a quaint and slightly perverted Jewish conspiracy to subvert the world's morals," says Dr. Louis Jolyon West. "After World War Two, psychiatry became respectable."

Caught up in the postwar euphoria, several of the leaders of American psychoanalysis set out to use the media to promote their profession. Dr. Will Menninger, who had founded the Menninger Clinic with his brother Karl and who served as chief consultant in neuropsychiatry to the surgeon general of the army from 1943 to 1946, urged moviemakers who had joined the war effort to produce films that would document the impact of psychotherapy on the emotional casualties of war. Later Menninger wrote of the change in public attitude toward psychiatry after the war, using a telling metaphor to describe this transformation: "Psychiatry struggled from the rear seat in the third balcony to finally arrive in the front row at the show."

Menninger sponsored one remarkable documentary directed by John Huston, *Let There Be Light,* that illustrated how army psychiatrists worked with shell-shocked soldiers. Huston's father, the venerable actor Walter Huston, provided the sober narration. In remarkably candid scenes shot at Mason General Hospital on Long Island, soldiers recalled the deaths of their comrades and described their own terror during combat. Many were still suffering from extreme stress that manifested itself in bizarre somatic reactions; some had lost the ability to use their legs or to speak coherently. Then these same soldiers were injected with sodium amytal and asked to free-associate, both about their wartime experiences and about their childhoods. In group-therapy sessions they shared their recollections of conflicts with their parents, which the psychiatrists believed had contributed to their later breakdowns. As a result of the therapy, their psychosomatic problems disappeared. The movie culminated with an almost ludicrous Hollywood ending—a baseball game with the fully rehabilitated soldiers joining ebulliently in the all-American pastime.

Even with this rosy finale *Let There Be Light* was deemed too disturbing to show to the American public; the Defense Department suppressed it for thirty-five years. The ostensible reason for the ban was that signed releases had not been obtained from the patients depicted in the film. But Huston believed the Pentagon's real motivation was the fear that the film's harrowing portrait of psychologically damaged soldiers could adversely affect military recruiting. In his autobiography Huston wrote, "I think it boils down to the fact that they wanted to maintain the 'warrior' myth, which said that our American soldiers went to war and came back all the stronger for the experience."

Still, vivid images of shell-shocked soldiers did find their way into mainstream Hollywood entertainment. In *Twelve O'Clock High*, a much-honored drama released in 1949, the protagonist is a proud general (Gregory Peck) who embodies the warrior code that Huston cites. Peck is the hard-as-nails commander of an American bomber squadron, and initially he has nothing but contempt for fliers who crack under pressure. As he undergoes grueling combat missions himself and sees several airmen killed in action, his iron facade crumbles, and his arm becomes immobilized as a result of conversion hysteria. Soon afterward he has a total breakdown. Although there is no psychiatrist in the cast of characters, *Twelve O'Clock High* is one of the most powerful pro-psychiatry movies of the period, for it convincingly demonstrates the shattering effects of emotional trauma.

Another drama about wartime stress, *Home of the Brave*, did include a psychiatrist ministering to shell-shocked soldiers. Arthur Laurents's acclaimed play appeared on Broadway in 1946 and was made into a movie three years later. In the film a black soldier experiences amnesia and hysterical paralysis after a buddy is killed in battle; a psychiatrist helps him to understand that he became severely disoriented when he caught a glimpse of his friend's racism.

After seeing *Home of the Brave* on Broadway, director Anatole Litvak hired Laurents to work on the screenplay adaptation of a book he had purchased for filming: *The Snake Pit*, a story of a young woman in a mental hospital. The movie, which came out in 1948, was produced by Darryl F. Zanuck, the head of Twentieth Century-Fox, who prided himself on being on the cutting edge of social issues. Zanuck had already won awards for making films about dispossessed farmers (*The Grapes of Wrath*) and anti-Semitism (*Gentleman's Agreement*), and now *The Snake Pit* offered him the chance to tackle the hot topic of mental illness. Other participants in the project had a far more personal interest in the subject of psychiatry. Anatole Litvak was in love with Dorothy Paley, the ex-wife of CBS founder William Paley; Arthur Laurents describes Mrs. Paley as an "analysis maven," and when her show-business pals were looking for an analyst, they invariably sought Dorothy Paley's advice. The star of *The Snake Pit*, Olivia de Havilland, had been analyzed, and so had her costar, Celeste Holm. Several psychiatrists were employed as technical consultants on the project. "We had analysts up to our armpits on that movie," Holm remarks.

In addition to exposing the subhuman conditions of mental hospitals, *The Snake Pit* conveys the reverence for Freud that typified movies of the 1940s. The main character, played by de Havilland, suffers a schizophrenic breakdown and is confined to a primitive mental institution, where she is rescued by a wise analyst played by Leo Genn. When he explains that her problems stem from her incestuous feelings for her father and her guilt over his death, his words are an epiphany. "It's like you were in a dark room and turning on the light," she gushes.

"The ending of *The Snake Pit* was bogus," Arthur Laurents acknowledges. "Suddenly it all comes together in thirty seconds. It just isn't that easy." In fact, the real-life psychiatrist—the director of Rockland State Hospital in New York—who was the model for the heroic analyst in the movie ended up committing suicide. Despite that grim footnote, *The Snake Pit*, like *Lady in the Dark* and *Spellbound*, helped to give psychoanalytic lingo a currency throughout the land.

The influence of psychoanalysis was not restricted to films that dealt explicitly with mental illness or psychotherapy. Indeed psychoanalytic references began turning up in the most unlikely places. In the smash-hit musical *Guys and Dolls*, which opened on Broadway in 1950, the hilarious song "Adelaide's Lament" contains a surprising subtext. Adelaide, the nightclub singer who has been engaged to the slippery Nathan Detroit for twelve years, has been reading a psychological tome, and she has learned that her persistent nasal infections may be a result of emotional stress rather than noxious streptococci. She croons of the multifarious "psychosomatic symptoms" and "neurotic tendencies" she has developed while waiting for her beau to set the date.

The fact that psychoanalytic language had even invaded Damon Runyon's world of gamblers and their molls suggests just how pervasive the Freudian catechism was becoming. This one song sums up many of the sexual and psychological assumptions of the period. In the view of the show's creators, Adelaide's psychosomatic ills stem from her anxiety at remaining single—the worst fate that a woman could confront. In an earlier day a fallen woman like Adelaide would have been presented as sinful. The value system of the 1950s saw her a little differently—as a bundle of neurotic symptoms, which could be purged by the joyful noise of wedding bells.

Joseph L. Mankiewicz's *All About Eve,* released also in 1950, delivers the same message. This classic movie owes a huge debt to Mankiewicz's enduring infatuation with analysis. In writing the script he brought incisive wit and psychological acuity to his characterizations of the aging, insecure actress Margo Channing (Bette Davis), the cold-blooded upstart Eve Harrington (Anne Baxter), and the long-suffering wife of the playwright (Celeste Holm).

In a colloquy with Gary Carey that served as an introduction to the published screenplay of *All About Eve* in 1972, Mankiewicz elucidated the movie's psychological underpinnings. Drawing heavily on psychoanalytic jargon, Mankiewicz declared that his motivation in writing the script was to explore the actor's unique problems: "what amounts to an obsessive need for the young actress/actor to acquire a substitute identity. A personality-proxy, really, wherewith she can attain acknowledgment, acceptance, even love and/or its many equivalents, from a society in which she is usually unable to function successfully as just herself."

Mankiewicz went on to say that he was particularly haunted by the problems of the actress as she approaches forty. "I *knew* these women," he told Carey. "I'd been in love with some—I'd worked with many of them." He spoke of Judy Garland and her terrible insecurities about her physical appearance, which led her to seek validation through performing, "that substitute-identity, the identity that existed only in a spotlight." Mankiewicz also observed that Garland had an inordinate fear of aging: "And with the passing years and accumulating fat and the deteriorating effect of the pills and drugs and booze that had somehow kept you going—kept you unaware, anesthetized as it were, in between spotlights—wouldn't the approaching finish, the approaching *blackout* of that spotlight-identity terrify you almost beyond reason, drive you to a despair of being capable even to go on existing without it? Roughly, that was Judy."

Margo Channing was a composite of Garland, Margaret Sullavan, Jeanne Eagles, and a number of other self-destructive actresses; *All About Eve* represented Mankiewicz's psychoanalytic dissection of the damaged performers he had known. But the movie, like *Guys and Dolls* (which Mankiewicz directed on screen), also contained the sexual prejudices that characterized Freudian analysis in that era. Although Mankiewicz created some of the most vivid female characters ever to grace the screen, he ended the drama with Margo Channing deciding to abandon her career and devote herself to the man she loves. Mankiewicz told Gary Carey that he wanted the film to dramatize realistic options for the aging actress: "The transition of their main performing arena from stage—to home. And the rapid narrowing of roles available, down to the ultimate two: wife and/or woman." It was the identical message that Moss Hart had woven into *Lady in the Dark*, a message reinforced by these writer-directors' Freudian analysis.

Mankiewicz used psychoanalytic insights not just as a screenwriter, but as a director as well. He frequently criticized Otto Preminger, who was known for screaming at actors and bullying them into submission. Mankiewicz's technique, by contrast, was to take his actors aside and talk to them quietly and privately. Nancy Guild, whom Mankiewicz directed in *Somewhere in the Night* in 1946, remembered that Mankiewicz spent two or three months with her before the start of production, probing for intimate details of her childhood and adolescence. Then when filming began and Guild had to attempt a difficult scene, she recalled that Mankiewicz "would sit with me for half an hour reminding me of things I'd told him about myself. . . . He was psychoanalyzing me all through the picture, breaking down my inhibitions."

If analysis had a profound impact on Mankiewicz's career, it did not seem to bring much order to his personal life. He was a compulsive womanizer, and he had numerous affairs throughout his stormy nineteen-year marriage to Rosa Stradner, an actress who came from Max Reinhardt's theater in Vienna. Rosa resented the fact that Joseph had pressured her to give up her career and devote herself to raising their two sons. She was a heavy drinker, suffered repeated mental breakdowns, and was hospitalized for a time at the Menninger Clinic.

When the Mankiewiczes moved to New York in the early fifties, Joseph sought out the eminent Dr. Lawrence Kubie to treat Rosa. Mankiewicz admired Kubie, but he acknowledged that the doctor was not a miracle worker. "Larry Kubie was very successful with Moss Hart," Mankiewicz said. "He was not successful with Rosa."

Mankiewicz made sure that his children were also seen by psychiatrists. That was fairly commonplace among the analytically attuned show-business families of the era. Chris Mankiewicz recalls, "My father used to say to me, 'You obviously have a lot of problems and a lot of hostility. You and I could never relate, so you need to talk to someone impartial.' Just as English families consigned their kids to private school so they didn't have to deal with them until they knew Greek and Latin, people like my father used psychiatry as a substitute for one-on-one dealings." Speaking of the distinctive rituals of growing up in Hollywood, Chris comments, "Most of us progressed from nannies to nurses to housekeepers to psychiatrists. There was always a surrogate parent around. So that they didn't have to interrupt their careers and their lives and deal with the issues that fathers and mothers should be confronting with their children, we were shipped out to professionals. That has got to be somewhat unique to the Hollywood experience. I can't think of a group of kids who more frequently were going to shrinks in the forties and fifties. The idea of just sitting down and rapping with your parents was inconceivable in my family. But the shrinks were always there."

Chris was a rambunctious youngster, and he was examined by a series of analysts. While he was growing up in Beverly Hills, his father sent him to Frederick Hacker, a Viennese-born psychoanalyst who had met Rosa Mankiewicz when he was working at the Menninger Clinic and who later became a close friend of the family. Hacker administered a battery of psychological tests to try to root out the sources of Christopher's pugnacity. Later, while attending prep school at Lawrenceville, Chris would visit a nearby analyst three times a week. And when he was in New York, he was dispatched to his mother's analyst, Lawrence Kubie. During one of his hours with Kubie, Chris complained that he did not see much of his father. When he walked in the door of the family's apartment after that session, Joseph L. Mankiewicz was glowering. "What do you mean telling Dr. Kubie that I'm never around?" Joseph demanded of his son.

"Here's a guy who didn't wait two minutes before calling my father to report on everything I told him," Chris says. "So much for the sanctity of the shrink's office!" Chris also claims that his parents dropped gossip that they had heard from Dr. Kubie about his other patients. "My mother was fanatic about classical music," Chris says. "And I remember hearing them excitedly talk about little tidbits that they had gotten out of Larry Kubie about Vladimir Horowitz. Kubie had very distinguished patients, and you're putting in his hands terrifically powerful gossip. It gave these shrinks a tremendous sense of power. They knew the inner workings of these legendary, fascinating people."

In 1957 Joseph Mankiewicz was filming *The Quiet American* in Rome, and he brought his family over for a visit. "My mother had a huge breakdown," Chris recalls. "She came down to our bedroom one night and started ranting and raving about our father fucking around, and particularly with his secretary, Rosemary. Finally she went to sleep. The next morning our father came down and said, 'I understand your mother was down here last night. She's a very sick woman. Is there anything she said that I should know about?' I said, 'Yes, she said you were having an affair with Rosemary.' He said, 'That poor girl Rosemary? That's a perfect example of how sick your mother is. I'm sending her off to Fred Hacker's sanitarium in Vienna.' Later in the summer we went to Vienna to see her. Then she went back to the care of Kubie in New York. The next year she killed herself. And a few years later my father married Rosemary. So, far from showing how sick she was, her accusations against my father were only an example of his constant philandering."

In September 1958 Rosa Mankiewicz committed suicide by swallowing an overdose of sedatives. A note to Dr. Kubie was found clutched in her hand. "The night my mother died," Chris recalls, "I was at the all-night movies in Times Square. It was my freshman year at Columbia. I rushed over to the apartment when I finally got the message, at three or four o'clock in the morning. Kubie was there. Later on, as we were going down in the elevator, he said to me, 'What are your feelings at this moment?' I said, 'This may seem strange to you, but I feel intensely happy, that a great weight has been lifted off my shoulders. The agony of my mother is finally over, and at least there will no longer be that terrible tension.' He said, 'That's the first honest emotion I heard expressed here tonight.' "

*   *   *

Chris Mankiewicz's tales of Dr. Kubie are mild indeed compared with those of Bill Hayward, another child of Hollywood who had a far more traumatic encounter with the autocratic analyst. Bill was the son of actress Margaret Sullavan and agent-turned-producer Leland Hayward. The Haywards and Mankiewiczes had been friendly in Hollywood; Joseph had produced some of Margaret Sullavan's first movies at MGM. Later both families moved to New York, and Chris Mankiewicz and Bill Hayward were schoolmates at Lawrenceville.

There were many other parallels between the two families: Both Joseph Mankiewicz and Leland Hayward were skirt chasers and obsessed workaholics; both Rosa Mankiewicz and Margaret Sullavan were fragile, high-strung actresses. But since Sullavan was a movie star and Rosa Mankiewicz was not, the Hayward children lived in an even more transparent fishbowl than the Mankiewiczes. "Our lives were a series of extremes," Brooke Hayward wrote in her best-selling memoir, *Haywire*. "A thanksgiving of riches was bestowed on us at birth: grace and joy and a fair share of beauty, privilege and power. . . . But there were also more expectations, more marriages (my mother four times, my father five), and more damage: more of us (three out of five) suffered mental breakdowns." Dr. Kubie, Rosa Mankiewicz's psychiatrist, was also the Hayward family's principal shrink. He supervised the treatment of Margaret Sullavan and her daughter, Bridget. Both of them ended up committing suicide.

Reeling from his parents' divorce and all the turmoil at home, Bill Hayward was the quintessential problem child. Like his friend Chris Mankiewicz, he delighted in defying parental authority. When he was fifteen, Bill decided that he would run away from prep school and elope with his girlfriend. The headmaster got wind of Bill's plan and called Leland Hayward, who drove down to Lawrenceville in a limousine and spirited his son back to Manhattan. The limousine stopped at Lawrence Kubie's office on East Eighty-first Street. "I had no idea what any of this meant," Bill Hayward says today. "I was a lamb to the slaughter."

Bill's emergency session at Dr. Kubie's office lasted several hours. The doctor's other appointments for the day were canceled. Kubie conferred with Bill, with Leland, with the two together. Finally Kubie took Bill aside and announced his decision. "In order to release the anxiety that my parents were going through—they would be unable to rest properly with the thought that I might elope at any moment—Kubie thought it was an excellent idea that I spend the night in a small private hospital in New York," Bill recalls. "I guess that's when I first realized I was in trouble, that I was in a game that I didn't know any of the rules to. We argued about that. Finally Kubie called an ambulance. Two guys came in and took me to the hospital. When I got there, they took all my clothes and ID and gave me some pills, which I thought I could resist. I couldn't. I was there about three or four weeks."

Bill was furious with his father and with Dr. Kubie. He refused to speak to the analyst until he realized that Kubie was the only one who could free him. Then he tried to ingratiate himself, but his fate was already sealed. "It developed that I was in a holding pattern until Kubie found a spot for me that would help me to mature," Bill says. "There's a naïveté that people in the fifties had. You thought you had rights. Finally Kubie came in one day feeling absolutely victorious. He thought it was a major coup to get me accepted into the Menninger Foundation in Topeka, Kansas. He even brought along photographs and architectural drawings. They were part of his sales pitch on how much I was going to like this place that I had no choice about going to. I remember looking at the pictures and seeing that there were no bars on the windows. I had been in this little dumpy room for three or four weeks. I was quite anxious to move along, and I thought Menninger's had to be better than where I was."

Bill's stepmother, Slim Keith, borrowed a plane owned by her friend William Paley to take young Hayward to Topeka. For the next two years Bill was confined at Menninger's. Twice he ran away; both times he was arrested and returned to the institution. The second time, his father flew out to confront him. Leland Hayward angrily told Bill that it was unfair to his other children for him to be spending so much money on one son's psychological rehabilitation. Consequently he had decided to cut Bill out of his will. The enormous sums Leland had already expended on the treatment of Bill and Bridget had not only put a serious dent in his pocketbook but in his enthusiasm for psychiatry. "He was becoming very disenchanted," Bill says. "The dollars were getting to Leland. He was not convinced this was the only way to deal with things, so it became a much better climate."

Bill looks back on the experience with mixed feelings. He did not regard the Menninger Clinic as a nightmarish place. The grounds were inviting. The therapists were caring. Famous movie folk like Gene Tierney and Edward G. Robinson were often checking in for extended stays. Although Bill was threatened with the notorious cold-pack treatment—where recalcitrant patients were wrapped in ice-cold sheets to calm them—he was never actually subjected to the torture. After his second escape attempt Bill had weekly sessions with Karl Menninger himself, and he was impressed with the doctor's wisdom and geniality. "We had long conversations about science," Bill says. "He could talk intelligently about anything."

Bill went on to work in Hollywood as a producer; one of his projects was a TV version of his sister Brooke's book, *Haywire*. But Bill became disillusioned with show business, and in his forties he enrolled in law school. Now a practicing attorney, he has investigated the legal rights of minors institutionalized in mental hospitals against their will. "Today it's a little bit different than it was in the fifties," he says, "but it's still not great. What stays with me is the horror of being locked up and having no legal mechanism to do anything about it."

Would his life have turned out differently if he had not been incarcerated as a teenager? "I don't know that the Menninger Foundation was anything more than a kind of holding tank until I grew up a little," Bill says. "But the worst thing about the experience was that it left me with problems with my father that lasted until he died. I never lost the anger against my father for having me locked up. I think he was too willing to listen to Dr. Kubie, but on the other hand, people were naive then. When a psychiatrist told you this is the best thing to do for your child, you listened. So perhaps it wasn't entirely my father's fault."

Hayward does not remember Kubie as a fierce, forbidding figure. "He was an elderly gentleman then, and he wasn't like a mean, tough guy," Bill says. "He was fatherly." Nevertheless Kubie was not inclined to doubt the correctness of his judgments. Like most Freudian analysts of his day, he believed that rebellious youngsters should receive treatment away from the influence of their parents and siblings. Lawrence Kubie's daughter, Ann Rabinowitz, says, "My father felt there were cases where a young person got sick in a particular situation and needed to be removed from the family situation in order to be treated. I remember he often said, 'If adults don't make the decision, who will?' " But in acting as he did, Kubie was also making life more convenient for his wealthy, self-centered friends. He insisted on the same unruffled existence for himself. Ann Rabinowitz admits that when she was growing up, her father was preoccupied with his work and was usually quite impatient with his own family. "My father didn't have an easy time with children," Rabinowitz says. "I have likened it sometimes to having a minister for a father. I have known ministers' children who said they were always supposed to have the word from God. There was an element of that in my family too."

Bill Hayward never saw Dr. Kubie after he was sent to Menninger's, but he heard his name again. "Years later," Hayward recalls, "in the mid- or late sixties a prominent director who was a friend of my father's came to me and asked me how I felt about my experience at Menninger's. I teed off on my father, who was still alive at the time. I didn't realize why this man was asking. Then I learned he was having trouble with his son. And immediately thereafter, under Dr. Kubie's care, his son was incarcerated. Kubie was obviously a quick hand with a key."

Psychiatry was not simply used to harness the children of show-business luminaries. It was also used to tame recalcitrant movie stars. The studio bosses initially viewed psychoanalysis with suspicion. "Both Marxism and analysis were objectionable to the studios," screenwriter Arthur Laurents remarks astringently, "because they were a source of rebellion. Analysis made you believe in yourself. *They* were the daddy, not the analyst."

Eventually, however, the moguls came to realize that they could use psychiatrists to control unruly actors. Louis B. Mayer was furious when Judy Garland first started seeing an analyst, fearing that the doctor might convince his valued protegée to abandon him. But a few years later Mayer decided to turn the enemy into an ally. When Garland was filming *The Pirate* in 1946, Mayer hired Dr. Frederick Hacker to provide his star with on-the-set therapy and keep her working. Soon Hacker was not only counseling Judy, he was sitting in on dailies with producer Arthur Freed and director Vincente Minnelli and offering his own suggestions on how to edit the film.

Mayer also summoned Dr. Augustus Rose, a neurologist from Peter Bent Brigham Hospital in Boston—where Judy had been hospitalized in 1949—to Hollywood to shepherd the tormented star through another movie, *Summer Stock*. Dr. Rose even helped persuade Judy's old friend Gene Kelly to costar in the film in order to supply a more supportive environment. If Judy panicked during a scene, Dr. Rose took her aside and calmed her until she could get back before the camera. Once, composer Saul Chaplin recalls, it took Rose hours to cajole Judy out of her dressing room. With the doctor's help she finally completed the picture, the last one she ever made for MGM. But the patch-up was only temporary and clearly served the studio's interest more than the patient's.

The sad history of actress Frances Farmer suggests how psychiatry could be used for more sinister purposes. Farmer, a promising actress from Seattle, worked for Samuel Goldwyn in the 1930s and then moved to New York to join the Group Theatre; she had a stormy love affair with playwright Clifford Odets and an equally turbulent marriage to actor Leif Erickson. Increasingly she came to resent her abusive treatment by the men who controlled the entertainment business, and her burgeoning feminism coincided with a growing commitment to left-wing causes. She also started drinking heavily and relying on amphetamines, which only made her more volatile and obstreperous.

Producers grew wary of hiring such a troublemaker, and her once-promising career stalled. In 1943, while working on a low-budget melodrama called *No Escape* for Monogram Pictures, Farmer was arrested after assaulting a studio hairdresser during a drunken argument. She cursed at the arresting officers and, when asked her occupation, replied insolently, "Cocksucker." Almost immediately she was transferred from the county jail to the psychiatric ward of Los Angeles General Hospital. A psychiatrist who examined her, Dr. Thomas H. Leonard, declared that she was suffering from manic-depressive psychosis, "probably the forerunner of a definite dementia praecox." As a result of Dr. Leonard's diagnosis (which has since been dismissed as meaningless gibberish), Farmer was confined to a sanitarium and given insulin shock treatment. Finally she was released into the custody of her mother, with whom she had always had a tense relationship.

Farmer's mother ultimately had her committed to the Western State Hospital in Steilacoom, Washington, one of many facilities that retained the services of Dr. Walter Freeman, at that time America's foremost psychosurgeon. Dr. Freeman had devised a revolutionary new technique for transorbital lobotomy. First he administered electroshock treatment until the patient passed out. Then he lifted the left eyelid, plunged a long needle under the eyeball directly into the patient's brain, and jiggled the cerebrum. With this quick fix Dr. Freeman was able to perform dozens of lobotomies in a single day. In his prime he made the rounds of mental hospitals all across the country, where he was called to quell troubled or violent patients.

Frances Farmer was returned to her mother in a more docile, almost vegetative state. She tried to resume her acting career in the late fifties and did a few cameos on television. When she appeared in 1958 on *This Is Your Life,* the host, Ralph Edwards, probed for details about her time in a mental hospital. Farmer, looking catatonic, barely uttered a word. Ultimately her comeback fizzled, and she moved to Indianapolis, where she hosted an afternoon movie series for a local television station. She died there of cancer at the age of fifty-six, all but forgotten in Hollywood.

In 1982 Jessica Lange played the doomed actress in *Frances,* a movie 180 degrees from the idealized picture of psychiatry immortalized in *Lady in the Dark.* By that time the extravagant hopes for psychoanalysis shared by the rapt believers of an earlier generation seemed almost laughably naive. But what happened to Frances Farmer was not unrelated to that delirious adulation. The showbusiness evangelists had fed the egotism of American shrinks by selling an image of the psychiatrist as seer. Doctors like Walter Freeman, the avid lobotomist, and Lawrence Kubie, the Freudian father who always knew best, became intoxicated with the idea of their own omniscience. Meting out cures and punishments to the psychological miscreants in their care, they acted as if they were every bit as infallible as their godlike counterparts on screen.

4. ROMEO AND MARILYN

By mid-century, psychoanalysis had captured the fancy of more than a few unlikely acolytes. Director Joshua Logan discovered just how far the Freudian fad had spread when he made the film version of *Bus Stop*, with Marilyn Monroe as the aspiring chanteuse, Cherie, and Don Murray as her cowpoke boyfriend.

In one scene Murray was supposed to awaken his lover with the comment "No wonder you're so pale and white. That's the sun out there." On the first take, however, the actor flubbed his line and said, "No wonder you're so pale and scaly."

Logan called "Cut," and Monroe turned excitedly to her costar. "Don, do you realize what you just did?" she asked. "You made a *Freudian* slip. . . . It's a sexual scene and you gave a sexual symbol. You see, you said 'scaly,' which means to say you were thinking of a snake. And a snake is a phallic symbol. You know what a phallic symbol is, Don?"

"Know what it is?" Murray retorted without missing a beat. "I've got one!"

That telling exchange between the good ol' boy and the some-time calendar girl occurred in 1956, not long after Marilyn began to study acting with her psychoanalytically inclined guru, Lee Strasberg, who was intent on molding her into a brilliant dramatic actress. Under Strasberg's influence Marilyn became an earnest devotee not just of Method acting, but of Freudian analysis as well. Ironically, when Marilyn was approached a few years later to costar in a film about the founder of psychoanalysis—a role that might have been the most challenging and profoundly serious of her career—she turned it down.

In 1961 John Huston—who had given Marilyn her first significant part, in *The Asphalt Jungle,* and who had just finished directing
her in *The Misfits*—was preparing an ambitious feature film based
on the life of Sigmund Freud. The first-draft screenplay was written
by Jean-Paul Sartre, and both Huston and Sartre had wanted Monroe to play Cecily, the neurotic patient whose sexual pathology
Freud analyzes as he begins to formulate his radical new theories.
It was a drama drenched in the high-mindedness that Marilyn
clearly craved. She was intrigued by the project and by the opportunity to team up once again with director Huston and with her
Misfits costar Montgomery Clift, who was slated to play Freud. But
according to Huston, Marilyn declined the part at the behest of her
analyst, Ralph Greenson. Dr. Greenson was a close associate of
Anna Freud, and Freud's daughter strenuously opposed any attempt
to depict her father's life on screen. Rather than displease her analyst, Marilyn refused the role.

When *Freud* was released in 1962, with Susannah York cast as
Cecily, it was a box-office flop. Huston later blamed the film's poor
reception on its clinical depiction of abnormal sexuality. "What [au-
diences] wanted was 'healthy' sex—the Marilyn Monroe kind of
sex," he decided.

There was of course an ironic disparity between Monroe's public persona as an avatar of "healthy sex" and the nymphomania,
drug dependency, and suicidal depressions that characterized her
private life—conditions that repeatedly led her to seek solace on the
analyst's couch. "It was an addiction," said her friend Lena Pepi-
tone, commenting on Marilyn's insatiable hunger for the Freudian
cure.

Of all Marilyn's analysts, none played a more prominent or more
controversial part in her tragic life story than her final father confessor, Ralph Greenson. It was not the only role that Dr. Greenson
performed as one of Hollywood's most visible psychoanalysts. Well
before he became a key player in Marilyn's life, he was already
something of a star on the local lecture circuit, and his home was
a favorite meeting ground for the town's intellectual elite. He even
served as the prototype for the hero of one of Hollywood's most
heartfelt tributes to the psychiatric profession.

Captain Newman, M.D., starring Gregory Peck as a dedicated
army psychiatrist during World War II, appeared in 1963 (the same

year that *Freud* was rereleased with the titillating subtitle, *The Secret Passion)*. But unlike *Freud, Captain Newman, M.D.* was an instant hit. Based on the best-selling novel by Leo Rosten, the movie depicted the struggle of a humane doctor to repair the shattered psyches of three battle-weary soldiers. Peck, fresh from his Academy Award–winning performance as Atticus Finch in *To Kill a Mockingbird,* was the cinematic paragon of decency and virtue. He was the ideal actor to embody Hollywood's exaltation of the psychiatrist as caring, courageous sage.

The avowed model for Captain Josiah J. Newman was Leo Rosten's close friend Ralph R. Greenson. But there was also a brasher side to Dr. Greenson, and that was reflected in the character of Captain Newman's wisecracking sidekick Jake Leibowitz (played in the movie by one of Greenson's patients, Tony Curtis). Most of the film's vignettes derived from Greenson's wartime experiences as chief of the combat-fatigue section at an air force rehabilitation hospital in Colorado. Greenson himself served as a technical consultant on the movie, although his contribution was never officially acknowledged. According to Greenson's widow, Hildi, Rosten advised the doctor not to include his name in the credits, lest any of his former patients recognize themselves and try to sue for a piece of the pie.

The relationship between Greenson and Rosten dated back to 1938, when Greenson was establishing his psychiatric practice in Los Angeles and Rosten was beginning to write for the movies. The two irreverent New Yorkers immediately hit it off. "We'd go out and shoot pool," Rosten recalls. "Greenson was in analysis himself, and he had a lot of time on his hands." Rosten, who had studied Freud's writings at the University of Chicago, was fascinated by the new science, and Greenson, an engaging crusader for the cause, took his friend to meetings of the analytic study group. Rosten reciprocated with invitations to more glittery gatherings. "I would bring him to dinner parties, and he began to get patients among the movie people," Rosten says. "Greenson was a remarkable storyteller—a real ham—and he would describe his cases in great detail. As an analyst he had to keep quiet all day, and that frustrated him. Soon he was telling his stories all over Hollywood."

"He was a very dramatic guy," agrees producer Julian Blaustein, who knew Greenson socially and who eventually tangled with him over the film biography of Freud, a project that Blaustein had initiated. Charles Kaufman, who followed Sartre as a screenwriter on *Freud,* also remembers Greenson as an avid raconteur. "He was always 'on,' " Kaufman recalls, "letting his emotions spill over. He should have been an actor."

If Ralph Greenson had an instinct for the dramatic, he probably came by it naturally. Born in Brooklyn on September 20, 1911, he entered the world with the unlikely name of Romeo Greenschpoon. He had a twin sister, and her name was Juliet. "My father liked Shakespeare and was a romantic," Greenson would explain. "My mother was weak from having given birth."

Greenson's father, Joel Greenschpoon, was the proprietor of a drugstore in the Williamsburg section of Brooklyn. He first met his wife when she answered his ad for a pharmacist willing to work long hours for low wages. A feisty, hard-driving woman, Katherine Greenschpoon had chosen a career in pharmacy because it did not require expensive schooling and it was one of the few professions open to refugees.

Impressed by Joel's knack for diagnosing his customers' aches and pains, the ambitious Mrs. Greenschpoon urged her husband to become a doctor. She managed the store while he attended medical school, and in 1914, three years after the birth of their twins, he earned his degree. Dr. Greenschpoon quickly developed a thriving practice in the tight-knit Williamsburg community. The family moved to a large, white colonial home situated majestically behind a high gate. In this lower-middle-class ghetto, the doctor's commanding residence was something of an anomaly—an emblem of the family's growing prosperity.

Life inside the Greenschpoon home reflected the cultural aspirations of these nouveau-riche Russian-Jewish immigrants. Mrs. Greenschpoon abandoned her pharmacy career and became an artists' manager, working with the legendary impresario Sol Hurok. Opera divas and drama troupes would entertain at the family's soirees. The quartet of Greenschpoon children—twins Romeo and Juliet, younger sister Elizabeth, and brother Irving—would perform as a quartet for the assembled guests.

Like his father, young Romeo was something of a stagestruck romantic, and through his mother's clients he was introduced to the theater at an early age. For a time Mrs. Greenschpoon managed the great Pavlova, and Greenson frequently went to see the sultry prima ballerina perform; he later confessed that he harbored romantic fantasies about her well into adulthood. But there were moments when he rebelled against the steady diet of classical music and high culture that his parents imposed upon their four children. In the grand baroque moviehouses of Brooklyn, he found a haven from the stifling regimen of music practice and academic study that dominated his home life.

He also chafed under the embarrassment of his name. When they first entered kindergarten, the Greenschpoon twins were immediately paraded around to all the classrooms. "We're Romeo and Juliet, and we are twins," they were told to recite in unison. With each new school year the ritual was repeated, eliciting predictable jeers from their classmates. Finally, at the age of twelve, Romeo announced that he would henceforth go by the name of Ralph, and a sympathetic teacher saw to it that his school records were changed accordingly. The nickname Romi stuck, however, and that is what friends and family called him throughout his life. (It was in 1937, following his internship at Cedars of Lebanon Hospital in Los Angeles, that he changed his last name to Greenson.)

After graduating from college, he set out in 1931 for the University of Berne in Switzerland, where he enrolled in medical school. "He was a young man in a hurry," recalls his wife, Hildi, whom he met in Berne while taking meals at the boardinghouse her mother operated. "He did his premed in something like two and a half years, attending night school. He knew those credentials wouldn't wash with a medical school in the U.S., so he applied at Berne, and they accepted him." Always a quick study, Greenson taught himself German in two months. "He especially liked the idea that he could read Freud in German," recalls Hildi.

With his medical degree in hand, Greenson traveled to Vienna, where he was psychoanalyzed by Wilhelm Stekel, one of Freud's earliest adherents and a founding member of the original Vienna Psychoanalytic Society. Though Stekel eventually aligned himself with the turncoat Adler—impelling Freud to refer to him as "that pig, Stekel"—he was well respected for his pioneering work on dream symbolism. As personality types, Stekel and Greenson had much in common. Peter Gay has described the grandiloquent Viennese analyst as "intuitive and indefatigable. . . . Though entertaining company, he alienated many with his boastfulness." It is a description that would apply to his American analysand as well.

Voluble and charming like his father, driven and ambitious like his mother, Ralph Greenson was adept at cultivating influential friends. He had mingled with celebrities as a child, and he was never intimidated by powerful people. When Greenson came to Los Angeles in 1936, he courted the imperious leaders of the psychoanalytic study group, Ernst Simmel and Madame Frances Deri, but they were leery of accepting him into the fold. His association with Stekel made him suspect in the eyes of these Freudian purists, and he had difficulty convincing them that he had not been permanently tainted by his earlier training. With the arrival of Otto Fenichel in 1938, Greenson found a more sympathetic mentor. He returned to the couch for four years of Freudian analysis under Fenichel and ingratiated himself with the brilliant German doctor, eventually earning a reputation as his most devout disciple.

Heading up the combat-fatigue unit at the Army Air Force Convalescent Hospital in Fort Logan, Colorado, during World War II— the interlude that gave rise to *Captain Newman, M.D.*—Greenson came in contact with the sorts of deeply traumatized patients rarely seen in civilian practice. He began publishing papers and found that the insights he had gained from treating casualties of war could be applied to other victims of emotional trauma.

Another thing he discovered in the army was a flair for public speaking. Blessed with quick wit and boundless self-assurance, Greenson was frequently called upon to deliver impromptu talks before the military brass. He delighted in expounding his ideas and, his wife, Hildi, recalls, "he also found that he could really *capture* an audience." Upon his return to Los Angeles after the war, Greenson used the oratorical skills he had honed in the army to enhance his reputation and expand his practice. His popular lectures on child rearing, a zesty blend of Freudian theory and Borscht Belt humor, played to packed houses at local schools, churches, and synagogues. "People got hooked on Greenson," says his wife. "When I once marveled that he never seemed nervous, his characteristic reply was, 'Why should I be nervous? Just think, these lucky people get to hear me!' "

"His voice would rise to a passionate pitch, or break into a helpless chuckle over his own joke," she once remarked. "He gave full vent to his emotions, was not artful or diplomatic, and at times was blunt and could offend the skittish or timorous."

That bluntness could also offend his colleagues. Leo Rangell, another prominent Los Angeles analyst, had worked with Greenson at the rehabilitation hospital in Colorado during World War II. A rather testy fellow himself, Rangell paints a decidedly different picture of Greenson from the adulatory one conveyed in *Captain Newman, M.D.* He claims that Greenson was so opinionated and domineering that the doctors working with him bridled. "He talked democracy, but he didn't treat his friends as equals," asserts Rangell's wife, Anita. "You had to slavishly serve him. When the rest of the group shunned him for his behavior, he came to Leo and said, 'Why didn't you tell me what I was doing? When I get back to Los Angeles, I'm going to have some more analysis.' He was absolutely charming about it."

But when Greenson and Rangell did return to Los Angeles after the war, neither of them displayed much humility. "Greenson wanted me to be a disciple of his," Leo Rangell declares. "Instead I became an independent person. He became very obstructive to my whole career." Following the deaths of Otto Fenichel and Ernst Simmel, Greenson attempted to maneuver himself into a position of authority within the newly formed psychoanalytic institute. That led to considerable friction within the ranks. It was not only the analysts who joined the rival Southern California Psychoanalytic Institute who mistrusted the ambitious Greenson; many of his brethren within the Los Angeles Institute, including Rangell, locked horns with him as well.

But Greenson also had his legion of admirers. Dr. Leonard Rosengarten, a dean of the Los Angeles Institute, has described him as "exciting, brilliant, creative, charismatic, amusing, witty, involved. Given a young and receptive audience, Romi was like an old bird dog ready to hunt. In all my years as a student or teacher anywhere, I've never seen another half so good." On the other hand, Dr. Norman Levy, one of the leaders of the dissident group, dismisses Greenson as a "showman." With wry understatement he adds, "Some of us were wary of that aspect."

Like his parents, Greenson enjoyed playing host to artists and intellectuals. Hildi Greenson describes the atmosphere of the elder Greenschpoons' social gatherings as proper but unpretentious. "It was that typically Jewish way of entertaining—not for dinner, but little sandwiches and things, cake and tea. Mama would put it all out on a very pretty cloth, and people would perform." A similar mood prevailed at the Greensons' comfortable Mexican-style home in Santa Monica, where celebrities and analysts would regularly congregate for chamber music, followed by cold cuts on paper plates. Unlike ostentatious Hollywood shindigs, these were parties where the scintillating conversation was the main attraction. Especially for newcomers from the East, who bemoaned the intellectual aridity of southern California, an invitation to the Greenson home was greatly prized.

One of those who remembers the liveliness of the Greensons' soirees is filmmaker Tamar Simon Hoffs, who had moved to Los Angeles in the mid-1950s with her husband, psychoanalyst Joshua Hoffs. "That's the only analytic 'salon' I can think of in which there was *fun*," she says. "You knew you'd always meet a cross-section of people—Anna Freud, Margaret Mead, Masters and Johnson, plus lots of Hollywood people. The talk at the place was fabulous."

Producer Henry Weinstein was another transplanted easterner who was a frequent guest at the Greensons' home. Weinstein had met Dr. Greenson through Celeste Holm, Weinstein's friend and Greenson's ex-patient. "I was totally taken by him," recalls Weinstein, who would later have a bitter falling-out with the analyst. "Coming to Los Angeles from New York was like coming to a cultural desert. Ralph Greenson was a breath of New York; he was extraordinarily committed and passionate. He reminded me of the title character in *The Last Angry Man*."

But not everyone was quite so impressed with Greenson's forceful manner. Producer William Fadiman, who had grown up with Greenson in Brooklyn, recalls that when the analyst entertained Margaret Mead, "he told *her* about anthropology. At his dinner parties he usually declaimed or hollered. He wanted to be the center of the action." Fadiman also remembers that while Greenson was remarkably incisive, his brutal candor could be hard to take. "One day he said to me, 'You'll have trouble with one of your four children,' " Fadiman remarks. "He was right, of course, but that's not exactly endearing."

Painter Tony Berlant, who was analyzed by Greenson, points out that the doctor conveyed a different image behind the couch. "He had a knack for ridiculing people in social situations," says Berlant, who sometimes ran into Greenson at parties. "But he was totally different when I saw him in his office. He was aware of this schism. He once told me that the therapeutic situation allowed him to be a kinder, more empathetic person."

Still, Berlant recalls that Greenson was not above manipulating certain patients when he had firm ideas about what was best for them. At the time Greenson was treating him, Berlant was a struggling young artist, and the analyst waived his customary fee because he had received a grant to study creative personalities. By contrast the patient who followed Berlant on the couch was a wealthy executive whom Greenson claimed to be charging one thousand dollars an hour. "Greenson let him know I wasn't paying a penny," Berlant says. Then the analyst would deliberately allow his sessions with Berlant to spill over into the next hour, forcing the executive to cool his heels outside. "He wanted to push the guy into quitting," Berlant explains, "because he thought that would be therapeutic for him."

Though always highly opinionated, Greenson could also be immensely charming. His innate self-confidence allowed him to initiate a friendship with Anna Freud, and that gave him influence in the high councils of international psychoanalysis. "She put him in charge of her armies here," Leo Rosten notes in amusement. When the diminutive doyenne came to Los Angeles for the first and only time, in 1959, Greenson invited her to stay at his home. He took her sightseeing, she swam in his pool, and they even drove out together to visit Palm Springs. The Greensons' hospitality stood in marked contrast to the cold formality with which she was usually treated. "People came to our house after one of her lectures," Hildi Greenson remembers. "Not a soul would sit down on the sofa next to her, to my amazement. I finally went over and sat down beside her, because I couldn't bear it—that she should be so isolated from everybody. They all had such respect. Royalty had truly come our way."

Greenson's ties to Anna Freud were also instrumental in establishing his relationship with Marilyn Monroe. Marilyn's New York analyst, Marianne Kris, was one of Anna Freud's lifelong friends. Kris's father, Oskar Rie, had been the Freud family pediatrician as well as one of Sigmund Freud's Saturday-night card-playing cronies. Marianne's husband, Ernst Kris, was an internationally recognized art historian and was himself a distinguished analyst. Along with Anna Freud, Marianne Kris was one of the leading lights in the field of child analysis. She also lived in the same building as Lee and Paula Strasberg on Central Park West. For Marilyn only a few flights of stairs separated her analyst's couch from the Strasbergs' apartment, where she often spent the night.

But Marilyn's four-year analysis with Dr. Kris was intermittent and largely unproductive. The neglect, abandonment, and abuse that had marked her desolate childhood made her an extraordinarily difficult case to treat. Moreover, her movie commitments, coupled with her erratic behavior and chronic tardiness, rendered the intensive process of psychoanalysis all but impossible. Nonetheless Marilyn became a rapt student of the Freudian science.

While she was filming *The Prince and the Showgirl* with Laurence Olivier in the summer of 1956, Monroe had come upon a disturbing passage in a journal kept by her new husband, Arthur Miller. She told Paula Strasberg, who had accompanied Marilyn to England to serve as her personal acting coach, that the passage "was something about how disappointed he was in me, how he thought I was some kind of angel but now he guessed he was wrong. That his first wife had let him down, but I had done something worse." Marilyn's time on the couch had taught her a thing or two about unconscious motivation, and she was quick to psychoanalyze her husband's behavior. When Paula tried to assure Marilyn that "if you keep a diary, you write all the things you think, good and bad," Marilyn responded, "Yeah, but I wouldn't leave my head wide open for the person I was thinking about to see. That's a little too Freudian."

"Even Freud said sometimes a cigar is just a cigar," Paula reminded her.

"This cigar was on purpose," Marilyn insisted.

As she grew increasingly preoccupied with the implications of her husband's diary entry, Marilyn fell into another of her numbing depressions. Olivier, who was also directing the picture, had by then lost all patience with both Monroe and her meddlesome protectress, Paula Strasberg. Marilyn's wild mood swings jeopardized completion of the film, and Olivier demanded that something be done. Just as Judy Garland's analysts would be called to the set to shepherd her through filming, Marilyn's analyst at the time, Dr. Margaret Hohenberg, was summoned to England to tend to her distraught patient. Dr. Hohenberg had a few sessions with Marilyn on location at Eggham, then sent her to see Anna Freud in London. Under their attentive care Marilyn did recover sufficiently to resume working, and filming was finally completed in November. It was Anna Freud who referred Monroe to Marianne Kris in New York.

Three years later, in early 1960, Marilyn experienced a similar breakdown while shooting *Let's Make Love* in Hollywood. By then her marriage to Miller was floundering, and she had embarked on a disastrous liaison with her costar, Yves Montand. When Montand suddenly cut off the affair, Marilyn became severely depressed and stopped coming to work. What Marilyn needed, Marianne Kris decided, was a psychiatrist in Los Angeles. Ralph Greenson, whose close ties to Anna Freud gave him legitimacy in her eyes, was the doctor she recommended.

At the time Greenson came to see Monroe in her bungalow at the Beverly Hills Hotel, he was well established as a favored Hollywood analyst. His younger sister, Elizabeth, was married to Milton "Mickey" Rudin, an entertainment attorney who was one of the town's major power brokers. People would joke about which brother-in-law had the more star-studded clientele, the lawyer or the analyst. At times the lists overlapped. Greenson's patient Frank Sinatra was a client of Rudin's, as was Marilyn Monroe. Among the analyst's other patients were Peter Lorre, Inger Stevens, and Vivien Leigh, whose public breakdowns had already become the stuff of legend. The story is told of Leigh inviting Greenson to attend a black-tie dinner one evening. When he dutifully showed up in his tuxedo, Leigh introduced him to each of the assembled "guests." Not a soul was actually in attendance, however, except for the analyst and his demented hostess.

Not even a patient as mentally unbalanced as Vivien Leigh could have prepared Greenson for the melancholy case of Marilyn Monroe. During his very first session with Marilyn, after she collapsed on the set of *Let's Make Love* in 1960, Greenson noted her slurred speech and dull affect. When she proceeded to rattle off the drugs she had been taking—Demerol, sodium pentothal, Amytal— he was alarmed. Like so many stars before her, Marilyn was adept at cajoling her various doctors into prescribing stimulants and depressants to keep her working throughout a difficult shooting schedule. Greenson, however, refused to accede; he insisted that she stop taking pills to deal with her insomnia, and she was impressed with his adamant stance. "I told her that she's already received so much medication that it would put five other people to sleep," Greenson later wrote to a colleague. "I promised she would sleep with less medication if she realized she is fighting sleep as well as searching for some obvious oblivion which is not sleep."

Greenson conducted only a few sessions with Monroe, but he did help her to make it through the picture. After the completion of *Let's Make Love* that spring, Marilyn flew back to New York and resumed her treatment with Dr. Kris. A few months later Arthur Miller and she arrived in Reno for the ill-fated filming of *The Misfits*, which Miller had specifically written as a showcase for his wife's dramatic talents. But the couple were barely on speaking terms by then, and the desert heat conspired with Marilyn's heavy drinking to leave her incapacitated much of the time. On the afternoon of August 6, 1960, she collapsed on the set, and was flown to Los Angeles, where she would spend ten days recuperating at a private hospital.

Dr. Greenson visited her there and prescribed a strict regimen to wean her from alcohol and drugs. But when she returned to finish filming *The Misfits*—her marriage to Miller now publicly at an end—she once again hit the bottle. A week after shooting was concluded, her costar Clark Gable succumbed to a fatal heart attack. There were reports that Gable's pregnant widow, Kay, believed that Marilyn's tantrums on the set of *The Misfits* had contributed to Gable's death by forcing him to wait for hours in the blistering sun.

Racked with guilt, Marilyn returned to New York and told Marianne Kris that she was contemplating suicide. As her emotional state deteriorated, Dr. Kris decided that she desperately required hospitalization. Marilyn, who thought that she was being sent for another round of detox and R and R, checked herself into the Payne Whitney Clinic in Manhattan. When she found herself confined to a locked room, however, she became hysterical. Marilyn's mother had been in and out of mental asylums all her life, and it was a pattern that the actress was terrified of repeating. She pleaded with the nurses to release her, then scribbled a letter to Lee and Paula Strasberg, imploring them to assure Dr. Kris that she was sane. Finally she was permitted to call her ex-husband, Joe DiMaggio, who managed to secure her release.

Marilyn's masseur, Ralph Roberts, has described her fury toward Dr. Kris after the disastrous episode at Payne Whitney: "She was like a hurricane unleashed. I don't think Dr. Kris had ever seen her like that, and she was very frightened and shaken. . . . Dr. Kris was trembling, and kept repeating over and over, 'I did a terrible thing, a terrible thing. Oh, God I didn't mean to, but I did.'"

Dr. Kris arranged for Marilyn to be transferred to the neurological unit of Columbia Presbyterian Hospital, a far less forbidding milieu. While she was there, Monroe wrote a letter to Dr. Greenson in Los Angeles. She felt that she could no longer trust Dr. Kris, and she was determined to woo Greenson into becoming her primary analyst. "There was no empathy at Payne Whitney," she wrote to Greenson. "The inhumanity there I found archaic . . . there were screaming women in their cells."

She went on to extol Greenson, expressing the hope that other psychiatrists would emulate the enlightened, compassionate approach that he had shown in treating her. "I think I had better stop because you have other things to do, but thanks for listening for a while," she said in closing.

That spring Marilyn told Dr. Greenson that she had decided to move back permanently to Los Angeles; she asked him to take her on as a regular patient. Greenson had reservations about doing so, but finally agreed. As Marilyn prepared for the move, she kept in constant contact with the analyst by phone. "He's my savior," she told Paula Strasberg. On June 1, 1961, her thirty-fifth birthday, Marilyn sent him a telegram:

> Dear Dr. Greenson,
> In this world of people, I'm glad there's you.
> I have a feeling of hope though today I'm three five.
>
> Marilyn

After settling into her new apartment on Doheny Drive, Marilyn embarked on a program of intensive therapy with Dr. Greenson. He knew that her therapy with Marianne Kris had been haphazard at best. Recognizing that the rigors of traditional psychoanalysis could not be applied to such a "borderline" personality—the term used to describe a constellation of symptoms that includes sexual compulsions, identity problems, and bouts of intense anger—he lit upon a far less orthodox approach, one that would stir bitter controversy among his colleagues.

The unusual course of treatment began when Greenson decided that the high-strung actress needed a less formal environment for psychotherapy than the customary office setting. At first he conducted the analytic hour at Marilyn's apartment. Then he began seeing her in the study of his own home in Santa Monica. After one of the first sessions there, Hildi Greenson remembers, Marilyn went home by taxi and then invited the cabbie to come inside. Greenson "realized this wasn't healthy," Hildi says, "so it was much better if she stayed around."

Marilyn was usually the last appointment of the day, and the analyst would often ask her to stay for supper. Instead of treating her with analytic detachment, Greenson embraced her into his family. Marilyn soon became chummy with the two Greenson children, son Danny and daughter Joan, and sometimes even assisted Mrs. Greenson with the household chores. "She'd help me in the kitchen," Hildi

Greenson recalls. "She'd say, 'I'm good at doing dishes,' and she would wash the dishes. She wouldn't sleep here, but she would often have dinner with the family. Sometimes she would bring us a bottle of champagne or something like that. When we'd have chamber music, my husband would invite her to come and listen. She'd sit in a corner and she'd turn away from the people and the musicians—just listening very intently, all huddled up."

It was not the first time that Marilyn found herself adopted by a surrogate family. She had been shuffled between foster homes as a child, and as an adult she was often taken in by her friends. She slept over at Lee and Paula Strasberg's apartment while she was studying at the Actors Studio, and earlier she had developed similar relationships with the photographer Milton Greene, her partner in Marilyn Monroe Productions, and Greene's wife, Amy, as well as with the poet Norman Rosten and his wife, Hedda. At her friends' homes Marilyn experienced the kind of informal domesticity she had never known as a child. With the Strasbergs' daughter, Susan, and the Rostens' daughter, Patricia, she acted as an attentive older sister, a role she clearly relished.

With Greenson's daughter, Joan, Marilyn developed a comparable attachment. When Marilyn had an appointment to see Dr. Greenson at his home, she would even show up early—very uncharacteristic behavior, and evidence of her eagerness to please the analyst. While waiting for Dr. Greenson, she and Joan, who was studying at a local art college, would go for walks around the nearby reservoir. Marilyn delighted in gabbing about boyfriends and offering tips on makeup. Once she taught Joan how to dance the Twist and, Joan's mother recalls with a smile, how to sashay with a sexy lilt and "give that little kick to the door as you come through."

Dr. Greenson encouraged their friendship and even went so far as to prevail upon Marilyn to attend his daughter's birthday party. "Surprise for our guests: Marilyn was invited, and she came!" Greenson told Norman Rosten, who related the story in his memoir of the actress: "After an initial shock, several boys took turns dancing with her, and soon all of them were on line." Greenson suggested that Marilyn's behavior at the party illustrated how sensitive she could be to other people's feelings. When all the boys lined up to dance with her, they ignored a black girl who, up to that point, had been the belle of the ball. So Marilyn went over and asked her to demonstrate a dance step she had been doing earlier. "Now, the point is, Marilyn knew the step, but she let this girl teach it to her,"

Greenson told Rosten. "She understood the loneliness of others." (Greenson himself did not seem especially sensitive to his daughter's feelings, considering that she was being upstaged at her own bithday party by Marilyn Monroe.)

With Greenson's son, Danny, Marilyn played a different role. She talked current events and left-wing politics, eager to seem committed and intellectually aware. Danny was then studying at UCLA, on his way to becoming a psychiatrist like his father. When Danny decided to look for a place of his own, Marilyn donned a black wig and accompanied him apartment hunting. One night she used that same disguise to slip into the packed auditorium of Beverly Hills High School, where she sat in rapt silence as Dr. Greenson delivered one of his famous lectures.

To Hildi Greenson, Marilyn "really was a waif." She describes the treatment her husband was attempting to effect as "adoption therapy," an effort to normalize Marilyn's field of relationships so that she could then be treated analytically. Mrs. Greenson remarks, "My husband said, when he wanted to bring her into the house, 'This is just not a case that one can analyze. She has to work through a great deal more before she can be analyzed.' She needed to become a whole person again."

His prescription for turning her into a "whole person" derived from the conviction that his own conventional lifestyle was something that Marilyn should emulate. Leo Rosten recalls Greenson's reply when he asked if the doctor wasn't "getting himself in too deep" by becoming so intimately involved with Monroe. "No," he answered, "I want her to have what I have. She needs at least one stable thing in her life." Some of her friends took a different view, suggesting that Marilyn had always been happiest around other "misfits" and outsiders—like her pal Truman Capote—and that she was tortured by her inability to fulfill the roles of wife and mother that society demanded of women at the time. By holding up his own family life as a model, Greenson may well have magnified his patient's deep-seated sense of deprivation and inadequacy.

Greenson's special treatment of Monroe could also be a source of resentment to other patients, especially other actresses. Celeste Holm had spent several years in analysis with Greenson in the early 1950s. She had entered therapy because she wanted to discover why she had, as she puts it, "three dopey marriages" in the course of half a dozen years. After her treatment concluded, she remained friendly with her analyst, and she was a frequent guest at his home. One evening in 1961 she found Marilyn at the Greenson dinner table. "I was jealous," Holm admits. "He hadn't invited me to dinner when I was in analysis." She had worked with Monroe on *All About Eve* a decade earlier, and Holm, a consummate professional, was thoroughly annoyed by the temperamental starlet. Now Marilyn was dining with her analyst, which struck Holm as simply another example of how everyone indulged the kittenish sex goddess. "Whenever Marilyn spoke in that feathery voice of hers," Holm recalls, "conversation stopped."

After dinner Holm and Greenson went for a walk. "What are you doing?" she asked the doctor.

"Celeste, this woman has no concept of family life," Greenson replied. "She was with Marianne Kris for years, but not one thing has touched her. So I'm trying to give her a model. I'm trying to give her some concept of the way it ought to be."

Another patient, actress Janice Rule, recalls similar feelings of envy when she learned that Monroe had been invited to attend chamber music recitals at the Greenson home. "You knew I love music. How come you never invited me?" she asked her analyst.

"You were never that ill," he replied.

"And of course," says Rule, "he was right—thank God."

While the Greenson family may have grown accustomed to having a star around the house, Greenson's fellow analysts were hardly so blasé. Viewed by many of them as self-important and abrasive, Ralph Greenson had already earned his share of enemies, and his rivals buzzed about the fact that he would so freely socialize with his famous patients. More than a few suggested there was something untoward, even sexual, about his relationship with Monroe. Greenson himself took no pains to conceal the fact that Marilyn was under his care. In fact, he seems to have flaunted his relationship with her. "You *knew* Romi was treating Marilyn Monroe," comments Tamar Hoffs. "Nobody had to tell you." Says Leo Rosten, recalling one occasion when he was a houseguest and Marilyn was in the kitchen, "Romi was furious with me because I didn't want to come down and meet her. I just stayed upstairs in Danny's room."

Greenson's wife and children were fond of Marilyn, but her volatile personality always held them at bay. "You couldn't help but like her," says Hildi Greenson. "But difficult! My God, she could flare!" When Marilyn heard about a spat between Joan Greenson and one of Joan's friends, she flew into a rage, rushing to Joan's defense. "She got furious and would not talk to that friend ever again," says Hildi Greenson. "Poor Joanie didn't know what to do. You always treaded on eggshells with Marilyn. You always had to be careful about what you'd say and how you'd say it."

Hildi Greenson also remembers the burden of coping with Marilyn's extreme dependency. "There were times when we were away on a trip," she says, "and we would get so many phone calls from her. The whole family had to help out. My son would have to go by and see her. She was bright and lovely and interesting, but there was something really very schizzy about her."

Dr. Greenson's own earliest diagnosis of Marilyn was that she did exhibit signs of schizophrenia, as well as "depressive reaction." Commenting on her attitudes toward the people around her, Greenson wrote, "As she becomes more anxious, she begins to act like an orphan, a waif, and she masochistically provokes them to mistreat her and to take advantage of her."

In Dr. Greenson's view, if Marilyn was ever to break this vicious cycle of neediness and masochistic provocation, she would have to rid herself of her cadre of hangers-on. She needed someone whom she (and her psychiatrist) could trust. Greenson set out to eliminate the old circle of hirelings, including her acting coach, Paula Strasberg, and her masseur and confidant, Ralph Roberts, both of whom bitterly resented this new Svengali in her life. In their place he brought in a woman named Eunice Murray to serve as the actress's companion and, in Mrs. Murray's words, "devoted assistant." Mrs. Murray had first met the Greenson family when she and her husband sold them the Santa Monica house that the Murrays had built. Mrs. Murray had remained friendly with the Greensons, and he would sometimes help to find work for her as a nurse-companion. After Dr. Greenson convinced Marilyn to hire her, Marilyn referred to the matron as "my caretaker." In fact, Mrs. Murray was also acting as Dr. Greenson's eyes and ears; the psychiatrist instructed her to report to him any unusual behavior on his patient's part.

At Greenson's urging, Marilyn purchased a small Mexican-style residence in Brentwood, not far from his own house in Santa Monica. It was the first home Marilyn had ever owned, and Greenson believed it would strengthen her sense of independence and responsibility. By early 1962, when she moved in, Marilyn and Mrs. Murray were busily selecting the colorful Mexican tiles that would replicate the look and feel of the Greensons' home. "It's like my doctor's house," Marilyn explained to Susan Strasberg, proudly showing off the little hacienda to her friend. "Of course, his is bigger."

Her psychoanalyst's allegiance to Anna Freud may not have been Marilyn's sole reason for declining John Huston's offer to costar as the deranged Cecily in his production of *Freud*. As Gloria Steinem has observed in her feminist reading of Marilyn's life story, had she agreed to perform the role of a father-fixated mental patient, Marilyn's emotional problems might have been seriously exacerbated. "Marilyn would have been called upon to enact the psychotic fate she feared most in real life," Steinem suggests, " . . . and to play the patient of a man whose belief in female passivity may have been part of the reason she was helped so little by psychiatry."

Instead of participating in this somber psychodrama, Marilyn chose to make a fluffy romantic comedy. She still owed one film to Twentieth Century-Fox under the terms of an old contract, and for the meager fee of $100,000 she reluctantly agreed to dispose of that obligation. She would star opposite her friend Dean Martin in *Something's Got to Give*, the remake of a 1939 Cary Grant–Irene Dunne programmer called *My Favorite Wife*. Dr. Greenson encouraged her to make the picture so that she could finally close out her commitment to Fox, which he believed was causing her professional frustration and personal anxiety. As it turned out, the pressures of filming this ostensibly harmless trifle would prove far more agonizing than any she could have confronted in filming Huston's *Freud*.

In 1962 Twentieth Century-Fox was a studio in turmoil. Darryl Zanuck, the flamboyant mogul who had almost singlehandedly molded the company, had slipped off to Paris six years earlier to nurse the careers of a string of starlet-mistresses. In Zanuck's absence Fox had fallen into the hands of an ex-exhibitor, Spyros Skouras, who, together with his hand-picked production chief, Peter Levathes, was rapidly running the studio into the ground. Levathes, a former advertising executive, was a Hollywood outsider whose principal qualification for his post seems to have been that he, like his benefactor Skouras, was of Greek extraction. In the spring of 1962, as preparations were under way for *Something's Got to Give* on the Fox lot, Darryl Zanuck was in Europe re-creating the invasion of Normandy for his monumental production of *The Longest Day*. At the same time, he was plotting to reinvade Hollywood and wrest control of Fox from the hostile Greeks.

Levathes' uneasiness about Zanuck's return was compounded by the wars raging on another front. Joseph Mankiewicz's production of *Cleopatra*, starring Elizabeth Taylor and Richard Burton, was running so far over budget that the studio was drowning in red ink. Taylor's public temper tantrums had already cost the studio untold millions, and the skittish Levathes was in no mood to indulge another prima donna named Marilyn Monroe.

Not long after *Something's Got to Give* started filming on the Fox lot, Marilyn began calling in sick. At first the company tried to shoot around her. She finally showed up for work for a couple of days, then disappeared again. Such erratic behavior was nothing new for Marilyn, as anyone who had ever worked with her could attest. For most of her career studio chiefs, producers, and directors had made allowances for these infuriating habits; they knew that her name on the marquee meant long lines at the ticket window. But now, as Fox teetered precariously on the brink of bankruptcy, other nerves besides hers were growing frayed. The front office was frantic, and Levathes demanded that producer Henry Weinstein lay down the law to his temperamental star.

Weinstein was torn. He sympathized with Marilyn, who was suffering from an acute sinus infection much of the time, and he also believed that her feelings of insecurity were genuine. On those rare occasions when she did arrive for work, Weinstein recalled, she would throw up at the studio gate. "We all experience anxiety, unhappiness, heartbreak," he reports having thought. "But that was sheer primal terror." Still, Levathes was turning the screws, and Weinstein, too, had a lot riding on the picture. A theatrical producer who had worked on only one previous film, Weinstein was as inexperienced at moviemaking as Levathes. Neither of them had the slightest inkling of how to cope with a creature as mercurial as Marilyn Monroe.

Director George Cukor, by contrast, was a Hollywood veteran who had handled a galaxy of high-strung stars, from the great Garbo to Judy Garland and Anna Magnani. Before filming *Something's Got to Give*, Cukor had worked with Marilyn on *Let's Make Love*, but even he found directing her to be a unique challenge. For one thing, he told his friends in exasperation, "if you needed to get in touch with Marilyn, you didn't call her secretary, her agent, or her lawyer. You called her psychiatrist!"

Henry Weinstein thought Marilyn's dependence on her analyst might give him an advantage. He and Dr. Greenson were friends of

long duration, and David Brown, whom Weinstein replaced as producer of *Something's Got to Give* when the old Zanuck regime was
purged by Skouras and Levathes, has indicated that it was Greenson
who recommended Weinstein for the job. Weinstein insists that is
not true, but the producer and the analyst did have innumerable
consultations during preproduction and filming.

Problems on the set were not all they discussed. Marilyn, who
was in the habit of calling people at all hours of the night, once
awakened Weinstein with the news that she had just come back
from an exciting adventure. She had located the address of her father, put on a disguise, arrived at his doorstep, and seduced him. A
shocked Weinstein promptly phoned Greenson, who dismissed the
story as another of Marilyn's extravagant fantasies. (It was not the
first time that Monroe told such a tale. According to another friend,
she once attended a dinner party in New York where the guests were
all asked to relate personal fantasies; Marilyn described donning a
black wig to disguise herself, searching out the aging Lothario who
had abandoned her pregnant mother, making love to him, and then
asking how it felt to be seduced by his own daughter.)

As Marilyn's conflicts with Weinstein and the studio intensified,
her visits to Dr. Greenson turned into a daily ritual. The analyst
cleared his calendar in order to accommodate her, and their sessions would sometimes extend for five hours at a sitting. Marilyn's
biographer Anthony Summers quotes a letter Greenson sent to a
colleague describing the grueling routine. "I had become a prisoner
of a form of treatment that I thought was correct for her, but almost
impossible for me," Greenson wrote. "At times I felt I couldn't go
on with this."

Greenson had delayed a planned trip to Switzerland with his
wife in order to help Marilyn make it through the filming of *Something's Got to Give*. In early May, however, he left the actress in the
care of his associate, Milton Wexler, and finally departed for Europe. Marilyn's anxiety about her analyst's absence was compounded by worries she had over a trip that she, too, was scheduled
to take.

On May 19 a gala fund-raiser was to be held at Madison Square
Garden to celebrate President John F. Kennedy's forty-fifth birthday. At the instigation of Marilyn's friend and the President's
brother-in-law, Peter Lawford, Marilyn had agreed to come on stage
and serenade the guest of honor with a breathy rendition of "Happy
Birthday." But Marilyn was so terrified by the prospect of appearing

before the throng that she called Greenson in Switzerland, who asked his son, Danny, to visit the distraught actress and lend moral support. Daughter Joan was enlisted to help Marilyn rehearse, and she offered a copy of the children's book *The Little Engine That Could* for inspiration. When Marilyn finally did make her appearance on stage before fifteen thousand adoring fans, they and the President of the United States were enchanted. "I can now retire from politics," said JFK, "having had 'Happy Birthday' sung to me in such a sweet, wholesome way."

If this had all been an expensive publicity stunt hatched by Twentieth Century-Fox, the flack who conceived it would have been hailed as a genius. But Peter Levathes, evidently oblivious to the value of free PR, was enraged that a star too "ill" to come to work had flown to New York to sing to the President. It was the last straw. He instructed Henry Weinstein to fire Marilyn from *Something's Got to Give*.

When he returned from Europe, Greenson was livid over the handling of Marilyn's dismissal. "He was furious that they fired her, and he bawled out Weinstein and probably whoever else he could get hold of," Hildi Greenson recalls. "Romi was very disappointed that Weinstein didn't have enough muscle to prevent that."

Weinstein acknowledges that Greenson had reason to be miffed, since no one had bothered to call him in Switzerland before the decision to fire Marilyn was finalized. "He might have been able to keep her propped up," Weinstein speculates, but the producer doubts that anyone could have saved her. "She was a very, very frightened, paranoid person," he says.

Celeste Holm, who first introduced the producer and the psychiatrist, suggests that in some sense Marilyn got caught in the middle of a power struggle between the two men. "Henry, of course, felt Greenson's strength," she says. "Anyone who knew Greenson felt it. But as a producer, he wanted to show that he was stronger than Greenson." And so he defied the analyst by aligning himself with the studio brass, who demanded that he take a hard line with Marilyn. Holm notes that, ironically, the whole affair did as much to damage Weinstein's budding career as it did to destroy Marilyn. "If he'd had any sense," says Holm, "he would have gone in and said, 'This is a great talent. You may not like her and she may be difficult to work with, but what we get on the screen is worth it.' That's what Moss Hart did with Judy Garland on *A Star Is Born*."

Greenson continued to minister to Marilyn over the course of the next few months. She had never before been fired from a picture, and she felt crushed by the brutal rejection and apprehensive about her future employability. Meanwhile, the studio added salt to the wound by mounting a carefully calculated publicity campaign making her out to be the villain in the embarrassing fiasco.

Career troubles were not all that preoccupied her that summer. She was upset that Arthur Miller's new wife, a photographer named Inge Morath whom he had met on the set of *The Misfits*, was now pregnant with his child. (Her own pregnancies when she was married to Miller had ended in miscarriages.) Marilyn was also feeling spurned by the Kennedys, who, like so many of the other men in her life, had toyed with her briefly and then abandoned her.

For Dr. Greenson, tending to this single patient had become an all-consuming occupation. He was tempted to have her hospitalized, but, remembering her hysteria when she was confined to Payne Whitney at the behest of Marianne Kris, he worried that she would crack again if she felt she was being incarcerated. Greenson later wrote a letter to a colleague in which he observed, "I should have played it safe and put her in a sanitarium, but that would have only been safe for me and deadly for her."

According to Greenson's version of events, on the afternoon of Saturday, August 4, 1962, he stopped by to check up on Marilyn at her home in Brentwood. "She seemed somewhat depressed," he recalled feeling, "but I had seen her many, many times in a much worse condition." A few hours later, as he was preparing to go out for dinner, Marilyn called him at home. They talked for a while, then he urged her to get some sleep. At three o'clock the next morning, he told authorities, he was awakened by a phone call from Marilyn's companion, Eunice Murray. Distressed to see a light still shining in Marilyn's locked bedroom, Mrs. Murray asked Greenson what she should do. Greenson immediately drove over to Marilyn's house.

When Greenson peered into the window of Marilyn's bedroom, he saw her lying facedown on the bed, the telephone receiver clutched in her right hand. After smashing the window pane with a poker, he managed to climb inside. An empty bottle of Nembutal sat atop the cluttered nightstand.

He turned to Mrs. Murray. "We've lost her," he said.

Later on the morning of August 5, Los Angeles Police Sergeant Jack Clemmons arrived at Monroe's house. He was the first law enforcement officer on the scene, and he claimed that he was troubled by Dr. Greenson's delay in calling the police after discovering her body. To this day Clemmons insists that Greenson had a hand in Marilyn's death. "It was the most obvious murder I ever saw," Clemmons told author Sandra Shevey in 1987, a charge he has made on numerous other occasions. Clemmons, a right-wing zealot who was once indicted by a grand jury for conspiring to libel California Senator Thomas Kuchel, resigned from the police department in 1965. His claim of "murder" is generally dismissed as ludicrous, but the oft-repeated charge continues to fan the flames of controversy. Because Greenson was among the last people to see Marilyn alive, and because he was the first person to find her body, he has been a prime target of the conspiracy theorists who, like Sergeant Clemmons, refuse to accept that her death was either accidental or suicide.

Marilyn's furtive trysts with President Kennedy and her alleged dalliance with his brother Bobby, combined with the murky circumstances surrounding her last night alive, have given rise to any number of bizarre scenarios. According to one, contained in a booklet for which Sergeant Clemmons supplied data and which was published two years after Marilyn's death when Robert Kennedy was running for the U.S. Senate, the politically liberal Dr. Greenson was a fellow traveler who acted as the agent of a Communist party plot to kill the actress because she threatened to expose her affair with Bobby Kennedy, the Reds' Manchurian candidate. According to an equally outlandish theory, Greenson was the agent of the Kennedys themselves, who wanted to silence Marilyn and save themselves from scandal. Still another alleges that she was killed by the CIA, which sought to discredit the Kennedys. In another, she was killed by the FBI, because J. Edgar Hoover wanted to seize her phone records and get the goods on Bobby. Yet another conjecture is that she was killed by the Mafia, to frame the Kennedys and drive them out of office. And one recent book even claims that Greenson himself had become so moonstruck over Marilyn that he murdered his patient in a jealous rage.

A somewhat more plausible hypothesis regarding Dr. Greenson's involvement in Marilyn's death is advanced in *Marilyn Monroe: The Biography* by Donald Spoto. Drawing upon toxicological evidence from a deputy district attorney who investigated the case, Spoto attributes the cause of death to an accidental overdose of chloral hydrate which, he speculates, Mrs. Murray administered rectally, at Greenson's behest, to help Marilyn get to sleep. According to Spoto, Greenson panicked when he realized that his hand-picked "nurse" had bungled the procedure. In order to cover up their incompetence, the author contends, Greenson concocted the story of Mrs. Murray's early morning phone call and then staged the window breaking. This "fatal enema" theory—which Spoto uses to exculpate the Kennedys of plotting to murder Marilyn—does have the advantage of cleaning up certain messy questions, such as why Mrs. Murray was doing laundry at midnight.

The credibility of Spoto's argument, however, is compromised by his extreme tendentiousness. To reinforce his claim that both Greenson and Mrs. Murray acted with villainous irresponsibility, he draws a portrait of the pair as evil incarnate. He even goes so far as to allege that Greenson once slugged Marilyn because he was enraged that she had sabotaged his vacation to Switzerland. Glibly psychoanalyzing the psychoanalyst, Spoto ascribes Greenson's love-hate relationship with the star to a pathological sibling rivalry with his concert pianist sister, Juliet, "whom he loved, admired, protected, applauded, and bitterly resented." Spoto sniffishly dismisses most of his rival biographers as purveyors of empty conspiracy theories, but his own book is suffused with a similar demonology. Instead of skewing the record to point the finger of blame at the Kennedys, the Mafia, or the CIA, he simply skews it to target the psychotic analyst and the wicked housekeeper.

Certainly it was no secret in Hollywood that Greenson was Marilyn Monroe's psychiatrist, but in the wake of her apparent suicide, he found his name splattered across the front pages of newspapers all around the world. The notoriety was not just cause for professional embarrassment but a source of personal anguish as well. For Greenson had developed an extraordinarily close relationship with his patient, one that had broken the so-called analytic incognito and led to a familial feeling between them that was as intense as it was unorthodox.

Reporters hounded the analyst, demanding to know if he had done everything possible to save Marilyn's life. Janice Rule, who was in analysis with Greenson at the time Marilyn died, remembers how "crucified" he felt by the press. She recalls that when she mentioned Marilyn's death during one session with Greenson, "he said something very moving: 'There is no way in my lifetime I will ever be able to answer any of this. I only worry how it will affect you as my patient.'"

"Marilyn's death was extremely painful for him," confirms Greenson's widow, Hildi. "Not just that it was so public, which was terrible in itself, but that Marilyn, he felt, was doing much better. He knew he hadn't quite brought her through, but she was better— and then to lose her, that was quite painful." About a week after her death, at his wife's urging, Greenson went to visit his friend Max Schur in New York. Schur had been Sigmund Freud's personal physician as well as one of the few confidants whom Freud trusted until the end of his life. For twelve hours straight Greenson poured out his feelings about Marilyn and her death, hoping that he could, in his words, "eventually *begin* to get over this."

Before his visit to Schur, Greenson had been so distressed that he could barely bring himself to keep his regular appointments. "It was awful," he said, "but I felt I had to go. And I went, and I *was* upset. And my patients saw me upset." Their reactions mirrored the range of attitudes he would find expressed by friends and strangers over the next several years. "Some of them saw no reaction in me, and were furious at me for being so cold and impersonal. They asked how could I come and work the next day, and how could I have taken such a patient anyway, and they were angry. Other patients felt sorry for me, and were sympathetic, and were crying. With some of them, I had tears in my eyes, and I couldn't hide it, and they saw it. And with some, I had tears in my eyes, and they didn't see it."

Seven years after the event, Greenson was still describing himself as "devastated" by Marilyn's death. "I don't know that I will ever get over it really or completely," he said. Noting that Marilyn had seen a number of therapists before him, he even came to question his own motives in presuming that he could somehow save her: "I was perhaps grandiose in thinking I could do something other than they did."

In an early study of neurotic gamblers, Greenson had discerned a connection between the gambler's willingness to "expose himself to fate" and "longings for omnipotence." His own decision to take on the case of Marilyn Monroe was an audacious gamble, and in the end, he felt, it was a gamble he had lost. "She was a poor creature whom I tried to help and ended up hurting," he ruefully admitted. Perhaps his own longings for omnipotence had clouded his judgment.

Still, Greenson was staunchly unrepentant about having taken the risk of treating her. "I knew it was a difficult case, but what should I have done? Turn it over to a beginner?" he would ask rhetorically. Despite his background as a disciple of the strict constructionist Otto Fenichel and his continuing role as one of Anna Freud's torchbearers, Greenson came to question the strictures of traditional Freudian analysis. In 1967 he published the first volume of his comprehensive textbook, *The Technique and Practice of Psychoanalysis*. In the introduction he noted with characteristic self-approbation that the previous works on the subject written by Freud, Fenichel, and others, "excellent as they are, are only outlines." He intended to fill in the picture by melding an encyclopedic knowledge of the psychoanalytic literature with his own practical experience treating patients. All too often, he observed, practitioners fall into one of two categories—the "conservatives" who are "rigid with orthodoxy," or the "secluded innovators" who are seen as "wild." If Greenson himself had once been an exemplar of the former, his controversial treatment of patients like Marilyn Monroe had steered him in the direction of the latter. His book—which is still considered a definitive text on technique—became an apologia for his own evolution from detached Freudian to an empathic healer intensely involved in his patients' lives.

One of Greenson's most important theories was that of the so-called working alliance. In developing this delicate relationship with a patient, Greenson pointed out, the analyst must inevitably enter a private world other than his own. "The origin of the urge to understand a patient can be traced back to the propensity to get inside another human being," he wrote in a famous paper on the subject. In establishing empathy with a patient, the therapist must be simultaneously detached and engaged, he argued.

"You can't sit there like a computer, or like a note-taker, or like a historian or a research worker or some neutral, neuter object observing a specimen of a creature in front of you," he told a group of students in 1969. He was especially mocking of "that blank wooden Indian face called the analytic posture. . . . I've seen more patients driven mad by that than by anything else." Instead, he contended, the therapist must "show a willingness to be involved with the person, within limits."

But who defines those "limits," and how does the therapist ever know whether he is exercising an appropriate restraint? Commenting on Greenson's relationship with Marilyn Monroe, Leo Rangell, Greenson's longtime adversary and a leading proponent of classical Freudian detachment, says, "This was seductive behavior, not ther-

-apeutic behavior." A glamorous movie star is precisely the kind of patient who must be treated "gingerly and unseductively," Rangell insists. "We all have very needy, traumatized patients. Very few of them end up in our families the way she did. She did because she was Marilyn Monroe! Even 'family therapy' doesn't mean therapy in the analyst's family."

"When Greenson or I would examine a student," Rangell declares, "such a thing would disqualify the student. And yet in the late stages of his career, when he was already a model for a lot of these people, he did not hesitate to do things that would only raise eyebrows. His earlier writings would never condone what he did."

Greenson's colleague Dr. Melvin Mandel is less sardonic but equally skeptical of Greenson's rationales for "adopting" Monroe as he did. "If it was true that she came from a tremendously deprived background," Mandel notes, "you couldn't go on with her in a strictly analytic way. It wouldn't work. I can imagine that's how he perceived it." Nevertheless Mandel wonders whether Greenson was motivated solely by the disinterested desire to help his patient. "You can never be sure of one's motivation in such a situation," Mandel suggests. "He liked having people like that around. And maybe she needed it. But how much did he need it too? If an analyst is enthralled with stardom and himself has an unconscious wish to be on stage (and Greenson *was* a superb performer), he may seek to identify himself with prominent people."

One therapist who tries to see the relationship between Greenson and Monroe in a larger cultural context is Dr. Lorraine Kaufman, the wife of screenwriter Millard Kaufman. Dr. Kaufman, who knew Greenson both professionally and socially over the years, points out that "Freud had supported the Wolf-Man" in much the same way that Greenson attempted to sustain Monroe. The Hungarian analyst Sandor Ferenczi went so far as to advocate familiarity, even affection, as a means of showing "humanness" toward a patient. (Freud once had to admonish Ferenczi for taking patients on his lap and showering them with kisses.) But, Dr. Kaufman notes, the impulse to lend such support comes out of an essentially European tradition. American psychiatry, in contrast, "grew out of American medicine, which is not familial, not community-oriented. The American tradition is to keep your distance, shut your door and not know your neighbor." Kaufman sees Greenson's treatment of Monroe as something that would be far less controversial in Europe, where doctors were wont to "offer shelter to an orphan in the storm."

*   *   *

The death of Marilyn Monroe marked a turning point in Ralph Greenson's life. He went through a long period of soul-searching and reassessment, taking on fewer private patients and immersing himself in his teaching and writing. He even decided to grow a beard, in a conscious effort to alter his physical appearance. Like the schoolboy who boldly announced that he no longer wished to be known as Romeo, he once again tried to reinvent himself. When Julian Blaustein saw the analyst with his new beard, he asked whether it had any significance. "I wanted to be somebody else," Greenson told him.

Says a younger colleague of Greenson's from this period, "He had lost a lot of the old fire. He wasn't the vigorous fighter he used to be. The beard was his way of turning himself into an elder statesman."

On occasion, however, he did rekindle the old fire, as when he railed against the gruesome film version of *The Exorcist*. When the picture was released in 1973, it quickly turned into a box-office smash, and a national phenomenon to boot. Front-page articles and network news features told of moviegoers all across the country fainting or vomiting in theaters as a result of the horrific spectacle. Priests and psychiatrists came forward to report their own cases of "demonic possession."

The author of *The Exorcist*, William Peter Blatty, had conceived the story as a celebration of the supernatural and a derogation of rational science. The film's hero is a priest-psychologist who has been plagued with doubts about his religious faith. Only when he abandons his role as secular counselor and reaffirms his belief in Christian mysticism can he save the twelve-year-old victim from Satan.

Such a message was bound to rankle a Freudian rationalist like Ralph Greenson. Outraged by the movie's spectacular success, Greenson penned an article for *Saturday Review*, lambasting the film's grisly sensationalism and taking it to task for the way it "degrades the medical profession and psychiatry." He described two acquaintances who came to him for treatment, a social worker and a university professor, both of whom suffered psychotic episodes after they saw *The Exorcist*. Many of his colleagues, he added, had received similar emergency calls from ostensibly normal individuals who were "freaking out" over the movie. Blaming the film for "pouring acid on our already corroded values and ideals," Greenson declared that it was not just a danger to "anyone whose emotional and mental balance is precarious" but to society as a whole. The analyst sounded a dire, apocalyptic warning, arguing that the movie's primary theme—"the devil made me do it"—absolved human beings of personal responsibility and so fed the pervasive "self-centeredness, greed, and immorality" reflected in worldwide calamities "from Bangladesh, Vietnam, Watergate, to the famine in India."

"We have to accept the fact that we are all part of the brotherhood of man," Greenson concluded, in his most somber (some might say sexist) tone. "We can and must do more to help our fellow man. Otherwise, we will become not just a sick society, but worse—a morally corrupt one. It is against this background that *The Exorcist* is a menace to our community. It should be X-rated."

As a postscript to Dr. Greenson's diatribe, the magazine printed a bemused response from its principal film critic, Hollis Alpert, who mocked the "censorial-minded" analyst for extrapolating from "a couple of hysterical cases" and building them "into a national attack of the jitters."

"I have some friends, a few cases here and there, who I feel were harmed, not helped, by psychiatric treatment," Alpert noted with asperity. "But should I go crying therefore, for all to hear, that psychiatrists are dangerous?"

That flap was one of Greenson's last forays into the media spotlight. He had a long history of coronary illness, and after his third pacemaker was inserted in the mid-1970s, he began to suffer from aphasia. "That was very hard for someone who had so many words for everything," observes Janice Rule. "He became enraged when he found that he couldn't express himself." Another friend and former patient of Greenson's, Celeste Holm, recalls introducing him to her mother, whom he had once counseled over the telephone following her own heart attack. "You don't look like an analyst," Holm's mother told the doctor, apparently expecting a more robust presence to match the authoritative voice she remembered hearing on the phone. Greenson lifted his shirt and showed her the scar from his pacemaker surgery. "We're just as mortal as everyone else," he replied. He died in 1979, at the age of sixty-eight.

*　　*　　*

"I will not discuss psychoanalysis, except to say that I believe in the Freudian interpretation," Marilyn Monroe once told an interviewer. With an irony she could not possibly have fathomed, she added, "I hope at some future time to make a glowing report on the wonders psychiatrists can do for you." Certainly Ralph Greenson, like Marianne Kris before him, was intent on performing whatever wonders he could for the desperate star. But there are those who argue that his methods were based on a paternalistic belief system that intensified, rather than mitigated, the most self-destructive aspects of her personality. Gloria Steinem speaks of Marilyn's "dangerous permission to remain dependent," a condition "that even her various psychiatrists may have reinforced." By indoctrinating her with "Freudian assumptions of female passivity, penis envy and the like," Steinem contends, psychoanalysis probably did Marilyn more harm than good.

Steinem's profile of Marilyn is especially intriguing in light of Greenson's case study of someone whom he identifies simply as "an emotionally immature young woman patient, who had developed a very dependent transference to me." It is not hard to recognize the striking resemblance between this unnamed patient and Monroe. Greenson wrote that when he told the patient of his plans to go abroad, she became extremely anxious about his leaving her. Doctor and patient attempted to get at the sources of her "clinging dependence," but made little progress. The situation changed dramatically, however, when she received a carved chess set as a gift. Now she realized that she could survive, Greenson wrote, because "as she looked at the set, through the sparkling light of a glass of champagne, it suddenly struck her that I looked like the white knight of her chess set. The white knight looked like a protector, it belonged to her, she could carry it wherever she went, it would look after her, and I could go on my merry way to Europe without having to worry about her."

Greenson related that he felt some misgivings as he left on his trip, but he also felt a trace of relief. "The patient's major concern about the period of my absence was a public performance of great importance to her," he wrote. "She now felt confident of success because she could conceal her white knight in her handkerchief or scarf; she was certain that he would protect her from nervousness, anxiety, or bad luck. I was relieved and delighted to learn, while in Europe, that her performance had been a smashing success." Not long afterward, however, Greenson received "several panicky transatlantic phone calls." The patient had misplaced her talisman and she "was beside herself with terror and gloom, like a child who has lost her security blanket." Reluctantly Greenson cut short his vacation and returned to care for his distraught charge. "I no sooner saw her than her anxiety and depression lifted," he reported. Doctor and patient then set about exploring "how she had used me as a good luck charm rather than an analyst."

Greenson cited this case history (which fits with his trip to Switzerland and Marilyn's performance at JFK's birthday party) in order to illustrate how the patient used her chess piece as a "transitional object" in the process of psychoanalytic transference. But it also suggests something about the phenomenon of countertransference, the analyst's emotional attachment to his patient. Greenson's willingness to cut short his trip and tend to his anxious patient probably did more to increase her dependence than to lessen it. And how much, one might ask, did the doctor really *want* to diminish her reliance on him? Being perceived as a "white knight" could be exhilarating under any circumstances. If the patient also happens to be the world's most glamorous movie star, how much more thrilling would it be?

More than one witness has attested to Marilyn's own recurrent fantasy of searching out and then seducing the father she had never known. In the psychoanalytic process of transference the analyst often becomes a father figure for the patient, and it is not unlikely that Marilyn did, if only in some unconscious way, repeat this pattern of seduction with her doctor. The question that Greenson's more skeptical colleagues asked was whether he, or any analyst, could know the extent to which he was blinded by her allure. "This was, after all, a woman who had seduced the whole world," one of them pointedly observes. "What made him think she couldn't seduce him too?"

There is a moment toward the end of *Captain Newman, M.D.* when the compassionate psychiatrist played by Gregory Peck learns of the combat death of a young soldier whose emotional traumas he had succeeded in healing. "Our job is to make them well," Peck cynically remarks, "well enough to go out and get killed."

In a sense, Captain Newman's disillusionment reflected the dilemma of the man who was his real-life inspiration. When Ralph Greenson devoted himself to the treatment of Marilyn Monroe, he surely had a sincere desire to help his patient. But to what end? So that she could go on feeding the fantasies of her fans and filling the coffers of the studios? Like so many other psychiatrists who fell into the all-consuming frenzy of moviemaking, Greenson frequently found himself repairing the patient in order to salvage a film—and the studio's investment. That is what Margaret Hohenberg had been called in to do for Marilyn on *The Prince and the Showgirl*, and what Greenson did on *Let's Make Love*, again on *The Misfits*, and finally on *Something's Got to Give*. Yet no one, not even her white knight, could go on mending the fragile star forever.

Despite the tragic death of Marilyn Monroe, Greenson never lost his infatuation with Hollywood. Leo Rosten recalls with affection, "Romi would often come to me and say, 'I have the greatest idea for a movie!' It was always absurd. He usually had the first scene down pat—the hero was seen fishing from the gondola of a balloon—something along those lines. But he could never go beyond that."

If Ralph Greenson delighted in his own creativity and loved to hobnob with filmland luminaries, he also understood the darker side of the movie business. That may explain why he could never get beyond the first scenes of his imagined scenarios. Having shared the real anguish of the idols who light up the screen, he knew better than anyone the fraudulence of Hollywood happy endings.

5. THE CONFIDENCE GAME

A decade before Ralph Greenson was thrust into the public spotlight as a result of the death of Marilyn Monroe, another shrink-to-the-stars found himself at the center of an even more morbid scandal. On August 28, 1951, Dr. Frederick Hacker, a Viennese emigré who was one of the premier psychoanalysts in Beverly Hills, received a frantic phone call from the housekeeper of Robert Walker. The young actor who had starred in such diverse films as *The Clock, Till the Clouds Roll By,* and *Strangers on a Train* was in a state of uncontrollable hysteria. Dr. Hacker rushed to Walker's home to take charge of the situation.

Walker's personal life had been troubled ever since his separation from Jennifer Jones, whom he had married at the age of twenty when both were struggling actors in New York. On their arrival in Hollywood they costarred in David O. Selznick's 1944 production *Since You Went Away.* But by the time they made that movie together, the couple (who had two young sons) were already estranged. Selznick aggressively pursued the comely starlet, and she soon found herself embroiled in a messy triangle. The affair between Selznick and Jones broke up two marriages; Selznick left his wife, Irene, the daughter of Louis B. Mayer, to marry his newfound protegée. Walker grew despondent after his divorce. He began drinking heavily, and his behavior became wildly erratic. In 1948 he was arrested on charges of drunk and disorderly conduct. Dore Schary, the head of production at MGM, where Walker was under contract, presented him with an ultimatum: If he did not submit to psychiatric treatment at the Menninger Clinic in Topeka, Kansas, he would be fired.

Schary's order was very much in keeping with the mood of the times in Hollywood. Studios were beginning to rely on psychiatrists to subdue temperamental actors, and Walker was one of a number of unstable performers shipped off to Topeka for rehabilitation. Frederick Hacker had trained at the Menninger Clinic, and it was Karl Menninger who referred Walker to Hacker. Once the actor left the sanitarium and returned to California, he began regular therapy sessions with Dr. Hacker.

On that night of August 28, 1951, when Hacker arrived at Walker's Brentwood home, he found the actor ranting incoherently. After consulting with his associate, Dr. Sidney Silver, Hacker decided to administer a sedative. Walker resisted at first, but a friend of the actor's named Jim Henaghan held him down while Hacker gave him a shot of sodium amytal. Almost immediately Walker went into shock. A fire department rescue squad summoned to the house could not revive him. There was a torrential rain that night, but after Walker was pronounced dead of respiratory failure, a dazed Dr. Hacker was seen wandering aimlessly outside without a coat, oblivious to the downpour.

On several previous occasions when Hacker had given Walker injections of sodium amytal, there had been no visible problems. It was a well-known medical fact, however, that the drug could accumulate in a patient's system and eventually produce toxic side effects. In addition, alcohol compounded the dangers of sodium amytal, and Walker had been drinking that evening. Before administering the injection, Hacker had failed to determine the level of barbiturates already in Walker's bloodstream.

Dore Schary, who was called to Walker's house immediately after the incident, later wrote about it in his autobiography: "Some doctors choose not to run the risk of using such a drug in treating someone who has been drinking. It is not always a fatal risk, but according to some doctors, it is advisable to have oxygen handy when using the drug because of the danger that the depressive effect of the drug, added to the depressive effect of a large amount of alcohol (which Bob had ingested), might cause a respiratory arrest." Schary also reported that there were bloodstains on Walker's arm where the needle had jabbed him while he was struggling with Dr. Hacker.

The authorities spared Dr. Hacker the embarrassment of a probing inquest. According to a *Los Angeles Times* story at the time, "The Coroner's office, holding a death certificate signed by two attending physicians, Dr. Frederick J. Hacker and Dr. Sidney H. Silver, said that there will be no investigation." Robert Walker was thirty-two years old when he died.

After Walker's death his eleven-year-old son, Robert Walker, Jr., was devastated. His mother and stepfather, David O. Selznick, decided to send the boy to a psychiatrist to help him deal with the tragedy. The psychiatrist they selected, astonishingly enough, was Frederick Hacker. "I didn't know Hacker had anything to do with my father's death," Walker says today. "He gave me a few psychological tests. I remember thinking even then that he seemed like a pompous know-it-all. But I don't blame him for what happened to my father. I just feel he didn't know any better. You can't blame somebody for being ignorant."

In speaking about the incident four decades later, some of Hacker's colleagues are far less forgiving. Says Dr. Alex Rogawski, a prominent Los Angeles analyst who had grown up with Hacker in Vienna, "Hacker killed Robert Walker. He actually killed him. But a doctor could get away with it back then. Today you would have a nice lawsuit."

In the early 1950s it was virtually unheard of to sue an esteemed physician for malpractice. When Hacker announced to the press that Robert Walker's death was accidental, the result of an unforeseeable combination of circumstances, almost no one thought to question his judgment. "It was handled incredibly adroitly," Alex Rogawski says. "Thank God you could not get away with that kind of thing anymore."

Speaking of the news stories that appeared after Robert Walker's death, Dr. Leo Rangell adds caustically, "That case didn't do Hacker any harm. It almost worked to his advantage, on the premise that any publicity is good publicity."

Frederick Hacker, who died in 1989 at the age of seventy-five, was never one to shy away from the media's gaze. He savored his stature as one of Hollywood's leading analysts, freely dropping names and intimate tidbits about his celebrity patients. Despite those fabled indiscretions, Hacker retained his popularity with the show-business crowd. His courtly manner and Viennese pedigree were major assets. "In those days in Hollywood," remarks Gottfried Reinhardt, another Viennese emigré who worked as a producer, "if you had an accent, you were automatically considered cultured."

Hacker's father had been a prosperous silver dealer whose customers included the Austrian royal family. Alex Rogawski attended the University of Vienna with Hacker, and he remembers that young Friedl, as he was known, was innately shrewd but only a mediocre student. Rogawski notes in amusement that while Hacker was Jewish, he prided himself on his blond hair and sometimes tried to pass himself off as Gentile. Nevertheless, when Hitler rose to power, Friedl was forced to flee his native Austria and seek refuge in the United States.

While training at the Menninger Clinic, Hacker made his first Hollywood contacts, including Rosa Mankiewicz, the wife of writer-director Joseph L. Mankiewicz. When she was hospitalized at Menninger's for nine months in 1942, Rosa became friendly with the young analyst, who enjoyed reminiscing with her about the artistic and theatrical life of prewar Vienna. Rosa's husband, Joseph, became one of Hacker's chief sponsors in Los Angeles. In addition Hacker was one of Karl Menninger's pets, and Dr. Karl referred many movie-star patients to him. "Menninger always loved tall people," says the diminutive Alex Rogawski with a chuckle, "and Hacker was tall."

Soon after his arrival in Los Angeles in 1945, Hacker set about creating his own answer to the Menninger Clinic. The first comprehensive psychiatric facility in Los Angeles, the Hacker Clinic was a stroke of entrepreneurial genius. With so many analysts flocking to Los Angeles after the war, it was impossible for all of them to establish their own practices. Hacker hired a cadre of these young shrinks and paid them meager salaries, with a substantial share of each patient's fee going to the boss. "Hacker was the first analyst to become a millionaire," said his rival, Dr. Martin Grotjahn. "At his clinic in Beverly Hills everyone made money for *him*."

Many of the analysts who worked for Hacker did feel exploited. Alex Rogawski, Hacker's childhood friend, had lent Hacker eight thousand dollars to help him get started in America. Rogawski was an internist practicing in Connecticut at the time. Later, when Rogawski became a psychoanalyst, Hacker urged him to come to California and join his clinic. Rogawski expected to be a full partner, but on his arrival he found that he was no more than one of Hacker's employees. When a change in the law required Rogawski to pass a medical examination in order to be licensed in California, he requested a reduced schedule at the clinic so that he could study for his exam. "What do you need a license for?" Hacker asked him in exasperation. "You can work for me for the rest of your life." Feeling like an indentured servant to the man whose career he had helped launch with his sizable loan, Rogawski signed a two-year contract with the Hacker Clinic in exchange for a part-time schedule. But Hacker was still irritated that Rogawski seemed so determined to strike out on his own. "You're one of the best horses in the stable," Hacker said to his former benefactor.

In addition to building his clinic and his star clientele, Hacker carved out a niche as a media pundit. A tireless glory grabber, he was one of the first psychiatrists to make a popular name for himself as an expert on a myriad of social ills. In 1955, as a witness at a Senate subcommittee hearing on the hot topic of juvenile delinquency, Hacker made headlines by testifying that movies could serve as a dangerous "trigger mechanism" affecting the behavior of maladjusted teenagers. The press quickly adopted Hacker as an authority on violence, and he spoke out on a number of high-profile cases. He was a court-appointed psychiatrist at the trial of Charles Manson, and he was consulted by the West German government after the terrorist killings at the Munich Olympics of 1972.

One of Hacker's first Hollywood patients was Robert Mitchum, who consulted the analyst in 1947 when his family decided that he needed psychiatric counseling for his reckless behavior. Mitchum was drinking, womanizing, and engaging in a few too many barroom brawls. (Later, when he was arrested for possession of marijuana, Mitchum wrote a letter to the court in which he cited his analysis with Dr. Hacker as evidence of his efforts at rehabilitation.) Hacker's diagnosis was that Mitchum was suffering from a state of "overamiability." In his eagerness to please the people around him, the actor was suppressing his own impulses and then acting out his frustrations in wild binges. At his analyst's urging, according to Mitchum, he began telling friends and associates to "go shit in a hat," and he felt much better. Mitchum and Hacker remained friendly after his treatment ended, and in later years, the actor claimed, Hacker would often invite him to his home to hash out perplexing cases.

"Some people considered Hacker too glib or too social," says writer-director Tom Mankiewicz. "But he was unbelievably bright. I think one of the reasons Fred did so well in show business was that he was a very funny man. A tremendous wit. You could talk to him about anything."

Tom's father, Joseph Mankiewicz, sent both of his sons to

Hacker for treatment when they were children, and as a young adult
Tom Mankiewicz sometimes returned to Hacker for counseling.
Tom also referred a couple of his girlfriends, including Tuesday
Weld, to Dr. Hacker. Joseph Mankiewicz had set the pattern by dis-
patching many friends and lovers to Hacker's couch. Among the
actresses whom Joseph tried to steer into analysis was an attractive
newcomer named Nancy Guild, who appeared in his production of
Somewhere in the Night in 1946. "[Joe Mankiewicz] was devoted to
sending people to psychiatrists," recalled Guild, who went to Hacker
briefly but was put off by the analyst's manner. "Hacker was very
impressed with names, which I don't like in a doctor, and I only
went four times," Guild said.

Joseph Mankiewicz's older son, Chris, also recoiled at Hacker's
pontificating and his willingness to talk about patients—including
Chris's own mother. When Kenneth Geist wrote his authoritative
biography of Joseph Mankiewicz, Hacker talked to the author at
great length about Rosa, providing elaborate diagnoses of her mental condition and explaining why she had committed suicide. "I
could not believe what he said about my mother," Chris comments.

The Schulbergs were another prominent clan with whom
Hacker ingratiated himself. Writer Budd Schulberg frequently ran
into the chatty doctor at the home of his uncle, the agent Sam Jaffe.
"Hacker was on the circuit," Schulberg says. "I was surprised at how
loosely he talked about his cases, including my relatives."

Producer John Kohn was married to one of Budd Schulberg's
cousins, and he, too, became leery of the loquacious analyst.
"Hacker used to talk about his clients," Kohn says. "This is supposed
to be privileged information, and he was kind of outrageous about
it. On the other hand, if he was discussing politics or a movie, he
couldn't have been more charming. But as a psychiatrist, the last
person in the world that I think you could trust your brain to would
be Hacker."

Hacker seemed to enjoy acting the part of scofflaw. "Fred was
once arrested for having an unbelievable number of parking tickets
that he didn't pay," Tom Mankiewicz says in amusement. "I used to
joke with him about it, and he said to me very seriously, 'You must
realize it is possible to cure cancer and die of the disease.' "

In his later years Hacker began to hold himself above the fri-
volities of Hollywood. Although he kept the Hacker Clinic going, he
spent more and more time back in Vienna, where he reveled in his
reputation as an international celebrity. He also lectured to audi-

ences around the world. In 1989, while he was appearing on a West German television program in Mainz, Hacker suddenly collapsed to the floor and succumbed to a fatal heart attack. He died as he had lived, in the public eye.

Highly visible Hollywood shrinks like Frederick Hacker were the ones most disdained by the rigid traditionalists of the psychoanalytic establishment. "Those who are publicized in the magazines," Leo Rangell declares, "are the less reputable psychiatrists and the ones who are most likely to misuse psychoanalysis." Rangell, the former president of the American Psychoanalytic Association and the International Psychoanalytic Association, has always been an outspoken critic of his Los Angeles cohorts. "Usually there's a seed of readiness to be corrupted in the people who settled here and were drawn to Hollywood," Rangell says. "When analysts are very charismatic, like Greenson and Hacker, that makes for great lectures and excited audiences. But in a one-to-one relationship where a person is unburdening his depressions, a charismatic influence behind the couch can be as much of a deterrent as an inviter of secret intimacies."

Another of those charismatic Hollywood healers whom Rangell reviles was Dr. Martin Grotjahn, whose roster of celebrity patients spanned half a century of Hollywood history—from Vivien Leigh and Danny Kaye to Warren Beatty and David Geffen. Grotjahn was also an inveterate ham who occasionally made guest appearances on TV talk shows. In 1979 he turned up on *The Merv Griffin Show*, ostensibly to promote his latest scholarly tome, *The Art and Technique of Analytic Group Therapy*. While Merv touted the book, Grotjahn bantered genially with the panel of other guests, including Cloris Leachman and best-selling author Gay Talese. As their badinage slipped over into the titillating topic of nude encounter groups and changing sexual mores, the doctor described one patient of his, a "multiorgiastic" woman who recalled "coming forty-eight times on the Fourth of July." Somewhat agape, Griffin asked Grotjahn what he had said to the woman.

"Congratulations," replied the doctor impishly.

While it is doubtful that his appearance did much to boost sales of *The Art and Technique of Analytic Group Therapy*, Dr. Grotjahn showed himself to be an immensely entertaining guest. But Merv was already quite familiar with Grotjahn's mordant wit; after all, the good doctor was not just a personal friend but his own analyst.

Two decades earlier Grotjahn, like Frederick Hacker, had become entangled in a highly publicized incident that brought psychotherapy out of the shadows and into the press. In 1953 Vivien Leigh was making an expensive picture for Paramount, *Elephant Walk,* about a fragile young woman who marries a tyrannical tycoon, goes to live with him on his plantation in Ceylon, and then falls in love with his foreman. Filming in the jungles of Ceylon, Leigh—who would later be diagnosed as a manic-depressive—grew more and more distraught, but she finally managed to complete the location scenes. Then the company flew back to Los Angeles to film the interiors on a soundstage at Paramount. Aboard the plane Leigh began to rave and tried to tear off her clothes and jump out of the aircraft. She was sedated, and by the time the plane landed, she had apparently regained her composure.

Her first day at the studio, however, she appeared to be on the verge of a relapse. When she arrived on the set, Leigh could not remember her lines. She took a drink to calm herself and began to weep uncontrollably. Imagining that she was Blanche Dubois in *A Street Car Named Desire,* the role that she had played on screen two years earlier, Leigh repeated one of the lines from the play: "Get out of here quick before I start screaming fire!" Then she shouted at the top of her lungs, "Fire! Fire! Fire!"

Her friend David Niven was enlisted to drive her home. Leigh's husband, Laurence Olivier, flew to Los Angeles from Italy, where he had just completed a film of his own. Olivier found the studio executives in a state of agitation. If Leigh had to be replaced now, all of the location scenes in Ceylon would have to be reshot. Olivier was equally worried; the couple's finances were shaky, and they were counting on Vivien's salary to tide them over. Olivier consulted his wife's Hollywood psychiatrist, Ralph Greenson, who confirmed that Leigh was gravely ill. The Oliviers were close friends of Danny and Sylvia Fine Kaye; indeed, according to a biography of Olivier by Donald Spoto, Danny and Sir Laurence were lovers over a period of ten years. Kaye urged Olivier to call in his analyst, Dr. Martin Grotjahn, for a second opinion. In his autobiography years later Olivier sardonically referred to Grotjahn as "the big maestro," the Hollywood psychiatrist who was "reputed to be the big white chief."

Greenson and Grotjahn were leaders of rival institutes, and whenever the two doctors met, they invariably locked horns. But they agreed to work together to get Leigh back on her feet. It was immediately clear, however, that they differed over a course of treatment. According to Grotjahn, Greenson believed that emergency methods like electroshock therapy might enable Leigh to complete the picture. Grotjahn claimed that Greenson boasted, "I will have that woman working next week."

Grotjahn, on the other hand, was far more pessimistic in his diagnosis; he felt that a lengthy hospitalization was required. "I gave a devastating evaluation," Grotjahn reported to the authors. "I told Olivier, 'Your wife is as sick as if she had been run over by a truck. You can prop her up and photograph her, but as a physician I must say, leave her alone.' Olivier was concerned about the money she would lose if she couldn't complete the picture, and the studio was concerned too. But I was not brought in to rescue a multimillion-dollar investment. I was thinking about the patient."

A few days later Leigh was released from her contract and sent to London, where she did undergo shock therapy. Olivier remained bitter about Grotjahn's intervention. In his autobiography he described Grotjahn's counsel quite mockingly. Olivier claimed that Grotjahn told him, "She must go to her home. You must take her there immediately; it is what she needs. She will recover there wonderfully quickly. She wants her mo-o-ther!" And Olivier added tartly, "On Vivien's side I would say there had been no great feeling of need for her mother since she stopped breast-feeding."

When Grotjahn read Olivier's book in 1982, he was stung. Scornfully calling him "Lord Oliver—I don't know why he uses the French pronunciation of his name," Grotjahn said that Olivier's reminiscence of their consultation "proved to me that he understood *nothing.*" While Grotjahn did like to emphasize the importance of "motherliness" as a treatment for many maladies, he insisted that he never meant that Leigh literally needed her mother in order to recover. Later Grotjahn heard that Leigh and Olivier both despised him and blamed him for Leigh's career troubles after the fiasco of *Elephant Walk.* But the doctor continued to believe that his diagnosis and prescribed treatment for the actress were correct.

Leigh's departure from *Elephant Walk* provoked a rash of stories in the press. With a major production forced to shut down in the middle of filming, it was impossible to keep the star's breakdown a secret. Gossip columnists gamely peeked under the shroud of mystery surrounding mental illness. Louella Parsons learned from one unnamed shrink that Leigh might be given shock treatment. "Although most people view these treatments with horror," Parsons wrote, "they're really not in the least as serious as the outsider may believe. They've restored many an upset brain to normality." Eager to edify her readers, Parsons went on, "These nervous breakdowns, this same psychiatrist tells me, must not be confused with real insanity. They're just temporary mental aberrations, and the brain needs just the same care that any other part of the body needs. If an arm or a leg becomes affected, it must be given a rest, and so with an overtired brain."

Vivien Leigh's brain did get its rest. Elizabeth Taylor took over her role in *Elephant Walk,* and the studio had to reshoot all of Leigh's scenes at considerable expense.

Martin Grotjahn, who died in 1990 at the age of eighty-six, always looked back on his encounter with "Lord Oliver" and Vivien Leigh as one of his most distasteful adventures in Tinseltown. He was never reluctant to discuss the case. Nor did he make much effort to conceal the identity of other celebrity patients. Like Frederick Hacker, Grotjahn was a bit notorious for his loose lips.

Grotjahn became a psychiatrist, he once said, because he came from "a very peculiar family." His great-grandfather, grandfather, and father had all been eminent physicians in Germany. When Martin entered medical school in Berlin, he had a daunting heritage to live up to. His father, however, died suddenly in 1931, and it was that traumatic event that spurred Grotjahn to undergo psychoanalysis. It was his first step toward becoming an analyst himself.

His relationship with his mother was equally difficult. When Martin was three years old, a younger brother named Peter was born. Martin described him as "a 'Sunday Child' of unusual beauty with his blue eyes and golden blond curly hair." Peter became gravely ill shortly after birth, an allergic reaction to his smallpox vaccination. As a result of that illness, his mother showered the younger child with affection. After Peter's recovery, Martin wrote in one of his autobiographical papers, "He remained my mother's only son and I found myself alone."

Once he settled in America, Grotjahn lost contact with his family, but he later learned what had become of them. His mother committed suicide. "They found her with a happy smile on her face," Grotjahn said. "All the forty women of her village, when it had become clear that Germany was going to lose the war, they all joined hands, sang their religious songs, and walked into the lake. All drowned." His brother, Peter, a soldier in Hitler's army, was killed in the Battle of Stalingrad.

Martin's father had been a socialist, and Martin, too, had left-wing sympathies, which increased his alienation from his mother and brother. In addition, Martin's wife, Etelka, also a physician, was part Jewish. In 1936, as the Nazi menace intensified, Grotjahn decided to get out of Germany, and Karl Menninger invited him to study and work at his clinic in Topeka, Kansas.

On arriving in America Grotjahn immediately felt a sense of liberation. As he wrote, "No longer was I greeted with the words: 'Martin Grotjahn, the son of Alfred Grotjahn?' Now I was Martin Grotjahn, period." But once again he was expected to yield to the will of a powerful father figure. "Karl Menninger saved our lives," Grotjahn said. "But he wanted me as a son. I was through with being a son. If I could have been a friend or a colleague, that would have been ideal. But Karl did not want that." After two years in Topeka, Grotjahn went to Chicago to work with Franz Alexander, who allowed him much greater independence.

Grotjahn served as a Navy psychiatrist during World War II. In 1945 he came to Los Angeles at the invitation of Ernst Simmel, who had been his analyst in Berlin. Before long, however, Grotjahn chafed under Simmel's imperious command, just as he had rejected the paternalism of Karl Menninger. "Simmel was a very small man," Grotjahn recalled, "and like many small men, he had a savior complex. He had peculiar dictatorial tendencies. He wanted to distribute every analytic patient and set every fee. Well, I didn't come out of the navy to take orders from the little savior."

Grotjahn broke with Simmel, quit the Los Angeles Psychoanalytic Institute, and joined May Romm and Frederick Hacker to form the new Southern California Psychoanalytic Institute in 1950. Because of his impressive résumé, Grotjahn headed up the institute's training program, and he served as training analyst for most of the initiates. That helped to win him a reputation in Hollywood as well. Grotjahn remarked, "If in Hollywood you say, 'I am only an analyst for doctors,' every movie star thinks, 'Only for doctors, and for *me*.' It's a wonderful advertisement."

Initially Grotjahn took up residence in downtown Los Angeles and saw patients in an adjoining room at his hotel. But a colleague, Dr. Philip Solomon, told him this was rather déclassé and invited Grotjahn to share an office with him on Bedford Drive in Beverly Hills. Dr. Peter Lindstrom, the neurosurgeon who was married to

Ingrid Bergman, occupied an office in the same building. Grotjahn and Solomon became friendly with Lindstrom and were frequent guests at his home, where they swam alongside Ingrid Bergman in her backyard pool. (Grotjahn remembered that Bergman enjoyed swimming in a comical, tight-fitting bathing suit with an arrow through the heart—a memento of her title role in the 1948 film *Joan of Arc*.) Both analysts made a number of celebrity contacts at those aquatic get-togethers. On one occasion Grotjahn had his fortune told by Marlene Dietrich.

One of Dr. Solomon's patients was Hedy Lamarr. She was determined to shed her image as a brainless sexpot and embarked on an intensive program of analysis. "I was almost like a foster father to her," says Solomon, who treated her over a ten-year period. Lamarr socialized outside the office with both Solomon and Grotjahn. On one occasion the psychiatrist René Spitz delivered a series of lectures on schizophrenic children at the Southern California Psychoanalytic Institute. "The work he had done was remarkable, but the lectures were lousy," Grotjahn recalled. "Then Phil and I came up with an idea. We invited Hedy Lamarr. Before the lecture Phil went up to him and introduced Hedy. She of course speaks German and made a great fuss about René. That day his lecture was wonderful!"

Grotjahn admitted that he was attracted to movie stars and excited at the prospect of working with them. First of all, they could afford to pay lavish fees. "We came here to America with two dollars and fifty cents," Grotjahn said. "I was very anxious to make money." In addition, he enjoyed the status he accrued by treating celebrities. "In Germany," Grotjahn observed, "you know your place. You are just a little doctor. So I felt very honored when these big-name people came to me."

He soon realized, however, that psychoanalyzing these prima donnas was far from an unalloyed pleasure. "Actors are almost impossible to treat successfully," Grotjahn observed shortly before his death. "The histrionic psychosis of the actor is one of the most difficult to treat. Actors have no proper identity. When someone assigns them an identity, they can do that very well. But when they get off the stage, they collapse. Richard Burton had no identity offstage. Marilyn Monroe did not like her assigned identity and did not know how to get out of it; death was the only solution. Even actors who seem to be the exception really are not. Katharine Hepburn, for example, has now assumed the personality of her assigned identity."

Grotjahn was frequently amazed at his star patients' self-involvement. A famous actress was once photographed by a tabloid shutterbug as she was leaving her analyst's office, and she insisted that Grotjahn treat her at her home from then on. He agreed and was greatly impressed by her magnificent garden. "After our session," Grotjahn reported, "I said to her 'I would like to see your garden.' She said, 'I've always wanted to walk through my garden. Let's go.' She had lived there for ten years!"

Another of his patients, Merv Griffin, invited Grotjahn once to visit him at his home in Carmel. Griffin was understandably proud of his hillside estate, which he considered a showplace. Grotjahn was more impressed with the view of Point Lobos from Griffin's veranda. "What's Point Lobos?" Griffin asked as Grotjahn began to wax rhapsodic about the scenic promontory. Astonished by his host's question, the doctor offered to give Griffin a tour. Later they drove to Point Lobos and got out of the car for a stroll. "Each time we came around a corner," Grotjahn recalled, "Merv said, 'Look, there's my house.' We walked a little farther, and he said, 'There's my house.' I said, 'Look *here*. This is Point Lobos!'" But Griffin "was only interested in looking at his own house."

When he was in the navy, Grotjahn had experimented with group therapy and had observed some spectacular results. After a few years in Hollywood, he decided to try the same techniques with his movie-star patients, and for the first time, he felt that he was making headway. "In individual therapy," Grotjahn observed, "stars still feel like stars. They feel I must do all the work. In group therapy they do the work."

Grotjahn knew that celebrities were often nervous about joining a group, fearful that their secrets would become juicy gossip for the other members. "But once they trust their group," Grotjahn explained, "they are tremendously relieved. Actors do well in group therapy because after a period of hesitation, they do not pretend anymore. They are free to be themselves. One thing I learned in group therapy was that *I* am more impressed by a star than the average American. I was so honored that a star would come to me. Other people in the group were not that impressed. I remember once I introduced a movie star into one of my groups, and a bank clerk—the most unsophisticated member of the group—said with great feeling to her, 'How can we help you?' The actress just broke open and said things she had never told me in our individual sessions. A group is a better mother than any analyst."

In a paper called "The Treatment of the Famous and the 'Beautiful People' in Groups," Grotjahn wrote, "The 'beautiful people' themselves are inclined to be narcissistic, suspicious, paranoid. They expect, hope and fear that everyone will notice them and talk about them. . . . It is a moving experience to see these narcissistic personalities accepting and being accepted by the group, to see them relieved of the obligation to be on display, allowed to be 'just like everybody else,' to see them attempt to be honest and free. To see this is a therapeutic experience for the patient, the group and, sometimes, the therapist."

Grotjahn also noted, however, that he had learned it was a mistake to include two movie stars in the same group. "When that happens," he wrote, "a murderous competition must be expected; the show is on, and these people perform instead of work." Grotjahn said that in his experience only one person in a group had broken confidence and gossiped about the secrets of the rich and famous. It was another psychiatrist. "I threw him out of the group," Grotjahn said, wincing at the memory.

If Grotjahn had a specialty, it was his treatment of comedians and comedy writers. He wrote a landmark psychoanalytic study of humor, *Beyond Laughter,* and his home was filled with his playful pen-and-ink drawings; many of them were caricatures of himself with impudent captions. Grotjahn always tickled his friends with his irreverent remarks. A fellow doctor once said to him, "You analyzed so many movie stars, Martin. Why did you not analyze Ronald Reagan? You might have saved the country a lot of trouble."

"He was too dumb to come to me," Grotjahn replied saucily.

If he disdained politicians and most actors, Grotjahn adored comedians and went out of his way to meet them. At a convention of the American Psychoanalytic Association, Grotjahn came up to Dr. Milton Wexler and begged his fellow analyst to introduce him to Elaine May, who was attending the conference with her husband, Dr. David Rubinfine. Wexler made the introductions but was agog to see what happened next. "Grotjahn actually knelt down and kissed Elaine's hand," Wexler recalls.

Grotjahn's own antic sense of humor made him amenable to the barbs of his patients. "I once went to a party," Grotjahn recalled, "and three of my patients did imitations of me. It is a great narcissistic pleasure to be imitated. The best imitation was done by Edie Adams."

Another of his analysands, Danny Kaye, turned his impression of Grotjahn into a recurring character on his TV variety show—a flamboyant Prussian psychiatrist who cheerfully spouted guttural gobbledygook. Those in the know instantly recognized Grotjahn's distinctive accent in Kaye's vivid impersonation.

Despite his affection for comedians, Grotjahn knew that their jokes could sometimes get in the way of effective therapy. "The only person who entertained me to the degree that it became a resistance was Zero Mostel," Grotjahn revealed. "He could keep me from him by making me laugh. He had the most spontaneous sense of the comical. Once when I went into the waiting room to call him, he got up and made a face as if he was stuck to the couch. Then he turned and investigated his enormous elephantine behind and said, 'Somebody spit his chewing gum on the couch.' He really seemed to be stuck. I started to apologize, and then I realized that it was all a performance. Danny Kaye would never do something like that. Danny performed only when he had studied it to the last detail."

After Mostel finished treatment with Grotjahn, he moved back to New York, but he would occasionally return for a consultation. After one session Mostel called Grotjahn from home and asked the analyst to repeat a critical judgment he had made concerning the comedian's marriage. "His wife was listening on the other phone," Grotjahn reported. "I should have suspected, but I didn't. I guess I hurt the wife because I never heard from Mostel again."

Grotjahn knew that his comedian patients were often anguished and depressed. Danny Kaye, for example, was not always the happy-go-lucky clown he appeared to be on screen. He was a temperamental man, plagued with questions about his sexual identity. "Danny had his miseries," says Dr. Louis Jolyon West, who was a friend of the comedian. "But in spite of all the Sturm und Drang, he and his wife, Sylvia, held their marriage together, and that was partly due to Grotjahn."

A sizable number of Grotjahn's patients were sexually ambivalent, and like most analysts of his generation, he firmly prodded them in the direction of a heterosexual union. A later patient of Grotjahn's was music and movie mogul David Geffen, who publicly acknowledged his homosexuality in 1992. In the 1970s he was dating both men and women, and one actress whom he saw briefly remembers that Geffen asked her to meet with his psychiatrist. She did, and Grotjahn reminded her of the financial perks of a romance with the extravagantly wealthy producer, dangling the prospect of glamorous vacations and a luxury car. Refusing the bait, she quickly ended her liaison with Geffen.

When he was seventy-five, Grotjahn suffered a heart attack, and he retired soon afterward. His hearing was also failing. "I thought perhaps I should retire when I started hearing my patients say things that they had not actually said," Grotjahn joked. He continued occasional private consultations with a few of his most celebrated patients, including Warren Beatty and screenwriter Robert Towne.

Patients like Towne often asked Grotjahn to read their scripts and offer a professional opinion. "I never charged for that," Grotjahn remarked. "I must say very rarely did I enjoy them." In 1988 Robert Towne's *Tequila Sunrise* was released, and Grotjahn was not surprised by the negative reviews. "I read Robert Towne's manuscript a few years ago," he confided. "What the critics say now is exactly what I felt. I expect my patients to be open, honest, frank, and direct. So when they want me to read a script, I feel the obligation to reward their openness with my openness. I have to be diplomatic if I don't like it. I don't say that it stinks. I say this gumbo is not to my taste."

Grotjahn did enjoy Towne's script for *Shampoo*, which starred another of the doctor's patients, Warren Beatty. Although the analyst was put off by the narcissism of most of the actors he treated, he admired Beatty for his multiple talents. "Warren is different from other actors I have seen," Grotjahn declared in our last interview with him in 1989. "He can do almost anything very, very well. But that is a superhuman temptation and can lead to great trouble. He does not know, is he an actor, a lover, a producer, a director?"

Another of Grotjahn's patients who retained a close relationship with him right up until his death was veteran sitcom writer and novelist Gail Parent. She had been a long-term member of one of his therapy groups and even met her second husband—a dentist—in Grotjahn's group. "One day we went for coffee together after group," Parent reports, "and that's how it started."

Parent knows that a romance between two members of a therapy group is generally frowned upon. "But it's hard enough to find somebody to connect with," she argues. "Why forbid it? I probably connected with him because I knew him that well and we were that comfortable with each other. Grotjahn is very free. He will allow love to flourish in a group."

When asked about this relationship, however, Grotjahn displayed his usual candor. "I don't restrict my groups from social contacts," Grotjahn said. "They are not children. Going to bed with each other is as important as talking together. But I told them they must report about it to the group, and usually this discouraged them. Frankly the development with Gail I don't think was a happy choice. But if I had thrown them out, they would have married anyway. I thought it was better to keep them going. I don't think that group members should marry."

Some of Grotjahn's patients might be surprised to know how freely he talked about them to strangers. But as he grew older, Grotjahn felt increasingly unfettered and immune from the censure of his straitlaced colleagues. "I am an honorary member of everything," Grotjahn said laughingly shortly before his eighty-fifth birthday. "I would have to fuck a patient on the street before they throw me out. I feel free and independent and old." Despite his occasional indiscretions, most of Grotjahn's patients adored him for his rambunctious wit and his keen intellect.

Grotjahn remained remarkably alert until his death in 1990. In a moving essay that he wrote at the age of seventy-eight called "The Day I Got Old," Grotjahn explained that nothing had ever slowed him down until he suffered his first heart attack three years earlier. Then all at once his world collapsed. Although he had been a furious workaholic for most of his life, he now had to face the prospect of retirement. Yet he adjusted with surprising equanimity to his enforced leisure. "I have no more worry about patients," Grotjahn wrote, "no more guilt that I don't understand them well enough, no more bad conscience that I don't know the way to help them . . . let other people worry now. I am through with work and worry."

The analytic encounter is meant to be as intimate and confidential as a conversation in a church confessional booth. As the examples of prominent analysts like Frederick Hacker and Martin Grotjahn make clear, however, the rules of confidentiality are not always held sacrosanct. But suppose an analyst were to reveal secrets of the couch not just to a few social acquaintances but to government authorities? During the McCarthy era rumors abounded of just such alarming breaches of trust.

Some psychiatrists had their own political agendas during this contentious period. Elia Kazan has suggested that his decision to cooperate with the House Un-American Activities Committee and testify against his former colleagues in the Group Theatre was spurred by the counsel of his psychoanalyst, Dr. Bela Mittelman. When Kazan told Dr. Mittelman, a Hungarian refugee with strong anti-Communist sympathies, that he wanted to defy the committee and refuse to identify any former Communists, the doctor asked him, "Wouldn't that make you unacceptable to the film industry?" Kazan agreed that it probably would.

"Wouldn't that be a terrible loss for you?" Mittelman continued. Kazan replied that he had considered the consequences and believed that he could still work in the theater and survive on his savings. According to Kazan, the doctor then prodded him, "I'm wondering if your fellow members would do the same for you if they were called upon to protect you by endangering their careers." His analyst's leading questions provoked Kazan to change his mind. A few weeks after his session with Dr. Mittelman, he met with the committee and offered his full cooperation.

Another therapist was known for having treated an entire battalion of HUAC informers. His name was Ernest Philip Cohen, and he has long been the subject of unresolved controversy. When Sterling Hayden wrote his best-selling memoir, *Wanderer*, in 1964, he tried to conceal his therapist's identity. Hayden indicated that the therapist had urged him to cooperate with the investigations into Communism in the motion picture industry, and the actor did give "friendly" testimony, first to the FBI and later to HUAC. During one session on the couch Hayden complained to his analyst, "Son of a bitch, Doc, I'm not sure I can take much more of this . . . . I'm thinking of quitting analysis . . . . I'll say this, too, that if it hadn't been for you I wouldn't have turned into a stoolie for J. Edgar Hoover. I don't think you have the foggiest notion of the contempt I have had for myself since the day I did that thing."

Hayden's Hollywood analyst was Phil Cohen. By the time he wrote his comprehensive history of the blacklist era, *Naming Names*, in 1980, Victor Navasky had identified more than a dozen of Cohen's patients during the 1940s and '50s. In addition to Hayden, they included actors Lloyd Bridges and John Garfield, writers Richard Collins, David Hertz, and Sylvia Richards, and agent Meta Rosenberg. Most of them were cooperative witnesses before the House Un-American Activities Committee.

Cohen was not a psychiatrist and never earned a degree as a psychologist, either, though he had done graduate work in psychology at the University of Chicago and later at the University of Washington. Cohen joined the Communist Party before coming to Los Angeles in 1942; upon his arrival he immediately set up practice as a lay analyst. Despite his rather flimsy credentials, Cohen was one of the few therapists sanctioned by the Communist Party, and that is how he attracted patients. The Party disapproved of psychoanalysis as a bourgeois indulgence, but if its members were going to bare their souls to anyone, it was best that they do so to a loyal comrade.

Cohen told Navasky that he dropped out of the Party sometime during the early 1940s, but he continued to espouse left-wing causes. When the country and the film industry began to shift to the right in the years after World War II, Cohen readily adapted to changing times. As someone who had himself become disillusioned with Communism, he was well equipped to counsel those members of the film community who wanted to save their careers by recanting publicly. Although Cohen claimed that he took a neutral stance with his patients, several reported that he pressed them to cooperate with the investigators from Washington. Screenwriter Sylvia Richards and actress-writer Elizabeth Wilson said that Cohen had helped persuade them to give friendly testimony to HUAC. William Wheeler, the chief investigator for the committee, was a close friend of Cohen's. According to Wheeler, Cohen told him, "If you subpoena one of my patients, I'll try to condition him to testify."

The most serious charge against Cohen was that he did not simply assist the snoops from HUAC but was actually in the employ of the FBI. "Phil Cohen came to my house for dinner one night," says the blacklisted writer-director Abraham Polonsky. "The first thing he said to me was, 'I've heard so much about you from all my patients.'" Polonsky, who was put off by the analyst's wagging tongue, told Victor Navasky, "I know [Cohen] was reporting confidences to the FBI. There's no question about that. And he was turning patients into stool pigeons."

"Word got around that Cohen worked for the FBI," says Polonsky's fellow screenwriter, Arthur Laurents. "That had a very frightening effect because people tell the analyst everything. It's as if your priest were going to tell what you had confided in him."

Cohen denied the charge that he was an FBI informer, but he did admit that he worked in "law enforcement" beginning in either

1948 or 1950, the same period when he was counseling Hollywood patients about their testimony before the House Un-American Activities Committee. Cohen insisted that the law enforcement work he was doing was "criminal" rather than "political." He held the rank of captain in the Inyo County sheriff's department in central California and became a special agent in the California Department of Justice under Governor Pat Brown. Cohen also admitted that after he left the Communist Party, Special Agent Mark Bright of the FBI interviewed him about his past participation. The two men became friendly. "He and I developed a personal relationship of sorts," Cohen told Victor Navasky. "As I got involved in law enforcement— these two events are not connected, the law enforcement and the political thing—then, obviously, he was one of my contacts at the bureau." One of Cohen's patients, Sylvia Richards, said that once she had decided to cooperate with the government investigators, "Phil set up a meeting with an FBI guy named [Mark] Bright."

When it was known that many of Cohen's patients were cozying up to the FBI and naming names to HUAC, his reputation plummeted. Cohen claimed that the Communist Party was surreptitiously trying to destroy his career. His clientele dwindled, and he became more heavily involved in "law enforcement work." Even if Cohen were not actually an FBI informer, patients would doubtless balk at revealing their most intimate secrets to a man who moonlighted as a sheriff's deputy.

Eventually Cohen moved to Santa Barbara and became a photographer, which had been his vocation before he studied psychology. He got a job teaching at an arts institute and tried to put his bizarre Hollywood past behind him.

A far more distinguished analyst, Judd Marmor, also treated many left-wing moviemakers who were faced with a crisis of conscience during the McCarthy era. Some of his patients, such as director Abe Burrows and screenwriter Isobel Lennart, ended up informing on their colleagues to keep their jobs. Others, such as actor Stanley Praeger, refused to cooperate with the House Un-American Activities Committee and were blacklisted.

Although Marmor felt revulsion toward the anti-Communist hysteria that was sweeping the country, he tried to maintain a posture of impartiality with patients who were struggling to arrive at a course of action. "That period was a horrendous blow to creativity," Marmor says. "It was a tremendous upheaval on both sides. Those who were determined to stand firm paid enormous penalties, had their family lives and their subsistence destroyed. And those who went along with it, either out of conviction or out of fear, were also plagued by enormous guilt. We live in a culture where from a very early point on, the concept of being a stool pigeon is a very derogatory thing."

Marmor never pressured his patients either to inform or to resist. "I was often asked to make a decision for them," he says, "and I refused. It's too personal a decision and too fateful a decision for an analyst to make unless he has delusions of grandeur."

In 1953, at the height of that anti-Communist frenzy, Marmor scrutinized those "delusions of grandeur" in a paper called "The Feeling of Superiority: An Occupational Hazard in the Practice of Psychotherapy." Marmor's essay expanded on some of Ernest Jones's criticisms of psychiatrists in his famous 1913 treatise, "The God Complex." Marmor pointed out the neurotic needs that may drive a person to become a psychiatrist—a hunger for prestige as well as a desire to solve one's own internal conflicts. He also argued that Freud's dictum that the analyst should remain "impenetrable to the patient" had encouraged many analysts to create an aura of secrecy and mystery about themselves, a professional image that only fed their vanity.

"The constant exercise of authority carries with it the occupational hazard of tending to create unrealistic feelings of superiority in the authority figure," Marmor wrote. He noted that patients who could afford psychoanalysis were often quite accomplished and successful themselves. "The seductive influence of an abundant flow of transference admiration from such sources may be considerable . . . . The psychotherapist has become the shaman of our society, the all-seeing father with the Cyclopean eye. He is endowed with God-like perceptiveness." Ultimately, Marmor suggested, therapists begin to view themselves in the same way: "The hazards and insecurity of their work, plus its ego-seductive aspects, plus its isolationism, tend to foster such defensive arrogance to a greater extent, perhaps, than do many other professions."

Marmor may not have been entirely free of personal ambition himself, but at least he was sensitive to the perils of grandiosity, and he never exhibited the overweening egotism that infected so many other prominent analysts. It was his humility, rather than his charisma, that people found attractive.

Even as a child, Marmor was no stranger to left-wing politics. He was born Judah Marmorstein in London in 1910. A year later his family moved to Chicago. His father was a Yiddish writer, historian, and literary critic who became the Chicago editor of the Jewish *Daily Forward*. He was also a dedicated socialist, and his son, Judah, was the only child who voted for Eugene Debs in his school's mock election of 1920. A few years later the family moved to New York. While he was a student at Columbia, Judah decided to become a psychoanalyst. Although his family had been steeped in Yiddish culture, in medical school he downplayed his Jewish identity and eventually Anglicized his name. Almost all the Jewish analysts of Marmor's generation went out of their way to discard their religious heritage. "In the New York Psychoanalytic Institute in the forties and fifties, if you went to a synagogue, you were looked upon as being neurotic," says Dr. Arnold Richards, a New York analyst who is also a leader of the YIVO Institute for Yiddish research. "Classes at the analytic institute were even held on Yom Kippur."

Despite their disdain for organized religion, analysts could be quite zealous about matters of psychoanalytic theory. After serving as a psychiatrist during World War II, Marmor followed some of his friends to southern California to set up a practice there. He was alarmed by the rigidity he found among the leaders of the newly formed Los Angeles Psychoanalytic Institute. "It is difficult to convey the quasi-religious fanaticism about classical Freudian doctrine that pervaded the small group of analysts in the original founding group of the Los Angeles Psychoanalytic Society and Institute," Marmor recalled. In 1948 Marmor presented a paper to the Society on Abram Kardiner, the distinguished New York analyst. According to Marmor, Ralph Greenson roundly criticized it because only two of fifteen references were to the writings of Freud.

That was the start of a long-lasting feud between Greenson and Marmor. "At the time Greenson was very rigid, very dogmatic," Marmor recalls. "And the essence of my own approach to my field has always been to be open. I don't believe there are final answers in any form of science. So there was a basic difference between Greenson and me." Marmor joined the rebel contingent led by May Romm, Frederick Hacker, and Martin Grotjahn in forming the new

Southern California Psychoanalytic Institute in 1950.

In addition to the referrals he got from Romm, Marmor made some contacts with the Hollywood set on the tennis courts. He was an avid player and often competed with screenwriter Albert Maltz and producer Julian Blaustein. Through them he acquired a number of show-business patients. But he met even more filmmakers through his political involvements. "I was a progressive person, liberal politically, and around the people I got to know socially were liberal writers, directors, producers," Marmor explains. "Gradually I became part of a circle. This was a very lively, exciting place before McCarthy."

One of his early analysands was the left-wing writer Arthur Laurents, who had first made a splash on Broadway with his play *Home of the Brave* and then came to Hollywood to work with Alfred Hitchcock on *Rope,* Max Ophuls on *Caught,* and Anatole Litvak on *The Snake Pit.* In the forties, living in New York, Laurents was in therapy with the lay analyst Theodor Reik, who did much to popularize Freud's theories in America, but whom Laurents now dismisses as a "charlatan." Laurents recalls that when he was writing his second play, *Heartsong,* Reik asked for ten percent of the profits because of all the encouragement he had provided. "I didn't have the balls to say to him, 'You're taking advantage of me,'" Laurents comments.

Reik also tried to bill the producer of the play, Irene Selznick, for his counseling services. The shrink came to a preview in New Haven and offered suggestions for improving the play. "He came, he saw, and he charged," Irene Selznick wrote in her autobiography. "He sent me a whopping bill, which even included traveling time."

Heartsong closed after a short run, so there were no profits for Reik to collect from either Laurents or Selznick. Soon after that ill-fated venture, Laurents moved to California and began a second round of analysis with Judd Marmor. "I knew I needed to get back in the oven and cooked a little more," Laurents quips. He considered Marmor, unlike Reik, to be a modest, ethical man genuinely concerned with helping his patients. "I revered him," Laurents says. "The main benefit of Marmor was his sense of values. When you are a neurotic, which I certainly was, and scared, and young, and you get a man you respect as a human being, that is very important. He made me feel my beliefs were valid."

Marmor indirectly encouraged Laurents to go back to New York and concentrate on writing for the theater. Laurents recalls one of their sessions when Marmor said to him, "I just want to point out something to you. The moment you say the word *movie*, within the next sentence will be the word *shit*."

"It was a good insight," Laurents says. "The point wasn't that movies were shit but that I regarded them as such. It was better for me to do what I really wanted to do, which was to write for the theater. Also, it was the whole period of the witch-hunt, and my beliefs were very strong, and Marmor endorsed them."

Laurents recommended Marmor to many of his show-business associates. "I was acolyte number one," Laurents jokes. One of the friends he referred was Shelley Winters, who felt frustrated by her image as a Hollywood sex toy. "You sort of hid your intellect and got by on cunning, presenting this sort of 'blonde bombshell' image," Winters once said of her early career in the movies. "If you have to be *the* most beautiful and *the* sexiest, then your feelings of insufficiency are multiplied. So I was very dissatisfied."

But Winters's analysis with Marmor was stymied by her own resistance. As she later said, "I think I mostly told him jokes. Anything that was painful I would make jokes about." She also arrived late for every appointment and would make sure she had a business meeting scheduled right after therapy so that she could leave early. "The fifty minutes got reduced to thirty minutes of jokes," she said. "After I had been with [Marmor] for a year, he became discouraged with my progress."

As he had done with Arthur Laurents, Marmor encouraged Winters to move back to New York, where she could establish herself as a serious actress in the theater. She did make her mark on stage and returned to Hollywood as a formidable dramatic actress, eventually winning two Oscars.

Marmor's judicious manner made him an adept mediator of the political factions within the analytic establishment. In 1973 he was elected president of the American Psychiatric Association, and his humane liberalism influenced the group when it made one of its historic decisions—removing homosexuality from the category of mental illness in the diagnostic listing of psychological problems. This had become a point of bitter contention within the APA. Freud himself had been tolerant of homosexuality, but many of those who followed him wanted to characterize it as a perversion. Marmor's training analyst, Lawrence Kubie, strenuously tried to "convert" his gay patients, and other psychiatrists who had done clinical studies of homosexuality—Edmund Bergler, Irving Bieber, Charles Socar-ides—made sweeping, disparaging generalizations about the mal-adjustment of all homosexuals.

In the early seventies a fierce battle raged within the APA. Bie-ber and Socarides fought to retain the prescriptive language against homosexuality, while three analysts from Los Angeles—Marmor, Robert Stoller, and Richard Green—advocated a change in classi-fication. "The classical analytic viewpoint was a stereotypic one: 'All homosexuals are destructive. All homosexuals can't make friend-ships,' " Marmor recalls. "It just didn't make any sense to me. The homosexuals I knew were different people, just as all the hetero-sexuals I knew were different people."

Under Marmor's leadership the APA's board of trustees voted in 1973 to delete homosexuality from the list of mental disorders. Bieber and Socarides were furious and pushed for a vote of the entire membership. To their surprise a majority of the psychiatrists voted to support the board.

Marmor was becoming a figure of repute, and his national renown helped him to attract some very esteemed patients, including Sam-uel Goldwyn. In 1969, after the legendary producer suffered a stroke, Marmor made house calls for several months, and Gold-wyn's spirits improved. The producer, known for his malapropisms, referred to his psychiatrist as "Dr. Murmur."

Marmor always tried to keep his Hollywood connections dis-creetly out of the papers, but one amusing tale did find its way into Leonard Lyons's syndicated column. In the early 1950s writer Abe Burrows and actor Stanley Praeger were both patients of Marmor's. One day they set out to play a practical joke on their analyst. They concocted a very elaborate Freudian dream and decided that during their next analytic sessions, each of them would recount it to Mar-mor in minute detail. Burrows came in and spent most of the ses-sion describing the dream to his analyst. Later in the day Praeger recounted the exact same dream. Marmor listened for a while and then commented with mock ingenuousness, "Stan, this is absolutely remarkable. You're the third patient who told me this today."

Marmor was too shrewd to fall for his patients' ruse that time, but he was not always so canny. In the late 1970s, Marmor was inveigled by another pair of Hollywood personalities, and for the first time in his career he found himself acutely embarrassed. Producer Ray Stark had come to Marmor for treatment after his son Peter committed suicide. Stark was one of the powers behind the throne at Columbia Pictures. Several of his most successful movies had been made for the studio, and he was a close friend of the studio's president, David Begelman. In 1977 Begelman, who was known to be a heavy gambler, was exposed for embezzling studio money by forging several checks. The Columbia board of directors was divided about what to do. One contingent, led by Begelman's immediate boss, Alan Hirschfield, and board chairman, Leo Jaffe, believed that it was wrong for a publicly held corporation to continue to employ an admitted felon. Another group, headed by Stark, believed that Begelman had kept the studio profitable and should be retained regardless of the checks he had forged. Stark also had reason to worry about losing his own favored status at Columbia if Begelman were dumped.

As reporters dug deeper into the scandal, the internal battle was heating up, and Begelman's position grew shakier. Finally Stark had a brainstorm. If Begelman could go into therapy with the respected Judd Marmor (who had treated Begelman once before, following his second divorce) and Marmor could pronounce him cured, the jittery stockholders might be reassured. Begelman began seeing Dr. Marmor three times a week between October and November 1977. But before long, Begelman and Stark were pressuring Marmor to extend his efforts on behalf of the beleaguered executive.

To counteract all the negative press he was getting, Begelman urged Marmor to set the record straight by granting an interview to *Wall Street Journal* reporter David McClintick, who was conducting the most thorough investigation of the case. Marmor did agree to meet with McClintick, and he offered his diagnosis that Begelman was suffering from "temporary emotional problems," which McClintick reported in *The Wall Street Journal*.

Ray Stark was still not satisfied. He told Alan Hirschfield that Begelman was making excellent progress in his therapy with Dr. Marmor. Stark continued to exert pressure, and finally Begelman was invited to address the board of Columbia Pictures. The day before Thanksgiving 1977, Begelman flew to New York and delivered a masterful *mea culpa* before the entire board, punctuated with just enough psychoanalytic lingo to make it all sound credible.

"Over the last six weeks," Begelman declared, "with the help of one of the finest doctors in the country, and indeed the world, I have learned a great deal about the roots of my misdeeds. The roots go deep, all the way back to my childhood and my relationship with my parents and with my siblings. In sum, the problem amounts to an unnaturally low self-esteem, a feeling of unworthiness, and an inability to accommodate success. Subconsciously I didn't like myself . . . in the therapy which I sought immediately upon the revelation of these acts six weeks ago, it became quickly clear to me that there were valid—not justifiable, but understandable in retrospect—reasons for these highly neurotic acts, which were not directed against Columbia or against any individual, but against myself."

Then his voice rose. "I appear before you," Begelman said, "with the acts revealed, with the investigation completed, with restitution made, or in the process of being made, and with my psychological health well on the way toward restoration. I am a man who was sick and is very nearly cured . . . . If you can summon up the mercy to grant me another chance, you will find that I will work day and night and do everything humanly possible to justify your faith in me. I will rededicate my life to the success of Columbia Pictures."

That was only the beginning of a well-orchestrated campaign to verify David Begelman's psychological rehabilitation. Three days later Judd Marmor himself flew to New York to meet with several powerful members of the Columbia board and add his professional opinion to Begelman's impassioned plea. According to David McClintick's subsequent history of the case, *Indecent Exposure*, Marmor labeled Begelman's problem "a neurotic disorder rather than a flaw of character." The doctor dismissed speculation that Begelman's embezzlement might indicate a lifelong criminal proclivity; this was an isolated incident of aberrant behavior. Marmor described the process of psychotherapy and told the board members, "I think the prospect of recurrence is absolutely minimal." Then he flew back to Los Angeles.

As a result of Marmor's endorsement, Columbia did agree to keep Begelman in his job—until public outrage became so vehement that he was finally ousted a few months later. The reports of Marmor's apologia for his patient led to many jokes in Hollywood about the "six-week Beverly Hills miracle cure." Marmor insists that some of the rumors were inaccurate. "I never said David was cured," Marmor declares. "I predicted that he would never do it again, which was correct. I had reason to believe that from my work with him. Some people took that as saying he was cured, which was just a distortion."

Marmor does regret that he ever spoke to McClintick. "I was reluctant to do it," Marmor says, "but David [Begelman] was so eager to have the total truth brought out, at least indicate that he was not a total crook, that I went along with it. But I now think it was a mistake."

What about his flying to an East Coast board meeting to speak on his patient's behalf? "That was a crisis, and I was doing some crisis intervention," Marmor says in his own defense. "He was not in traditional analysis with me. The patient had a life problem. He was going to be fired, and it would have been a real disaster, which it turned out to be anyway. But I felt that if I could talk to them and indicate that what he had done was a neurotic aberration, that justified it. I was convinced from having worked with Begelman that this would not occur again. They wanted to keep him. They were pleading with me, 'We want to keep him. We consider him a very talented man and very valuable to the studio. But we're afraid to keep him. Is he going to do it again?' I said, 'No, I can say unequivocally that he will not do it again.' That's basically why I went there. I was asked to go there to answer those questions, with his approval. And on that basis they kept him for a while before it got out of control."

As soon as Marmor's role in the Begelman affair became public knowledge, he was accused of being co-opted by a criminal. Arthur Laurents, who had venerated Marmor ever since being analyzed by him twenty-five years earlier, was deeply shaken. "I thought it was unseemly," Laurents says. "I wrote to Marmor and told him what I thought. He said to me, 'It's none of your business,' and I said, 'Yes it is.' My image of the man was shattered."

Within the analytic community there was also a widespread sentiment that Marmor had allowed himself to be manipulated into behaving unprofessionally. Marmor's colleagues charged that he had erred by speaking publicly about a patient and that he had used the respectable mantle of psychoanalysis to keep a thief in his job. Dr. Alex Rogawski, who had known Marmor for thirty years, was sorely disappointed in his old friend. "Ordinarily Judd is very discreet, so I don't understand how he did that," Rogawski says ruefully. "It became a whitewash, and we shouldn't be involved in such cases. It's like the psychiatrist who proposed the Twinkie defense in San Francisco."

Dorothy Colodny, the daughter of Marmor's old friend May Romm and a retired psychiatrist herself, has also known Marmor for many years. When asked her opinion of Marmor's involvement in the Begelman case, Colodny says tersely, "I don't know whether he was gullible or corrupt, and which would he rather be?"

There are many forms of seductiveness in Hollywood. Marilyn Monroe epitomized one obvious kind, but producers and moguls have a different, no less compelling brand of magnetism. Ray Stark and David Begelman may be ruthless businessmen, but they can also be witty and immensely ingratiating. Tossing off self-deprecating jokes and delicious confidences about their famous friends, they know how to make a stranger instantly feel like a crony. It is tempting to respond to the attention of a charismatic power broker, and as Marmor frequently pointed out in his own writings, analysts can be all too human—and blind to the consequences of their own hubris. "You may have a famous star, director, producer, or writer look up to you," Marmor says of psychiatry in Hollywood. "It's very intoxicating. You can begin to feel you're the Great White Father."

Just as Ralph Greenson's name is forever linked to Marilyn Monroe, Judd Marmor will never erase the stigma of his embarrassing involvement with the wily moguls Stark and Begelman. Marmor's honorable accomplishments and scholarly essays may earn him a niche in the psychoanalytic pantheon. To connoisseurs of Hollywood confidence games, however, he will be remembered as just another hapless pawn—a wise old doctor outsmarted by a couple of show-biz sharpies.

6. ACTING OUT

When Lee Strasberg died in 1982, Stella Adler asked her acting class to stand and observe a moment of silence. "A man of the theater died last night," she announced solemnly. After the silent meditation, she added, "It will take a hundred years before the harm that man has done to the art of acting can be corrected."

Stella Adler's sardonic eulogy suggests the powerful but highly controversial influence that Strasberg exerted on an entire generation of American actors, an influence that was inextricably intertwined with his reverence for psychoanalysis. Strasberg was the artistic director of the Actors Studio, an outgrowth of the Group Theatre, which he had co-founded with a band of fiery young actors (including Stella Adler) in order to bring unvarnished realism to the American stage. Strasberg's trademark "Method" style of acting, as practiced by pupils like Marlon Brando, Geraldine Page, and James Dean, would be the approach favored by the most esteemed American actors for decades to come.

Strasberg had adapted the Method from techniques introduced by the great Russian theoretician of acting, Konstantin Stanislavsky; both Strasberg and Stella Adler had studied with Stanislavsky's disciple, Richard Boleslavsky, who had emigrated to the United States in 1923. Adler, who later went to study with Stanislavsky himself, claimed that Strasberg distorted the teachings of the Russian master. Stanislavsky had encouraged the use of the imagination in the actor's craft, but Strasberg highlighted another aspect of Stanislavsky's technique—the reliance on so-called "affective memory." Strasberg urged actors to elicit the truth of a scene by dredging up the profound memory of a similar emotional moment that they had experienced in their own lives. The exercises that he led were not unlike an analytic session, in which a patient would dig deeper and deeper into his past, trying to recapture not only the events that had transpired but the feelings surrounding them. The goal in analysis was to purge those demons from the past by confronting them. At the Actors Studio the aim was to channel those buried emotions into a performance so as to heighten the reality of the scene.

"Analysts have come to our sessions," says Frank Corsaro, who followed Strasberg as director of the Actors Studio, "and I remember one of them said, 'You get results much more quickly than we do.' Some actors come to the Actors Studio almost for therapy."

While Corsaro says that he refuses to accept a student who is seeking a surrogate shrink, Strasberg actively encouraged his pupils to unburden themselves. In Strasberg's heyday, a class at the Actors Studio was often hard to distinguish from an intense session of group therapy. Classes at the Studio met twice a week. During these sessions an actor or a pair of actors would present a scene that they had rehearsed for weeks. Afterward they would candidly discuss the preparation they had done, including the emotional memories they had tapped. Strasberg himself would then interrogate the actors, and other members of the Studio would also query the players. At last Strasberg would deliver his summary evaluation.

"I realized that the key to Method acting is the ability to be publicly private," says Bruce Dern, who studied with Strasberg in the 1950s and has vivid recollections of his forceful manner. "When Lee would do his comments on a scene, and he would sense a resistance from the actor or actress on going further in dealing with certain emotions, he would literally write vocal prescriptions for analysis. He would say, 'There is a big wall between you and me. For you to grow as an actor, somebody's got to get you through that. You should see a doctor.' At other times he might ask, 'Are you in analysis? Are you going to a psychiatrist? Who is it?' Then Dane Clark or Eli Wallach might raise his hand and ask, 'Is he on Fifty-seventh Street?' At the time I hadn't been in analysis, and I wasn't sure if it was an intrusion or an invasion of the actor's privacy."

Others voiced the same concerns about Strasberg's prying. "He sometimes got into areas that were better left to a psychiatrist," Anne Jackson said. "When I observed Lee's classes," says director Sidney Lumet, "I felt an emotional voyeurism at work, which in my view didn't have a hell of a lot to do with acting."

Bruce Dern notes that it was actresses—including Anne Jackson, Geraldine Page, Kim Stanley, Kim Hunter, and Janice Rule—who particularly thrived in Strasberg's classes during the 1950s. "The strongest, most eloquent work at the Studio," Dern declares, "was done by the women, particularly the women who were in analysis. Most of them were in their thirties. They were not married, or if they were, they had been in multiple marriages. They had problems, and they wore their problems on their sleeves. They were transparent. I saw them crumble week after week, in scene after scene. Men could never do that."

Strasberg had a special affinity for female movie stars, especially those who could strip themselves naked emotionally. He adopted a select few—Jennifer Jones, Marilyn Monroe, Jane Fonda—as protegées and set out to transform them into luminous dramatic actresses. Not surprisingly, these were all women who had a pattern of attaching themselves to Svengali-like mentors; and they all had a devotion to psychoanalysis. In dealing with these malleable personalities, Strasberg was a virtual Pygmalion. As his daughter, Susan, observed, "The girls dreamed he would make them stars; the stars, that he would make them actresses. He seemed to be alternately teacher, surrogate father, and psychiatrist."

Of all the actresses who studied with Strasberg, probably no one was more strikingly transformed than a B-movie player who was born Anne Italiano. When she won a contract at Twentieth Century-Fox in 1951, Darryl F. Zanuck changed the twenty-year-old starlet's name to Bancroft. Over the next five years Anne Bancroft made eighteen movies—a flock of turkeys including *Don't Bother to Knock* (which also featured Marilyn Monroe as a psychotic babysitter), *Demetrius and the Gladiators,* and *Gorilla at Large.* During the same period she married and divorced a real estate developer and then drifted into a series of unfulfilling romantic liaisons with vacant young actors and other nonentities. As Bancroft later summed up her early days in Hollywood, "Every picture I did was worse than the last one, and every man I was in love with was worse than the last one."

In 1956 she entered psychoanalysis put an end to this downward spiral. "I had squelched ambition," she decided. "I never realized that ambition is a healthy thing to have. I thought nice girls didn't have it." Her analyst encouraged her to move back to New York to test herself in the theater, and she enrolled in acting classes there, first with Herbert Berghof, and then with Lee Strasberg. Her training at the Actors Studio complemented her ongoing analysis.

"At the Studio I learn a lot about my real-life problems," Bancroft told one interviewer. "I also get a chance to work out many emotions that would make trouble for me if they were bottled up. For instance, I can act out my destructive tendencies where they can't hurt anyone."

Bancroft's metamorphosis was one of the most extraordinary in the annals of American acting. In 1957 she appeared in the last of eighteen stupefying B-movies, *The Girl in Black Stockings*. In January 1958 she opened in *Two for the Seesaw* on Broadway and, later that season, won the Tony Award for best actress. The next year she won another for *The Miracle Worker*. On December 21, 1959, she was on the cover of *Time* magazine. When she returned to Hollywood for the movie version of the *The Miracle Worker*, her first picture since *The Girl in Black Stockings*, she turned in a performance that earned her an Academy Award.

Bancroft talked about her amazing transformation in dozens of interviews, and she gave the Actors Studio and her six-year analysis most of the credit. To other aspiring actresses Bancroft's sudden ascent to the very peak of her profession was the best possible advertisement for the practical benefits of psychoanalysis. In 1962 she told Earl Wilson, only half facetiously, "The only men in my life from now on will be my father, my agent, my press agent and my psychiatrist." Two years later she added a fifth man when she married comedian Mel Brooks. It may have seemed like an improbable match, but the squat Jewish jokemeister and the willowy dramatic diva were united by a common devotion to the religion of psychoanalysis. The five-year analysis that Brooks underwent was instrumental in abetting his own transition from Catskills comic to Hollywood auteur. In addition, he once quipped, psychoanalysis helped him to overcome his habit of "vomiting between parked cars."

Both of the plays that catapulted Anne Bancroft to stardom, *Two for the Seesaw* and *The Miracle Worker*, were written by William Gibson and directed by Arthur Penn. There was a unique synergy among these three artists. Like Bancroft, Penn and Gibson were profoundly influenced by psychoanalysis. Gibson was married to a prominent analyst, Dr. Margaret Brenman, who had trained at the Menninger Foundation and then went to work at Austen Riggs sanitarium in Stockbridge, Massachusetts. Austen Riggs was the model for the fictional psychiatric clinic depicted in William Gibson's novel, *The Cobweb*, which was turned into a star-studded, fairly ridiculous 1955 movie, once described as *"Grand Hotel* in an insane asylum." The cast included Richard Widmark, Lauren Bacall, and Charles Boyer as therapists and John Kerr, Susan Strasberg, and Oscar Levant as patients, with the venerable Lillian Gish as an administrator of the sanitarium. (At one point during filming, the temperamental Levant, who had visited a score of analysts during his life, balked when receiving advice from his director, Vincente Minnelli. "Don't try to tell *me* how to play crazy!" Levant exploded. "I'm crazier than you could ever *hope* to be!")

William Gibson, who taught a drama workshop at Austen Riggs, was fascinated by his wife's psychiatric colleagues, and Margaret Gibson was equally drawn to her husband's world. She interacted with show-business personalities in several ways. She met some of them, such as Margaret Sullavan and Jules Munshin, when they were hospitalized at Austen Riggs. She met many more through her husband and Clifford Odets, who had been William Gibson's mentor at New York University. In 1981 Margaret Gibson wrote an exhaustive biography of Odets, a book that is richly psychoanalytic in its approach.

Dr. Gibson sometimes utilized her professional skills to aid her husband's theatrical ventures. For example, during the rehearsals for William Gibson's first Broadway hit, *Two for the Seesaw,* she was enlisted to assuage the nervous star, Anne Bancroft. The play chronicled the unlikely romance between a Greenwich Village kook and a starchy midwestern lawyer, played by Henry Fonda. "Hank was an inaccessible, unpleasant person," Margaret Gibson says. "On that play he was so uptight and inhibited, and he was awful to Annie." Dr. Gibson served as ad hoc therapist for both Bancroft and director Arthur Penn. "I talked to Arthur about what I thought was going on with Fonda," Dr. Gibson says, "and I also talked to Annie. Every night after rehearsals she was on the floor with how mean Hank was to her both on and offstage. I told her, 'He is treating you so badly because he is seeing daily that you are commanding the stage. You are such a threat to this man, who is supposed to be the star.' " Dr. Gibson's counsel sustained Bancroft right up until the triumphant opening night.

In 1963 Penn and William Gibson were brought in by an ailing Clifford Odets to work on the musical version of Odets's 1937 hit, *Golden Boy,* which he had originally written for the Group Theatre. This story of a Jewish prizefighter torn between his conflicting impulses as a virtuoso violinist and a pugnacious pugilist had been retooled as a vehicle for Sammy Davis, Jr., a song-and-dance man who had no experience with such a demanding role. Davis's erratic behavior soon required another frantic SOS to Margaret Gibson. "Sammy was one of the most gifted people I ever met," Dr. Gibson says, "but many people don't know that he was illiterate. He couldn't read or write because he never learned. When he was two and a half, he went on the road with his father and his uncle as a performer. He never went to school. He felt insecure working with William Gibson and Arthur Penn. During rehearsals he would often panic, because he felt that he was totally unable to fulfill the commitment of serious acting that the play required. On dress-rehearsal night he disappeared. Bill and Arthur were furious with him, so it became my assignment to handle him. I found him and sat down with him and analyzed what these panics were about. I reminded him how excited Clifford was when he first met him. In a way it's such a cliché, but if you can help the person find in themselves a little self-regard, usually you can help them to move on."

The ministrations of a professional analyst like Dr. Gibson were obviously not a regular part of the rehearsal process. But many directors who fancied themselves amateur analysts attempted to use the same techniques in their ongoing work with actors. The career of Elia Kazan, arguably the most important American director of the 1950s, epitomized the benefits of a psychoanalytic approach to acting and directing—as well as its shortcomings. Kazan had been one of the cofounders of the Actors Studio in 1947, and he shared Lee Strasberg's reverence for analysis. Kazan himself had spent years on the couch, first with the Hungarian-born Dr. Bela Mittelman and later with an associate of Karen Horney's, Dr. Harold Kelman. The director's analytic background powerfully affected his working methods. Kazan was fond of dissecting the personal lives of the actors he was auditioning. For instance, when he was directing *Cat on a Hot Tin Roof,* Kazan decided to cast Barbara Bel Geddes as the sexually voracious heroine because of his own assessment of the actress's psychological makeup. "I'd known her when she was a plump young girl," Kazan wrote in his autobiography, and he believed "that when a girl is fat in her early and middle teens and slims down later, she is left with an uncertainty about her appeal to boys, and what often results is a strong sexual appetite, intensified by the continuing anxiety of believing herself undesirable." That was his appraisal of Bel Geddes: "I knew how much a working sexual relationship meant to this young woman and that in every basic way she resembled Maggie the Cat. I trusted my knowledge of her own nature and life and therefore cast her."

Kazan also used his understanding of psychoanalysis to goad actors into giving more intensely felt performances. In directing the 1955 film *East of Eden*, Kazan observed that Raymond Massey, who was playing James Dean's stern father, disliked his temperamental young costar, believing him to be undisciplined and surly. Kazan told Dean exactly what Massey thought of him, hoping that Dean's resentment would spill over into his scenes with Massey. The ploy worked to infuse the father-son scenes with a palpable tension.

When Kazan directed *Sweet Bird of Youth* on Broadway, he decided that the key to the character of Chance Wayne was the aging stud's alienation from the other people in his provincial hometown. To ensure that Paul Newman would convey that sense of isolation and discomfort, Kazan rounded up the other men in the cast before the first preview in Philadelphia and told them, "From now until the play opens, I don't want any of you to socialize with Paul. Let him feel that you don't like him and that he's alienated from you. Right now you're too chummy with him, and it shows up in the play." The actors obeyed Kazan's instructions and snubbed Newman. Although Newman tried to learn what he had done to offend them, none of them disclosed the truth. Finally, the day after the play opened on Broadway, the actors revealed Kazan's strategy to Newman. "Kazan said that from that point on, the play was never the same," remarks Bruce Dern, who had a supporting role in *Sweet Bird of Youth*. "After that, the electricity was gone."

Kazan was manipulative to the extreme, but his shrewd instinct for casting and his genius at drawing emotional performances from actors like Brando, Dean, and Newman testified to the rewarding interplay between psychoanalysis and art. In other respects, however, the impact of analysis on Kazan was more dubious. Kazan's friend Budd Schulberg (who wrote the screenplays for two of the director's most memorable films, *On the Waterfront* and *A Face in the Crowd*) recalls that Kazan frequently sang the praises of his analysts. Schulberg, however, views their influence on the director with more cynicism. "Kazan came out of analysis with his guilts removed about any wrong thing he might have done," Schulberg says. "If you cheated on your wife, it's all right because that's you and you must be yourself. It removes accountability. Kazan felt relieved from problems about his wife, Molly, who was a wonderful woman and a tremendous force in his life. He had put her through hell."

There was another aspect of his life in which Kazan's analysis influenced him greatly. After he directed Archibald MacLeish's play *J.B.*, Kazan confessed to his analyst, Dr. Harold Kelman, that he had no real regard for the play. In fact, although he was then the most admired director in America, he was dissatisfied with most of the work he had done. After a few months of treatment, Dr. Kelman gave him the reason for his frustration. "He told me that although I'd successfully impressed a great number of people with the plays and films I'd done," Kazan said, "my best and truest material was my own life: my parents, my childhood, my dreams, my intimate life, the desperation and panic I felt." Dr. Kelman was taking the basic tenet of psychoanalysis—that mental health comes from bravely confronting one's own personal and family history—and applying that principle to the creative arts. It was Kelman who encouraged Kazan to write about his own life, a fantasy that the director had harbored but never realized. In 1963 Kazan wrote and directed *America America*, the story of his uncle's journey from Turkey to the United States. Then he put aside his film and theater work to concentrate on his newfound career as a novelist.

While this mid-life transition may have proven personally rewarding for Kazan, it was less rewarding for his audiences. Kazan was far better at interpreting other people's stories than he ever was at creating his own. He made splendid contributions to the American theater directing Tennessee Williams's *A Streetcar Named Desire* and Arthur Miller's *Death of a Salesman*, and his best films—*On the Waterfront* (written by Budd Schulberg), *East of Eden* (adapted by Paul Osborn from John Steinbeck's novel), and *Wild River* (again written by Paul Osborn)—are among the landmark films of the 1950s. All of these works benefited from Kazan's personal experience; *Death of a Salesman* and *East of Eden* drew much of their passion from Kazan's feelings about his tortured relationship with his overbearing father, and *On the Waterfront* dramatized the complex emotions surrounding the act of informing—a drama that Kazan himself had acted out two years earlier when he testified before the House Un-American Activities Committee. All these works had a personal charge to them, but Kazan was enriching scripts by fine writers, and the collaborations produced soaring works of art. *America America, The Arrangement, The Understudy,* and Kazan's other novels may have their merits, but they are not in the same league.

An analyst has no legitimate interest and probably no expertise in making artistic judgments; his role is to encourage the self-realization of the patient. Apparently Dr. Kelman succeeded in this regard with Elia Kazan. Since Kazan tapped into the wellspring of his personal past and poured those memories into his writing, he claims to have lived a far more fulfilling life. But the hard truth is that Kazan's work over the last three decades has been inferior to his earlier achievements. Kazan's enemies on the left predicted that his work as a director would decline after his friendly testimony before the House Un-American Activities Committee. That proved not to be the case; Kazan's best films were made after he testified in 1952. It was the legacy of Sigmund Freud, not Joseph McCarthy, that finally sabotaged his career. Psychoanalysis encouraged him to reveal himself proudly, when a certain measure of self-abnegation had accounted for his greatest accomplishments as an artist.

Like Lee Strasberg, Kazan encouraged the actors with whom he worked to enter psychoanalysis. Kazan sent Marlon Brando to his first analyst, Dr. Bela Mittelman, and Brando remained a patient of Mittelman's for years. When Brando wanted to extricate himself from his contract to appear in *The Egyptian,* a lumbering Twentieth Century-Fox costume picture, he had Dr. Mittelman call the studio and inform Darryl Zanuck that the star was too "sick and mentally confused" to complete the picture.

That was not the only benefit Brando derived from analysis. He often used psychoanalytic insights to try to outmaneuver his fellow actors. After Samuel Goldwyn hired Brando for the screen version of *Guys and Dolls,* Brando learned that Frank Sinatra would be his costar. Brando had no musical experience, and he was not happy about the prospect of sharing the screen with one of the world's great crooners. To give himself the advantage in their scenes together, Brando employed a devious tactic. He knew that Sinatra hated retakes, so he began deliberately flubbing his lines in order to drag out the shooting and leave Sinatra feeling exhausted and angry.

Brando used similarly hostile gestures off the set as well. He once met James Dean at a party and lambasted the young actor for imitating his mannerisms. Then he ended the conversation by playing on Dean's insecurities and advising him solicitously, "You ought to see a psychiatrist." Jay Presson Allen, a writer prominent in both theatrical and film circles for over thirty years, knew Brando well. She notes that psychoanalysis "was enormously useful to Marlon. He used the insights it gave him to manipulate the people around him. He was a very apt student."

In the long run Brando's analysis contributed to his growing disdain for his own art. His time on the couch supplied him with elaborate jargon to explain the actor's stunted psychological development. In 1960, when he made *One-Eyed Jacks*, the only movie he also directed, Brando explained why he was tired of performing: "Acting by and large is an expression of a neurotic impulse. . . . The truth is that actors are actors because it gives them sustenance for their narcissism. Acting enables them to experience a false form of love and attention, the same kind of attention given any exhibition." That crude textbook analysis provided the rationale for a cynical, venal approach to his work. Early in his career Brando had selected his projects very carefully and brought passionate conviction to most of his roles. Later on he seemed to choose his movies mainly on the basis of the salary he could command, and he gave performances—in films like *Superman, The Formula,* and *Christopher Columbus*—that verged on self-parody. That attitude of contempt was something that his years of therapy may have done more to engender than allay.

Elia Kazan did not simply proselytize for analysis to actors like Marlon Brando, whose background in live theater predisposed them to absorb both Stanislavskian and Freudian precepts. Kazan was also willing to preach the gospel to the stars born and bred in Hollywood, who were belittled as vacuous nonactors by most other members of the theatrical elite. It was Kazan who first urged Marilyn Monroe to enter analysis, and he was also instrumental in reshaping the career of another dyed-in-the-wool creature of Hollywood, Natalie Wood. A child star at the age of eight (she had appeared with Orson Welles in *Tomorrow Is Forever* and then played the precocious child in *Miracle on 34th Street*), Wood had never appeared on stage and had been too busy making films to take time off for acting classes. She was eager, however, to work with Kazan, whom she knew could enhance her reputation as a serious actress. In 1960 she coveted the lead in *Splendor in the Grass* and asked Norma Crane, an Actors

Studio veteran, to coach her for her audition with Kazan. The director felt that if he could eliminate some of the bad habits Wood had acquired as a studio contract player, he might be able to tap into a real sense of vulnerability. For her screen test, Kazan later said, "I used paint remover on her, took off her glamorous clothes and put her in front of the camera, naked and gasping."

Kazan was not Natalie's only mentor. Shortly before winning the role in *Splendor in the Grass* she joined the throng of young actresses who were entering analysis in search of legitimacy. Her analyst, Dr. John Lindon, turned into her most trusted attendant as she underwent a series of personal and professional crises. Her steamy love affair with her *Splendor in the Grass* costar, Warren Beatty, broke up her marriage to Robert Wagner, but then the romance with Beatty cooled, leaving Wood feeling bereft. She also faced career problems in the 1960s. After becoming a top box-office draw in *Splendor in the Grass*, *West Side Story*, and *Love with the Proper Stranger*, she made a string of flops. The nadir came in 1966 when she played the title role in *Penelope*, a misfired comedy that featured Dick Shawn as a quack psychiatrist inept at treating the befuddled heroine.

Natalie's real-life psychiatrist, Dr. Lindon, tried his best to keep her afloat. She spent her lunch hour with him almost every day for eight years. She refused to accept any acting jobs that would require an interruption of the regimen—a decision that was hardly beneficial to her stalled career. In 1966 Warren Beatty tried to persuade Wood to star opposite him in the first movie he was producing, *Bonnie and Clyde*. But the prospect of three months on location in Texas away from Dr. Lindon terrified the actress, and she turned down the role. Beatty persisted and came to her home one afternoon to make one last appeal. The two ex-lovers got into a screaming match. After Beatty left, Wood swallowed a bottle of sleeping pills. Her friend and sometime secretary, Mart Crowley, who was living in a guest house on her property, discovered her slumped on the stairs and immediately phoned Dr. Lindon. Crowley drove Wood to Cedars of Lebanon hospital, where Lindon registered her under a pseudonym so that the press would not learn of her suicide attempt.

That near-fatal incident pushed Wood into more intensive therapy with Lindon. Over the next several years she gradually regained her equanimity, a recovery that she credited to her sojourn on the couch. "I'm as grateful for that experience as for anything that ever happened to me," she told journalist Tommy Thompson. "If it wasn't for those years of analysis, I'd probably be dead." Like many Hollywood analysands, Wood became a fervent evangelist, urging her friends and family to find salvation in the analyst's chamber. Several of her close friends—including screenwriter Tom Mankiewicz and the fluttery socialite Edith Goetz (whose husband, producer William Goetz, had cast eight-year-old Natalie in her first major movie)—became patients of Dr. Lindon's. Wood also became an avid reader of psychiatric case studies, and two of the books she personally optioned for filming were Hannah Green's story of mental illness, *I Never Promised You a Rose Garden*, and Frances Farmer's memoir of her own incarceration in a mental hospital, *Will There Really Be a Morning?* (Both movies were eventually made with other actresses.)

In 1969 Natalie married producer Richard Gregson and had her first child. Three years later she divorced Gregson and remarried Robert Wagner. The wedding took place aboard a fifty-five-foot yacht, where the band played "The Second Time Around." According to Natalie's sister, Lana Wood, Dr. Lindon was included in a small group of intimate friends at the wedding party. He circulated among the guests with a tape recorder, encouraging them to offer congratulatory messages to the happy couple. Later, he was sometimes invited to dinner parties at the Wagner home, and Wood introduced him quite nonchalantly as her analyst. "Natalie was just insane about him," confirmed Edith Goetz, who entertained Dr. Lindon at her own elegant soirees.

Analysis may have helped some fragile performers to survive for a time, but evaluations of the psychoanalytic approach to acting that Elia Kazan and Lee Strasberg popularized are sharply divided. On the one hand, the best Method actors plumbed their characters' inner lives with sharp insight. In Brando's famous "I coulda been a contender" speech in *On the Waterfront,* or in the scene of James Dean reaching out to touch his estranged mother in *East of Eden,* the visceral impact of the performances was stunning; viewers felt as if they were eavesdropping on the most private human encounters, witnessing raw emotion stripped of all defenses. But Jay Presson Allen voices a common criticism of Method acting when she says, "We turn out the most realistic actors in the world, but we consistently fail to turn out actors who can deal with the classics. You can see the difference between American actors and English

actors, who are not analytically influenced. They're involved with
style, but we're involved with probing reality. Both schools can
bring forth astonishing actors. Maggie Smith, for example, is an
extraordinary technician. If I were casting a stylish comedy, I would
lean toward the Brits almost all the way. But not many English
actors tear your heart out as the best American actors do."

Even Elia Kazan acknowledged the validity of critiques like the
one Jay Allen makes. When he staged the *Oresteia* with a cast from
the Actors Studio, Kazan was appalled by the results: "Although
they were devoted and worked hard, although they were attractive
people for whom I felt affection, they had, almost without exception, poor speech. It was, and still is, parochial and even ethnic, 'off
the streets,' perfect for *On the Waterfront*. The unconscious premise
of all too many of them was: If I have the emotion, that is all I need."

The technical inadequacies and the lack of basic professional-
ism associated with Method acting have been the bane of innumerable directors and producers over the years. Stories abound of
hopelessly self-absorbed actors who caused lengthy delays in filming
because they could not find the psychological "motivation" to perform a simple bit of business necessary to move the story forward.
Alfred Hitchcock came face-to-face with this maddening intransi-
gence when he directed Montgomery Clift in *I Confess*. Hitchcock's
businesslike treatment of actors contrasted sharply with the psychological coddling favored in the Actors Studio, and Hitchcock had little patience for Clift's finicky demands. The climax of *I Confess* takes
place at the historic Château Frontenac in Quebec. To establish the
scene, Hitchcock wanted the priest played by Clift to look up and see
the word *Hotel* on the roof of the grand Gothic structure. But Clift, a
veteran of Lee Strasberg's classes, balked at performing this routine
action. "I don't have any motivation to look up at that moment," Clift
told the director. The Master of Suspense conceded the point but explained that he needed the character to look up simply in order to
identify the locale so that he could cut to the interior of the hotel.
Actor and director batted the point back and forth for hours, but Clift
refused to budge. Finally Hitchcock solved the problem by sending
a message to a gaffer on a high scaffolding, instructing him to call
Clift's name. The crew member hollered to the actor, Clift reflexively
looked up, the camera caught the moment, and the scene was
wrapped—without any Method acting.

*   *   *

Ten years later Clift had the chance to dig far deeper into his psyche when he starred in Hollywood's most unabashed tribute to the founder of psychoanalysis, John Huston's production of *Freud*. Unfortunately, by that time Clift was so debilitated by alcohol and drug dependency that he was closer in spirit to the psychotic patients depicted in the film than he was to the wise doctor he was portraying. (Marilyn Monroe once said of Clift, "He's the only person I know who is in worse shape than I am.")

When Clift was hired to play Freud, he viewed the movie as an opportunity not simply to celebrate the sage of Vienna but to pay homage to his own analyst, Dr. William Silverberg, with whom he had developed an intimate relationship that verged on *folie à deux*. Like Clift, Silverberg was homosexual, and in addition to socializing frequently, the two men sometimes vacationed together in Maine. When he presented a copy of his book, *Childhood Experience and Destiny*, to Clift, Silverberg penned a special inscription: "To Monty, my hero, Billy."

Despite—or perhaps because of—his excessive identification with his patient, Silverberg was completely ineffectual at treating Clift's crippling alcoholism. When Clift's medical doctor urged the actor to seek treatment at the Menninger Clinic, Dr. Silverberg vetoed the idea; he could not bear to lose his hold on the magnetic star. In their sessions together toward the end of Clift's life, according to Clift's secretary, Lorenzo James, Dr. Silverberg spent as much of the hour confiding his own problems as he did listening to the travails of his analysand.

Like his star, director John Huston viewed the film of *Freud* as an act of reverent homage. Huston's fascination with psychoanalysis had been sparked when he made a wartime documentary about shell-shocked soldiers, *Let There Be Light*. "Making that film was like having a religious experience," Huston commented. He went back to the altar when he directed *Freud*, which grew out of what Huston himself described as "an eighteen-year-old obsession based on the firm conviction that very few of man's great adventures, not even his travels beyond the earth's horizon, can dwarf Freud's journey into the uncharted depths of the human soul."

In preparing *Freud*, Huston teamed up with two of his collaborators on *Let There Be Light*—producer Julian Blaustein and screenwriter Charles Kaufman. But the project almost ran aground because of stubborn opposition from Anna Freud. Ralph Greenson, who knew Kaufman socially, arranged for him to meet with Anna

Freud in London. "She was extremely nice, but it was a futile idea to try to get her blessing," Kaufman recalled shortly before his death in 1991. "The idea of an actor putting on a false beard and impersonating the great man in her life would never be acceptable to her."

Anna Freud proposed to Kaufman and Blaustein that if they agreed not to proceed with the film while she was alive, she would grant them all film rights to her father's works after her death. She said to her lawyer, "Please point out to Mr. Blaustein that I am sixty years old." Blaustein replied acerbically, "With modern medicine, what kind of guarantee is that?"

Blaustein eventually left the project, and Kaufman prepared a story treatment for the film that was vetted by a battery of lawyers to ensure that no one was defamed. Huston then hired the existential savant Jean-Paul Sartre to write the script. It turned out to be 1,500 pages long, so Kaufman was rehired to pare it down to manageable size.

Despite its tortuous road to the screen, John Huston retained his high hopes for *Freud*. Shortly before the movie's release, he declared, "We have attempted to accomplish something new in story telling on the screen—to penetrate through to the unconscious of the audience . . . to shock and move the spectator into at least a subliminal recognition or awareness of his own hidden psychic motivations." The picture may not have achieved that lofty goal, but it was still an audacious effort, and far less simplistic than most of the Freudian melodramas that preceded it. Structured like a mystery story whose denouement was Freud's discovery of the Oedipus complex and infantile sexuality, the film conveyed a substantial amount of scientific information in an entertaining format.

Although *Freud* was too didactic to please the avant-garde, it did catch the fancy of most middlebrow reviewers, who described it in tones of hushed reverence. Writing in *The New York Times*, Bosley Crowther pronounced the movie "as daring and dramatic as the probing of a dark, mysterious crime," and he sang the praises of Huston's direction: "so graphic, so expressive of the rhythms and moods of troubled individuals, so illustrative in its use of cinema's styles, that it drags the viewer into the picture with the disturbance of a patient on the couch." Philip K. Scheuer of the *Los Angeles Times* was equally bewitched, and his prose was almost as tremulous. "Not all the traumatic experiences in the enthralling, remarkable motion picture called *Freud* are confined to the screen," Scheuer wrote. "Each viewer may well have the sensation that he is undergoing one himself—that he is finding out things about himself which are closer than his skin."

Freud came out in 1962, a year that probably witnessed the fullest flowering of Hollywood's love affair with psychoanalysis. Several important movies of 1962 dealt overtly with psychiatry, and many others evinced a strong psychoanalytic bent; they explored the inner torment of complex characters, probing their unconscious motivations and conflicts. For example, *Lawrence of Arabia,* the year's Academy Award-winning best picture, was a new kind of screen epic, one that exposed the neurotic tendencies of its flamboyant, masochistic hero. The brilliant political thriller *The Manchurian Candidate,* which was also released that year, was rife with Freudian symbolism. Angela Lansbury gave a chilling performance as a voracious gorgon locked in an intense love-hate relationship with her prissy, repressed son, Laurence Harvey. In the climactic scene, when Lansbury reveals her diabolical scheme to engineer a Communist takeover of America, she ends her "aria of evil," as one critic called it, by kissing Harvey passionately on the lips—a daring scene for its day, and one that brought the movie's Oedipal undercurrent explicitly to the fore.

Of the movies released that year that dealt directly with psychiatry, *Tender Is the Night* was by far the most extravagant. It had been in a state of gestation for almost as long as Huston's *Freud.* In 1948 David O. Selznick had bought the rights to F. Scott Fitzgerald's novel about a psychoanalyst whose life is destroyed after he marries a beautiful but deeply troubled patient. Selznick envisioned it as a vehicle for his wife, Jennifer Jones, a lifelong therapy addict who identified intensely with the character of the quavering Nicole Warren. "Everyone tells me I'm perfectly cast," Jones remarked. "But Nicole is such a tortured, neurotic person, it's a dubious compliment."

Partly because of the downbeat nature of Fitzgerald's story and partly because of Selznick's reputation for reckless spending, it took him almost a dozen years to scrounge together the necessary financing to make the film. In 1959 Selznick moved to Zurich to begin scouting locations. That was not the only reason for the move. Jennifer had discovered a new analyst—Dr. C. A. Meier, a Swiss disciple of Carl Jung—whom she adored. The intensely protective Selznick could not bear to be separated from his wife, so he simply packed up shop and moved with her to the Dolder Hotel in Zurich. He also brought all his employees with him. "Selznick had moved his entire operation from Culver City to Zurich," says producer Gottfried Reinhardt, who came to visit a screenwriter working for Selznick and found a large Hollywood contingent ensconced at the hotel. "I was flabbergasted," Reinhardt adds.

By the time filming began in 1961, Selznick had been forced to relinquish the reins as producer. Twentieth Century-Fox considered him an impossible perfectionist and hired Henry Weinstein, a newcomer from Broadway (who would later work on Marilyn Monroe's abortive last project, *Something's Got to Give*), to replace Selznick. Fox was in dire financial straits at the time, and the studio tried to keep the movie's costs under control by using as many of its contract players as possible. That is how such miscast performers as Tom Ewell and Jill St. John ended up with major supporting roles. Jason Robards was cast as Fitzgerald's dissolute hero, Dick Diver, after William Holden and Richard Burton turned down the role. Robards had already played a Fitzgerald-like novelist in Budd Schulberg's *The Disenchanted* on Broadway, which is one reason why Selznick hired him. The film's director, seventy-four-year-old Henry King, had met Fitzgerald on the Riviera back in the 1920s and took an instant dislike to the novelist. Jason Robards recalls King telling him, "We have a lot of lousy actors on this picture. And we should get all this Scott Fitzgerald shit out of the script."

King, a cantankerous Hollywood veteran whose credits stretched back to the silent days, had as little use for psychoanalysis as he did for F. Scott Fitzgerald, which may be why the movie turned out to be something of a muddle. But Robards, like Jennifer Jones, was deeply involved in therapy at the time he made *Tender Is the Night*. Indeed, he developed an ongoing attachment to his own psychiatrist, Dr. Ferruccio Di Cari, which was comparable to the symbiotic relationship between Montgomery Clift and William Silverberg as well as the intimate tie between Natalie Wood and John Lindon.

Robards met Dr. Di Cari in a most unusual manner. The doctor, an ardent theater buff, came backstage after one of Robards's Broadway performances to congratulate the actor. Di Cari was an Italian emigré who, in addition to practicing psychiatry, dabbled in playwriting and lectured around the world on the legend of Pinnocchio, one of his obsessions. When he met Robards in the actor's dressing room, Di Cari mentioned that he was a psychiatrist, and

Robards joked that he might look him up. Shortly afterwards he did just that. Robards was drinking heavily, and his marriage to Lauren Bacall was in peril. A dozen years later he was divorced from Bacall, still drinking, and still in therapy with Dr. Di Cari. Finally, during a revival of Eugene O'Neill's *A Moon for the Misbegotten* in the mid-seventies, he went on the wagon for good. "I'm sure that my analysis had something to do with my quitting," Robards says, "but it took years."

By that time Robards and his psychiatrist had developed a close personal friendship. In fact, according to Robards, their roles eventually reversed. Robards reports, "He'll say to me, 'I'm having trouble with my relationships. Can you help me? I helped you. You can return the favor at least.'" Robards frequently dined with Di Cari at the mansion on East Sixty-first Street that the doctor had purchased from Gypsy Rose Lee, and Di Cari attended Thanksgiving dinner at the Robards home. And when Robards's youngest son was born, Di Cari was named the child's godfather.

Besides the big-budget productions of *Freud* and *Tender Is the Night*, two grittier films of 1962 explored dramatic relationships between psychiatrists and patients. Stanley Kramer's *Pressure Point* cast Sidney Poitier as a dedicated psychiatrist trying to uncover the reasons for the violent antisocial behavior of a young racist played by Bobby Darin. And *David and Lisa*, which cost less than $200,000 to produce, turned out to be the most influential of the year's many cinematic psychodramas. Hailed as one of the first American "art films," it won Academy Award nominations for its writer, Eleanor Perry, and its director, Frank Perry, and it earned a tidy profit as well.

The project had been brought to the Perrys' attention by Eleanor's daughter from her first marriage, Ann Bayer, who was then a student at Sarah Lawrence. She had read Dr. Theodore Rubin's fictional case study, *Lisa and David*, the story of two young people who fall in love in a mental hospital, and suggested to her mother that it could make an effective movie. Eleanor agreed, and the Perrys cajoled friends and theatrical associates into providing the financial backing.

In the story David is a brilliant but disturbed young man who is terrified of being touched; Lisa is a schizophrenic who speaks only in rhymes. At first David disdains his psychiatrist, but eventually he responds to the doctor's compassion and concern. By the end of the film, the boy has become so thoroughly enraptured by his mentor that he confesses—in a late-night conversation over chocolate cake and milk—that he is thinking of becoming a psychiatrist himself. In the poignant final scene he reaches out to the isolated Lisa and asks her to take his hand. Writing in *The New Republic*, Stanley Kauffmann praised the film for its warmth and humanity, though he did have reservations about the characterization of the psychiatrist, played by veteran actor Howard Da Silva. "The kindly analyst is as straitened a role as the kindly priest," Kauffmann remarked, summing up the idealized view of psychiatry conveyed in most movies of the early 1960s.

Janet Margolin, the actress who played Lisa, was only eighteen when she was cast in the film. She recalls that Frank Perry, like most directors of the era, urged her to get a bead on the character by delving deeply into her own psyche. "Frank didn't want us to visit mental hospitals and try to imitate the patients," Margolin says. "He wanted us to draw everything out of ourselves. I got to use all my years of being a troubled, lonely, sensitive, high-strung, miserably shy girl."

In addition to launching Margolin's career and that of her costar, Keir Dullea, the movie also gave considerable prominence to the author of the original novel, Dr. Theodore Rubin. He went on to publish twenty-seven books and even wrote a sequel to *David and Lisa*, which imagined a reunion of the two characters after two decades. He tried to interest Dullea and Margolin in turning it into a movie, but Margolin declined. "It was as bad as *A Man and a Woman: Twenty Years Later*," she says.

David and Lisa, however, remained one of the landmark films of the decade. Despite its simplifications, it had as powerful an impact on audiences of its day as films like *Spellbound* and *The Snake Pit* had on an earlier generation. "After *David and Lisa* came out, I became a hero of the New York Psychoanalytic Institute," Frank Perry says. He and Eleanor were wined and dined by the most prominent New York analysts.

"The movie had a considerable effect on getting people into the field of psychiatry, and on raising money for mental health," Theodore Rubin says. "It showed disturbed people as human beings." Rubin also found the movie a boon to his bank account. "Frank Perry put the book in the smallest possible print on the screen," Rubin complains. "But it sold more and more copies over the years.

It's been translated into several languages and has by now sold a couple of million copies. It began to be used in a lot of college classes. It has the advantage of being extremely short, so students love it for a book report." A poster from the movie hangs on the wall of Dr. Rubin's office, right above his couch.

The year 1962 also saw the release of Arthur Penn's film version of *The Miracle Worker,* based on William Gibson's powerful drama about the young Helen Keller and her dedicated teacher, Annie Sullivan. The movie earned Penn his first Academy Award nomination, and both Anne Bancroft and Patty Duke won Oscars under his direction. That film represented the convergence of a team of people with intense ties to psychoanalysis. Even sixteen-year-old Patty Duke would soon join the fold. Duke credited her psychiatrist with helping her to lay to rest the destructive influence of the Svengali-like personal managers who guided her career as a child star, and she eventually wrote two best-selling books about her personal bout with manic-depressive illness.

The Miracle Worker is a glowing tribute not simply to education but to selfless, intensely concentrated therapy. In her work with the unruly Helen Keller, Annie Sullivan behaves very much like a strict Freudian analyst. She insists that Helen be separated from her over-indulgent parents so that she alone can conduct her "treatment" of the child in an isolated, pristine environment.

In directing the drama, Arthur Penn was able to draw on his personal experience with precisely that kind of imposing therapist. He had been psychoanalyzed by a strong-willed European refugee named Dr. Rudolph Loewenstein, whose self-confident manner was comparable to that of the determined Annie Sullivan. Born in Switzerland, Loewenstein took his training at the Berlin Institute under the tutelage of Freud's disciples Karl Abraham and Hanns Sachs. When the war broke out, Loewenstein narrowly escaped from Germany, first to Vichy France, where his life was saved by a man he had never seen before—a Gentile who substituted himself in a line of suspects when the Nazis were rounding up Jews. (The story of his escape, which he frequently recounted in later years, was transformed by Loewenstein's patient, Arthur Miller, into the play *Incident at Vichy*.) Loewenstein settled in New York and eventually acquired a star-studded clientele that included Mike Nichols, Miller, and Penn.

Penn sought treatment from Loewenstein in the early 1950s because he seemed unable to break certain self-destructive patterns in his professional life. He repeatedly passed up opportunities to advance his career. "I was not sure if I really wanted to succeed," Penn says. With Loewenstein's guidance he began to pursue his directing career more singlemindedly.

Penn's familial history raised thornier problems during his four-year analysis. "My parents were divorced when I was very young," Penn notes, "and I didn't see my father probably at all until I was about fourteen and then only for a few years, a few difficult years, before he died, so that nothing was ever resolved. That unresolved material remained to be digested or left stuck in your throat like a great glob of suet. Those things reside there sort of like a psychological boil. One result of psychoanalysis was that I could put it to rest."

After he had dealt with some of the personal issues that dogged him, Penn says, he was ready for "psychoanalytic insight into my work, so it became not just self-directed but other-directed."

Indeed, of all major American directors, Penn may have been the most overtly psychoanalytic in his approach—even more than Elia Kazan or Joseph L. Mankiewicz. His very first film, *The Left-Handed Gun*, made in 1958, was a treasure trove of Freudian motifs. Based on a television play by Gore Vidal, but considerably altered and embellished by Penn, *The Left-Handed Gun* was a psychological study of Billy the Kid (played by Paul Newman). Billy's father died when he was a boy, and his first crime, according to the film, occurred when he shot a gunman who insulted his mother. The basic oedipal triangle is given many additional twists throughout the film. At one point Billy seeks refuge in Mexico with an older man, a kindly gunsmith. But the young outlaw betrays his benefactor by seducing the gunsmith's wife. At the end of the film, when Billy is on the run from a posse and wants the Mexican couple to shelter him again, they reject him because of this sexual betrayal. Racked with guilt, Billy allows himself to be killed by Sheriff Pat Garrett, another paternal figure.

All of Penn's subsequent films show a marked psychoanalytic influence as well. Troubled father-son relationships appear in many of them, from *The Chase* to *Four Friends* and *Target*. The most poignant scenes in *Alice's Restaurant* concern Arlo Guthrie's vigil at the bedside of his dying father, Woody, who is in the terminal phases of Huntington's chorea. Arlo finds a father substitute in Alice's husband, Ray, who forms a commune in Stockbridge, but ultimately the young man leaves Ray to strike out on his own. The search for a surrogate father is a recurring motif in Penn's films, no doubt reflecting his feelings toward his own absent father. *In Little Big Man* the impressionable hero (Dustin Hoffman) is adopted by a number of unreliable mentors and finally finds a haven with a wise old Indian patriarch.

Penn has also focused on fraternal rivalry in several of his films, notably *Bonnie and Clyde,* and he suggests that this theme, too, draws its urgency from his complex relationship with his own brother, the respected photographer Irving Penn. "I can't suggest I would be particularly adept at a film about a son who had a mother infatuation," Penn notes. "That was not within the lexicon of my emotional and psychological formation. I would know something about brother competitiveness and friendliness and father alienation. Those tend to be the scripts I'm attracted to. After all, those are the dynamics of life as I know them. Analysis is a way of understanding, a way of making use of a broader range of materials out of your own existence that you might quite understandably flinch from and flee from. Analysis makes it accessible to you."

Freudian imagery also permeates Penn's work. *The Miracle Worker* contains expressionistic flashback sequences emphasizing the influence of Annie Sullivan's childhood on her current vocation. *Mickey One,* Penn's experimental film about a night-club comic on the run from the mob, is filled with visual symbols of oedipal guilt and castration anxieties. *The Chase,* Penn's overblown melodrama about Southern racism, posits a Freudian interpretation of bigotry, underscoring the link between sexual frustration and violence.

Some of these films are rather simplistic in bearing down on Freudian interpretations of character. *The Miracle Worker,* for example, suggests a neat causal link between Annie's inability to save her brother's life when they were children and her determination to rescue Helen Keller from darkness. Penn's most telling and subtle use of psychoanalysis can be found in *Bonnie and Clyde.* The script by Robert Benton and David Newman had presented Clyde Barrow as a homosexual trying to prove his manhood through crime. Penn suggested changing the homosexuality to impotence. Scenes in which Bonnie and Clyde fondle a gun clearly imply that the weapon is a substitute for Clyde's ineffectual penis. Clyde finally becomes potent when he reads a poem about him that Bonnie has published in the newspaper. Fame is an aphrodisiac to Clyde, and once he is immortalized as a dangerous man, he can express himself sexually. Unlike some of Penn's other films, *Bonnie and Clyde* is psychologically acute rather than reductive; its characterizations are vibrant and layered with revealing touches.

One of the most memorable scenes in the film is the reunion between Bonnie and her family. It is after Bonnie and Clyde abduct a young undertaker that Bonnie suddenly has a desire to see her mother one last time. Penn attributes the impact of this haunting sequence to his knowledge of psychoanalysis. Originally the reunion with Bonnie's mother occurred early in the script, but Penn decided that the sequence would have more significance if it served as "an adumbration of her death," as he puts it. "If we could place it appropriately," he goes on, "the audience, without being bludgeoned, would have a certain sense of the ominousness of it. That then dictated the aesthetics of it. When we came to shoot the scene, I thought it would be wonderful if it had a slightly different visual aspect from the rest of the film. What we chose was the idea of the slightly faded photograph. We put some window screen over the lens, and we also chose to shoot in an old metal foundry that had all rusted. Everything was rust-colored. And we shot at the end of the day, when things take on a grayness, and dressed people in monochromatic tones. What started out as an insightful replacement absolutely galvanized the picture. It is a scene that takes place somewhere around the areas where psychiatry and psychoanalysis have concentrated. Through psychoanalysis you recognize that things like graduations, anniversaries, birthdays, reunions tend to be episode-producing events."

Like Joseph L. Mankiewicz, Elia Kazan, and Lee Strasberg, Penn has also used avowedly psychoanalytic techniques in working with actors, although he is conscientiously less manipulative in his approach. His own experience in analysis taught him how a good therapist can draw intimate secrets from a patient, and Penn tried to mimic that method to inspire trust in the actors he directed. He would begin the rehearsal process by delving into every actor's life history. "You need a body of shared information with actors when you come to certain difficult scenes and want them to call upon material that's not easily accessible," Penn says. "I glean that by taking a nonjudgmental posture so that they feel at ease telling me. Then you have to remember it at the appropriate time and bring it up again: 'Remember when you were telling me about your brother and how you felt then? I think if you could invest that in this scene . . . ' Very often when I say that, the actor will say, 'Yeah, now I've got it. Right.' Often the reason they didn't think of it is that they didn't want to touch that material unless they felt in a sympathetic climate. I think that's what a director has to do. So in that sense it is a quasi-therapeutic job."

Psychoanalysis not only influenced Penn's art, it also permeated his social life. A few years after his analysis with Rudolph Loewenstein ended, Penn and his doctor struck up a friendship. They had many acquaintances in common, and they would sometimes encounter each other at parties. "We decided to become friendly," Penn says. "Rudy felt it would not be a problem." Clearly Loewenstein enjoyed his social interaction with Penn, who was by then one of the leading directors in America and an intimate of many of Broadway's biggest stars.

Even after they became friends, Penn sometimes returned to Loewenstein for therapy. The doctor justified this dual relationship with his patient by saying that he was no longer practicing orthodox psychoanalysis with Penn, and Penn felt that his informal therapeutic sessions were helpful in getting him through some crises. When he directed *Bonnie and Clyde* in 1966, for example, Penn felt under pressure to deliver a hit. "I developed a lot of anxieties while I was doing *Bonnie and Clyde*," Penn says, "and I went back to Rudy to deal with that. I went to him about ten times, and the problem resolved itself."

Loewenstein was not the only analyst who became a close friend of the director's. Through William and Margaret Gibson, Penn met Erik Erikson, whom Dr. Gibson had brought to work at Austen Riggs. At one point Penn, the rapt disciple, made a short film of Erikson offering a psychoanalytic interpretation of Ingmar Bergman's *Wild Strawberries*. Penn's wife, Peggy, whom he married in 1956, volunteered as an assistant to Erikson in Stockbridge and became so enthusiastic about his work that she decided to become a therapist herself. She has served as director of clinical training at the Ackerman Institute for Family Therapy in New York.

Partly because of his wife's involvement in family therapy, Penn now has some mixed feelings about the religion of Freudianism that he once embraced. "There was an exquisite orthodoxy to it," Penn says wistfully. "But analysis was a long, arduous, expensive process—not the best recommendation. How many people can afford it?" In addition, the application of psychoanalytic theory to drama tended to be one-dimensional and sometimes foolish, Penn now recognizes. "Psychoanalysis was such a wonderfully available gimmick that it began to appear everywhere," he notes. "There were an awful lot of nights on Broadway where we sat through the same damn play. It was resolved with a Freudian oedipal configuration. That was the explanation, bang bang bang. It was very simplistic and got to be an enormous cliché. But in those days you would make psychoanalytic associations even in everyday conversations. You would talk about mother fixations. That was how my generation spoke."

Penn has also become more skeptical of the close friendships that developed between analysts and artists in theater and film. "Analysts were interested in the arts, interested in artists," he says. "People tended to congregate at dinner parties, and lo and behold, there would be two or three analysts. They would treat very important people, and somehow this interchange took place, and they would find themselves semi-stars. People would say, 'He's Tennessee Williams's analyst; he's Bill Inge's analyst.' Those who were less than strict with themselves began to enjoy the notoriety, which was a kind of corruption of the analytic movement. Analysts often expressed their own rapture with theater by becoming overly involved with patients working in the theater."

To explain this infatuation, Penn points out that refugee analysts like his own doctor, Rudolph Loewenstein, were often stripped of their credentials when they arrived in America and had to reestablish themselves. "A lot of these analysts had to take an M.D. exam," Penn observes, "and it was a severe travail for them. They were not young, they were studying in what was for them a foreign language. So there was a period when these people with enormous status in a previous life in Europe were now reduced to a kind of internship again. They paid heavy dues, maybe ten years of heavy dues. Therefore when they broke out of that, they craved some recognition in their new country, something that was probably naturally given to them as Herr Doktor Professor in Germany and Vienna. They began to measure their prominence in terms of the prominence of their patients. They were all susceptible to that, even the very brightest and the very best."

Another of the analytically inspired films to appear in the landmark year of 1962 was Sidney Lumet's compelling screen version of Eugene O'Neill's masterpiece, *Long Day's Journey into Night*. The play was one of the most important works of art ever to incorporate

Freudian psychology. O'Neill had been profoundly influenced by Freud, and in one of his earlier plays, *Strange Interlude*, he had the characters verbalize their subconscious feelings in asides to the audience. But *Long Day's Journey into Night* represented a far more subtle expression of psychoanalytic theory. This searing drama illustrates the dark passions and guilty secrets hidden just beneath the surface of everyday life. In one of the great passages in the play, the older son, Jamie, who has appeared to be deeply solicitous toward his sickly younger brother, unleashes the hatred that he harbors, recalling his jealousy when he saw himself supplanted in his mother's affections. It is the oedipal drama removed from the textbook and transmuted into art. Jason Robards, who had extensive experience in analysis, interpreted the role masterfully on both stage and screen.

Like O'Neill and Robards, Sidney Lumet was also enthralled with psychoanalysis. "Analysis is unfashionable now," Lumet says, "but I'm loath to think where I would be without it." Lumet, who has been married four times, had trouble sustaining relationships, and he entered analysis with an orthodox Freudian named Eilhard Von Domarus to deal with his compulsions. "If I asked Von Domarus why he didn't say anything," Lumet recalls, "he would respond, 'Why do you feel that way?' "

Lumet soon tired of the inscrutable doctor. In the 1950s he consulted Dr. John McKinney, who had been chief of psychiatry for the navy during World War II. "He was less rigid than Von Domarus," Lumet says. "He was frustrated by the length of time that analysis took." To shorten treatment, McKinney experimented with LSD in the 1950s and '60s, before it became the hallucinogen of choice to the hippie generation. Lumet took LSD three times under McKinney's supervision; one session lasted eleven hours. "It unlocked incredible memories," the director reports. "One was from infancy, and I checked it with my father, who confirmed that it was true."

McKinney argued in favor of legalizing LSD before a congressional committee, and he submitted a tape of one of Lumet's sessions as part of his testimony. Ultimately McKinney lost the battle for legalization, but before the drug was officially outlawed, many prominent personalities used it under psychiatric supervision. Henry and Clare Boothe Luce took the drug under the direction of Dr. Sidney Cohen, a Los Angeles psychiatrist who was studying its effect on actors and other creative people. Cary Grant experimented with LSD in the fifties under the guidance of Dr. Mortimer Hartman, one of Dr. McKinney's fellow crusaders for legalization. Grant later said of his many LSD trips, "The experience was just like being born for the first time; I imagined all the blood and urine, and I emerged with the first flush of birth." He and Timothy Leary even compared notes on their LSD adventures. In 1968, however, when Grant was going through a bitter divorce from Dyan Cannon, she testified that he had forced her to take the drug and had been abusive when under its influence. At the divorce proceeding, Dr. Judd Marmor, the psychiatrist who achieved notoriety when he publicly defended the check-forging mogul David Begelman, examined Grant and testified in court that LSD had not damaged the actor but, on the contrary, had "helped cure his shyness and anxiety in dealing with other people."

As for Sidney Lumet, despite the insights he gained through LSD, his treatment with Dr. McKinney failed to clear his head completely. In the 1970s he consulted a younger psychiatrist, Dr. Christopher Zois, who was an advocate of short-term therapy. "Analysis has always had drawbacks as a method of treatment—the time involved, the cost, and the unpredictability of the outcome," says Zois. So he tried new techniques, including videotaping his sessions with patients. "It did accelerate the process," Lumet recalls. "I would ask, 'Did I say that?' and he could show me right away that I did."

Lumet's openness to newer forms of therapy offers a clue to his personality and to his trademark as a director—his uncommon versatility. Lumet's eclectic tastes led him to undertake some abysmal projects for which he was clearly ill suited—a Gothic melodrama, *Child's Play,* and a big-budget musical, *The Wiz.* But his adaptability was also a key to his remarkable endurance. In the late 1960s, when Arthur Penn was one of the hottest directors in Hollywood, Lumet had trouble getting anyone to hire him. Penn, however, went into decline in the 1970s and 1980s, whereas Lumet rebounded and has been one of the most steadily employed directors in the business. His resilience had a good deal to do with his willingness to experiment, and he attributes his venturesome spirit to his time on the couch. "Before analysis I don't think I could have conceived of myself as anything but a totally realistic director," Lumet says. "A picture like *Network* or *Murder on the Orient Express* would have been impossible for me to do earlier, not just in terms of technique but because I simply wouldn't have seen it. I came to see realism as only one style. That greater openness came through analysis, just as one began to discover there are other ways to live."

Lumet contends that his years of therapy also had considerable influence on his work with actors. "I found it enormously helpful in terms of delving into character, discussing with actors the motives and intent of the character," Lumet says. But he parts company with directors like Arthur Penn and Elia Kazan in his attitude toward the Method acting that had transfixed a generation. Lumet began as a child actor with the Group Theatre, so he knew Lee Strasberg well, and he has directed many of Strasberg's students over the years. "One of my strongest objections to Lee and certainly among the actors of his that I worked with was their very sparse imagination," Lumet says. "I felt the atmosphere in his class was one that encouraged a kind of display, where feeling per se was the end result, as opposed to what I prefer in acting, when feeling is only the first step in the process. I can always recognize a Strasberg student because somewhere in rehearsal I'll hear, 'Sidney, you know what I need here?' And as soon as I hear that, I'll jump on it in a subtle way and say, 'No, what do you think the *character* needs?' " Lumet's criticism is essentially the same complaint that Stella Adler lodged—that Strasberg promoted self-indulgent soul-searching instead of cultivating the actor's imagination.

This has been a source of disagreement between Lumet and Strasberg's star pupil Al Pacino, whom Lumet directed in *Serpico* and *Dog Day Afternoon*. "As I've pointed out to Al, he uses the word *I* a lot," Lumet says. In *Dog Day Afternoon* Lumet helped Pacino to do some of his best work by urging him to transcend his own persona. In preparing the memorable scene where Pacino's character, a bisexual bank robber, becomes a folk hero by shouting, "Attica! Attica!" to the assembled crowds, Lumet told his star, "Do Mussolini, go out there and have a good time."

"He laughed and knew exactly what I meant," Lumet recalls, "and he did it. There was a helicopter overhead and a thousand people in the streets, and I think the reality of that situation just lifted him up on a wave and really tossed him over the top. I wish he would do more of that."

Although he was never the uncritical champion of Method acting or Freudian analysis that other directors of his generation were, Lumet does feel something has been lost in the smashing of old idols. "I think that lack of analytic awareness has a great deal to do with the kinds of movies we see now that are totally geared to the present and the momentary feelings and sensations," he observes. His own films, including *Long Day's Journey into Night, The Pawn-*

broker, Daniel, and *Running on Empty,* underscore the impact of the past on the present, the tenacious grip of the characters' early life experiences. But this has become an unfashionable theme, Lumet notes. "In modern moviemaking there is no pre-life to the characters," he says. "They exist only for the time of the picture itself, and they're not burdened by anything in the past. Steven Spielberg's movies are totally of the moment. It's interesting that this has come with a generation of moviemakers that is anti-analytic."

Notwithstanding Lumet's indictment, at least one younger filmmaker defies contemporary fashion and staunchly upholds the analytic tradition. Writer-director Nicholas Meyer, who was born in 1945, has more in common with the filmmakers working in that year than with the members of his own baby-boomer set. "I lived through the sixties," Meyer says, "and people had flowers in their hair and were smoking weird things and listening to Bob Dylan. If my life depended on it, I couldn't quote you a line of Bob Dylan. When I was five years old, I figured out that Mozart was the best, and nothing has ever caused me to change my mind."

In his attitude toward psychoanalysis, too, Meyer is a classicist. "Debunking Freud has become facile," Meyer says. "Yes, you can criticize his views of women or some other subject. But the fact remains that Freud discovered the unconscious. He identified a new continent, just like Columbus."

In his best-selling 1974 novel, *The Seven-Per-Cent Solution,* Meyer created a distinctive tribute to the father of psychoanalysis. He imagined a meeting between Freud and Sherlock Holmes, who pool their deductive powers to solve a murder in nineteenth-century Vienna. In the course of their work together, Freud even psychoanalyzes Holmes and discovers the source of the detective's misogyny in a repressed childhood trauma, when young Sherlock saw his father kill his mother after discovering her in an act of adultery. Both the novel and the 1976 film version are lighthearted but unabashed celebrations of psychoanalysis. Meyer, who also wrote and directed *Time After Time,* an homage to another nineteenth-century prophet, H. G. Wells, as well as two *Star Trek* movies crammed with high-toned references to Shakespeare and Dickens, refuses to engage in what he calls the "sublimated father-bashing" of so much modern writing about Freud.

In Meyer's case a debunking of Freud might have smacked of

overt father-bashing, for his own father, Dr. Bernard Meyer, was a distinguished Freudian analyst. *The Seven-Per-Cent Solution* had its roots in Nick Meyer's childhood conversations with his father. When he was a boy, he says, he always tried to get his father to elucidate what he did for a living. Dr. Meyer explained, "When a person comes to see me, I listen to what they say; I try to hear how they're saying it; I try to hear what they're not saying. I look at how they comport themselves and how they're dressed. I am, in short, searching for clues as to why they are not happy."

"It sounds to me like detective work," young Nicholas responded.

Nicholas Meyer's mother died when he was a teenager, and his father sent him to a New York psychiatrist, David Rubinfine, to help him through a traumatic period in his life. When he moved to California to pursue a career as a filmmaker, Nick Meyer reentered analysis with Dr. Lewis J. Fielding, the psychiatrist who made headlines when his office was ransacked by the Watergate plumbers searching for records of his patient, Daniel Ellsberg, after Ellsberg released the Pentagon papers. Meyer went to Fielding four times a week for ten years. "I suppose choosing this treatment must have represented a kind of unconscious knuckling under to my father's sway," Meyer says of his analysis. "But it made sense to me. I am a plodding type of person in all areas of my life. I don't believe in instant solutions."

Meyer's personal history has given him a unique insight into the relationship between directing movies and psychoanalysis. He offers a provocative description of the connection between the two processes when he compares the relationship of patient and analyst to that of a director and a film editor. A director is often so overwhelmed by the logistics of shooting a complicated scene that at the end of the day he simply turns over an undigested lump of film to his editor. "If he's a good editor and he understands what you were doing," Meyer suggests, "he will put together that scene and play it back to you. You sit there and say, 'Yep, that's right. I think you need a close-up of the mother, and maybe we hold on the poison going into the coffee a little too long, but basically you've got it.' If he's a *really* good editor, he'll show you things implicit in the scene that you never even realized were there. If he's a bad editor, he'll put the scene up in front of you and you won't recognize it. It's so far from what you intended that it doesn't ring a revelatory bell. There's been a misunderstanding.

"In my analysis I would go in to my doctor, and I would spin out what might be called the dailies of my mind. I would talk about what I came to say, and then since he doesn't say anything, you run out of programmatic content, which is when it gets really interesting, and you start saying random things, what you had for breakfast, who said what on the phone. The analyst says nothing. But all the time he's trying to make sense of these associations. Finally, forty minutes into the hour, he comments, 'What you seem to be saying is . . . ' and he plays it back to you, in much the same way an editor plays back film. If he's a good analyst and he's understood you, there is in fact a pattern to these associations, which you recognize as he distills it for you. If he's a *really* good analyst, you're slightly surprised as you realize what you've actually been going on about in your apparently random associations. If he's a bad analyst or he's not the analyst for you or if he's having an off day, as sometimes happens, you listen to it and it doesn't ring a bell. People say, 'Doesn't it make you crazy that the analyst doesn't talk?' That's the hardest thing for some people to understand. He's not a guru; he has no instructions. He's just a poor schmuck trying to get through it with you. He's the editor who plays back your material."

Meyer has remained so enthusiastic about analysis that he even composed a scholarly article for a psychiatric journal. "Lost Boys Wandering Around the Peter Pantheon," published in 1985 in the *Annals of the American Society for Adolescent Psychiatry,* is one of Meyer's proudest achievements. He speaks of it with more pleasure than he does of his best-selling novels and hit movies; he hands out reprints as if they were cigars. "I wrote the article a few days before my thirty-fifth birthday," Meyer reports. "I must have written ten drafts. I gave it to my analyst as a present, and he said, 'This is good enough to be published.' Subsequently I got invited to address a convention of psychiatrists."

The article discussed the characters of Peter Pan, Henry Higgins, and Sherlock Holmes as expressions of their creators' adolescent fixations. At the end of his literary exegesis, Meyer related these fictional characters to his own arrested development and gave psychoanalysis the credit for prodding him into adulthood.

Nick Meyer's father would, no doubt, be proud. In an era when psychoanalysis has fallen out of fashion, at least one grateful disciple doggedly defends the faith.

7. COMIC RELIEF

The airborne camera zooms in on a bucolic hideaway nestled in the spectacular mountains above Big Sur, right on the edge of the Pacific. Cut to a tight shot of a blissful couple, Natalie Wood and Robert Culp, speeding along in their sports car toward this rustic nirvana. The frenzied intercutting continues as the "Hallelujah Chorus" floods the soundtrack, rising to a crescendo. Then as the camera swoops inside the gates of the fabled Esalen Institute, several stark naked women step into a hot tub, joining a corpulent gentleman absorbed in reading *The New York Review of Books*.

This memorable opening of Paul Mazursky's first directorial effort, *Bob & Carol & Ted & Alice*, was something of a cinematic milestone. Made in 1969, the film titillated audiences with its coy glimpses of full frontal nudity. At the same time, it exposed a medley of quirky new forms of psychotherapy that were just beginning to sweep the country. That exhilarating journey to Esalen signaled Hollywood's disenchantment with orthodox psychoanalysis, which just a decade earlier had been seen as the only road to salvation.

Leo Rangell, the dean of Freudian analysts in Los Angeles, still recoils at the memory of that startling set piece. "You see Natalie Wood and her husband driving up Route One toward Big Sur in a wild, orgiastic ride," Rangell says. "Right off the bat you have a combination of excitement and imminent breakdown. You don't know where it's going to lead—over the hill into the sunset, or down the cliff into the ocean?" Rangell calls the movie a perfect reflection of "southern California, where all this was going on, *after* psychoanalysis had reached its zenith, then faced competitive avenues of treatment. And the film industry and the arts and the people in the vanguard would give everything a trial. Southern California, the home of Hollywood and activism and exuberance, has always been a center for the fragmentation of the psychiatric field."

Bob & Carol & Ted & Alice was the first important movie to express Hollywood's growing infatuation with alternative therapies. Immediately after checking in at Esalen, Bob and Carol join a touchy-feely group encounter led by a guru who urges the participants to bare their emotions: "We talk a lot about love, but we don't feel it a lot." In the course of this twenty-four-hour marathon the eager apostles perform sensitivity exercises, then pound on pillows to release their aggressions. Whenever one of them has a breakthrough "insight," the others celebrate with a group hug. The process of rigorous psychoanalysis, whereby a solitary patient probes the dark recesses of his tortured psyche under the guidance of an impassive analyst, seems no more than a distant memory.

Although dozens of Hollywood moviemakers have expressed a fascination with psychotherapy in their work, no one has ever presented quite so many cinematic variations on the therapeutic encounter as Paul Mazursky. In fact, if knowledgeable moviegoers were asked to identify the filmmakers most closely associated with psychiatry, two names would surely top the list: Paul Mazursky and Woody Allen. Yet both Mazursky and Allen express greater ambivalence toward the religion of psychiatry than the believers of an earlier generation. Although both are longtime devotees of analysis, they cannot suppress a puckish sense of humor about the rituals of the couch.

Mazursky and Allen have much in common. Both hailed from Jewish families in Brooklyn, started out as performers, then turned to writing and directing. Each of them made his directorial debut in 1969, a year of uncommon cultural turmoil, when antiestablishment warfare and the nascent sexual revolution triggered a new wave of irreverent filmmaking. Yet for all their similarities, a striking paradox divided them. Whereas Mazursky moved to Los Angeles and chronicled a panoply of sexual high jinks in his freewheeling California comedies, he has remained fairly traditional in his own personal life; he has stayed married to the same woman, a librarian and social worker, for more than thirty years, and he is the devoted father to two daughters. Allen, the diehard New Yorker and devout Freudian, has persistently mocked Los Angeles hedonism, but his own personal life—awash in multiple affairs, nymphet mania, and even a quasi-incestuous roundelay—played more like an outrageous California farce than anything Mazursky ever invented.

*   *   *

Growing up in a middle-class Jewish neighborhood, Mazursky had no firsthand experiences with psychiatry. "The only thing I knew about therapy was I'd heard of Sigmund Freud," he says. "When I moved to Greenwich Village in the early fifties, I actually met a couple of people who would say, 'I have to go now. I'm going to see my psychoanalyst.' That was new to me."

In other words, a decade before he made *Bob & Carol & Ted & Alice,* psychoanalysis was still a modish pastime for arty writers and actors. Mazursky, who had the insecurities typical of young performers, decided to follow the example of his more bohemian friends. In 1957 he started seeing an analyst in training, the only kind of analyst that a struggling actor could afford. "He was a Russian," Mazursky recalls, "and the whole idea then was, 'Let us begin this process that is going to take a long, long, long time.' So you started out depressed right away. You were going to pay for it forever, and talk about your dreams forever, never hear any feedback. That's what it was like for almost two years. I'd always look around to see if he was sleeping."

Finally, after one unsettling incident, Mazursky decided to call it quits. "One day the analyst showed up forty-five minutes late," Mazursky recalls. "I waited in front of his office for almost the full session. A cab pulled up in front of the building, and he got out, dead drunk."

The analyst confessed that he was an incurable alcoholic. "Then what business do you have being a therapist?" Mazursky screamed at him. That encounter may have convinced Mazursky that analysts have feet of clay, but he still believes that his therapy was productive. "It helped me to move to California," he says. "I wanted to start a new thing."

Mazursky began a second round of psychotherapy after he settled in Los Angeles and was hired to write for Danny Kaye's television show. He consulted a therapist named Donald F. Muhich, who had many show-business patients. Mazursky had become fairly successful as a sitcom writer, but he wanted to branch out, and Muhich encouraged him to try his hand at feature films. When *I Love You, Alice B. Toklas,* a satire of the hippie movement that Mazursky wrote with Larry Tucker, became a box-office hit, Mazursky got the chance to direct his first movie.

In 1968 Mazursky and Tucker saw a story in *Time* magazine

about Esalen that showed a picture of noted Gestalt psychologist Fritz Perls in a hot tub with a group of naked novitiates. "It looked funny," Mazursky says, "so Larry and I wrote a treatment." But Mazursky decided that the script needed more authentic details. So he and his wife, Betsy, took an excursion to Esalen. They participated in a forty-eight-hour marathon with about a dozen other new recruits. "You got so tired after about fifteen or sixteen hours that you'd say anything," Mazursky remarks. "I did feel an elation after the weekend. I'll never be sure whether the elation was because I knew I had a movie. My wife and I *had* looked in each other's eyes and cried for a day or two. We felt great. And though we never went back, we did tell everybody, 'Boy, we just had a great zap.'"

When he returned home, Mazursky used his own experience as the springboard for the script for *Bob & Carol & Ted & Alice*. He and Tucker focused on a couple not unlike the Mazurskys, who feel so rejuvenated by their weekend marathon that they begin questioning all the old rules of marriage. Natalie Wood and Robert Culp played the adventurers, and Mazursky cast two relative newcomers, Elliott Gould and Dyan Cannon, as their more timid friends, Ted and Alice. In the course of the story Bob and Carol experiment with sex and drugs and try to lure their more conventional friends into the kinky maelstrom. They smoke marijuana together, openly discuss their extramarital flings, and even toy with the idea of a spouse-swapping orgy—though they do lose their nerve at the last second, while sprawled naked together in a king-size bed.

One crucial scene in the movie shows the straitlaced Alice consulting a psychoanalyst, who helps her to sort through her feelings about her friends' new lifestyle. In auditioning actors to play the psychiatrist, Mazursky found himself dissatisfied with the available choices. By that time he was no longer in regular treatment with Donald Muhich, though he still sought the ministrations of the cherubic shrink when he needed what he calls "an injection, a patch-up" for a temporary crisis. Muhich had acted in college and still dreamt of performing professionally. "Don always told me he wanted to be an actor," Mazursky says, and so the director decided to give Muhich the part in *Bob & Carol & Ted & Alice*.

At first Dyan Cannon was nervous about playing the scene with a real therapist, especially since Mazursky wanted Muhich to improvise in order to keep the actress on edge. "He did things that were not in the script," Mazursky notes, "like hold his ear a certain way and rub it or stare at her. I can't think of an actor who could have done it as well. There's information in the heads of these people that just makes them respond very differently to what we're saying and doing."

The result of this unorthodox casting was one of the wittiest and most original psychiatric interludes ever captured on celluloid. Even psychiatrist Irving Schneider, who has written very critically about many of Hollywood's portrayals of his profession, has called the analytic hour between Cannon and Muhich "the best and most realistic therapy session ever portrayed on film."

The entire scene conveys a tart, skeptical attitude toward both the psychiatrist and the patient. Mazursky cannot resist presenting Muhich's character as a figure of fun. His long sideburns suggest a doctor aching to be hip, and his fish-eye glances and constant pinching of his own cheek are sly touches. Mazursky's most biting gibe at the psychiatrist's expense comes at the end of the scene. Alice has been talking about her husband's frustration over her growing frigidity. She looks at the doctor and says, "Sex is very important to a man, you know that." A sheepish Muhich replies in a tremulous voice, "It seems that our time is up for today." Suddenly his patient spews forth a volcanic torrent of pent-up feelings, trying desperately to reach some understanding of her troubled marriage. Still glancing at the clock, however, the doctor tells her, "We should take that up on Thursday," as he practically pushes her out the door.

Although Mazursky comically underscores the dollar-driven nature of psychotherapy, the scene is not a simplistic put-down of analysis. Many of the doctor's questions to Alice are quite perceptive. At one point he interrupts her pointedly, "Are you aware that earlier you said you *like* your husband and you *love* your child?" And when she inadvertently substitutes Bob's name for Ted's in a classic Freudian slip, the psychiatrist calls her attention to her unconscious wishes. Despite the constraints of the analytic hour, Alice does gain new insight into herself as a result of the shrink's trenchant probing.

Nevertheless Mazursky took more than a little flak from the psychoanalytic establishment after the film was released, and Muhich was criticized even more strongly for accepting a paying job in a movie created by a sometime patient. His critics claimed that Muhich was exploiting the doctor-patient relationship to satisfy his own ambitions—a criticism that Mazursky pooh-poohs. "I always said to Don that I wish there was a published list of the doctors who attacked him so that people would know which therapists to avoid,"

Mazursky remarks. "Because the one quality I think a therapist must have is humor. If they don't have any humor or irony, how could they perceive some of the situations that people come to discuss, which are often filled with bizarre contradictions? I think part of the reason people were pissed is they thought we were undermining the sanctity of the temple, showing the inner workings. Why shouldn't we show it? We show doctors doing operations. Maybe the real reason they were pissed is that they didn't get the part."

Over the next several years Muhich continued to practice psychotherapy, but he also kept his hand in show business. In 1970 he helped develop a television series called *Matt Lincoln,* starring Vince Edwards as a psychiatrist. But the show was an early ratings casualty. Gradually Muhich grew more restless and dissatisfied. He wandered around the country, though he stayed in touch with Mazursky and soothed the director's ailing ego when the need arose. Mazursky reports, "I'd call him and say, 'I just got some bad reviews, could you help me?' And he'd say, 'Well, I can't really help you with the bad reviews, but come in and we can talk.' He once treated me on the telephone for two months. He was living in the Midwest, and I was here. I was having a writer's block where I really felt rotten. So he said, 'You could pay me to come to California, you could fly here and stay here for a while, or we could try it on the phone and see how it goes.' So we did that, and it worked. After two months I was writing a script again. Muhich has helped me a lot. He's a brilliant man."

But it wasn't just the patient whose needs were being addressed during these ongoing therapeutic encounters. "The only problem was that Don would ask me for a job during the sessions," Mazursky reveals with an affectionate chuckle. "He would say to me, 'You know, I don't have to just play the therapist. There are a lot of other parts I could play. I read the script, and I think I could do such-and-such.' I'd say, 'Well, you probably could, but I don't think you're right for that part. I'm sorry to reject you so summarily.' He had a sense of humor about it."

The director did continue to turn to Muhich, however, when he was looking for an actor to play a therapist. In Mazursky's 1973 romantic comedy *Blume in Love,* the psychiatrist had a bigger role than in *Bob & Carol & Ted & Alice;* he was prominently featured in several scenes with his patients, the divorce lawyer, Blume (George Segal), and his estranged wife, Nina (Susan Anspach). "I figured I was lucky once, so I'll cast him again," Mazursky says. In this movie, too, Muhich cuts a slightly comical figure. With his wide paisley ties, he looks more like a Hollywood agent than a staid analyst. And some of his earnest pronouncements are uproarious. In a session when Blume confesses his impotence, Muhich counsels him soberly, "Sometimes after people get divorced or separated, they go through a period of sport-fucking."

Over the years Muhich became a familiar member of Mazursky's repertory company. In *Willie and Phil* in 1980 he played a draft-board psychiatrist, and in the wild 1986 comedy *Down and Out in Beverly Hills,* he played a pet psychiatrist trying to analyze an anorexic canine. In writing *Moon Over Parador,* a farce about an actor who agrees to impersonate a dead South American dictator, Mazursky even contemplated a scene in which the hero, confused about his identity, would consult a Latino analyst, but that character never made it to the final script. "I would have gotten Muhich with a mustache," Mazursky says. "It would have been hilarious, but I didn't know quite how to do it."

The change in Muhich's role from a quite respectable Freudian analyst in *Bob & Carol & Ted & Alice* to the doggie psychiatrist of *Down and Out in Beverly Hills* might seem to suggest a dramatic decline in Mazursky's own esteem for the profession. As Irving Schneider speculated in the *American Journal of Psychiatry,* "We can only wonder if Mazursky sees psychiatry itself going to the dogs." Mazursky insists that one should not read any sense of disillusionment into this rather curious progression.

Still, he remains deeply ambivalent about the whole experience of psychotherapy. "There is a certain sarcastic, cynical, satiric side of me that makes fun of it," Mazursky says, "yet I want you to know that I believe in it. In *Bob & Carol* and in *Blume in Love,* the therapist throws cold water on the pretending the characters are doing."

Mazursky's divided attitude emerges most clearly in the final scene between George Segal and Donald Muhich in *Blume in Love.* Frustrated by his inability to put his life back together after his divorce, Blume tells the analyst, "Sometimes I think this is a waste of time. That it doesn't really do any good."

"Sometimes it doesn't," the shrink agrees.

"Then why do you do it?" Blume persists.

"Sometimes it does," the doctor replies. "And until we find something better, what else is there to do?"

Immediately after this scene, Blume tries another ploy to woo his ex-wife. He goes to her home and rapes her. So much for the reasonable approach fostered in analysis, Mazursky seems to be saying.

A more worshipful view of therapy (and a more politically correct view of the war between the sexes) was expressed in Mazursky's acclaimed 1978 movie *An Unmarried Woman*. One of Hollywood's first unabashedly feminist films, the picture starred Jill Clayburgh as a Manhattan housewife named Erika whose life falls apart when her husband walks out on her. With the help of a sensitive therapist, Erika learns how to put the pieces back together.

To play the psychiatrist, Mazursky auditioned a slew of professional actresses. But just as he had failed to find an actor who could play the analyst in *Bob & Carol & Ted & Alice*, he was once again disappointed in the results of his casting call. "There was an essential quality that they didn't have," Mazursky says of the actresses who read for the part. "I couldn't verbalize it, but they all seemed like actors pretending to be psychiatrists."

Just when he was about to give up, filmmaker Claudia Weill had an idea for him. Weill's mother was a psychologist at Sarah Lawrence, and she had a friend and colleague who, Weill thought, might fill the bill. Dr. Penelope Russianoff was a successful, if somewhat unorthodox Manhattan therapist, and she was a striking presence. Originally Mazursky had conceived the character of Tanya, the psychiatrist in *An Unmarried Woman*, as a "petite, thirty-five-year-old European." Upon reading that description in the script Mazursky sent her, the fifty-nine-year-old, six-foot two-inch, American-born Russianoff was perplexed. "What the hell? That's crazy," she remembers saying to herself. Still, she figured that if Mazursky was serious about casting her for the part, she wasn't about to pass up a shot at stardom. When the director came to meet Russianoff at her Upper West Side penthouse, he instantly reconceived the character of Erika's therapist. Russianoff's artless manner captivated Mazursky. At the same time, he thought her apartment-office would make an ideal setting for the intimate sessions that he imagined between Erika and Tanya. The loftlike chamber, with its comfortably overstuffed pillows and gold-colored floor cushions, looked like a cross between an opium den and the site of a middle-aged slumber party.

For Russianoff, landing the part was the realization of a lifelong dream. The daughter of a prominent geneticist named Raymond

Pearl, she had harbored fantasies of becoming an actress since childhood. Because of her physical size, however, young Penelope was invariably cast in the male roles at the all-girls school she attended. Her greatest triumph was playing Jesus Christ in a Passion Play. "The mothers all cried," she notes with some pride.

Opting for a more practical career, she studied psychology at the University of Michigan, where she began to formulate a number of idiosyncratic theories, including a decidedly heterodox view of incest. Even today she is quite outspoken in questioning the taboos that surround that subject. "It's very frightening," she says, "because if Daddy takes his little girl on his knee and they go horsey-horsey, the mother's apt to say, 'Oh, don't do that. You might be stimulating her.'" She elaborates on the origins of her own laissez-faire attitude: "One of the first cases I ever had when I was a neophyte at the University of Michigan involved a young woman who had had intercourse with her father and with her brother. She viewed it as one of the greatest experiences of her life. One day she was tired, and a teacher asked her what the trouble was. Somehow the teacher got the idea that sexual abuse was going on, which wrecked the whole family—demolished the family. I felt that if nobody had ever known about it, it would have been just fine."

After graduating from Michigan, Russianoff earned her Ph.D. at Northwestern and went on to become a disciple of the "nondirective" psychologist Carl Rogers. While she built a thriving therapeutic practice, she also found ways to satisfy her impulse to perform, whether lecturing at the New School or leading psychodrama workshops.

"I'm lucky in the sense that I'm a creative person," Russianoff says, "and the very nature of my work fits in with the creativity." In the early 1960s, searching for yet another artistic outlet, she decided to take clarinet lessons and ended up marrying her clarinet teacher, Leon Russianoff. He was her second husband, and someone whom she describes as an improbable Mr. Right: "Eight inches shorter than me, blind in one eye, and a Jew from Brooklyn." With Leon's encouragement she even started playing jazz drums when she was well past sixty.

While she had a curiosity about all the arts, Russianoff had long considered film the most intriguing. She was friendly with the experimental filmmaker Maya Deren (whose *Meshes of the Afternoon* was an early avant-garde favorite), and once she even tried writing a screenplay, though she lacked the patience to finish it. When Paul

Mazursky suddenly showed up at her door with the offer of a movie role, she felt it was destiny calling.

Although *An Unmarried Woman* contains only two scenes showing Erika in therapy with Tanya, those interludes (which were largely improvised) do make an indelible impression. Rarely had the intimate details of a woman's sexual development been discussed on screen with such unvarnished candor. Erika's memory of her first menstrual period—"the wet, warm feeling in my crotch"— was a startlingly intimate revelation, especially for an American movie.

"One of my hidden goals in doing the film," Russianoff said shortly after the movie opened in 1978, "was to desensitize people to the fear of therapy." She was understandably dismayed, therefore, when several of her colleagues took her to task for her portrayal. One of them called her "a discredit to the profession," and another chastised her for recommending that Erika take a "vacation from guilt," since, in this therapist's view, guilt was indispensable to growth. Writing in *Psychology Today*, anthropologist Lionel Tiger lambasted the movie and termed Russianoff's performance "quite nauseating." Russianoff had to resume therapy with her own analyst, Dr. Lionel Ovesey, to sort through her feelings about such "negative reactions."

On the whole, however, Russianoff's immersion in moviemaking exhilarated her. "When I went to view the film, it had my name alone on a wide-angle screen," she says. "I couldn't believe it. I mean, it was too overwhelming." There was even talk of an Oscar nomination. "The assistant director felt that I should have at least been considered as supporting actress," she says. "I thought, 'Oh, that would be nice.' But inside I shuddered. It really wouldn't be fair. Think about all these people who've been waiters and waitresses for years, who've studied and studied, waiting for their big moment, and then I walk in—that would be too much! I just knew it wouldn't happen. It would be rough for the industry."

Her fifteen minutes of fame did turn Dr. Russianoff into an identifiable personality, even if one fan insisted that she recognized her from *Annie Hall* and another thought she was Julia Child's sister. As for her patients, most of them took her newfound celebrity in stride, though a few found it disturbing. "I had one patient who had been an actress for about thirty-five years and never had such a great part," Russianoff recalls. "She sweats away, and suddenly *this* happens. It was unfair from her viewpoint, and from my viewpoint too. So she left me as a patient."

If Russianoff's sudden stardom threatened certain old relationships, it opened the door to new ones—or so she imagined. "I have a lot of friends who are enormously successful," Russianoff says, "but in fields that aren't as dramatic as the movies." She hoped to widen her circle by becoming "close personal friends" with Mazursky, but that was not to be. "I wanted to be a friend of Jill Clayburgh's too," she confides. "When you're in a movie, there's an intensity about everything—about the actors with each other and about the actors with the crew. I had no idea that when they go on to the next movie, and the old one is out the window, that's it! Goodbye! This is a common thing, and you just have to accept it."

The unkindest cut of all came when she concluded filming her last scene, the party during which Erika is startled to spot her therapist on the arm of another woman. Suddenly a voice was heard booming through a megaphone: "Okay, Penelope, come here. That'll be all." Russianoff walked over to collect her paycheck and then looked around. "I was going to say good-bye to Mazursky," she recalls. "I started to cross the set, and the guy with the megaphone said, 'Penelope, please get off the set. You are finished.' I must say, my heart was broken. It always brings tears to my eyes to think about that moment."

The spectacle of Paul Mazursky's pair of performing shrinks adds an unusual twist to the saga of psychiatry in Hollywood. Most analysts only wanted to hobnob with movie stars; Muhich and Russianoff actually longed to share the screen with them. Mazursky, an unashamed ham who seldom passes up an opportunity to act in another director's movie, may have been more sympathetic to the fantasies of his therapists than other filmmakers would have been.

More than a decade after the release of *An Unmarried Woman*, Penelope Russianoff still thinks about resuscitating her short-lived movie career. She retains her membership in the Screen Actors Guild and proudly notes that a small residual check keeps coming for her work in the 1978 film.

"I always wanted to do another part," Russianoff says wistfully. "Mazursky told me the same thing happened with the other therapist he used." Like Donald Muhich, Russianoff aspires "to do a part that's not a psychologist." She thinks it would be fun to play a female bartender—"something where I could knock off some pithy one-liners." And she dreams of working with a "truly great director, who could handle me and tell me what to do. I know I would be just spellbinding."

Once, when Woody Allen's secretary contacted Russianoff's husband to track down a particular mouthpiece for his clarinet, Russianoff cheekily asked if she could have the name of Allen's casting director. But the prospect of actually auditioning for Allen intimidated her. "I can't possibly memorize a part," she confesses. Although she passed up that opportunity, she still has hopes of meeting Allen. "I want to be in a Woody Allen movie," she states unabashedly. *"With* Woody Allen."

Russianoff may never snare a part in a Woody Allen movie, but her director, Paul Mazursky, *has* managed to cast Allen in one of his. In the 1991 comedy, *Scenes from a Mall*, Allen played a sportswriter married to a popular radio psychologist and author of a best-selling marriage manual entitled *I Do! I Do! I Do!* Once again Mazursky tweaked the therapist, played by Bette Midler, suggesting that this self-proclaimed expert on personal relationships was completely oblivious to her own husband's extramarital affair. The casting of Midler and Allen seemed irresistible on paper but fell flat on screen. A far more inevitable match was Allen and Mazursky, two therapy fiends who seemed tailor-made for each other.

Allen has done even more than Mazursky to popularize psychiatry for both moviegoers and aspiring moviemakers. Writers who came of age in the 1960s were mesmerized by Allen's tales from the couch. "Because of Woody Allen," says comedy writer Gail Parent, "analysis became a very hip thing to do, a thinking person's thing to do. That's why I started analysis. I wanted to be a New York intellectual, neurotic comedy writer. And how could you be that without a psychiatrist?"

If Woody Allen was instrumental in inflating analysis, he also had a hand in bursting the balloon—partly through the potshots he aimed at the talking cure in his comedy routines and movies, and even more devastatingly when his personal life exploded in scandal in 1992. The news of his affair with the adopted daughter of his lover, Mia Farrow, caused even his most fervent admirers to gape in disbelief. How, they wondered, could someone who had been through so much psychotherapy have acted in such a patently nutty manner?

During the lurid custody battle that Allen fought with Mia Farrow, their all-consuming involvement in psychotherapy was a frequent subject of court testimony; it was revealed that their son Satchel started therapy at the age of three, and their daughter Dylan started when she was five.

Long before he plunged into a love affair with Soon-Yi Farrow Previn, Allen's interminable analysis had become the stuff of legend. In his 1973 farce *Sleeper,* Allen himself poked fun at the snail's pace of his treatment. The character he plays is cryogenically frozen and wakes up in the twenty-second century. Hopelessly disoriented, he complains, "I haven't seen my analyst in two hundred years . . . . If I'd been going all this time, I'd probably almost be cured by now."

The same year that *Sleeper* was released, Allen gave an interview in which he compared his analysis to the case history of another show-business luminary: "It's worth it if you can see an end to it. But with me, it's like Cole Porter's leg—that endless series of doctors who treated him after his horse fell on it. It's like someone saying to you, 'Well, we're going to try to work together and you must have faith, but we can't guarantee anything and there may be a lot of operations.' Porter went to doctors for twenty-five years and they worked and worked on his leg—and finally they amputated it. I feel the same thing."

Allen began his arduous journey after he was kicked out of New York University. In 1957 the dean told him, "You are not good college material. I think you should get psychiatric help because it doesn't look good for your getting work." When Allen replied that he was already gainfully employed in show business, the dean pondered for a moment and then said, "Well, if you're around other crazy people, maybe you won't stand out."

Two years later Allen did heed the dean's advice and began seeing an analyst. He has been going ever since. Over a period of three decades he has consulted a dozen different analysts, with only a few brief interruptions. Unlike Paul Mazursky, who dabbled in Esalen and Gestalt psychology, Allen has stayed the course with a strict, Freudian regimen. "I've had very, very pure experiences, classical Freudian kinds of austere experiences, where nothing is really made easy and no real advice is ever given, and you really have to work hard to make your gains," Allen says. "I find that is something that I've grown up with in my life in general. It may just come from a Jewish family, the idea that nothing pleasurable can ever be good for you."

Allen has always taken a dim view of less rigorous therapy. In

Manhattan the pretentious writer played by Diane Keaton sings the praises of her trendy analyst, a fellow named Donnie. "You call your analyst Donnie?" Woody asks in astonishment. "I call mine Dr. Chomsky. Either that or he hits me with the ruler." Donnie is in the habit of phoning his patient late at night and weeping; the last we hear of him, he is in a coma as a result of a bad acid experience.

This character epitomizes the New Age shrinks who confound Allen. "A very well-known actor told me years ago that he'd meet his analyst, and they'd go walking in the hills together and that kind of thing," Allen recalls. "And I, *mired* in lying down on the couch five days a week and never hearing an utterance, never hearing an exhaling of breath, I was so amazed to hear that. Maybe it works. But anything other than the harshest kind of strict treatment, I've grown up being suspicious of."

At the same time, Allen expresses doubts about the efficacy of his own severe treatment. "Analysis has never been what I hoped it would be," he says. "I had great visions of it when I was much younger. I thought, 'God, this is really going to make a major change in my life. It's going to buoy me tremendously.' And it hasn't. But it's been somewhat of a help."

One thing it did help him do was find choice material for his comedy. In one of his earliest nightclub routines he described a softball league consisting of several rival therapy groups: latent paranoids versus neurotics, nail biters versus bed wetters. Allen played for the neurotics. "I used to steal second base, then feel guilty and go back," he quipped.

Allen's very first movie script, for the 1965 farce *What's New, Pussycat?*, featured Peter Sellers as a Teutonic shrink, Dr. Fritz Fassbender, who is far more concerned with satisfying his own libidinous urges than with helping his Don Juan patient, Peter O'Toole. One of Allen's most sophisticated later comedies, *Zelig*, expressed a more affectionate—but equally wry—view of psychiatrists. Mia Farrow played the owlish Dr. Eudora Fletcher, who treats the title character for his curious compulsion to blend into his surroundings; she falls in love with the pipsqueak in the process. Indeed virtually every one of Allen's movies has included some mention of psychiatry, frequently coupled with a playful suggestion that the analyst may be just as discombobulated as the analysand.

But Allen is not always so lighthearted in his approach to analysis. His first serious drama, *Interiors,* contains a scene in which Diane Keaton is speaking to an unseen analyst, expressing all her torment: "My emptiness set in a year ago, my paralysis . . . . Increasing thoughts of death just seemed to come over me." Alas, the words are not intended as parody.

The same solemnity has sometimes infected the filmmaker's off-camera comments on the talking cure. In a rather dour interview with *The New York Times Magazine* in 1979, Allen responded to a question about how his analysis (which at that point had lasted twenty years) was progressing. "It's very slow," Allen replied. "But an hour a day, talking about your emotions, hopes, angers, disappointments, with someone who's trained to evaluate this material—over a period of years, you're bound to get more in touch with feelings than someone who makes no effort."

That comment provoked a savage rejoinder from Joan Didion in *The New York Review of Books:* "This notion of oneself as a kind of continuing career—something to work at, work on, 'make an effort' for and subject to an hour a day of emotional Nautilus training, all in the interest not of attaining grace but of improving one's 'relationships'—is fairly recent in the world, at least in the world not inhabited entirely by adolescents." Didion concluded her attack by sarcastically noting, "The message that large numbers of people are getting from *Manhattan* and *Interiors* and *Annie Hall* is that this kind of emotional shopping around is the proper business of life's better students, that adolescence can now extend to middle age."

Allen tries gamely to defend himself against the charge of self-indulgence. "Creative people have got to spend a certain amount of time in self-obsession," he asserts. "Psychoanalysis and psychotherapy deal with those very things that the artist is concerned with, his feelings about life, his feelings about himself. For an artist, what's so terrible to spend an hour in the day, to lie down on the couch and just talk freely about your deepest feelings on any subject? It's dramatic and fascinating. And as you can face certain problems with a larger view, a more generous view, with more grasp of them and perspective on them, you have a chance to have a larger view in your writing."

There is certainly evidence of this creative evolution in his films. Allen's early movies, such as *Take the Money and Run* and

Bananas, were entirely self-fixated, with his own nebbishy character dominating the story. As he gained a broader perspective on his own personal anxieties through analysis, Allen has branched out artistically and managed to populate his movies with a richer gallery of well-defined characters quite unlike himself. That is the great achievement of novelistic movies such as *Hannah and Her Sisters* and *Crimes and Misdemeanors.*

In addition, the progression in his films from the light, jokey comedies to the more personal and ambitious comedy-dramas can probably be traced to the self-scrutiny encouraged by psychoanalysis. For example, *Radio Days,* a pungent reminiscence of Allen's childhood in the 1940s, shows a clear analytic influence. The quarrelsome parents call to mind Allen's description of his own bickering mother and father, and many vivid domestic details have the feel of intimate memories conjured up during free association on the couch.

But some critics contend that analysis, by making Allen more self-conscious, destroyed the spontaneous humor of his most original work. In *Stardust Memories* Allen puts these sentiments into the mouths of the extraterrestrial aliens who ambush filmmaker Sandy Bates and inform him that they like his movies, "especially the early funny ones." Over the course of his long analysis Allen began to take himself more and more seriously. His insatiable desire to be accepted as a tragic artist on the order of his idol, Ingmar Bergman, may be one of the least salutary results of his protracted couch trip. In rapturously reviewing Bergman's autobiography for *The New York Times,* Allen explicitly related Bergman's art to Freud's revolutionary insights. "As the Freudian revolution sank in," he wrote, "the most fascinating arena of conflict shifted to the interior . . . Bergman evolved a style to deal with the human interior, and he alone among directors has explored the soul's battlefield to the fullest." Unfortunately, Allen's ersatz Bergman dramas—*Interiors, September,* and *Another Woman*—sink into dreary ponderousness.

Although he keeps trying to attach himself to brooding writers and European auteurs, Allen has considerably more in common with Borscht Belt comics than he does with Bergman, Strindberg, or O'Neill. He seems perfectly at home in the boisterous world of *Broadway Danny Rose,* far less comfortable in the Kafkaesque universe of *Shadows and Fog.* It is revealing that even Allen's most humorless films have their roots in pop culture. *September,* a chamber drama drenched in Chekhovian melancholy, wears its angst on its sleeve. But the story itself—the saga of the daughter of a famous movie star who has lived in torment ever since she was charged with murdering her mother's gangster boyfriend—was clearly based on all the tabloid gossip about Lana Turner, Cheryl Crane, and the killing of Turner's lover, Johnny Stompanato.

In *Another Woman*, Allen's lugubrious 1988 drama, the protagonist is a philosophy professor played by Gena Rowlands. At the beginning of the film she takes a new office that happens to adjoin that of a psychiatrist. The walls are paper-thin, and Rowlands becomes haunted by the sessions she overhears between the analyst and a suicidal patient (Mia Farrow). As she listens to this unseen woman's laments, Rowlands begins to question the purpose of her own life and plunges into existential despair. Allen's plot was probably inspired by more show business lore, including the famous story about a Hollywood writer-director who was sitting in the waiting room of his psychiatrist's office and overheard his wife's analytic session, in which she confessed to a torrid extramarital affair.

In the more scintillating comedy-drama *Crimes and Misdemeanors,* Allen conducts a weighty examination of the triumph of amorality in a world where God has turned a blind eye to human depravity. But the narrative vehicle for this momentous theme is a tale of hit men and jilted lovers borrowed from innumerable B-movies. Allen's sensibility is pure show biz, and that may be why his loftier aspirations seem so strained. Like Paul Mazursky, who flails when trying to imitate Fellini and Truffaut (in such films as *Alex in Wonderland* and *Willie and Phil*), Allen stumbles when he tries to fill the shoes of Ingmar Bergman. "I would feel incomplete if I couldn't look back on my life at one point and say, 'I made a serious film that was accepted,' " Allen comments dolefully. "I don't think that a great comic work of art can ever equal *War and Peace* or *Crime and Punishment* or *Othello* or *The Trial*. A couple of films by Chaplin are great, and a couple by Keaton and the Marx Brothers. But I don't feel that they're as fulfilling a human experience as *The Bicycle Thief* or *Persona*. I once read a review that John Lahr wrote, and one of his critical comments about me was that I confused serious with solemn. That hit me; it was a good insight. I do like solemn things. I like that slow, very serious unfolding of a very heavy story." His intensive, slow-going psychoanalysis has doubtless heightened Allen's perverse predilection for grim, somber art.

Ironically, psychiatrists themselves have often criticized Allen's films for not taking human problems seriously enough. Irving Schneider has accused both Allen and Paul Mazursky of making light of emotional torment. "In their works," Schneider wrote, "audiences have had difficulty distinguishing between real pain and self-indulgence, between the need for therapy and an addiction to therapy."

Other psychiatrists have raised similar concerns. "Unfortunately, what most people think about therapy is the Woody Allen concept of therapy, which is basically a bored human being indulging himself," says Dr. Christopher Zois, who has treated a number of celebrities, including director Sidney Lumet. "I've been in practice for years, and I have never seen that kind of patient. In my view neurosis is as painful as a broken leg. A lot of people might consider getting some kind of help if they see something on screen they can identify with. And yet their impression from Woody Allen's movies is that therapy is a waste of time—for the self-indulgent, the wealthy, the narcissistic."

No doubt that impression was only confirmed by the news that, after thirty-five years of psychotherapy, Allen had embarked on an unseemly affair with his lover's daughter. His taboo-breaking dalliance might well be interpreted as a by-product of his self-indulgent brand of treatment. Nonetheless there was something incongruous about Allen's decision to take up with a young woman whom he had known since she was nine years old and whose mother was his intimate companion. For he had constantly portrayed himself on screen as an honorable figure. The characters he played may have been tempted to stray from the straight and narrow, but they inevitably pulled back from the brink of calamity. In a memorable scene in *Manhattan* Allen's Isaac Davis chastises his best friend, Yale, for stealing his girlfriend and then rationalizing his unprincipled behavior. Yale lashes out at the self-righteous Isaac: "You think you're God!"

"I gotta model myself after somebody," Isaac responds with a sheepish shrug. He then points to a nearby skeleton—their conversation takes place in a biology lab—and says, "It's very important to have some kind of personal integrity. I'll be hanging in a classroom one day, and I want to be sure when I thin out that I'm well thought of."

Indeed the characters whom Allen himself chooses to portray are always obsessively concerned with their ethical image. The other men in his movies are the philanderers and perverts. In *Han-*

nah and Her Sisters Michael Caine's character has the lusty affair with his wife's sister, while Allen's character turns to Catholicism and Eastern mysticism in a search for salvation. In *Crimes and Misdemeanors* Allen plays a high-minded documentary filmmaker appalled by the fast-talking, double-dealing TV producer who woos and wins his girlfriend. In one of the movie's funniest scenes, Allen's unmarried sister, who has resorted to advertising in the personals columns, describes her nightmarish date with a man who seemed to be a mild-mannered intellectual but proved to be a degenerate rapist. Weeping, she is at first reluctant to reveal what happened. "Tell me, what's so terrible?" her solicitous brother implores. Finally she blurts out the truth: "He sat over me and went to the bathroom." Allen lets out a shriek of horror. "That's so disgusting," he moans. "Oh my God, that's the worst thing I ever heard in my life!"

In *Husbands and Wives* Allen's Gabe Roth resists the blandishments of the seductive twenty-year-old college student played by Juliette Lewis; he allows himself one passionate kiss but refuses to go any farther. A series of other older men, we are told, did not exercise the same self-control; they hopped into bed with the pouty Lolita. Allen had paved the way for condemnation of his real-life entanglement with Soon-Yi Previn by so often casting himself in his movies as a spokesman for virtue and propriety.

What may have been more dismaying than any moral lapse was the loss of Allen's sense of humor during his May-December romance. When Allen issued a press release declaring that Soon-Yi is "a lovely, intelligent, sensitive woman who has and continues to turn my life around in a wonderfully positive way," he sounded like the simpletons who pop up in his films for the sole purpose of being burlesqued—like the vacuous young lovers whom Alvy Singer encounters on the street in *Annie Hall*. "I'm very shallow and empty, and I have no ideas and nothing interesting to say," the dopey blonde comments when asked for the secret of her blissful romance. "And I'm exactly the same way," her moonstruck boyfriend pipes up.

Most commentators compared Woody's fling with Soon-Yi to the story line of *Manhattan,* in which Isaac Davis has an affair with a seventeen-year-old high school student named Tracy (Mariel Hemingway). But in that movie it is Isaac who breaks up with Tracy because he feels embarrassed by such an age-inappropriate relationship. Only at the very end of the movie does Isaac decide that he was wrong to yield to conventional morality, and he resolves to win Tracy back. Of course it is relatively easy to ask for the audience's approval of a romance with a bright, wholesome girl who sips ice cream sodas. If the child-woman in that movie had been the hero's adopted stepdaughter, the conclusion would not have had such a lyrical, bittersweet poignance.

Husbands and Wives, made twelve years later when Allen was acting out just such a deviant drama in his own life, turned out to be one of his most daring and evocative movies. His bizarre midlife crisis did not blunt his artistry. Conceived in the style of a cinema verité documentary, complete with hand-held camera movement and interviews with an offscreen filmmaker, *Husbands and Wives* imagines modern romance as a series of violent squalls without structure or satisfying resolution. While his personal life was in turmoil, Allen was creating this masterful chronicle of several marriages and love affairs coming apart: his own darkly comic scenes from a crack-up.

Beyond issues of morality or artistry, however, a perplexing question remained unanswered. As Allen waged an ugly custody battle with Mia Farrow and confessed to taking "sexy" nude photographs of his quasi-stepdaughter, one could not help wondering how this notoriously meticulous filmmaker—and very private person—had allowed himself to become the center of a sex scandal that even knocked the Royal Family off the tabloid front pages.

In *Husbands and Wives* Gabe Roth confesses his attraction to "kamikaze women" and his involvement in a series of destructive romantic relationships. In an interview a few years before he made that movie, Allen spoke about his own neurotic tendency to embrace dangerous, doomed love affairs. "That's a real common problem that people have, this repetition compulsion to do that," he said. Even though such liaisons are painful, people pursue them, he suggested, "because they're getting a very significant payoff in some form of their life, emotionally, erotically, intellectually. Somewhere they're getting it from choosing trouble. I've done that in my life. I've been guilty in my life of not making wise choices and then swearing up and down the line that I'm going to make a wise choice the next time, and then making an equally foolish choice, and then doing it again after that, totally blinded to the fact that I'm doing it. Over the years you begin to get some perspective on it. At least I hope so. I could go out tomorrow and do it again." Allen finally abandoned the kamikaze women for a worshipful schoolgirl. As his character murmurs in *Crimes and Misdemeanors,* "Human sexuality is just so mysterious, which I guess is good in a way."

Movie directors have a natural tendency toward megalomania, which is magnified by the obsequious treatment they receive on the set. When the playwright David Mamet directed his first film, *House of Games,* about a psychiatrist engaged in a deadly battle of wits with a con man, he was startled by the authority he was handed. "The amount of deference with which one is treated is absolutely *awesome,*" Mamet said of his new vocation. A sense of unchecked power is an occupational hazard for any director. But for an auteur of Woody Allen's stature, it is especially treacherous. No director is more revered—or more isolated—than Allen. Studios give him carte blanche, actors sign on for his movies without even reading his closely guarded scripts, and critics award him their highest accolades. On top of that, his interminable analysis—decades of navel gazing—may have instilled in Allen an added feeling of entitlement that even the most arrogant Hollywood directors never dared to own.

For such an unapologetic egotist, "relationships" of any kind are excruciatingly difficult to maintain. Certainly Allen and Mia Farrow had a most unconventional union for twelve years. They never actually lived together, and when he dumped Farrow for her daughter, Allen ignored the effects of his actions on Mia and the rest of her brood. In fact, he blithely admitted that he had never paid any attention to his presumptive step-children. "I was not involved with the other kids," he told an interviewer for *Time* magazine. "I spent absolutely zero time with any of them, particularly the girls . . . . I was only interested in my own kids." This apathy toward Farrow's "other" children had persisted during the decade that he shared her bed, fathered a biological child with her, and adopted two orphans with her. Within his own hermetically sealed frame of reference, Allen evidently felt that his absolute indifference toward Farrow's children lent credibility to the claim that he was innocent of incest. Maybe so, but it also revealed his utter obliviousness—not just to Farrow and her family but to the way he would be judged in the court of public opinion. Allen was behaving like those ridiculous old goats in his own movies, the satyrs who lust after young flesh and fail to see that the rest of the world is laughing. "The heart wants what it wants," Allen declared with solipsistic silliness when asked to explain his liaison with Soon-Yi. "I didn't find any moral dilemmas whatsoever."

It took more than three decades, but Allen's Freudian calisthenics finally did away with that stubborn bit of excess baggage—his Jewish guilt. Allen may have sometimes questioned the effectiveness of psychotherapy, but in his case it had one tangible result: it finally obliterated his superego, leaving him a randy, reckless combination of ego and id. In David Mamet's *House of Games* the main character is a therapist who commits murder and gets away with it. She is encouraged to banish guilt by her own analyst, who tells her, "When you have done something unforgivable, I'll tell you exactly what to do—you forgive yourself." The protagonist absorbs that credo, and when she is asked to inscribe a copy of her best-selling book in the very last scene, the homicidal shrink writes two precious words: "Forgive yourself." That was fiction, of course, but many real-life therapists have offered the same cheerful counsel. It is a message that Woody Allen, the century's most famous therapy addict, at long last took to heart.

8. THE HEARTBREAK KIDS

Amid all the furor surrounding Woody Allen's offscreen shenanigans at the time that *Husbands and Wives* was released in 1992, a provocative subplot in the film went virtually unnoticed. Woody's character is not the only middle-aged lech smitten with the seductive coed played by Juliette Lewis; her analyst, too, has become deliriously fixated—stalking the girl like a depraved erotomaniac.

Movies that expose the dirty little secret of doctor-patient sex have almost invariably raised the hackles of the psychiatric profession. This time, however, the embarrassing scandal involving the filmmaker himself gave the shrinks the last laugh. A decade earlier Woody Allen's sometime writing partner, Marshall Brickman (who worked with Allen on *Sleeper, Annie Hall,* and *Manhattan*), wrote and directed a wicked comedy about an on-the-couch romance that generated a lot more heat within the analytic community.

First titled *Valium,* later *Analysis,* and finally *Lovesick,* Brickman's 1983 movie proved to be one of the most incendiary of all cinematic treatments of psychiatry. The film's protagonist, Dr. Saul Benjamin, is a respectable psychoanalyst, drolly played by Dudley Moore. The cast of characters includes half a dozen other shrinks, whom Brickman skewers with subtle aplomb. When Saul grows disillusioned with his practice and returns fees to a patient who had not been helped one whit by years of treatment, an elder of the analytic society asks in horror, "You gave money *back* to a patient?" In another scene Saul consults his own training analyst, played by John Huston, whose only advice to him is "Relax, take a tranquilizer." As Saul enumerates his problems, Huston begins to snore. When Saul jabs his mentor to awaken him, Huston reflexively bleats the analyst's retort of last resort, "So, Saul, what do *you* think?" In the final scene Alec Guinness, making an ethereal cameo as the ghost of Sigmund Freud, tells Saul that he is off to Mexico to study hallucinogenic drugs and primitive religion. Saul is agog. "But what about psychoanalysis?" he asks the revered founder. "It was an interesting experiment," Freud replies with a shrug. "I never meant it to become an industry."

It was not just this pointed mockery of analysis, however, that struck a raw nerve with the psychiatric establishment. The plot of *Lovesick* revolves around the turmoil that erupts when Dr. Benjamin falls in love with a patient, a gifted young playwright named Chloe (Elizabeth McGovern). He inherits her from another analyst (Wallace Shawn), who was romantically obsessed with her, and almost immediately Dr. Benjamin finds himself equally bewitched. He dreams about ravishing her and even breaks into her apartment in a helpless, sex-induced trance. When she finds him there, Chloe admits that she shares his romantic yearnings, and they fall into bed together. Although Saul is ostracized by his fellow analysts for this breach of professional ethics, the film suggests that the relationship is enriching for both doctor and patient. Dr. Benjamin not only becomes a more satisfied human being, he even turns into a more dedicated therapist; he gives up his affluent, narcissistic patients and begins working with homeless schizophrenics.

Other films—including *Spellbound, The Dark Mirror,* and *Dressed to Kill*—had already dramatized erotic entanglements between psychiatrist and patient. But what made Brickman's movie so subversive was that it encouraged the audience to applaud the union of doctor and patient and regard the opponents to their romance as foolish fuddy-duddies. Brickman treated the ethical dilemma as little more than a newfangled complication in a lighthearted romantic comedy. As Krin and Glen O. Gabbard observed in their book *Psychiatry and the Cinema,* "It can be argued that *Lovesick* is the most insidious depiction of a psychiatrist acting on erotic countertransference feelings that has ever appeared on film."

Countertransference is defined as the emotional reaction that the therapist has to a patient, the flip side of transference. In traditional psychoanalysis, transference is one of the crucial steps in treatment. By projecting onto the therapist positive and negative feelings toward key people in one's life—parents, siblings, spouses, and lovers—the patient comes to understand those complicated relationships during the analytic process. But what happens when the analyst begins to project onto the patient the longings and dissatisfactions in *his* life? Beginning with Freud, analysts have recognized that they would at times have intense emotional responses to a patient, but the goal is to master those feelings so that they do not interfere with treatment. By presenting a fable in which the psychiatrist simply surrenders to his impulses—and is then rewarded for expressing them—Marshall Brickman knew he was playing with fire. "It was like putting a whoopee cushion on the principal's chair," says Brickman, a long-term analysand himself.

Still, he never anticipated the intense acrimony that the film would stir. Typical of the denunciations it received was one written by Dr. Richard Johnson for the newsletter of the Southern California Psychoanalytic Association. Johnson attacked the movie for doing "the psychoanalytic image a serious disservice," and he speculated that the story probably grew out of its creator's unresolved anger toward psychoanalysis. "It had a cartoon effect similar to that expected from a hostile cartoonist who has an incompletely analyzed negative transference," Johnson declared. Even more troubling to the doctor was the economic impact such a portrayal could have. Taking issue with Brickman's lampoon of the analytic elders, Johnson wrote, "I feel that this public smearing, as tempting as it is to tweak authority figures, hits a destructive note to an already flagging credibility of the psychoanalytic movement . . . . The large, relatively uninformed general public will have again been subtly indoctrinated to reject psychoanalysis as a science or legitimate clinical technique."

Dr. Jacqueline Bouhoutsos, a psychologist who once chaired the ethics committee of the California State Psychological Association and also served as a member of the Motion Picture Association of America's rating board, describes *Lovesick* as "an awful distortion." Bouhoutsos sounds a dire warning: "*Lovesick* plays right into the fantasy that a lot of women patients have and encourages this kind of behavior, not only for the women but also for the therapist. Yet in studies we have done, this kind of relationship turns out to be damaging to the patient in ninety percent of the cases. It leads to hospitalization or suicide."

Mental-health professionals were not the only ones to take up the cudgel against *Lovesick*. Frances Lear, then married to television mogul Norman Lear, mounted a personal campaign against the movie. "One might think, watching this nasty little film, that sex under these conditions is no more than a naughty psychotherapeutic act," Lear complained in a vitriolic letter to the *Los Angeles Times* in February 1983, shortly after the movie's release. "Nowhere is there a hint that sex between patient and analyst is, as responsible physicians attest, as devastating an emotional experience as incest itself . . . . Did the author pitch the film as a funny little number about young-old sex, this season's prurience winner? Is the mindset of motion picture executives so irresponsible as to knowingly produce a film that distorts and approves a tragic social problem? I tremble at the answer."

Lear continued to assail the movie whenever she could. "Frankly, her reaction astounded me," says the movie's star, Dudley Moore. Marshall Brickman was equally astonished by Lear's vehemence. "She thought I was the anti-Christ," Brickman recalls. "She felt it was reprehensible that the analyst went unpunished. To her it was yet another example of Hollywood having no ethics."

Frances Lear, who went on to become the founding editor of *Lear's* magazine, still trembles slightly at the mention of *Lovesick*. "I thought it was appalling," she says. Lear has been in therapy on and off for more than fifty years, and one reason she was so outraged by the movie is that she was herself seduced by one of her psychiatrists. "It's a kind of rape," Lear argues. "If you are a woman patient, you are obligated to do as the therapist says. Doctor-patient sex is still not as out in the open as it should be. It is heinous, and the psychiatric community is not doing squat to change it."

There is no shortage of examples to support Lear's claim. In 1975 Julie Roy sued her psychiatrist, an illustrious German-born analyst named Renatus Hartogs, for seducing her during treatment. At the same time that he was writing a monthly column for *Cosmopolitan*, "The Analyst's Couch," Dr. Hartogs was urging his patient to strip naked and lie down *with* him on the couch. In upholding the jury's judgment against Hartogs in a New York civil court, Judge Allen Murray Myers said, "A patient must not be fair game for a lecherous doctor." In 1981 Evelyn Walker won $4.6 million in damages against a distinguished San Diego analyst named Zane Parzen, who eventually lost his medical license as a result of several cases of sexual abuse. Among other kinky misdeeds, Parzen was accused of commanding a female patient to duck-walk across the room and unzip his pants with her teeth. Several years later Dr. Jules Masserman, a past president of the American Psychiatric Association, also surrendered his medical license after a patient sued him for repeatedly injecting her with Amytal and then having intercourse with her while she was unconscious.

Dr. Jacqueline Bouhoutsos estimates that as many as 12 percent of male therapists may be guilty of sexual misconduct with their patients. "It has to do with power and exploitation," Bouhoutsos says. "Sometimes the therapist is a sociopath."

In the annals of sex between psychiatrists and patients, many cases shocked outsiders. But the liaison that most clearly paralleled the situation in *Lovesick*—and may have actually inspired it—involved a prominent New York psychoanalyst named David Rubinfine and the brilliant comedienne Elaine May.

Like the character Elizabeth McGovern played in *Lovesick*, May was a promising young writer when she first entered analysis. Born Elaine Berlin in 1932, she was the daughter of two performers in the Yiddish theater. As a child she moved with her family to Los Angeles, and when she was just sixteen, she married Marvin May, who worked in an aircraft factory. The marriage got her away from home but ended in divorce after a few years. Then Elaine moved to Chicago and began hanging out with a group of comic actors that included Alan Arkin, Shelley Berman, and Zohra Lampert. May developed an almost symbiotic rapport with a shy, German-born comic named Mike Nichols. The story they tell is that their comedy act was born in a Chicago train station, when Nichols sat down next to May and began impersonating a Russian secret agent; without missing a beat May followed suit, and the two of them were soon improvising a whole KGB encounter while their fellow commuters looked on in amazement.

Nichols and May, who had a brief romantic fling that turned into an enduring platonic friendship, started performing with the Compass Players in Chicago, then moved to New York and made a splash in avant-garde nightclubs. Their hilarious sketches ridiculed intrusive Jewish mothers, arty singles, bored suburbanites, and other choice specimens of the Eisenhower era. It was only natural that many of their routines involved psychoanalysis, one of the favorite pastimes of fifties intellectuals. In a sly skit called "Transference," May impersonated a Viennese shrink whom Nichols claimed reminded him of his mother. At first May explained that this is a typical delusion of the analytic process; then she asked solicitously, "Are you eating?"

One skit called "Merry Christmas, Doctor" contained an eerie foreshadowing of events in May's own life. Again Nichols played the patient and May the analyst. As their session began, he told her that he had to cancel their appointment on Christmas Eve so that he could be with his wife and children. At first the psychiatrist seemed only mildly disgruntled. "I want to analyze this reluctance to come in on Friday," she declared sternly. Gradually, however, her jealousy became more and more transparent, and she finally broke into uncontrollable sobs at the prospect of losing her patient—even for a single hour—to his family.

Both Nichols and May were in analysis at the time they created this sketch. Nichols was being treated by the Swiss refugee Dr. Rudolph Loewenstein, who was president of the American Psychoanalytic Association. May's analyst was Dr. David Rubinfine. When May began seeing him in the late 1950s, Rubinfine was one of the rising stars of the New York Psychoanalytic Institute and Society.

Born in Chicago in 1921, Rubinfine trained as a physician at the University of Chicago, then did his residency at the Menninger Clinic in Topeka from 1946 to 1948. He worked under Dr. Milton Wexler, who remembers that Rubinfine was not just a gifted therapist but an amateur magician who delighted both the staff and patients with sleight-of-hand performances. "He was marvelous with his hands," Wexler recalls, and as a result, Rubinfine was promptly enlisted to assist the chief neurosurgeon at the clinic. "Neurosurgery was very slow, very tedious," Wexler says. "David hated it, but he was so damn good with his fingers that he could manipulate a scalpel and all the instruments very well. So they wouldn't let him off the hook. One day David was opening a sardine can and cut his fingers so badly that he ripped the tendons open. From that moment on he couldn't perform surgery; he was too clumsy with his fingers. Everyone said, 'David, what kind of unconscious have you got that you ruin your hands in order to get out of neurosurgery?' "

After Rubinfine moved to New York to take additional training, he developed a special interest in children and adolescents. But he also built a stellar clientele that included, among others, Alger Hiss and concert pianist Elly Kassman, who was married to one of Rubinfine's psychoanalytic colleagues, Dr. Bernard Meyer. After his wife died of cancer, Dr. Meyer sent his teenage son, Nicholas, to Rubinfine for treatment. "He was very effective with me," says Nicholas Meyer, who became a successful novelist and filmmaker. "He was responsible for keeping me alive at a very difficult point in my life."

Rubinfine was unquestionably a dedicated therapist, but he was at least as passionate about his extracurricular activities. "He was enamored of show business and show people," says Milton Wexler. "He loved them to distraction, and he was a showman himself."

Dr. Margaret Brenman Gibson, another of Rubinfine's former supervisors and the wife of playwright William Gibson, agrees with Wexler's assessment. "David was a very bright man, and a slightly out-of-control romantic," she says. "I think he would have liked to be in the theater."

Michael Pressman, a film and television director, married Nicholas Meyer's sister, Constance. Through her, he became acquainted with David Rubinfine, who remained a friend of the Meyer family. Pressman also heard tales of Dr. Rubinfine from the actor Herbert Berghof, who ran a New York theater company and who costarred in one of the movies that Pressman directed, *Those Lips, Those Eyes*. "In his days in New York, Rubinfine was seeing patients all day and pulling the curtain at the Herbert Berghof studios at night, because he had the bug," Pressman reports. "I thought Rubinfine was a very charismatic eccentric—flamboyant and charming and funny. Many people would say he probably should never have been an analyst, that he might have been better suited as an actor, director, or writer. He was in love with the arts in a way that I think confused his work."

Pressman first met Dr. Rubinfine at a social gathering where Alger Hiss, another friend of the Meyer family, was also present. "Alger quite casually introduced Rubinfine as his doctor," Pressman recalls. Later, when he got to know Rubinfine better, Pressman could not resist asking the analyst whether he thought Hiss, who had been convicted of perjury, had been falsely accused of being a Russian spy. Rubinfine was convinced of his patient's innocence. "That man was not capable of telling a lie," Rubinfine confided to Pressman. "I had to teach him how to tell a white lie."

Composer Stephen Sondheim knew Rubinfine socially in New York, and he remembers one incident that suggests how Rubinfine's desire to mix it up with the cultural elite could create embarrassment. Rubinfine hosted a dinner party to which he invited Sondheim, director Harold Prince and his wife, and Prince's analyst. Rubinfine was aware that Prince was one of his friend's patients, but he thought they could all socialize together happily. Instead the unexpected appearance of his psychiatrist mortified Prince. "Hal could not have been more surprised," Sondheim says. "You don't invite somebody's analyst without telling them."

Rubinfine's love of theater helps to explain what he found so enticing about Elaine May. She was not just a magnetic new star, but one of the funniest women in America. Rubinfine, who had a huge portrait of Buster Keaton hanging above his desk, was also known for his dry sense of humor. "He even looked a little like Keaton," says one of his patients, Marty Gwinn Townsend. "He had the same long face."

Milton Wexler notes that while Rubinfine was infatuated with May's world, she was equally fascinated by his. "Elaine loved the idea of psychiatry, and psychoanalysis particularly," Wexler says. "She was even interested in theory—the whole idea of the unconscious and what brings laughter, things like that. And I can certainly understand why David was attracted to Elaine. She is so witty and so sharp. But I don't think it's the best idea to find your wives on the couch."

As their analytic sessions progressed, Rubinfine and May found themselves more and more drawn to each other. Marshall Brickman, the creator of *Lovesick,* acknowledges that he speculated on the turning point in their relationship. "There must have been a session," Brickman muses, "when Rubinfine said, 'Miss May, I must talk to you. I can't conceal from you any longer . . . ' She went in there obviously and twirled him around. She was fascinating, brilliant, attractive. Who's going to be able to withstand that? Well, he didn't."

In Brickman's *Lovesick,* when the pillars of the analytic society learn that Dr. Benjamin has fallen in love with a patient, one of them asks the ultimate leering question: "Tell me, did they have sexual relations on the couch?" Equally blunt questions were asked about Rubinfine and May. "Did Elaine and David have an affair while she was still in treatment?" Dr. Margaret Gibson asks. "We will never know."

Clearly something very unconventional was going on in her analysis. Elaine May married lyricist Sheldon Harnick in April 1962 and then filed for divorce two months later. Not long afterwards, Rubinfine let it be known that he was leaving his wife of twenty years to marry his patient. But if the subject of transference and countertransference was a source of comedy in the Nichols-and-May routines and, later, in Marshall Brickman's movie *Lovesick,* there was nothing funny about the fallout from the Rubinfine-May romance. Rubinfine and his wife, Rosa, had three daughters. His family was torn apart when he moved out. Milton Wexler, who had first met Rosa Rubinfine in Topeka in the 1940s and had played host to the entire family at his vacation home in Lake Tahoe, flew to New York to counsel Rosa when her husband left her. "I tried to comfort her in some way," Wexler says. "But she just couldn't take the idea of David and Elaine. It was very tragic."

On April 30, 1963, Rosa Rubinfine committed suicide by swallowing an overdose of sedatives. She was forty-two years old. Less than six weeks later, on June 8, 1963, David Rubinfine married Elaine May.

If the news of Rubinfine's impending marriage to his patient had scandalized the analytic world, his wife's suicide added several layers of insult to injury. "It rocked the community," says writer Jay Presson Allen. "Rubinfine was drummed out of the corps."

Before the scandal Rubinfine had been rising steadily within the ranks of the New York Psychoanalytic Institute and the American Psychoanalytic Association. He was named to the faculty of the Center for Advanced Psychoanalytic Study at Princeton in 1960, and in 1961, when he was just forty years old, he became a training analyst at the New York Psychoanalytic Institute, a post reserved for the most respected analysts. When he revealed that he was going to marry Elaine May, Rubinfine was stripped of his position as training analyst and ostracized by the New York establishment.

Arthur Penn directed the popular Nichols-and-May show on Broadway in 1960, and he got to know both performers extremely well. Mike Nichols's analyst, Rudolph Loewenstein, had also been Penn's analyst. After his analysis ended, Penn continued to socialize with Loewenstein and with many other prominent New York analysts. When David Rubinfine married Elaine May, Penn found himself privy to some of the debate within the analytic community. "Often I would be at a dinner party and the topic of David and Elaine would come up," Penn recalls. "Friendships were strained by this case. Some analysts defended him and some attacked him. Some felt that they were all compromised by what he had done. It was a beaut of a scandal, exacerbated by Elaine's prominence."

Dr. Erika Freeman, an analyst who treated many members of the New York theatrical set, was critical of both Rubinfine and May. "When Elaine May was told that Rubinfine's wife had committed suicide," Freeman reports, "she said, 'What a hostile thing to do.' In a sense she was right, but it was hardly her place to say it!"

*   *   *

One of the New York psychiatrists who was most disturbed by the Rubinfine case was Dr. Victor Rosen, an analyst ten years older than Rubinfine. Rosen, who was elected president of the American Psychoanalytic Association in 1965, had been a good friend of Rubinfine's. According to Rosen's daughter, Winifred, her father was "horrified when David married Elaine. Partly he felt it was a smirch on all their reputations. He also felt it wasn't good for David." Perhaps Rosen identified with Rubinfine. Winifred Rosen remembers the two analysts as being very much alike. "They both emanated a kind of sweetness," she says.

But Winifred also believes that her father was upset by Rubinfine's breach of ethics because the case touched him personally. "My father must have been denying his own situation," she says. For at the time the Rubinfine scandal exploded, Victor Rosen was involved in a very intensive analysis with a young patient of his own whom he would marry just a few years later. The ruckus that ensued was almost as intense as the furor surrounding the Rubinfine-May case, though it was perhaps less titillating because the patient for whom Rosen left his wife was not a celebrity. Since Rosen was an even more eminent analyst than Rubinfine, however, the psychiatric establishment was even more shaken by it. In addition to his prestigious positions in the New York Psychoanalytic Institute and the American Psychoanalytic Association, Rosen had many friends among the New York intelligentsia, including Lionel and Diana Trilling, Howard Fast, and William Styron.

His unseemly liaison outraged his psychoanalytic colleagues, and Rosen, like Rubinfine, was shunned. In her book *Psychoanalysis: The Impossible Profession*, Janet Malcolm mentioned "two analysts who had sinned against the mores of the analytic community . . . Their sin was to marry a patient." Malcolm did not name them but wrote that one analyst got into a "messy triangle" during the analysis, while the other went out with his patient shortly after the analysis ended. The first was Rubinfine and the second Rosen. As Malcolm explained, "They were removed from the roster of training analysts, they were divested of their various functions in the ruling structure, they were dismissed from their teaching posts." Malcolm noted that both eventually left New York and commented that the banishment of the two doctors raised issues about "the dogma of the psychoanalytic movement as well as the mores of the profession."

To Rosen this repudiation came as something of a shock. Because he occupied a loftier perch within the analytic hierarchy than Rubinfine, he felt insulated from the censure of his confreres. As Winifred Rosen remembers it, "When David Rubinfine announced that he was marrying Elaine May, his patient, he knew that he was doing something wrong. My father had a very different attitude. Of course he was much more powerful than Rubinfine, so he said, 'I'm about to marry Elise Snyder, my former patient, and I don't see anything wrong with it.' He did not eat crow. He asserted his right to do it. He was completely blind."

Rosen's story was at least as startling as Rubinfine's. Dr. Rosen began treating Elise Snyder when she was a medical student; he was some thirty years her senior. Her analysis eventually lasted seven years, and Rosen was her training analyst when Snyder decided to become a psychoanalyst herself. After Snyder's analysis ended, Rosen asked her to help him edit a paper he was writing; within a few months their relationship had turned into a full-fledged romance. Both Rosen and Snyder were married to other people. Rosen's wife became despondent when he left her, and at one point she required emergency medical treatment. Their daughter Winifred says, "My father acted badly. All he could think of was the shame of it when the ambulance came to our building and my mother was carried through the lobby."

That was not Dr. Rosen's most bizarre notion. When Winifred, who had just graduated college, told her father that she wanted to resume therapy to deal with some of the issues raised by her parents' separation, Rosen suggested that she seek treatment from Elise Snyder. "My dad didn't want me talking about the situation to an outsider," Winifred says. "He didn't want any of this to be known. So he sent me to Elise, which was completely weird. He said, 'I know that anybody would think this is very unconventional, but she's so talented.' I had a number of sessions with her that were indescribable. My father was in love, so he was insane by definition."

Winifred Rosen remembers the sudden change in her father's status. At her sister's wedding, right before Victor Rosen announced that he wanted a divorce, the guest list read like a Who's Who of prominent New York analysts. Then Dr. Rosen's world collapsed. The conservative members of the New York Psychoanalytic Institute stopped speaking to him, though a few of his more liberal friends remained supportive. "His case polarized the Institute," says Winifred Rosen. "But I think there was a general agreement that he had way overstepped the bounds. He was removed as a training analyst against his violent protestations. It turned quite ugly. I remember he said they made him drink hemlock. Then his anger turned inward."

Rosen was devastated by his colleagues' rejection, and he grew increasingly bitter and depressed. A few years after marrying Snyder, still feeling like a pariah, he left New York to accept a teaching position at Yale. Even though that might sound like an enviable appointment, "to him it was a defeat," his daughter Winifred says. Rosen and Snyder took up residence in Deep River, Connecticut. He was drinking heavily, but his wife forced him to give that up. "That drove him into secret drug use," Winifred Rosen reveals. "A lot of his downfall was drug-related. It all started because he thought he had a gall bladder problem, and when he had an attack, he did what all doctors do—he medicated himself. When he finally had his gall bladder removed, it turned out he didn't have a gall bladder problem. He had a hiated hernia. But it was also discovered that he had a tremendous tolerance for Demerol."

As he took more drugs, Rosen became more and more isolated. The downward spiral that began when he married his patient could not be halted. "The taboo is a good taboo," Winifred Rosen says. "You shouldn't marry your patient. Elise had been my father's patient for seven years, so he knew everything about her, and she knew almost nothing about him. Talk about an inequality of power! Then their roles reversed. I remember toward the end of his life he said, 'She de-cerebrates me!' Their marriage was falling apart when he died. His real problem was he couldn't open up to anybody. He was a mess at the end."

In certain ways Rosen's tragic story was prefigured by the classic story of analyst-patient romance, F. Scott Fitzgerald's *Tender Is the Night*. In the novel Dick Diver is a brilliant young psychoanalyst in Zurich when he begins treating a beautiful and wealthy schizophrenic, Nicole Warren, who has retreated into madness as a result of being sexually molested by her father. Dr. Diver cures her and falls in love with her in the process. Although his training analyst tries to warn him of the dangers of countertransference, Dick marries Nicole and moves with her to the south of France. There he surrenders to the languor and luxury of her world, abandoning his psychiatric practice and research. At first Nicole continues to suffer occasional mental lapses, but over the years she gradually grows stronger while Dick becomes more and more dissipated. As their original roles are turned upside down, she finally leaves him for another man; at the end of the novel he is completely broken. Victor Rosen's disintegration after his marriage to a patient echoes Dick Diver's decline.

The role reversal of David Rubinfine and Elaine May after their marriage was not quite so dramatic, but it also bears some resemblance to the archetypal story of Dick and Nicole Diver. "David Rubinfine thought of himself as an orthodox analyst," says his former supervisor, Dr. Margaret Gibson. "And to become sexually involved with a patient was a sin for an orthodox analyst. In the book of great rules in the sky, he had to feel very guilty about that whole thing. If you then add to that Rosa's suicide, which of course was her way of saying how *she* liked the whole idea of his leaving her, he had to have had a very unhappy life thereafter."

"I'm sure he felt very bad," Milton Wexler agrees. "But I don't know whether it would change his behavior. He was absolutely crazy about Elaine right to the day of his death."

At first, just as in the fictional marriage of the Divers, Rubinfine's role was to bolster May. In 1966 she was in Hollywood, acting in her first movie, the film version of a Broadway comedy called *Enter Laughing*. Janet Margolin, who was costarring in the movie, remembers seeing David Rubinfine accompany Elaine May to the set every day. "She seemed slightly fragile at the time," Margolin says, "and he was there holding her hand. Movie sets can be so awful, and you feel so lonely. I remember thinking, 'God, wouldn't it be great to have somebody who buffered you on the set.' It looked great to have somebody taking care of you that way."

Gradually, however, Rubinfine and May switched roles. May, who had been in the subordinate position as Rubinfine's analysand, soon became the stronger and more accomplished partner. "David and Elaine often had dinner with us in Stockbridge," Margaret Gibson recalls. "When I saw them together, they seemed like any couple we knew—*meshugah*, more or less happy and unhappy, up and down. My memory is that Elaine ran the show in their marriage, which might have been a very great relief after being on her back on the couch for five years."

Both Rubinfine and May were sensitive to the shift in their relationship as well as to the embarrassing scandal their romance had generated. When she gave a rare interview to gossip columnist Joyce Haber in 1968, May was not eager to have her husband identified as a psychiatrist. "Why don't you just say I'm married to a doctor?" she asked waggishly. "It'll make my mother happy."

For a time Rubinfine's involvement in his wife's work seemed to solidify the bond between them. Arthur Penn directed a play by May, *A Matter of Position,* in the Berkshires in the late 1960s. Rubinfine was a constant backstage presence. "David was there a lot, being very much engaged in the whole process," Penn reports. For her part May encouraged her husband's participation. Janice Rule remembers acting in a play in New York, not long after Rubinfine and May were married. "I asked Elaine to help me out because I had a very ineffectual director," Rule says. "I would go to their home after rehearsals, at eleven-thirty at night. Elaine was an insomniac anyway. She would not work on the scene unless I had somebody to act with, so David would stay up too. He loved working with us."

Rubinfine and May made an engaging, sometimes madcap pair in their first years together. Ralph Greenson's widow, Hildi, remembers one occasion when her husband was hospitalized for coronary illness. "David and Elaine came storming into the hospital at eleven o'clock at night with a bag of green apples," Mrs. Greenson recalls. "They said, 'We heard you like apples.' So that was when they came for a visit." Mrs. Greenson describes Rubinfine as "capable of being very wild and crazy, just like Elaine. I liked him very much, but I realized he was a totally unreliable person. So was Elaine. When we went to New York, they would say, 'We'll see you tomorrow, we'll call you.' You never heard from them."

In 1971 May made her debut as a film director with the shaggy-dog comedy *A New Leaf,* in which she also costarred with Walter Matthau. The following year she scored a triumph directing her own daughter, Jeannie Berlin, along with Charles Grodin, in *The Heartbreak Kid,* a cynical but hilarious comedy about a man who falls in love with another woman on his honeymoon. (The premise was not so different from May's experience in abruptly ending her own two-month marriage to Sheldon Harnick in order to pursue the love of her life.)

May's film career was moving into high gear, but she was also developing a reputation as an impossible perfectionist. Hollywood's wariness of women directors, coupled with her own headstrong nature, led to many wrangles with studio executives. On her third film, *Mikey and Nicky*, a dark view of male camaraderie starring her friends John Cassavetes and Peter Falk, May committed professional hara-kiri. The production budget was $1.8 million, but the cost rapidly escalated to $4.3 million. She finished shooting the movie in August 1973 and then spent two years editing 1.4 million feet of film. In the fall of 1975 she was still fiddling with the picture and asked Paramount for an additional $180,000 to complete it. The studio balked and ordered her to turn over the film immediately. She delivered it with two reels missing.

According to documents on file in New York Supreme Court, May went to her husband's New York apartment (by then they were keeping separate residences) when she received the order from Paramount. Following his wife's visit, Rubinfine admitted in a deposition, he went to the Carter Studio in New York, where the film was being stored and processed. He removed two reels of film and hid them overnight in the trunk of his car. The next day he delivered them to the home of a friend in New Britain, Connecticut. Then Rubinfine telephoned Peter Falk in California to inform him of the theft of the film. Soon afterwards the film was removed from the friend's home, though no one would say who had taken it.

Paramount brought charges of criminal contempt against May and Rubinfine in New York Supreme Court, and in his ruling the presiding judge declared that the couple had submitted no affidavits contradicting "the many serious allegations made against them." Finally, however, in the fall of 1976, May came to terms with the studio. The reels of film were returned, the criminal charges were dropped, Paramount supplied additional money to complete the picture (which eventually cost $5 million), and it was released a few months later—three years after the conclusion of shooting. *Mikey and Nicky* received some favorable notices but was a disastrous failure at the box office, putting a kibosh on May's directorial career until Warren Beatty gave her another chance on the equally catastrophic *Ishtar* a decade later. She continued to earn huge fees as a screenwriter and script doctor (on such films as *Heaven Can Wait* and *Tootsie*) but failed to win studio approval for her own personal projects.

May's career problems and Rubinfine's excommunication from the psychiatric establishment surely put added strain on their marriage. They decided to live separately, though they remained on friendly terms and never divorced. Rubinfine settled permanently in California in the mid-1970s, while May commuted back and forth between New York and Los Angeles. As Arthur Penn says, "David and Elaine couldn't stay married, but they loved each other." Each of them explored other relationships. For a time Rubinfine was keeping company with the estranged wife of another prominent Los Angeles analyst. One of Rubinfine's patients, Marty Gwinn Townsend, was curious about his unorthodox marriage and once asked him about it. She remembers that Rubinfine told her, "We have a terrific arrangement. I love Elaine. She loves me. We live separately."

While he continued to see patients, Rubinfine remained irresistibly attracted to Hollywood and enjoyed mingling with stars and studio executives. "David loved show business," says producer Julian Schlossberg, who also worked as May's personal manager. "He always wanted to hear what was grossing and what wasn't grossing." Through Elaine May, Rubinfine had plenty of ties to the Hollywood set. When director Robert Benton was doing research for his suspense thriller about a psychiatrist, *Still of the Night,* several friends suggested that he consult with David Rubinfine. Benton scheduled an appointment with the analyst for the day after the Academy Awards ceremony in April 1980. Both times that he mounted the podium of the Dorothy Chandler Pavilion to accept the Oscars he won for writing and directing *Kramer vs. Kramer,* Benton tripped on a stair. The next morning, when he went to meet Rubinfine, the first thing the analyst said to him was, "I thought it was very interesting that you stumbled both times when you went up the steps."

"Suddenly I had a notion of what it was like to be a patient," says Benton, who had never been in analysis. "I never even heard of analysis when I was growing up in Texas. David helped me gain new insight. He was tolerant of me as an extremely naive person."

His patients revered Rubinfine and appreciated his wide net of social contacts. One patient was sometime actress Judy Walker, the wife of actor Robert Walker, Jr., who was also treated by Rubinfine. "David was very open," Judy Walker says. "He had no rules. He came to his patients' birthday parties." He also got a kick out of using his connections to help advance their careers. "David gave show-business advice," Judy Walker reports. "He kept wanting me to make it as an actress. He set up appointments for me to see [agent] Sue Mengers, for example. He really wanted to see me grow as a woman, and if that meant setting up an appointment with a top agent, he would do it."

Another patient, Marty Gwinn Townsend, was working as a singer, and she, too, remembers that Rubinfine was eager to lend a helping hand. "He was seeing other people in the music business," Townsend says, "and he really wanted to use those contacts to help me." One of the doctor's good friends was Mo Ostin, the head of Warner Bros. Records, and Rubinfine urged Townsend to give him a demonstration tape that he could pass on to Ostin. "I never did it," Townsend explains, "because I was afraid that it would get in the way of our relationship. What if Mo Ostin rejected me? How would that affect my relationship with David? If I had been more desperate, I might have done it. I knew David was offering from the goodness of his heart, but it scared me."

Later, when she began dating Kim Townsend, an English professor at Amherst College, Marty asked Rubinfine to meet her new beau and assess their prospects. Dr. Rubinfine joined Marty and Kim and another friend of Marty's at a Santa Monica restaurant for dinner. "I was stunned by the oddity of the occasion," Kim Townsend recalls. "But then I'm a stuffy English professor from the East. This friend of Marty's was a disruptive presence at the dinner. She kept calling me by Marty's former boyfriend's name. But Rubinfine handled it all with panache. He came up with a verdict on the spot. I passed. I must admit I had stage fright before that dinner. In the modern age I suppose being judged by your girlfriend's psychiatrist is the equivalent of trial by fire."

Lovesick, the irreverent movie comedy about a psychiatrist who falls in love with a patient, ends on a blissful note. Dudley Moore's Dr. Benjamin feels liberated when he is thrown out of the priggish analytic society for his transgression. In the final scene he is reconciled with his lover in Central Park, and as dawn breaks over the city, a romantic panning shot around the park suggests that the happy couple have achieved a state of harmony with nature.

The real-life stories that parallel the screen fable did not end so idyllically. Depressed by his banishment from the New York Psychoanalytic Institute, Victor Rosen became heavily addicted to drugs, and soon his second marriage was on the rocks. He attempted suicide but was discovered in time, rushed to a hospital, and revived. The next time he was determined to succeed. On February 5, 1973, at the age of sixty-one, Victor Rosen drove his car deep into the woods near his Connecticut home, parked in a desolate spot where he was sure he would not be found for hours, and swallowed a bottle of barbiturates. His death was not reported as a suicide, so at least he was spared one last public indignity.

David Rubinfine's demise was not quite so ghastly. But he, too, died at the age of sixty-one. He was a heavy smoker and refused to quit, despite his worsening heart condition. On the morning of November 21, 1982, he suffered a fatal heart attack at his Santa Monica apartment. It was several hours later that his friend Peter Falk broke down the door of the apartment and found Rubinfine's body.

Falk, Marlo Thomas, Walter Matthau, and Jack Lemmon were among those who delivered eulogies at his funeral. Elaine May was also there, along with several of Rubinfine's patients and his numerous Hollywood friends. One patient, Judy Walker, attempted to talk to one of Rubinfine's daughters from his first marriage, but she rebuffed the contact, keeping very much to herself and avoiding the show-business crowd.

The scandals involving David Rubinfine and other analysts who broke the taboo against doctor-patient sex put psychiatrists under harsh critical scrutiny. Even before David Rubinfine married Elaine May, what Margaret Gibson calls the "iconic" image of the analyst had begun to erode, but the lurid gossip surrounding the lovesick shrinks accelerated the debunking process. "People make the assumption sometimes that psychiatrists or psychotherapists should be more perfect themselves," Nicholas Meyer observes. "They're just people."

Winifred Rosen raises a provocative issue when she suggests that her father's tragedy grew out of his inability to reconcile the discrepancy between the outside world's idealized view of the psychiatrist as an omniscient healer and his own painful awareness of his all-too-human flaws. "In a way that is the very same discrepancy that celebrities and stars have to deal with because they're so identified with the larger-than-life parts they've played," Rosen observes. "That may be why celebrities and psychiatrists were so drawn to each other. I wonder if anyone has ever compared the suicide rate of performing artists and that of analysts. I suspect they would both be higher than normal."

9. BREAKING THE RULES

In 1983, the same year that *Lovesick* took a mischievous look at psychiatrist-patient sex, another bittersweet comedy punctured the same taboo. *The Man Who Loved Women,* loosely adapted from François Truffaut's movie of the same name, starred Burt Reynolds as a bed-hopping Lothario unable to resist a shapely pair of legs. The tale is narrated by the protagonist's psychoanalyst (Julie Andrews), who recalls the sexual adventures that he described during their hours of therapy together. In one of these sessions the libidinous hero confesses to his therapist that he has fallen in love with her. The next scene shows the two of them naked in bed together.

The doctor-patient fling in *The Man Who Loved Women* did not provoke the same fury that *Lovesick* stirred, perhaps because sex between a female analyst and a male patient was less threatening to the predominantly male psychiatric establishment. Besides, the story line of the film was far less controversial than the unlikely collaboration that created it. The script was written by the film's director, Blake Edwards, his son Geoffrey Edwards, and Milton Wexler. Dr. Wexler, one of Hollywood's most prominent analysts, had been trying for years to have one of his screenplays filmed. *The Man Who Loved Women* marked the first screen credit for the seventy-five-year-old psychoanalyst. What made the occasion so remarkable was that Blake Edwards was his long-term patient, and Edwards was still in therapy with Wexler at the time they cowrote the picture.

Of all the renegade analysts of Hollywood, few have been more defiant than Milton Wexler. Others may have strained propriety and flouted the analytic canons, but no one did it quite so cavalierly as

Dr. Wexler. His collaboration with his patient on *The Man Who Loved Women* was not the first time Wexler strayed from the straight-and-narrow path of his profession. He had already enlisted many of his patients—including Blake Edwards; actresses Jennifer Jones, Carol Burnett, and Sally Kellerman; producer Jonathan Krane; architect Frank Gehry; and Claire Pollack, the wife of director Sydney Pollack—as major contributors to a medical research organization that he created, the Hereditary Disease Foundation. The ethical bylaws of the American Psychiatric Association state that a psychiatrist "must not exploit the treatment of a patient for his own financial gain or to promote his personal advantage." Wexler's critics charged that by using his patient connections to launch a screenwriting career, and by letting his patients bankroll his own foundation, he had violated this cardinal principle of the profession.

Milton Wexler's screenwriting debut may have set tongues wagging within the inner circles of the analytic institutes and among the cognoscenti at Hollywood cocktail parties. But Wexler never received the same public scrutiny as another Hollywood shrink who struck up an untoward partnership with a patient at around the same time.

Eugene Landy, a psychologist who treated Brian Wilson of the Beach Boys, was a sixth-grade dropout. He had worked briefly for RCA Records and as a writer for *Teen Screen* magazine before returning to school at the age of thirty-two and earning a Ph.D. in psychology from the University of Oklahoma. Drawing on his showbiz savvy, Landy was one of the first psychotherapists to prepare his own press kit. The flamboyant shrink described himself to one interviewer as a "hyperkinetic, perceptually disoriented, brain-damaged person."

Landy weaned Brian Wilson from drugs by using his trademark "twenty-four-hour therapy," a comprehensive plan that required a cadre of deputies to monitor the patient around the clock. In a chapter he wrote for the 1981 *Handbook of Innovative Psychotherapies*, Landy explained his revolutionary concept: "The success of 24-hour therapy rests on the extent to which the therapeutic team can exert control over every aspect of the patient's life." The therapists' aim, he said, was to "totally disrupt the privacy of their patients' lives, gaining complete control over every aspect of their physical, personal, social and sexual environments." Landy's fees for this unorthodox treatment ranged from ten to twenty thousand dollars a month. His celebrity clients included Rod Steiger, Richard Harris, and Alice Cooper.

With Brian Wilson, however, he went several steps further. While he was serving as Wilson's therapist, Landy also began acting as Wilson's executive producer and business manager; he even co-wrote several songs with the musician, claiming a 25 percent share of all royalties.

In February 1988 the California Board of Medical Quality Assurance charged Landy with ethical violations, stating that his participation "in the various dual, triple, and quadruple relationships has caused severe emotional damage, psychological dependency and financial exploitation to his patient." In 1989 the agency revoked Landy's license to practice as a psychologist, declaring that "the patient abuses were heinous."

In defending his affiliation with Wilson, Landy cited the screen-writing collaboration of Milton Wexler and Blake Edwards as an ostensibly respectable precedent. "Most people feel a doctor can't write songs or write at all—or manage or produce," Landy said. "But look at Blake Edwards's psychotherapist. He's written screenplays with his patient, who's also his friend."

Milton Wexler's creative and business partnership with Edwards did indeed raise ethical issues similar to those that led to the revocation of Dr. Landy's license. But Wexler is a very different personality from the "hyperkinetic" Eugene Landy, who favored blue jeans, cowboy boots, floral shirts, and tinted glasses, and who has been aptly likened to Jackie Mason. The tall, dapper Milton Wexler is the antithesis of such a crude tummler. "Milton is like a Connecticut Yankee," says his friend Jane Attias, whose family has known Wexler for many years. One of his former patients, the wasp-ish writer Peter Feibleman, agrees. "Milton is much more a New England character than a Hollywood or California character," says Feibleman. "I live in New England, and my sense of him is that he belongs in that landscape."

In fact Wexler is a native Californian—born in San Francisco in 1908. Writing, he declares, was always his first love, but that seemed like an impractical career ambition to a boy raised in an upwardly mobile Jewish family. "My brother was going to be a doctor, and that sort of meant I had to be a lawyer," Wexler says. He earned a law degree at New York University and practiced law for a few years before calling it quits. While he was in law school, he discovered Freud and devoured his writings. In 1939 Wexler went back to graduate school at Columbia University, earning a Ph.D. in clinical psychology. He took analytic training with Theodor Reik, another maverick lay analyst. Reik had ingratiated himself with Freud, who vigorously defended him when Austrian authorities tried to bar him from practicing therapy without a medical degree. Reik ran into the same problem after he settled in New York. He frequently irked the members of the medical establishment by challenging their dicta, and they tried to have him stripped of his credentials. This time it was Milton Wexler who rushed to Reik's defense. Wexler's background as a lawyer came in handy; he composed a letter on his legal stationery and sent it to the attorney general of the state of New York, protesting Reik's harassment at the hands of the medical psychiatrists. "They never dared to prosecute him," Wexler says with some satisfaction.

After serving in the navy during World War II, Wexler joined the staff of the Menninger Clinic in Topeka, Kansas, where he specialized in the treatment of schizophrenia. His early work with schizophrenics helped shape his unconventional modus operandi and sowed the seeds of his reputation as a rule-breaker. Wexler believed that the formal distance between doctor and patient required in orthodox Freudian analysis was completely ineffective in reaching psychotic patients, and he began experimenting with more direct intervention. He describes one breakthrough he had with a schizophrenic woman who for years had spoken nothing but gibberish. "She was a very powerful lady with big muscles," Wexler recalls. "One day I walked over to her, and she kicked me in the testicles. I was outraged, and on a reflex I slapped her right in the face. She said, 'Why did you do that?' It was the first coherent sentence she had spoken. I thought I had found a new approach to schizophrenia."

Wexler cited that experience in an article advocating a far more directive, literally hands-on approach with schizophrenic patients. He showed a draft of the article to his boss, Karl Menninger, who was horrified. "You can't say that you slapped a patient," Menninger told him. "Don't you know your career is over the minute you publish that?" Wexler revised the piece and worded his argument more gingerly, saying only that he had responded in kind to a patient's physical attack. Nevertheless, he became known in analytic circles as a bold experimenter willing to use any pragmatic means necessary to get results.

In 1951 Wexler left Kansas for greener pastures. Fifteen years earlier he had married Leonore Sabin. He did not know at the time that her family was afflicted with Huntington's disease (then called Huntington's chorea), a fatal neurological disorder that gradually destroys both the body and the mind. Leonore's father had died of the illness when she was a child, and she subsequently learned that it was a hereditary disease with a fifty-fifty chance of striking other family members. In the late 1940s all three of her brothers began to exhibit symptoms of Huntington's. To provide financial support for Leonore's family, Dr. Wexler decided to set up an analytic practice in Beverly Hills.

Wexler was tantalized by the prospect of living and working in the movie capital. He had enjoyed encountering the stars—such as Robert Walker—who came for treatment at Menninger's, and he recalls meeting the Academy Award–winning actress Luise Rainer once on a vacation. "What a lovely, charming, delightful woman!" Wexler exclaims. "I thought if all Hollywood people are this engaging, it must be a marvelous place to live."

Upon settling in Los Angeles, Wexler struck up an alliance with Ralph Greenson, who was instrumental in introducing him to the show-business crowd. On Sundays they often met for brunch at writer-producer Dore Schary's house, where the cream of Los Angeles society would gather—sometimes to hear Schary read his latest play or screenplay. The two analysts eventually became office mates, compared cases, and coauthored professional articles. When Greenson went on vacation, Wexler filled in for him; it was Wexler who treated Marilyn Monroe shortly before her death in the summer of 1962, while Greenson was in Switzerland.

Other Los Angeles analysts, who had heard about Wexler's innovative approaches to schizophrenia, referred their most difficult patients to him. John Altoon, a promising young painter, suffered a psychotic episode and came to Wexler for treatment. "He recovered rather rapidly," Wexler says, "and all the artists became interested in me."

Wexler's first therapy group consisted of Altoon and several of the artist's ex-girlfriends. That expanded into a larger collection of artists including Ron Davis, Ed Moses, and Frank Gehry. Although Wexler became known for specializing in group therapy, he had no special background in conducting groups. He began treating the artists together largely as an economy measure. "I had to shoo them out and put them in a group," Wexler explains. "I told them, 'Forget about individual therapy, you guys are going to bankrupt me.' They never paid their bills!" But he soon discovered that group work could be extremely effective. "There was a lot of catharsis in those interactions," Wexler says.

The analyst's growing reputation was enhanced by the reflected glory of his successful patients. Frank Gehry's association with Wexler was especially important in this regard. When he first entered therapy, Gehry was a journeyman architect doing home remodeling. Several years later he was winning prizes and prestigious assignments all over the world. "Frank would make casual remarks about my being responsible for his success," Wexler says. "I'm not responsible. He's just a great architect." But Wexler did encourage Gehry to follow his own example and break the rules. "I may have given him permission to defy the world or say the hell with the critics and even the customers," Wexler acknowledges. "But suddenly other architects would come to me and expect me to make them great architects."

While his professional career was advancing, Wexler found himself confronted with a stark personal crisis. In 1968 Leonore Wexler was diagnosed with Huntington's disease. Wexler had divorced her four years earlier. What their daughter Nancy described as Leonore's growing sadness and listlessness had driven a painful wedge between the couple. But even after their divorce Wexler continued to contribute to her financial support. In addition to his alimony payments, his ex-wife's hospital bills for the next ten years, until her death in 1978, were overwhelming. Wexler faced another daunting financial burden if his two daughters, who were also at risk for Huntington's, should become ill. That alarming prospect set him on a new course, one that required a full stable of well-heeled patients.

In 1922 Sigmund Freud encouraged one of his analysands, an American psychiatrist named Horace Frink, to leave his wife and marry one of Dr. Frink's former patients, Angelika Bijur, the wife of a New York millionaire and a wealthy heiress in her own right. Freud diagnosed Dr. Frink as a latent homosexual and warned him that his problems might intensify if he stayed in his present marriage; on the other hand, Freud suggested, a marriage to Mrs. Bijur could cure him. When Frink resisted the idea of his latent homosexuality, Freud wrote to him, somewhat whimsically, "Your complaint that you cannot grasp your homosexuality implies that you are not yet aware of your phantasy of making me a rich man. If matters turn out all right let us change this imaginary gift into a real contribution to the Psychoanalytic Funds." These funds had been established to promote psychoanalytic research and were personally controlled by Freud himself.

At Frink's suggestion Mrs. Bijur also came to Vienna and met with Freud, who urged her to marry Frink and thus help sublimate his homosexual tendencies. When Angelika Bijur's husband learned of Freud's role in this bizarre matchmaking scheme, he wrote the master an outraged letter and threatened to expose him: "Great Doctor, are you a savant or a charlatan?" Horace Frink and Angelika Bijur did indeed divorce their respective spouses and marry each other, but their marriage lasted less than two years.

Half a century later, as he was creating his own research foundation, Dr. Milton Wexler also played Cupid to a pair of wealthy charges, actress Jennifer Jones and tycoon Norton Simon. Jones, an emotionally fragile, chronically dependent woman, had been in therapy since the age of twenty-four, and she became a fervent champion of psychoanalysis; she encouraged her friends and her children to partake of its wonders. "Mother was always happiest if every member of her family was in analysis," says her son, Robert Walker, Jr.

When she first entered treatment, Jones was trying to adjust to her sudden ascent to stardom as well as to the turmoil in her personal life. Her first major film, *The Song of Bernadette*, won her an Academy Award as best actress of 1943. At the time she made that movie, she was still married to Robert Walker; but then she entered into an extramarital affair with David O. Selznick, who had discovered her and signed her to a long-term contract two years earlier. Selznick himself was an analytic enthusiast. He was on the couch of May Romm, who served as his consultant on both *Spellbound* and *Since You Went Away*, an inspirational wartime drama in which Walker played Jones's fiancé, a soldier who is killed in battle. In that movie the grief-stricken Jones visits a beneficent psychiatrist, aptly named Dr. Golden, who helps her to come to terms with her loss.

That cinematic encounter set a pattern that Jones would act out in real life as she sought the counsel of a long succession of eminent shrinks, including Selznick's doctor, May Romm. After marrying Selznick in 1949, Jones went on to sample the wares of analysts all over the world.

Despite her lengthy analysis, Jones's emotional condition deteriorated over the years. Robert Walker's gruesome death at the age of thirty-two contributed to her feelings of guilt, and her marriage to Selznick was burdened by his compulsive gambling, his addiction to amphetamines, and his mania for control. Managing her career turned into Selznick's full-time occupation. When Vincente Minnelli directed Jennifer in *Madame Bovary* in 1949, Selznick would fire off dozens of instructional memos, even about such minute matters as his wife's eyebrows. "It would be sheer folly to tamper with them to the slightest extent," Selznick wrote Minnelli. "I will appreciate it if you will leave them strictly alone, and will assume this to be so unless I hear from you further." Twelve years later, when Jennifer made *Tender Is the Night,* Selznick insisted that she have her coiffure done at home every morning so that he could make sure every hair was in place before she departed for the studio.

Selznick's fanatical protectiveness only heightened his wife's dependency. When the overbearing producer died of a heart attack in 1965, Jones was utterly bereft. By that time her movie career was already in decline. Following the failure of *Tender Is the Night,* the only roles she got were in low-budget potboilers.

On November 10, 1967, Jones checked into a Malibu motel under the name Phyllis Walker. She took a handful of Seconals, then called her physician and told him that she wanted to die. She drove to a deserted cliff overlooking Point Dume and climbed down to the beach. Her doctor meanwhile notified the Malibu sheriff's station, and several officers rushed to the scene, where they discovered the actress lying unconscious in the shallow surf.

Shortly after that incident—her third attempt at suicide—Jones was referred to Dr. Milton Wexler. "She came to me to try and stop that kind of behavior," Wexler says. During the next few years, through intensive therapy with Wexler, Jones underwent a remarkable transformation. She gained confidence and became one of Hollywood's premier hostesses and a shrewd businesswoman as well. Wexler ministered to her during some very difficult crises, including the suicide of her twenty-one-year-old daughter, Mary Jennifer Selznick, who plunged to her death from the top of a Los Angeles skyscraper in 1976.

Just as he had with his schizophrenic patients in Topeka, Wexler took a very active role in running his Hollywood analysands' lives. He was not content to sit back and listen silently, in the conventional Freudian style. Instead he gave forceful direction, often telling his patients exactly what he thought they should do. But this peremptory approach was precisely what malleable personalities like Jennifer Jones seemed to crave.

In 1971 Jones was introduced to Norton Simon. As the head of Hunt Foods Co., the hard-driving Simon had built the tiny firm into a major international conglomerate. His art collection alone was worth more than a billion dollars. Simon had divorced his wife of thirty-seven years in 1970, a few months after his unsuccessful bid for the U.S. Senate and a year after his son had committed suicide.

Jones said that one of the main things that drew her to Simon was their shared "profound involvement" in psychiatry. Simon himself had been in therapy since the early 1950s, and he was almost as enthusiastic an acolyte as Jones. On their second date Jones asked Milton Wexler to tag along. "I brought my psychoanalyst along to look him over," Jones remarked. "I was gold-digging for a project I was working on, the Huntington's Disease foundation." That organization, of course, was Dr. Wexler's own charitable foundation.

A few days later Simon invited *his* psychoanalyst to size up Jennifer. The two shrinks gave their blessings, and a month after Simon and Jones first met, they were married. As Jones later observed, they had a rather unusual prenuptial agreement. "Norton said to me, 'I'm a crook and you're a crook—what do you want?' So he gave a substantial sum to the Huntington's Disease foundation and didn't get much from me but a dowry of chipped china and worn Porthauldt sheets." Simon also threw in a three-million-dollar painting by the seventeenth-century master Francisco de Zurbarán.

For Milton Wexler the nuptials represented not just a personal triumph for his most famous patient but also a considerable financial boon to his own fledgling foundation, which he had launched in 1968, right after learning of his ex-wife's illness. A major scientific research fund required the patronage of wealthy sponsors, and Wexler was not averse to accepting donations from the occupants of his couch. Over the next several years his therapeutic practice became filled with show-business personalities; it also became inextricably intertwined with the work of his foundation.

One of Wexler's mentors, Karl Menninger, had set the pattern by seeking donations from the Hollywood crowd—including his patients and their families—for his psychiatric research foundation. But Menninger found the Californians somewhat parsimonious. After one of his fund-raising trips to the Coast, he wrote to his training analyst, Ruth Mack Brunswick, "Although we got a few thousand dollars, we were on the whole very disappointed, as we had hoped to get about a hundred thousand dollars out there."

Milton Wexler proved to be far more adept at drawing big bucks out of his celebrity patients and their friends. Jennifer Jones became his number-one backer. She made her last movie in 1974, playing Fred Astaire's charred love interest in *The Towering Inferno*. After that she devoted herself to managing her husband's art collection, creating her own Jennifer Jones Simon Foundation for Mental Health and Education, and toiling on behalf of Dr. Wexler's Hereditary Disease Foundation. "In many ways it gave Jennifer life," Wexler says with paternalistic pride. In 1977 Jones made a personal pitch for Wexler's organization before members of the Senate Appropriations Committee. "She became a very important factor in Washington," Wexler adds. "Jennifer can walk into the Senate dining room and be recognized by everybody there and have a wonderful time and feel very significant."

Jones and Norton Simon donated huge sums to support Wexler's research organization. Other patients—including Blake Edwards, Dudley Moore, Sally Kellerman, and Frank Gehry—were also named to the board of directors of the Hereditary Disease Foundation. At Wexler's group-therapy sessions, which always included at least half a dozen of Hollywood's prime movers, the foundation was a regular subject of conversation. In 1975 literary agent Nancy Hardin joined Wexler's group, which then met twice a week in his Beverly Hills office. "In the first few weeks," Hardin recalls, "everyone started talking about a benefit that was being run by Jennifer, a fashion show at the Beverly Wilshire Hotel." Hardin emphasizes, as do most of Wexler's other patients, that Wexler never solicited contributions directly. "It was just something you'd hear about," she explains. "I first found out about the fund raiser because it was being discussed in group. Finally I volunteered that I was feeling left out and miserable. Jennifer invited me to come, sort of as her poor relation, because at that time I didn't have a lot of money. After a while I wanted to pull my weight and contribute."

Others give a similar account of how they came to donate money. "Knowing Milton, you would just naturally become involved," Blake Edwards says, "because of the story of his two daughters and the fact that it's possible they could come down with Huntington's [disease]. Getting to know about him, little by little, it was a foregone conclusion that I would get involved with the foundation and try to do what I can to help out. Once a year we bring the scientists out. They show up at one of the board members' houses. We give a party for them, and they have this workshop where they all meet and brainstorm. You get to meet all these Nobel laureates in your house, and they appreciate it so much. They're kind of wonderfully naive about Hollywood." Those patients invited to the parties were the biggest contributors to the foundation. Anyone who put up at least $1,500 a year received a donated print by Ron Davis or Ed Moses.

The "fashion show" of which Nancy Hardin speaks took place on April 3, 1976. Dubbed the "Shower of Stars," the fund-raiser at the Beverly Wilshire Hotel turned into one of the splashiest social events of the decade. Wexler's patients delivered the star power, which generated the kind of publicity that few other charities could match. Gregory Peck was chairman of the gala; Cary Grant acted as doorman; Walter Matthau, Jack Nicholson, Warren Beatty, Kirk Douglas, and Jack Lemmon were enlisted as fashion commentators. Cher, Carol Burnett, Jacqueline Bisset, Anjelica Huston, Diahann Carroll, and Sally Kellerman modeled the designer rags. Among the 750 guests were Elizabeth Taylor, Candice Bergen, Alfred and Betsy Bloomingdale, Barbara Walters, and Rosalind Russell. Dr. Wexler gratefully introduced the evening's hostess: "a woman of great dignity, great generosity, deep caring, who brought this all together—Jennifer Jones Simon." Then Jones herself took the podium and declared, "Helping is just another form of loving, and I want to thank you all for being such great lovers."

Reporters who covered the affair never mentioned that many guests and sponsors were Dr. Wexler's patients. One article referred to Wexler only as a "scientist," rather than as a psychoanalyst.

Over the years Wexler continued to earn glowing press for his foundation—largely as a result of his connections. In 1986, *60 Minutes*, the most formidable investigative show on TV, did a human-interest story about Wexler, his daughters, and the work of his foundation without reporting that many of the foundation's major donors were also Wexler's patients. Diane Sawyer (whose husband-to-be, Mike Nichols, was an intimate of Wexler's show-business cronies) narrated the segment and interviewed Wexler and his daughters.

Other members of the fourth estate joined the lovefest. Advice columnist Ann Landers has on occasion been scathingly critical of the psychiatric establishment. In the summer of 1992 she devoted an entire column to touting a book called *You Must Be Dreaming*, which accused Dr. Jules Masserman, a past president of the American Psychiatric Association, of repeatedly raping his patients. Landers attacked the APA for failing to expel Masserman. She wrote, "The psychiatric community does, indeed, take care of its own, but Ann Landers takes care of *her* own too, and this column will be read by 90 million people."

Landers's pen could swing both ways. She is a close friend of Milton Wexler's, and he has often escorted her to parties. She could hardly be considered a disinterested observer. Nevertheless, in 1983 she gave his foundation an extraordinary plug. Responding to a letter from a couple who wanted the name of a worthy charity, Landers recommended the Hereditary Disease Foundation: "No other foundation comes close," she wrote. "Its integrity is exemplary." Nine years later Milton Wexler's daughter Nancy, the president of the foundation, sent a note of thanks to Ann Landers, which was printed in her daily column: "Since you gave us that generous accolade nine years ago, we have been named as beneficiary in a number of wills from people throughout the country. In some instances, the entire estate has been donated to the Hereditary Disease Foundation. This is a remarkable testimonial to the trust that people have in you, Ann Landers." It was also a remarkable testimonial to the financial clout of Milton Wexler's well-placed friends. "I would like my readers to be aware that I know your organization intimately, having served on the board for 16 years," Landers replied to Nancy Wexler. "Those of you who want to support a truly fine cause need look no further."

No one denies that the Hereditary Disease Foundation has done valuable research work in seeking a cure for a horrific illness or that it is a well-run and worthy charity. But does that justify an analyst's enlisting vulnerable patients to support a foundation that was created in part to aid his own family? Wexler insists that he never strong-armed patients for money. But when asked whether some of them might not feel a subtle pressure, knowing that they would please their analyst by contributing, he replies, "Maybe they do. It's possible. But I don't feel that hurts them. I believe in that foundation. I think it's one of the best foundations in America. If my patients give to a foundation which does some remarkable work, if they have the gratification of knowing that we have advanced the cause of genetics monumentally, I don't see what's wrong with that."

One of Wexler's patients who did see something wrong was

writer-director David Seltzer. "I admire Milton as a smart man," Seltzer says, "but I question the use of power, which is abject and total, in getting patients to contribute money to your favorite charity."

Nor is it simply the effect on patients that is at issue. What happens to the objectivity of the analyst when he needs and wants his patients' financial support for a fund that he oversees? Nancy Hardin, for one, believes that Wexler did tend to play favorites. "I do feel that rich people were more important to Milton than those who couldn't contribute quite so much," Hardin says. "Some people like Jennifer really did give an awful lot. It would not be human not to give them some preference."

Those who know him are quick to point out that Wexler was not seeking personal enrichment from his wealthy patients. By all accounts he lived rather modestly; he preferred Clifton's cafeteria to Morton's, and when he entertained at his Santa Monica apartment, it was usually with spaghetti dinners rather than Beluga caviar. But regardless of the setting, he seemed to delight in rubbing elbows with the cultural elite. "Some people say Milton only goes to parties and cultivates famous people because of the foundation," Nancy Hardin comments. "I don't believe that. I feel he likes famous, high-up people."

In contrast to traditional analysts who scrupulously avoid any social contact with patients, Wexler attended parties and premieres with his analysands, spent Thanksgiving and Christmas with some of them, and joined them in all sorts of other extracurricular activities. During the 1970s, when the "human-potential" fad est swept through the entertainment business, Wexler decided to see what all the fuss was about. He signed up for a VIP seminar in San Francisco run by Werner Erhard himself. "I went up there with Jennifer," Wexler nonchalantly remarks, "because she was interested in the experience too. We had a ball."

Wexler also took trips with other patients. He once cruised down the Nile aboard Max Palevsky's chartered yacht, part of an elite sailing party that included writer Peter Feibleman and Feibleman's companion, Lillian Hellman. Sometimes Dr. Wexler's patients would rent a vacation home near his own Lake Tahoe retreat, and the analyst would even help to make the necessary arrangements with the real estate agent. Wexler claims that in such instances he was only following the example of his own analyst, Theodor Reik, who frequently took his patients along with him when he traveled.

But other analysts object in principle to such cozy camaraderie, arguing that it can compromise the therapy. "Let's assume that a patient becomes very angry at his therapist," says Dr. Samuel Klagsbrun, the director of Four Winds Hospital in Katonah, New York. "If they have this buddy-buddy relationship, and they go to parties together, will the patient express anger, disappointment, criticism, conflict? How much is the friendship covering up rage or the range of complicated, difficult emotions that patients need to express if therapy is ongoing? In effect you are robbing your own patients of an opportunity to work with you."

Or as Los Angeles psychoanalyst Melvin Mandel puts it, "You can be very effective as a friend. But if you're going to be a psychoanalytic therapist, you must maintain distance from your patient. If you allow that to get eroded by an excessive identification with your patient or by some desire to be liked or taken in by your patient into a circle, or a desire to take your patient into your circle, it begins to contaminate that professional relationship. Instead of seeking out a very difficult, dirty, hard truth, you tend to smooth over something. Ideally analytic work is done like surgery, in a sterile environment."

Notwithstanding the disapproval of his colleagues, Wexler persisted in blurring the line between therapy and friendship. Most of his patients savored their social ties with his extended family, though a few were put off by its glittery ambience. "I think a famous person corrupts a therapy group," says David Seltzer. "I've seen groups change when a celebrity joins. There just comes into the room a self-consciousness and a sense of excitement, and I think what you're trying to accomplish is the opposite; you're trying to diffuse people's self-consciousness. Everyone wants to be loved by a famous person. So you will start being your best self. You're not going to want that celebrity to know you went behind the barn and did this or that. You want to be invited to their parties. I can't imagine a group in Hollywood without at least one superstar, and Milton Wexler certainly hit the jackpot."

Most other analysts who specialized in group therapy conducted several groups, and they would take care to place their famous patients in separate groups. But Wexler had only one group, which sometimes had as many as twenty-five members, and it was top-heavy with stars. Newcomers who joined the fold were instantly dazzled. "I walked into group, and there was Jennifer Jones, an idol from my childhood," Nancy Hardin recalls. "And Frank Gehry and so many others. When I told friends on the East Coast about the group, they said it sounded like a social club. To some extent it was. I hated to miss it because it was the most interesting place to be, the best soap opera in town. I wanted to hear what happened every week." Yet Hardin concedes that the group was not always so blissfully communal. Cliques formed, and some members would be excluded from others' parties, or they might not be invited for a weekend retreat at someone's ranch in Santa Barbara. "Feelings got hurt, and sometimes you wouldn't be as honest because you wanted to be invited," Hardin says.

The group could foster professional conflicts as well as petty social rivalries. In 1976 Hardin secured a plum job as vice president of production at Paramount. As a Wellesley-educated former book editor, she was expected to bring prestige projects to the studio. Another Paramount vice president, Don Simpson, represented a different constituency; an aggressive hustler, he was tagged to discover macho action pictures, and he ended up coproducing such testosterone-driven hits as *Beverly Hills Cop* and *Top Gun*. Simpson was no fan of psychotherapy. He had grown up in Alaska and scorned anything associated with high-toned intellectuals. "Don had a love-hate relationship with the group," Hardin says, "just as he had a love-hate relationship with the Ivy League. He was threatened by both." The two vice presidents jockeyed for the favor of their boss, Michael Eisner. Often, Hardin says, Simpson would try to sabotage her by deliberately scheduling executive meetings at the hour he knew Wexler's group met.

Once, another member of the group, a producer who sometimes did business with Paramount, shared with Simpson a couple of the unflattering comments that Hardin had made about both Simpson and Eisner during supposedly confidential group therapy sessions. Simpson gleefully informed Hardin that her fellow analysand had spilled the beans. "I called Milton at home because I was so upset," Hardin says. "That might have cost me my job."

That was not the most traumatic incident that Hardin endured during therapy. One night as the group was sharing intimate secrets in Wexler's penthouse office in Beverly Hills, they were distracted by a noise coming from the anteroom. Wexler went out to investigate and returned with a man holding a gun to his head. The thief had been rummaging through some empty offices after hours, and when he reached the penthouse, he was startled to discover a klatsch of rich celebrities unburdening themselves. He proceeded to unburden them of their money and jewelry.

News of the holdup quickly made the rounds in Hollywood. "A lot of people in the industry who were actually at that session heard the story pitched back to them by writers who had been told about it and thought it was a great premise for a TV movie," Nancy Hardin says. Hardin herself recounted the tale to her friend Nora Ephron, who included a scene of a robbery during group therapy in the novel and screenplay for *Heartburn*. When the episode turned up in the movie version, which featured Meryl Streep as the heroine and Maureen Stapleton as her therapist, it seemed like an outlandishly farcical interlude; only a few insiders recognized the real-life inspiration.

Wexler's group shared many close encounters, which helped to intensify the bond among them. Long before *The Player* joked about AA meetings as fertile ground for Hollywood networking, Wexler's therapy group became one of the town's secret power units. At times lucrative movie deals were cemented in between personal confessions. Blake Edwards was in a quandary when George Segal dropped out of *10*—his tale of a lusty composer trying to adjust to middle age—on the first day of filming; but Edwards had to search no farther than Dr. Wexler's group to find a replacement. "Suddenly one night," Edwards says, "I looked over and thought, 'I've been sitting here all this time, and the man I'm writing about in the movie is facing me.' "

That man was Dudley Moore. Just like Edwards's fictional character, Moore compulsively pursued young women who could rate a perfect 10. "I never would have known that Dudley was ideal for the part if I hadn't known his psychoanalytic profile," Edwards notes. The director took Moore aside after their therapy session ended, told him about the movie, and they started shooting a few weeks later.

Edwards also met his business partner of several years, Jonathan Krane, in the group. Krane was a financial whiz kid who had achieved great success as an international tax lawyer before he turned thirty. "But I hated the law," Krane says. "That was one of the reasons I went into therapy." Krane was soon enraptured by the show-business luminaries he met in Dr. Wexler's group. "They were much more interesting than the lawyers I knew," Krane says. Wexler, as a former attorney himself, encouraged his patient's career change, and Blake Edwards, who had come to know Krane as an articulate presence in group, brought him into his company to produce half a dozen movies.

Krane made another important contact at those therapy sessions. Sally Kellerman, the husky-voiced actress who had first come to prominence playing "Hot Lips" Hoolihan in Robert Altman's *M*A*S*H*, was a long-term member of Wexler's group. She had sought treatment after her first marriage broke up and her personal manager died; therapy helped to restore her equilibrium. When Jonathan Krane joined her therapy group, Kellerman found rejuvenation of a different kind. She was instantly attracted to Krane, whom she once described as "a Jewish Warren Beatty."

"After about six months Sally asked me out," recalls Krane, who is almost fifteen years younger than Kellerman. "We immediately told the people in the group we were dating. The problem with a lot of relationships is that there is no one to comment on it. But it's impossible to have a relationship in front of a bunch of other people and not have it be more honest." Of their unusual courtship Kellerman once said, "I'm thrilled to have met him there [in group therapy] because it's like belonging to the same church."

The couple tied the knot on May 11, 1980, at the Malibu estate of Jennifer Jones and Norton Simon. Dr. Wexler was there, as were most members of the group. "Jonathan's family was not at the wedding, but the group was," Nancy Hardin reports with some amusement. Frank Gehry personally redesigned the newlyweds' hilltop home.

Such fond fraternization among the members of Wexler's charmed circle did not delight everyone. "It was too incestuous for me," says David Seltzer, who eventually defected from Wexler's group to join one organized by another popular therapist, Evelyn Silvers, the onetime "Revlon girl" and former wife of comedian Phil Silvers. Dudley Moore also joined Silvers's group, though he decided to stay in Wexler's group as well. When the members of Wexler's group learned that Moore was part of another Hollywood group run by a rival therapist, they were apoplectic. Who knew what secrets he might be telling Silvers's patients about *them*? "It was felt as a complete betrayal," says Hunter Murtaugh, who was working as a Paramount executive at the time. "Everyone wanted to banish him from our group. Of course if you had a real job, if you worked for Con Ed, would you have the time or money to go to two groups? It was a big issue to the patients, though Milton found it amusing."

*   *   *

Wexler's patients were not the only ones who benefited from the industry contacts they made in group therapy. The analyst himself was more than happy to cut a deal. Ever since he was a teenager and penned a play about Rasputin, Wexler had had the itch to become a professional writer. He churned out dozens of stories, screen treatments, and screenplays in his spare time. On occasion he had asked patients such as Jonathan Krane and Nancy Hardin to take a look at them. "He shows these things to anybody who will read them," Hardin says.

Linda Palmer, a novelist who was married to Warner Bros. chief Ted Ashley, recalls that in one session she had with Wexler he pulled out a script. "It was about Huntington's disease," Palmer says. "He wanted me to give it to Ted." According to Palmer, she refused and left Wexler for good after that session.

Blake Edwards was far more receptive to his analyst's literary aspirations. Edwards was another habitué of the couch. "I couldn't have had a family if I hadn't gotten into therapy," Edwards says, "because I'm too fucked up. I'm a major hypochondriac."

To alleviate his real and imagined ills, Edwards started popping pills when he was a young man and became dependent on them. He was also beset with sexual confusions. "From my very early days in Hollywood," Edwards says, "I gained a reputation for being a homosexual. I don't know whether it still exists, although I hear that occasionally it does come up. If I were gay, I would have no trouble with it, particularly now. Quite the contrary was true of me, which may indicate that I have a stronger feminine side than a lot of men care to admit. I have always been the worst woman chaser in the world, and for a while I was suspicious that maybe I was trying to cover up something as far as being a homosexual. Maybe by chasing women I was trying to prove desperately that I wasn't gay. Therefore I got into therapy." Eventually Edwards came to realize that although he had had "some homosexual fantasies" and "homosexual childhood adventures," his strongest desires were heterosexual.

In fact, his womanizing seemed to control his life. It destroyed his first marriage, to actress Patricia Walker, and led to a series of self-destructive relationships. Then he fell in love with Julie Andrews, when he directed her in *Darling Lili* in 1969. By that time Edwards was in treatment with Milton Wexler, the third therapist he had consulted. The marriage to Andrews lasted, partly because she, too, was a devotee of psychoanalysis. Her doctor, Gerald Aronson, was a friend of Wexler's from his days at the Menninger Clinic. Aronson was another veteran Hollywood shrink, whose star patients included Marlon Brando and Anthony Perkins. Andrews saw Dr. Aronson every day for years. She also notes that she and Edwards have had "many a joint session" with either Aronson or Wexler.

Edwards preferred Wexler to his previous analysts because Wexler was not a classical Freudian obsessed with childhood miseries; he was more interested in helping Edwards solve his present problems—his occasional writer's block, his hypochondria, as well as his lingering sexual compulsions. Edwards had intensive private sessions with Wexler in addition to group therapy. "They were fascinating times in that group," Edwards says. "They were all such bright people and so wonderfully emotional—and such children." Edwards was so high on the experience that he even persuaded his daughter, Jennifer, an aspiring actress, to join the group with him. Though that was a highly unorthodox arrangement, Dr. Wexler had no trouble accepting it.

Edwards's immersion in analysis proved to have a profound impact on his work as a writer-director. His early films were mostly genre pieces—lightweight slapstick comedies (*Operation Petticoat, The Great Race, The Pink Panther*) and suspense thrillers (the *Peter Gunn* TV series, *Experiment in Terror*)—or they were dramas adapted from other writers' work (*Breakfast at Tiffany's, Days of Wine and Roses*). The box-office debacle of the extravagantly over-produced musical *Darling Lili* almost ended Edwards's career, and he retreated to Europe for several years in the 1970s. (The major obstacle to that move, he once said, was that it required a separation from Dr. Wexler.) Then his fortunes rebounded with three highly lucrative sequels to *The Pink Panther*, which he had directed a decade earlier. The profits from those films, together with his share in merchandising spin-offs, made him a multimillionaire. With that financial cushion Edwards felt liberated artistically. Beginning with *10*, which he wrote soon after returning to Los Angeles (and to Dr. Wexler's therapy group), his films became increasingly personal and psychologically self-conscious.

The early scene in *10*, when Dudley Moore spies Bo Derek on her wedding day and pursues her in a feverish trance, was a comic emblem of Edwards's own compulsions. Edwards freely admitted that the promiscuous hero of that movie—a character type whom he would also scrutinize in *The Man Who Loved Women* and *Skin Deep*—was his alter ego. *Switch*, which focused on such a Don Juan reincarnated as a woman, expressed Edwards's fascination with ambisexuality, a theme explored earlier in *Victor/Victoria*, in which Julie Andrews played a woman impersonating a man impersonating a woman. *That's Life!* was an especially intimate self-portrait, about a hypochondriacal architect trying to deal with his feelings of personal failure on the occasion of his sixtieth birthday. Milton Wexler had not only "saved his bacon," as Edwards put it, but had helped to transform the very nature of his work.

Edwards had an equally significant impact on Wexler. Over the years Wexler became as close to Blake Edwards and Julie Andrews as he was to Jennifer Jones and Norton Simon. "Time has made us friends as well as patients," Andrews says. "I think it's just something that happens after a certain amount of work's been done." If the Simons offered the promise of huge sums of money for Wexler's foundation, Blake Edwards had something else to offer—the screenwriting opportunity that the analyst craved.

When he was working on *10*, Edwards asked Wexler's advice on a dream sequence he was contemplating. Wexler eagerly sat down and wrote three or four possible dream sequences and handed them to the director. "He didn't use them, but he did comment on the fact that they were well written," Wexler says. During the next few years Edwards asked his therapist for more advice on his movie scripts. Edwards cannot recall the specific moment when they decided to collaborate. He describes the process as a slowly evolving redefinition of their relationship. "There came a time when it became less clinical, and more friendship," Edwards says. "That didn't preclude the clinical side. We were both perfectly capable of dropping into that when it was needed. But in twenty years I learned an awful lot about the man I was dealing with. He had always wanted to be a writer and writes a lot, constantly. So one day I said, 'Hey, Milton, why don't we just put the therapy in one slot over here when I really need it, and in the meantime let's write something together.' And he said, 'Sure, I'd love to.' "

When Edwards began preparing *The Man Who Loved Women*, he decided to give his elderly analyst his big break. In refashioning François Truffaut's tender romantic comedy, Edwards added a female psychiatrist to the cast of characters and even dramatized a sexual liaison between the analyst and her hedonistic patient. Edwards immediately asked Dr. Wexler for his advice on the script. At first Edwards hired Wexler as technical consultant, then decided that his analyst's contribution had become so integral that he deserved a cowriting credit. Dr. Wexler was also on the set during shooting, and Julie Andrews, who played the psychiatrist, remembers that he offered a number of suggestions on how to act the part convincingly. "Obviously I pinched all I could from what I'd learned and seen," Andrews says. "Milton did supervise the screenplay, and he guided us so that we did not go wrong."

The Man Who Loved Women was a commercial flop, but the experience intensified Wexler's appetite for filmmaking. Even before that he had enjoyed visiting the sets of Edwards's movies and gabbing with the actors. "Guys like Richard Mulligan and Jack Lemmon were just a pleasure," Wexler says. Now, at last, he had a chance to become a full creative partner. In 1986 Edwards and he collaborated again, but this time the analyst played a much larger role in shaping the screenplay. Unlike *The Man Who Loved Women, That's Life!* was not based on another writer's story; it was created from scratch by Wexler and Edwards. In fact, on the screen it was Wexler who received first credit as writer.

Edwards put up the entire two-million-dollar budget for the film himself. He also recruited friends and family to participate for deferred salaries. Jack Lemmon, who had worked with Edwards several times before, signed on to play the lead, and Lemmon's wife, Felicia Farr, and son, Chris, also joined the cast. Julie Andrews was enlisted to play the protagonist's wife, a singer who discovers a tumor in her throat that may be malignant. Andrews's daughter, Emma Walton, played one of the couple's children, and Edwards's daughter, Jennifer, played another. The executive producer of the film was Jonathan Krane, a friend from group therapy; and Krane's wife, Sally Kellerman, another Wexler patient, was cast as a next-door neighbor. This glossy home movie was even filmed at the Edwardses' Malibu beach house.

The script was equally unconventional. Edwards and Wexler wrote a thirteen-page treatment summarizing all the events that were to take place in the course of the story. Then Wexler wrote detailed, psychologically oriented character sketches for each member of the cast. Utilizing the outline and the notes prepared by Wexler, the actors got together and improvised the scenes. Edwards describes the process: "Milton would be on the set, because we didn't have a script. It was almost like group therapy. We would sit and talk about this character and what they would say and what they wouldn't say and where they were coming from, and he would kind of conduct a seminar in a way that we eventually would get up and shoot."

Dr. Wexler was exhilarated by the making of *That's Life!* and thrilled to see Oscar-winning actors take their cue from him. "We improvised as we went along, so I'd be telling Jack Lemmon what to say to Julie in bed and how to be hysterical about the blood count or something like that," Wexler remembers. "I wish I had started writing much earlier."

The film may have been a lark to make, but like *The Man Who Loved Women*, it went belly-up at the box office. It also suggested the perils of having a psychotherapist as creator: it was riddled with earnest truisms and naked self-indulgence. Most reviewers pronounced the picture well-meaning but banal. *The New Republic*'s Stanley Kauffmann summed up the prevailing sentiment when he dismissed *That's Life!* as "a ragout of old movies" and derided "the triteness of every situation and all the dialogue."

Caveats about the aesthetic merits of *That's Life!* were overshadowed by the ethical questions surrounding Dr. Wexler's decision to become his own patient's writing partner. In an interview with *The New York Times* right before the movie opened, Wexler tried to deflect some of the inevitable carping. "Every strict Freudian will think this collaboration is anathema," Wexler declared unabashedly. But then he turned the judgment around by suggesting that these "strict Freudians" were stuck in a time warp. "I was a classical analyst 100 years ago in New York," Wexler said, "but now I'm too old to be so stuffy. In this case, I think the collaboration was helpful because somewhere there's the problem of [Edwards] being blocked in his work and if I help him with that, then fine."

Wexler went on to justify the partnership by arguing that the concept of transference, which requires that the analyst remain a blank screen to his patient, was outmoded. "I don't think transference is so important anymore," Wexler said. "I think that support systems and the real opportunity to identify with the therapist and have a real relationship with him are more important."

But abstruse arguments about the purity of "transference" were not entirely pertinent. To Wexler's critics the issue was not an academic peccadillo but a far more basic concern—that the analyst might be exploiting his patient for his own gain. Dr. Leo Rangell, former president of the American Psychoanalytic Association and the International Psychoanalytic Association, denounces Wexler's conduct because it is "to the enhancement of the analyst rather than the analyst serving in a therapeutic mode. I knew an analyst in New York who as a hobby wrote detective novels. Other analysts are artists and sculptors. But that's all in a different category from using someone who comes in and exposes himself to you for gain. Not necessarily monetary gain—though with funds and foundations it gets into that too—but ego gains." To Rangell such extracurricular involvements undermine the very purpose of psychotherapy. "The patient comes in," Rangell argues, "and is urged and even instructed to reveal intimate material with the promise not only of confidentiality but of not being used. These people may tell you about the experience—Blake Edwards raved about it—but that doesn't make it right. One can never know how objective an analyst can be with a patient like that if he wants to share credits with him on a picture."

Wexler is well aware of such adverse criticisms, but he blithely dismisses them. "I know there are canons of ethics that say you can't have a dual relationship," Wexler says with a sigh. "That's something for social workers to play around with if they want to pretend that they are totally pure. The tradition that they're defending is so silly. To think that the analyst who sits behind the patient is a nonentity on whom everything is projected is ridiculous. I don't think it's very long before the patient knows whether I'm bright or stupid. If the patient says, 'You're a stupid son of a bitch,' you can't say, 'That's obviously what he thought about his father.' Maybe you *are* a stupid son of a bitch. If I write scripts with my patients, if I have dinner with my patients, all they know is that I'm some kind of person. The idea that you can't have any relationship with your patients outside the office seems to me unreasonable, unfair, and just plain silly. I had no qualms whatsoever about collaborating with Blake."

Wexler had been something of a heretic from his first days as a practicing analyst in Topeka, and he scoffs at his hidebound colleagues. "I used to hear hours and hours of debate among analysts," Wexler says, "as to whether it's okay to give a patient a Kleenex if snot is running out of his nose and he's crying his eyes out. A lot of analysts would say, 'No, you can't do that, because it will infect the transference.' This is crazy! If people knew how neurotic most analysts are, if they had an inside look at the analytic institutes, they probably would swear off analysis forever."

*   *   *

As the criticism directed at Milton Wexler continued to grow louder among his analytic rivals, something happened to neutralize the controversy. He had a stroke and retired from practice in the spring of 1988. By the fall of that year he had recovered sufficiently to be feted by his friends and patients at a celebration honoring his eightieth birthday and the twentieth anniversary of his foundation. The committee sponsoring the gala at the Chiat-Day advertising agency included many of Wexler's patients and other show-business pals—Julie Andrews, Candice Bergen, Blake Edwards, Peter Falk, David Geffen, Norman Lear, Jack Lemmon, Sophia Loren, Henry Mancini, Walter Matthau, Elaine May, Max Palevsky, Sydney Pollack, Milton (Mickey) Rudin, and Edie and Lew Wasserman. Marylouise Oates, the society reporter for the *Los Angeles Times*, wrote a celebratory story about the party headlined STAR ANALYST GETS THE STAR TREATMENT. "In his 30 years of Southern California practice," Oates noted without irony, "Wexler has managed to become an integral part of his patients' lives. 'We all love Milton,' was the constant refrain throughout the evening."

The party had the aura of a valedictory, but the old soldier was not quite ready to fade away. By 1991, when he was already eighty-three years old, Wexler had returned to practicing therapy on a part-time basis. Although his eyesight is failing and he still suffers some aftereffects from his stroke, he has resumed treating individual patients and even convenes his group occasionally. Several veteran participants such as Nancy Hardin say that it feels more like a nostalgic social gathering than a true therapeutic encounter. Nonetheless Wexler does charge his customary fee.

Jennifer Jones Simon left the group but still has private therapy sessions with Dr. Wexler. "Milton has been with Mother forever," chuckles Jones's son, Robert Walker, Jr. "He'll never get away from Mother. They'll never get away from each other. In the great hereafter they will be forever in a relationship." Emulating her mentor, Jones has even become a paraprofessional therapist herself. She now spends at least six hours a week volunteering as a lay counselor at the Southern California Counseling Center in Beverly Hills. Commenting on her career change in a rare interview with entertainment journalist Robert Osborne in 1992, Jones said, "I don't think people are much interested in movie stars anymore. The so-called 'glamorous people' of today are the scientists and the psychiatrists."

Wexler also stays in close touch with Blake Edwards. The analyst has written a script based on Saul Bellow's novel, *Henderson the Rain King,* which he hopes Edwards will someday direct. It may be the ideal swan song for the preeminent psychoanalyst to the stars. Bellow's story revolves around a charismatic rogue who embarks on a grand adventure. Driven by a burning desire for fulfillment and recognition—a chant of "I want, I want" that resonates in his head—the restive Henderson wanders through Africa until he finally discovers a gullible tribe that embraces him as a god. It is a theme that surely strikes a personal chord for Milton Wexler, who has learned a thing or two about ego trips and hero worship during his own reign as one of the most revered shamans of Hollywood.

10. THE INTRUDERS

Milton Wexler may have the distinction of being the first psycho-analyst to share screen writing credit with a patient, but he was hardly the first to insinuate his way into the filmmaking process. Ever since May Romm combined her role as David Selznick's ther-apist with that of his technical adviser on *Spellbound,* there has been a steady proliferation of such curious collaborations. Not content merely to minister to the stars and moguls, many Hollywood shrinks set out to influence the actual content of movies.

Shortly after *Spellbound* was released in 1945, humorist S. J. Perelman cast a satiric eye on the phenomenon. "The latest group of specialists to be smiled upon by the cinema industry are the psy-choanalysts," Perelman wrote in *The New Yorker*. "The vogue of psy-chological films started by *Lady in the Dark* has resulted in flush times for the profession, and anyone who can tell a frazzled id from a father fixation had better be booted and spurred for an impending summons to the Coast."

Noting that *Spellbound* had listed the services of Dr. Romm among its opening credits and that another psychiatrist had just been observed coaching Joan Crawford for a forthcoming role as a schizophrenic, Perelman foresaw a time when such advisers would be standard fixtures in the movie mecca. To illustrate the phenom-enon, he described an imaginary encounter at the corner of Holly-wood and Vine between a couple of pompous analysts named Sherman Wormser and Randy Kalbfus. When Kalbfus mentions that he's temporarily holed up in a motel room with a couple of female extras, Wormser comments that he hadn't realized his col-league had separated from his wife.

"Don't be archaic. She's living there, too," Kalbfus replies. "Once in a while I fall into the wrong bed, but Beryl's made her emotional adjustment; she's carrying on with a Greek in Malibu. Interesting sublimation of libido under stress, isn't it? I'm doing a paper on it."

S. J. Perelman may have treated such bedazzled shrinks as comic fodder, but the analysts themselves took their mission far more seriously. A year after Perelman's story was published, Dr. Lawrence Kubie, one of the analytic community's leading spokesmen and the psychoanalyst to many creative artists, offered a decidedly more earnest view of psychiatric consultation in Hollywood. Noting, as Perelman did, the surge in psychologically oriented films (including *Lady in the Dark*, which was the brainchild of Kubie's patient, Moss Hart), Kubie wrote an essay for *Hollywood Quarterly* in which he proposed that a panel of distinguished psychoanalysts be assembled to advise moviemakers on matters of technical accuracy related to psychiatry. Brimming with righteous fervor, he also urged the creation of a permanent foundation, endowed by the film industry and presided over by analysts, to study the impact of film on American culture and to elevate the quality of cinema. In support of his ideas Kubie made what Irving Schneider has described as "a remarkable statement, but one in keeping with the psychoanalytic optimism of the time." The enactment of his proposal, Kubie declared, "could not fail to help the film industry as a whole to achieve maturity and to realize its extraordinary undeveloped potentialities. At the same time, there can be little question that it would open up vast new empires of expanding markets and save large sums of money annually lost on unsuccessful films."

Those statements reflect not just the optimism but the grandiose desires of many analysts who became consultants to the movie business. Impressed by the power of film to penetrate private consciousness and mold public opinion, Kubie believed that the cinema could be turned into "the most significant educational implement we have ever known." From his standpoint, dramatizing psychological insights, proselytizing for psychoanalysis, fostering the "maturity" of the film industry, educating the masses, and achieving colossal grosses were all exquisitely consistent goals.

Although Hollywood never did get around to creating an official advisory board along the lines Kubie envisioned, filmmakers did routinely seek the approval of psychiatrists in order to win credibility and stave off controversy. In the 1940s and 1950s producers relied on these experts primarily as a source of information about technical matters related to the depiction of psychiatric procedures and specific mental illnesses. In recent years, however, the consultants have come to perform a far broader function—assessing character motivation, arguing plot points, and even suggesting marketing ploys for the finished product.

Among the filmmakers who have been their biggest boosters are Sherry Lansing and Daniel Melnick, two prominent producers and executives who worked together on such pictures as *Kramer vs. Kramer* and *Making Love.* Lansing, who became the first woman to head a major studio when she assumed the presidency of Twentieth Century-Fox in 1980, first entered psychoanalysis twelve years earlier, when she was twenty-five. She had been recently divorced and was having second thoughts about pursuing her acting career. The analyst who treated her turned out to be a Freudian autocrat who urged her to stop working, find a husband, and learn to "bake pies."

"He was a Machiavellian, truly destructive person," Lansing recalls. "I thought that all analysts were like him. They were like that in the movies I had seen—the doctor who tells you everything and overanalyzes everything. I hated analysis at that time."

A few years later, when she had given up acting and gone to work as a development executive, Lansing discovered Dr. Joshua Hoffs, an urbane analyst with lots of ties to the Hollywood set. Hoffs, whose wife, Tamar, is a filmmaker, was more sympathetic to Lansing's professional aspirations than her first analyst had been. Indeed Lansing gives Hoffs major credit for her remarkable ascent up the corporate ladder. "I never would have been president of Twentieth Century-Fox if it hadn't been for Dr. Hoffs," she says. "I would never have dared to think I could have the job. I remember that he asked me once, 'Why don't you run a studio?' I was a vice president at the time, and I said, 'A woman could never do that.' He asked why not, and I kept saying, 'I don't know.' He gave me confidence, a sense of self." Lansing's sessions with Dr. Hoffs provided her with "light-years better self-esteem," she raves. "It was the best gift I could give myself—worth more than a new house, a new car, or a new anything." By the time she concluded her five-year analysis with Hoffs, she was a zealous fan not simply of the doctor's but of psychoanalysis in general. Now, she reports, two of her closest friends are analysts, and she solicits their opinions on any script she plans to produce.

For Lansing's mentor Daniel Melnick, the devotion to psychoanalysis took root much earlier. As a college student Melnick contemplated becoming a psychiatrist himself, but he was too squeamish to make it through medical school. Instead he went to work in the entertainment business. As a television executive in the 1960s, Melnick began consulting with psychiatrists on an informal basis to help determine audience tastes. "I was always inclined to look for aids to programming decisions," he recalls. "I also tried to be guided by psychological truths in working with writers."

When he moved on to become a movie executive at MGM and Columbia, he continued the practice. "I have discussed ideas with analysts but have never been able to utilize their services as fully as I would like," Melnick says. "The studios feel it is all mumbo jumbo, and the marketing departments are very threatened."

But Melnick himself is convinced that psychotherapists are a valuable resource in making both creative and commercial judgments, and he remains one of their most enthusiastic champions. In 1982 he produced *Making Love* for Twentieth Century-Fox, the studio then presided over by Sherry Lansing. The subject matter of the film—a married man coming to terms with his homosexuality—was considered quite audacious for the time, and Melnick and Lansing were intent on dealing with it in a scrupulously "responsible" manner. They called in Dr. Michael Bleger, a Los Angeles psychologist with a large gay clientele, to act as a consultant on the project. "I wanted to get the behavior right, and Dr. Bleger was so anxious that there be an accurate, nonjudgmental portrayal that he contributed his services," Melnick says. "I did make an honorarium payment to a gay center."

Dr. Bleger's advice was not confined to matters of characterization. He also offered tips on how to sell the film to a popular audience. Barry Sandler, the movie's screenwriter, was one of Bleger's patients, and he recalls discussing the film's commercial prospects during a session with the psychologist, who avidly followed the box-office tallies for all the major releases. "I told him that I thought our film could do as well as *Ordinary People*, which I thought had been a big success," Sandler says. "Bleger shook his head and told me *Ordinary People* had only done twenty million in rentals!"

Making Love turned out to be a commercial flop, but Melnick still felt that Dr. Bleger's insights into audience tastes were quite astute. When Melnick produced the teen dance movie *Footloose* two years later, he invited Bleger to assist in designing the marketing campaign. Bleger suggested that teenagers are especially anxious whenever they have to return to school, so Melnick decided to release *Footloose* in February, to coincide with the beginning of the second semester, in order to tap those anticipatory emotions while they were still raw. The picture did strong business, and Melnick credits the psychologist's input for guiding it to the right audience. "He was quite helpful. I'd like to keep him on retainer," Melnick says, noting that the employment of such unorthodox prognosticators is not unprecedented. "There used to be a fortune-teller consulting for television," he remarks.

Earlier, while working as an executive at Columbia, Melnick oversaw production of *Midnight Express*, Alan Parker's harrowing film about a young American drug dealer trapped in a Turkish prison. With its graphic scenes of torture and brutality, as well as its veiled homoeroticism, *Midnight Express* was bound to stir controversy. Melnick remembers pondering "how far we could go before we threatened an audience so fundamentally that they'd be alienated from the film." Without informing either director Parker or the film's screenwriter, Oliver Stone, Melnick asked a few psychiatrists to review the script and then solicited their opinions over dinner. "They helped in shaping the material and shaping the marketing campaign," Melnick says. Later Melnick did discuss the ideas with Parker. "Alan embraced some and rejected others," Melnick recalls. "We changed it to make it more accessible and less threatening."

Dr. Martin Wasserman, one of the analysts whom Melnick consulted, explains some of the changes he proposed. He notes that one troubling aspect of *Midnight Express* had to do with its impact on younger teenagers. "There were a lot of unconscious homosexual things going on," he points out. "We felt that if you gave it some expression, instead of leaving it all unconscious, a child could understand what was happening." He urged the filmmakers to make the homosexuality more overt, to avoid what he calls "homosexual panic" on the part of a youngster who might be confused about his own inchoate sexuality. That advice led to the inclusion of a scene in the prison shower, during which the protagonist does engage in some fairly explicit homosexual contact with another prisoner.

Wasserman recalls other instances when his advice was not so readily accepted. "I had a strong opinion, but it wasn't necessarily what the American public wanted to see," Wasserman admits. "Sometimes they've taken my advice, sometimes they've done totally the opposite—and made money, which they wouldn't have made if they'd listened to me."

He cites his friend Sherry Lansing's production of *Fatal Attraction* as one example of a box-office smash that might have fizzled if she had heeded his counsel. The original ending of the film, in which the Glenn Close character commits suicide so that her paramour would be charged with her murder, proved so downbeat to preview audiences that it was eventually scuttled in favor of a more lurid, if incredible, finale in which Close terrorizes her lover's family and ends up being shot by his wife. "I thought the first ending of *Fatal Attraction* made more psychological sense," Wasserman says. "It would have been more reasonable in terms of her character. But from what they tested, the second ending would have made more money."

As Wasserman notes, psychological truths and commercial success do not always go hand in hand. "Who are you really consulting *for?*" he asks. "The producer, the writer, the director, the studio? Maybe they're just hiring a gun, so you're basically there to support a position. Are psychiatric consultations just a rubber stamp?" Wasserman doesn't have an answer to that question, but he suggests that consultants delude themselves if they overestimate their influence. "You're there to educate, to give some information," he says. "When we get lost is when we feel we really have power, or know better than the filmmakers."

As Dan Melnick points out, television companies have traditionally been more receptive than movie studios to the intrusion of such psychiatric advisers. Cowed by nervous sponsors, TV producers have typically enjoyed less freedom than feature filmmakers when dealing with ticklish subject matter, and they have regularly sought (or bought) the approval of the mind mavens in order to prove their good intentions. For example, Dr. Alvin Pouissant, a professor of psychiatry at Harvard Medical School and a well-known expert on child behavior, regularly perused the scripts for his friend Bill Cosby's weekly television series, suggesting ways to make the relationships among the characters more psychologically credible and the story lines more edifying. "Part of Bill's appeal is his self-deprecating humor," Dr. Pouissant told Edward Silver in *The New York Times.* "It plays well, but I think I've toned it down a bit." The doctor's intention, according to Silver, was to counteract "what he sees as the silly-male, strong-female aspects of the Huxtables' relationship, which reproduces in a professional context the stereotype of the black welfare family."

At the network level, psychiatrists have played a far more controversial role. They advise the censorship departments (euphemistically called broadcast standards and practices) in monitoring sex, violence, and language in program content and also in promoting what they like to call "prosocial" values. The reigning dean of such consultants is Dr. Melvin S. Heller, a genial Philadelphia psychiatrist who has enjoyed a long association with ABC. His 1984 monograph "Sexuality, Television and Broadcast Standards" has been the standard manual used for regulating the sexual content of ABC programs, and he has frequently been called upon to examine scripts for the network. "I've reviewed all the pilots each year for new shows that are coming up," Dr. Heller says with pride. "I've got some pretty good programming ideas."

Heller came to his job by a rather circuitous route. After a stint as the chief (and only) psychiatrist at a federal penitentiary in Terre Haute, Indiana, he took a position at Yale, where he built on his experience working with prison inmates to do scientific research into criminal behavior. "I thought maybe I could learn something about violence and its causes," he recalls. "And you can't be in psychiatry very long without learning a great deal about sex."

Drawing on his research, Heller authored a couple of academic studies that came to the attention of Alfred Schneider, the veteran vice president for policy and standards at ABC. Under pressure to reduce the amount of violence on television in the wake of the Robert Kennedy and Martin Luther King assassinations in 1968, ABC commissioned Dr. Heller to do an in-depth study of the impact of televised violence on the viewing public.

By correlating the behavior patterns and viewing habits of juvenile delinquents, Heller concluded that "television can do an enormous amount of damage if it demonstrates novel, imitative techniques of harming people. I think the fusion of sadistic violence and erotic stuff affects certain predisposed people in an arousal fashion, and can come to no good."

But how could a network censor—whom Dr. Heller prefers to call an editor—know when such a volatile "fusion" was taking place? Heller suggests a rather provocative answer in his little handbook entitled "Sexuality, Television and Broadcast Standards": "The editor is alerted to arousal not by a considered sense, but by an immediate erotic sensation. It is your visceral response or feeling rather than your intellectual faculty, which identifies arousal—unless yours is the only such reaction. As Justice Stewart so pithily remarked: when proposed material arouses, you will 'know it when you see it.' And if it does, it needs editing."

With regard to the depiction of nudity, Dr. Heller deems it acceptable so long as it falls into the category of "tribal nudity, à la *National Geographic*," which is "invariably covered by at least a small frontal apron." This, Dr. Heller argues, is no problem "if that is the way the tribespeople normally go about, and their nudity is not unduly ogled, or otherwise exaggerated for the audience, by the camera. It is not the editor's role to distort otherwise sensitive depictions of authentic tribal life by adding sarongs or imagined trappings of decency." When a high-ranking executive at ABC pressed him to permit frontal nudity in the landmark telecast of *Roots*, Heller condoned it in the film's opening scene, which shows the Africans disembarking from a slave ship. In that context, Heller decided, the nudity could legitimately be shot "à la *National Geographic*."

Niggling over nudity, or even over scenes of violence, has been less controversial among writers and directors than efforts to control the presentation of social issues. Despite Dr. Heller's jolly persona, his opponents in the creative community see him as a chilling force, working to drain television drama of any challenging ideas. Writer-producer David Rintels, for example, locked horns with Dr. Heller over *The Execution of Raymond Graham*, a 1985 docudrama that questioned the validity of capital punishment. The psychiatrist wrote an elaborate memorandum criticizing Rintels's script for its "bleeding heart viewpoint" and warning the executives at ABC that it could make the network look like "an irresponsible sob sister." He urged that every argument against capital punishment in the script be balanced by an equally persuasive plea for the death penalty. (Heller also blue-penciled a couple of raunchy scenes, including one shot of a nude centerfold, for which he proposed substituting "an equally socko pose in a bikini instead.")

"I try not to write polemics," Rintels says in defense of his script. "But to say that every debate has an equal A side and B side turns everything into vanilla custard. There are arguments in life that have winners and losers."

As far as Dr. Heller is concerned, however, his kind of "editing" does nothing at all to lessen the dramatic impact of a story. "We're all *for* controversy, because controversy and conflict are dramatic," he declares. "But we have a license to entertain, not propagandize. The biggest sin that network television can make is misinforming the public. When you misrepresent an issue, then you've got a very ignorant or crazy society, like in Iran."

To Dr. Heller, protecting the public from such misinformation is a grave responsibility. "We have a duty not to poison the air-waves," he says, dismissing objections like those voiced by David Rintels as mere caviling. "I'll tell you what writers and directors think," he says in consternation. "They think, 'You guys are a bunch of nerds. We're creative and you're interfering with our artistic free-dom.' That's all very good, but these are the same people who would bring us *Deep Throat* if they could! If you only saw some of the scripts we had to X out!"

Ideally, Heller believes, he or someone like him should be con-sulted well before the script has even been committed to paper. "If I can't look at the thing till they're ready to go to rough cut, they're ready to lock the thing up anyway," he says. "It's necessary to get broadcast-standards people in at the very earliest beginnings of the concept." All too often, he complains, he sees the finished product when it is already beyond repair.

"A good psychiatrist is the last person who would want to con-trol," Dr. Heller insists. Nonetheless, he implies, *someone* has to protect the public from the avarice and prurience of the networks. "If you let the thing loose," he warns, "you'll have three networks vying to see who can show *Deep Throat* first."

While most psychiatrists, such as Martin Wasserman and Melvin Heller, prefer to keep a low profile about their media consulting, a few have been quite aggressive in publicly marketing their services. Arguably the most visible of these professional script doctors is Car-ole Lieberman, M.D., a pert, opinionated Beverly Hills shrink who once worked as a cabaret singer and off-Broadway actress. A mem-ber of the Writers Guild of America, Dr. Lieberman runs a regular ad in the guild's monthly magazine urging other writers to avail themselves of her expertise in order to make their scripts "MORE PSYCHOLOGICALLY ACCURATE AND POWERFUL." Included in the ad, just below a head shot of the smiling doctor, are several blurbs about her work, culled from *The Wall Street Journal, Daily Variety,* and *The New York Times.* Dubbed the "doyenne of plot consultants" by the

Times, Dr. Lieberman explained her modus operandi to a reporter for that paper. "Because of my experience as a writer and actor," she said, "I believe I can assist in the expression of the creator's original intent. In cases where they get stuck, I might trace the story line back into the writer's unconscious mind."

Sessions with Dr. Lieberman, for which she charges upward of $150 per hour, are not simply in the interest of creating more compelling story lines. She also has a social mission to perform. Like Dr. Heller, she frets about the power of television to shape values and corrupt impressionable minds, and she suggests that trained psychotherapists are needed to keep the airwaves pure. "Television is not just something to be gobbled down every day after work," she has declared. "For many, many people, it's the strongest influence on their lives. A psychological consultant should be part of the crew for each show, like the gaffer or cameraman."

In a 1990 op-ed piece for the *Los Angeles Times,* Lieberman extended that argument to include movies as well as TV. Assailing the Motion Picture Association of America's rating system, which had just replaced its prohibitive X category with the neutral-sounding NC-l7, she issued a portentous call to arms. "If the movie industry wants to retain the privilege of self-regulation and stem the dangerous tide of censorship that is menacing any vestiges of creativity left in America," Lieberman warned, "it needs to be more responsible. Just as the regulation of air and water shouldn't be turned over without ongoing scrutiny to industries that pollute those resources, similar scrutiny should be given to the entertainment industry, which affects an even more precious resource—our *minds.* Unfortunately, the creative freedom of all artists risks extinction because too many have greedily polluted viewers' minds with psychologically destructive imagery." To remedy that blight, Lieberman proposed a radically overhauled rating system, to which she assigned the acronym MIND (Movies Influence Neuropsychological Development). Based on a new formula of her own devising, the rating board would measure films according to a quantified scale of sex and violence and then identify them as "Child-Safe," "Teen-Safe," or "Adult-Safe." In addition, the membership of the board would have to include a specified number of psychotherapists in order to give, in Lieberman's words, "expert opinion regarding psychologically damaging content." To receive any rating at all, Lieberman argued, "a movie would need a psychotherapist script consultant/technical adviser on staff to deal with psychological accuracy and suggest alternatives to psychologically damaging content."

Lieberman's ideas for psychiatric policing of movies might seem oppressive, but they are not without precedent. Almost two decades before her article appeared, Motion Picture Association of America president Jack Valenti had already decided to put a psychiatrist in charge of the rating system. The man he selected for the job was a dapper, honey-tongued Long Island analyst named Aaron Stern, whose brief, controversial reign ultimately convinced Valenti that critics like Dr. Lieberman are dead wrong in arguing that movies should be monitored by a mind doctor. Looking back on Dr. Stern's tenure, Valenti evinces no nostalgia. "I will never again have a psychiatrist or psychologist on the rating board," he states flatly.

Dr. Stern was introduced to Valenti in 1969, when Stern was teaching at Columbia University and practicing psychiatry in Great Neck, New York. One of Stern's neighbors was Robert Benjamin, a United Artists executive, who frequently invited the analyst to attend private screenings of his studio's films. At one such screening— of Ken Russell's rendition of D. H. Lawrence's *Women in Love*— Valenti also happened to be present, and following the movie, Valenti found himself enthralled by Dr. Stern's incisive commentary. "He gave a splendid, luminous analysis of the film," Valenti recalls. "People who speak well impress me."

In fact Valenti was so impressed that he asked Stern if he might be interested in serving as a part-time consultant to the MPAA's rating board. The rating system, which Valenti had hatched just one year earlier, was designed to replace the old Production Code, by which movies had been censored since the 1930s. The Code had been conceived and enforced in close cooperation with the Catholic Legion of Decency. Now, as Hollywood entered a more permissive era, it seemed somehow appropriate that it should turn for guidance to the new priesthood of psychiatry. In forming the rating board, Valenti had already named a child psychologist, Dr. Jacqueline Bouhoutsos, to serve alongside several veterans of the Production Code staff. Valenti believed that a distinguished psychoanalyst like Dr. Aaron Stern could lend additional prestige to the rating board. "I thought Aaron would add stature and insight," he says.

In addition to his academic and medical credentials, Stern carried the enthusiastic recommendation of United Artists chairman

Arthur Krim, who already counted himself a special beneficiary of the doctor's sage counsel. Early in 1969 United Artists was preparing to release *Midnight Cowboy,* John Schlesinger's movie version of James Leo Herlihy's gritty novel about the relationship between a Bowery derelict (Dustin Hoffman) and a male prostitute (Jon Voight). With its graphic portrayal of the street hustler's world— including scenes of fellatio, sodomy, and sex-for-hire—*Midnight Cowboy* tested the boundaries of screen permissiveness. But it was also a sensitive drama by a highly regarded filmmaker, and the rating board decided it deserved an R rating, rather than the more restrictive X, which was rapidly coming to be synonymous with hard-core pornography. Krim solicited Dr. Stern's opinion on the rating, and Stern urged Krim to forgo the R rating and self-apply an X instead. Despite its artistic seriousness—the movie went on to become the only X-rated film ever to win an Academy Award as best picture—Stern believed that *Midnight Cowboy* should not be viewed by impressionable young people, even if their parents approved, since it appeared to be advocating a deviant lifestyle.

During a radio interview in 1971, Stern attempted to explain his convoluted reasoning: "One of the things about *Midnight Cowboy* that was of concern was that it was a film that dealt with a homosexual frame of reference. That's no problem for an adult. If you choose the homosexual life, that's fine, that's your choice, and you have every right to it. But before you make that choice, you should understand what homosexuality stands for. If you're a thirteen- or fourteen-year-old and you've never had intercourse with a woman that is gentle, tender, communicative, sensitive, and if the way in which it is depicted by John Schlesinger in the film is your *only* criterion for evaluating intercourse—and if you recall the scene with Brenda Vaccaro, they get into a power struggle over who's on top, and the next day she then says, 'You're one of the greatest I've ever had, and I'm telling my girlfriend about you'—to a kid in the audience who's never known more meaningful interaction, he could completely distort this and be stripped away of his opportunity for meaningful choice."

While Stern's suggestion that watching a single movie can determine an adolescent's sexual orientation might seem a bit silly, his arguments proved persuasive enough to sway the nervous executives at United Artists, who followed the analyst's advice and released the movie with an X rating. Ironically, in 1970, after the Code and Rating Administration was roundly criticized in the press for the X on *Midnight Cowboy* that the studio had self-applied, the film was finally rerated R, the classification that the rating board had intended to grant in the first place. Almost no one raised a peep of protest.

Upon Stern's appointment to the MPAA as a consultant, he immediately began shaping the board's agenda. He decided that the rating process was not sufficiently rigorous, and he proposed sweeping new guidelines to regulate film content. He recommended that whenever sex was portrayed in a G or GP (later changed to PG) film, it had to be "within the context of a loving relationship." Any scene that treated sex as "discharge" (to use Stern's own terminology) was strictly verboten in all but R- or X-rated films.

Stern further recommended that violence in unrestricted films should always be "represented as a force in the service of law and order." Thus the extreme violence of policemen or soldiers might be acceptable, but that of rebels and revolutionaries was not. He was also concerned with upholding conventional assumptions about right and wrong. For films in the G category, his directive read, "The broadly practiced social mores are not challenged." For films in the GP category, it read, "The broadly practiced social mores are not significantly challenged."

Dr. Stern was mightily pleased with his new definitions, and he shared them not just with the rating board but with top studio executives. To his surprise the reaction was overwhelmingly negative. In August 1971, shortly after Stern disclosed his proposals to rate films on the basis of the social criticism they conveyed, Samuel Z. Arkoff, the crusty chairman of American International Pictures, sounded the alarm in an address before a meeting of theater owners. "There seems to be another new and previously uncharted concept that Dr. Stern has apparently adopted which I consider more threatening than any other area—the concept of thought control," Arkoff declared. "He has told me that he feels any film that questions the validity of the existing social structure should not be seen by young people under seventeen except in the company of their parents. Such films are to be rated R or X. To me this is an absolutely terrifying concept, alien to America." Arkoff went on to accuse the doctor of "using the whole country as a guinea pig for his own psychiatric beliefs." Of course Arkoff's company was the leading purveyor of teenage exploitation films at the time, and he had a lot to lose if his target audience was suddenly restricted. But he was not alone in vehemently opposing Stern's new ideas. Reeling from the barrage of criticism, MPAA president Jack Valenti decided to bury Stern's inflammatory proposals.

Like the television watchdog Melvin Heller, Dr. Stern was not content simply to evaluate a finished product. He would confer privately with filmmakers and studio executives while scripts were being written, shot, or edited. That way he could indicate how a film might be tailored to win a desired rating. When Ernest Lehman adapted Philip Roth's best-selling novel *Portnoy's Complaint* in 1972, Dr. Stern made a house call to Lehman and went over the project with him in some detail. Later he told the rating board, "If Ernie Lehman wants to make a film about momism, that can be accommodated in R. But if he is going to emphasize masturbation, that will make it X."

Critics charged that such informal consultations with filmmakers could lead to self-censorship, and Stern did tangle with some strong-willed directors who resented having to cut their films at the psychiatrist's behest. John Boorman, the director of *Deliverance*, battled Stern over that film's homosexual rape scene, though he did finally agree to a few minor snips in order to win an R rating. On the other hand, several filmmakers actually seemed to welcome the analyst's input, or were at least willing to humor him in order to get the rating they desired. Ernest Lehman, for one, claimed that Stern never urged him to edit his script of *Portnoy's Complaint* "or launder it or self-censor it with a rating in mind," and other directors also rushed to Stern's defense. Responding to an article about the ratings that appeared in *The New York Times*, Sam Peckinpah publicly stated his "appreciation of the extraordinary cooperation of Dr. Aaron Stern, who bent over backward to keep the intent of *Straw Dogs* intact." According to Peckinpah, his film may have been trimmed here and there, but Dr. Stern helped him to maintain the "integrity" of its controversial rape scene, and he was proud of the results—despite the objections of what Peckinpah called "one or two possible women's lib freaks who read into the intent of the picture something which never existed." The director went on to describe his dealings with Stern as "not only highly satisfactory, but a plus for the film. In fact, some of his suggestions, not enforcements, I used for the European version, because it made a better picture."

Don Siegel, the producer-director of *Dirty Harry*, wrote that "without the attempt of Dr. Stern to censor films, there would be no distinction between hard-core pornography and films such as Kubrick's *A Clockwork Orange*, Peckinpah's *Straw Dogs*, and, for that matter, *Dirty Harry*. I found Dr. Stern to be sympathetic with the aims that I, as one of the creators of *Dirty Harry*, was seeking. I felt he didn't inhibit my creative integrity. In fact, some of his suggestions proved to be beneficial to the film." The star of the movie, Clint Eastwood, echoed the sentiment. "In my dealings with Dr. Stern and his board, I found it was most educational to get their feelings and objective opinion on a film, and in many cases it was even beneficial to the final film released," Eastwood wrote.

A few weeks after these letters appeared in the *Times*, the paper's principal film critic, Vincent Canby, leveled a withering attack on their authors. Hollywood's "censorship machinery," as Canby called the rating system, was "not only ineffective and confusing, it also has the dreary subsidiary effect of persuading supposedly mature filmmakers to act like children in desperate need of nannies"— a clear swipe at the filmmakers who lauded Stern for his "beneficial" advice. "I couldn't care less whether someone of the stature of Sam Peckinpah thinks that Dr. Stern's advice made, say, *Straw Dogs* a better film," Canby wrote. "Peckinpah is old enough to make movies on his own. . . . It's very depressing to hear him, of all people, carrying on in praise of public moralists who spend their days measuring frames of pubic hair, counting four-letter words, and trying to figure out whether a certain sex act indicates sodomy or is just a variation on the conventional frontal approach."

Besides filmmakers like Peckinpah, Siegel, and Eastwood, Dr. Stern had managed to cultivate a number of other unlikely allies, including *Playboy* publisher Hugh Hefner. "Hef," as Stern referred to him, had made a foray into moviemaking in 1971 with an R-rated version of *Macbeth*, and the two men quickly developed a mutual-admiration society. Stern enjoyed dropping in at the Playboy Mansion, and "Hef" became one of the analyst's chief supporters. "I am very happy that Aaron is in there," he told Leonard Gross of the *Los Angeles Times*. "The code permits films to be made today that couldn't be made before. The rating system permits a person willing to accept an R or an X to have virtual total freedom."

The problem was that almost no studio *was* willing to accept an X, since few exhibitors would show X-rated movies and newspapers in many major markets refused to accept advertising for them. The rating itself was viewed as box-office poison. As an MGM censor explained to one reporter, "None of us wants an X. MGM won't even release one. The whole basis of the industry is to make money." In order to avoid the leprous X, directors were forced to cut scenes they might otherwise have included. "Dr. Stern has worked with us many times," the censor noted. "We've called him in to talk to a producer, and he's been very helpful. What you've got to explain to a producer is that he's got a PG script except for— pardon the language—the word 'fuck' three times. The word's not important to the story. So he takes it out and gets his PG. That's the best rating there is—just a little bit of salt and spice." This sort of ratings-minded tinkering, critics charged, was not so different from the censorship practiced under the old Production Code.

Stern himself dismissed such charges as hopelessly naive. "Be careful about that word 'artistic creation' in motion pictures," he warned pedantically. "When you make a film, it is one of the most powerful forces for influencing the human mind. Even a bad film— I mean bad in terms of box office response—is sometimes seen by hundreds of thousands of people. It's not like a book where it can die on the shelf with a distribution of 5,000 copies. A bad movie can be seen by almost a million people. . . . When you go up on that screen and promiscuously rip defenses away from an audience, you at least must take the responsibility of forewarning the person who comes in so he makes the choice to undergo that experience. You don't merely show it on the screen as two hours of entertainment, because it goes beyond that. It has depth, it has quality, it has creative intrusiveness."

During the first year and a half that he worked for the rating board, Stern had to confer with his new Hollywood friends on quick, monthly visits to the Coast. But it was not long before he craved more constant contact. In July 1971, when Eugene Dougherty, a holdover from the old Production Code office, stepped down as head of the Code and Rating Administration, Stern decided to take over the post. He moved into a new suite of offices at the rating board's headquarters, situated above a Rexall drugstore in West Hollywood, and even made room for his analyst's couch. One reporter who visited him there was so incredulous when he spotted that unusual accoutrement that he asked Stern if he still saw patients. "Absolutely," the doctor replied. "I said I wouldn't take the job if I couldn't."

Stern and his wife took up residence in a posh Beverly Hills home and plunged into the good life—playing tennis, collecting art, and entertaining the rich and famous with private screenings in their state-of-the-art projection room. Prominent Los Angeles analysts like Judd Marmor and Leo Rangell were also invited to these cinematic soirees. "It was kind of fun in the days before VCRs to sit in a plush armchair and watch a movie," says Dr. Rangell's wife, Anita.

The ratings czar became something of a regular on the Bel-Air circuit. Linda Palmer, who was married to Warner Bros. chief Ted Ashley, remembers accompanying Dr. Stern and his wife to a private screening at producer Mike Frankovich's estate. In addition to the usual Hollywood chitchat, Stern offered helpful tips on ratings. At one point, Palmer recalls laughingly, Stern told their host, "Don't worry, Mike, *balls* is a PG word."

Soon Dr. Stern was shmoozing with all the town's top honchos. In addition to Frankovich, Ashley, and Hef, his pals included directors like William Friedkin and actors like Warren Beatty. Not everyone was a fan, however. On one occasion TV host Dick Cavett invited the analyst to appear on his show to talk about the rating system. As Stern drifted into an elaborate apologia, Mel Brooks, another guest on the program, began squirming in his seat. Reacting to the shrink's sonorous disquisition, Brooks clutched his side and moaned in mock agony, "Doctor, Doctor, I have a pain!"

In December 1972 a particularly acerbic article about Dr. Stern appeared in *Saturday Review,* written by Jack Langguth. Quoting Stern's ominous comments about "political overtones" to his hush-hush plans for redesigning the rating system, and alluding to his ambitious scheme for "how the rating system will eventually dovetail into the whole audio-visual structure," Langguth painted a devastating portrait of the analyst-turned-censor. When Stern told Langguth that by rating movies he was somehow fighting repression, the reporter sardonically noted that "he sounded very much like that U.S. Army major who said he had to destroy that Vietnamese town in order to save it." For the most part, however, Langguth was able to skewer Stern by quoting the doctor's own self-serving prattle. On the subject of Stanley Kubrick's *Clockwork Orange,* he reported that Stern confided, "I flew to London to talk with Stanley about that X rating. At first he was angry. But I told him that we couldn't give *Clockwork* an R just because he had speeded up the camera on that *ménage à trois* scene. Because, if we did that, then any hard-core pornographer could speed up his scenes and legitimately ask for an R on the same basis. We would have created a precedent. By the time we finished talking, Stanley saw my point." (As Langguth noted, Kubrick did eventually cut thirty seconds of footage from two scenes in the film, and the MPAA rerated *Clockwork Orange* R when it went into wide release.)

Reacting to all the bad press he was receiving, Stern portrayed himself as a hapless scapegoat. "What the media have done to me just fills the industry's needs," he declared, lambasting his Hollywood detractors. "These people all talk about art," he scoffed. "They've never had so much freedom, and yet they keep making these perverse demands. It's not freedom they want, it's indulgence." According to Stern, he was being crucified by a petulant band of narcissists. "Of course, I've been a pain in the ass to the industry," he said defiantly. "But the industry needs what I stand for. They want to use my credentials, and they hope my ideals won't be noticed—that's the American way."

In December 1973, as the controversy surrounding Stern's handling of the rating system continued to mount, he made a rather remarkable move. He resigned his post at the MPAA and, at the invitation of Columbia Pictures corporate president Alan Hirschfield and Columbia production chief David Begelman, entered into a contract with the very "industry" he had publicly reviled. Given the title "head of special projects," he was empowered to create an entirely new division within Columbia Pictures, developing advanced audiovisual products for markets around the world—including hotels, college dormitories, hospitals, and nursing homes.

Stern's boss at the MPAA, Jack Valenti, was en route to Iran for the Teheran Film Festival when Stern announced his resignation, and he could not be reached for comment. Today he talks frankly about the direction in which Stern steered the rating system. The rating board went awry, Valenti suggests, when Stern took it into "the ill-lit corridors that psychiatrists get into from time to time." The board has no business "making judgments on psychiatric attention or inattention to detail," Valenti adds. "Ordinary people, not acolytes of Sigmund Freud, should be making the judgments. I may not want my seven-year-old hearing the word *cocksucker*, but I don't need a psychiatrist to tell me that."

Insiders who were familiar with Stern's facility for ingratiating himself with filmmakers and studio brass while he headed the rating board saw his move to the executive suites as a predictable progression. "He got involved in this and seemed to be taken over by it," says Dr. Martin Wasserman. Director Arthur Penn concurs. "He became contaminated by his association with producers," says Penn, who recoiled at Stern's use of "psychoanalytic jargon to offer glib explanations and justifications for censorship." Another director, Sidney Lumet, was equally put off by the analyst's unctuous manner. "He always seemed so Mr. Showbiz," Lumet says.

When he moved into his new quarters at Columbia, Dr. Stern seemed to have finally found his element. But the honeymoon was quickly over. Eight months after joining Columbia, Stern left the studio in a huff. He filed a $20-million breach-of-contract suit, charging that the company had failed to grant him access to its film library, the cornerstone of his far-reaching audiovisual venture. In addition he alleged that Columbia failed to pay him the $75,000 in salary (and a like sum in expenses) that he had been promised.

For a while it looked as if Dr. Stern's ambitious plans to conquer Hollywood had hit a snag. Then, on December 30, 1975, came the surprising announcement that he had just made a deal to develop and produce three of his own original stories. Even more surprising, the deal was with Columbia Pictures, the same studio he had sued the previous year for breach of contract. With nary a hint of their past troubles, Columbia president David Begelman declared, "We are most pleased to have concluded arrangements with a man of Aaron Stern's background and talent and are happy to have him with Columbia." Stern's twenty-million-dollar lawsuit against the company had been quietly settled behind the scenes.

Stern's relationship with the crafty Begelman—who would eventually lose his job in the infamous check-forging scandal that rocked Hollywood in 1977—raised more than a few eyebrows, but Stern felt he had a handle on the mercurial studio head. The doctor told at least one associate that he believed Begelman suffered from "boot-strap disease," a condition that he subsequently explained at some length. For a man like Begelman, who lives out the Horatio Alger saga that is the American dream, success can become an intoxicating drug. "By advancing far beyond his origins," Stern said of this sort of rags-to-riches hero, "he becomes extremely vulnerable to 'bootstrap' disease—having 'pulled himself up by his bootstraps' to a station in life that is far beyond the position he started from, he lives with the fear that he will lose it all and be forced back to the point from which his climb originally began." The "bootstrap" sufferer becomes so addicted to the "narcissistic inflation of success" that he insulates himself from failure, for fear of tumbling back to his humble origins. Soon he becomes a remote potentate, surrounded by sycophants. "Admission to previously inaccessible places is now possible," Stern noted. "You have connections and influence. You have moved . . . into the self-inflated regions of arrogance and grandiosity."

To some observers that diagnosis sounded suspiciously like a self-portrait. The son of Yiddish-speaking immigrants from the Polish-Russian border, Aaron Stern had little exposure to the world of high culture or privilege that analysts like Lawrence Kubie and Ralph Greenson had known as children. "Half the Jewish boys in Brooklyn wanted to go to medical school," Stern told an interviewer in 1972; he was one of the few who made it. He pulled himself up to become not just a doctor, but a Hollywood producer to boot! Remarks Thomas Baum, one of the writers hired to develop Dr. Stern's original screen stories for Columbia, Stern enjoyed the distinction of being "the only analyst with a three-picture deal."

Baum recalls the slightly surreal atmosphere at the Century City headquarters of Betair Productions, a company whose name derived from the combination of Stern's first name and that of his wife, Betty. Hollywood trade papers were piled alongside medical journals, "easy-listening" radio music was piped in to soothe the anxious, and a celebrity Rolodex sat temptingly on the novice producer's desk. The inner sanctum even sported his analyst's couch, for the benefit of his few steady patients.

Susan Rice, another of the screenwriters whom Stern hired to develop his original stories, remembers the analyst-producer as "slick, gray-haired, and condescending." The script she was enlisted to write had to do with sexual surrogacy, and Stern viewed it as a groundbreaking piece of work. According to Rice, Stern "earnestly felt he was going to do an enormous service" by making the film. "He was going to help people deal with their sexuality. He wanted to do something revolutionary."

Because the story centered on a female surrogate, Stern and the director on the project, John Avildsen, would ask Rice probing questions about sexual dysfunction in women. "They would expect me to validate it from my own life," she recalls. At first she resisted this psychoanalytic exercise. Later, when she tried suggesting some interesting quirks of behavior that *were* drawn from her own experience, Stern summarily cut her off. "Oh, no, no woman would ever do that," Rice recalls him saying.

"He had a sort of clothing for female sexuality that I had to fit into," Rice says. And because Stern was both psychiatrist and producer, he could be doubly persuasive. "He was wearing both hats at once," Rice notes. "*Dr.* Aaron Stern got him a certain deference. He was always calculating your normalcy." (At the same time, there were certain advantages to working for a doctor-producer. Once, when Rice mentioned that her insomnia was interfering with her writing, Stern obligingly prescribed a sedative.)

In the end Rice's sexual-surrogacy script, like the other two screenplays Dr. Stern had hoped to produce for Columbia, failed to reach the screen. Earlier Stern had tried developing a project called *Coldsteel and Neon* with his sometime chum Warren Beatty, but that, too, withered on the vine. Disillusioned with the vagaries of moviemaking, Stern finally abandoned his producing hopes, packed up his finely tailored suits, and returned to the East Coast. "He was just a gust of wind that came through here," says Dr. Leo Rangell, one of the Los Angeles analysts whom Stern courted during his glory days. "As fast as he came, he left."

Stern hung out his shingle in suburban Connecticut and set about completing his magnum opus, *Me: The Narcissitic American*. Published in 1979, the book is a rambling, humorless sermon about the decline of American culture at the hands of the author's bête noire, unbridled narcissism. In it Stern asserts that if "power is a form of narcissistic prostitution, then the media is the world's best brothel for procuring it." Awed by the power of the media to influence our lives, and presumably chastened by his own abortive efforts to harness this potent force, his rhetoric rises to an ominous crescendo: "Any stone dropped into the huge ocean of the media generates waves that will pound into infinity. Throughout the ages people have appeared who sought to dominate the entire world— from Genghis Khan to Adolf Hitler. . . . The first tyrant to master the media may succeed where others have failed. The media can serve us or it can rape us. The choice is ours to make. If we demand the expression of more loving values, we can control the growing narcissistic infestation spread by the media. If we don't make that demand, the narcissistic infestation will not only continue, it will grow and overcome us all."

Spurned in his efforts to become the new Sam Goldwyn, the embittered exile was starting to sound like a latter-day Cotton Mather.

*   *   *

Paul Mazursky, who remembers having had a "couple of run-ins" with Dr. Stern over rating board decisions, cites the psychiatrist's love affair with Hollywood as testimony to the seductive power of the movie business. "The odds are overwhelming that if Freud lived here, most of the big executives would have gone to him," Mazursky says with a laugh. "Eventually Freud would have had a three-picture deal too—probably his own production company. 'And Sigmund Freud Presents: Judy Garland and Sixteen Other People Who Have Been My Clients.' Just imagine, if you've been their analyst, you could tell the actors, 'I got a part you *can't* turn down.' "

S. J. Perelman displayed a similarly bemused attitude toward the susceptibility of mental-health professionals to the lure of Tinseltown. Back in 1946, when he wrote "Physician, Steel Thyself," his droll narrative about the movies' new breed of psychiatric consultants, Perelman began by noting, "A psychiatrist suddenly pitchforked into Hollywood, the ultimate nightmare, must feel rather like a small boy let loose in a toy store, but I wonder how long he can maintain a spirit of strict scientific objectivity." Indeed, it doesn't take long for Perelman's staid protagonist, Sherman Wormser, M.D., Ph.D., to shed his conservative vestments in favor of a snappy pea-green play suit. "Chameleon-like," the narrator says, "he soon developed a sense of protective coloration."

For Wormser's colleague, Randy Kalbfus, the turning point comes when he realizes that mere consulting will never generate enough income to buy the eighteen-room hacienda in Beverly Hills that he covets. "Original stories—that's the caper," Kalbfus declares, confiding that Zanuck has already offered a princely sum for the script he's been working on, "and it isn't even on paper."

When Perelman's story first appeared, it was little more than an absurdist flight of fancy. In the ensuing decades, as eminent analysts such as Milton Wexler and Aaron Stern actually moved from psychiatric consultation into writing and producing "original stories," the tale has come to seem more like prophecy than whimsy. Whether adapting "chameleon-like" to their new surroundings or simply surrendering to their own delusions of grandeur, these real-life heirs to Drs. Wormser and Kalbfus have proven that, in Hollywood at least, life does have a curious way of imitating satire.

11. THE FEMININE MYSTIQUE

"How wise our educators that they pester the beautiful sex so little with scientific knowledge," the young Freud wrote to his friend Emil Fluss in 1873. Women, he assured Fluss, "have come into the world for something better than to become wise."

Although Freud's later comments on "the dark continent" of womanhood were somewhat more ginger, he was seldom less patronizing, and the masculine bias built into traditional psychoanalysis has long been a complicating factor in the roles women perform as champions or opponents of Freud's legacy. Karen Horney, one of the first psychoanalysts to grapple with the consequences of that ambiguous role-playing, complained that by treating women as failed men, Freudian theory promoted a "dogma of the inferiority of women." And although Freud himself was willing to recognize and support aspiring female analysts, they tended to be those who acted the part of "masculine woman"—a term he applied to his disciple Joan Riviere—and thus conformed to his views of male superiority.

Freud's circle of female devotees did include a few exceptions to that austere prototype, most notably the beguiling Marie Bonaparte, princess of Greece and Denmark and great-granddaughter of Napoleon's brother, Lucien. After being psychoanalyzed by Freud, "our Princess"—as he proudly referred to her—became Freud's faithful confidante and amanuensis, introducing him to the moneyed nobility of Europe and providing financial backing for his publishing ventures. Psychoanalysis failed to cure the princess's frigidity, but she remained so in thrall to Freudian theories of passive female sexuality that she even submitted to a novel surgical procedure, the lowering of her clitoris, in the hope that it would facilitate vaginal orgasms. "All my life I was to attach a value to nothing but the opinion, the approval, the love of a few fathers chosen higher and higher, and the last of whom was to be my great master Freud," Marie wrote in her memoirs. As historian Paul Roazen has observed, "Freud encouraged the transference Marie had set up toward him," for she occupied a niche quite different from that filled by such unadorned intellectuals as Joan Riviere, the upstart Karen Horney, or his own devoted daughter Anna. The Princess, Roazen notes, "fit into the category of those beautiful and narcissistic women for whom Freud seems to have had a special fascination."

In the years since Freud was first captivated by the Princess Marie, male analysts have continued to reserve "special fascination" for certain of their more glamorous votaries. Nowhere has that infatuation been more evident than in Hollywood, where at least one alluring acolyte succeeded in charming her mentors much as "our Princess" enchanted Freud. Under the tutelage of some of America's most prominent analysts, onetime chorus girl and sometime movie star Janice Rule became not just a practicing psychoanalyst but a published theoretician on the psychology of acting. Her 1973 article entitled "The Actor's Identity Crises (Postanalytic Reflections of an Actress)" remains to this day one of the most frequently cited treatises on the actor's unique personality.

Two decades before that scholarly essay appeared in the *International Journal of Psychoanalytic Psychotherapy*, Rule herself was the subject of a very different sort of article. When her face graced the cover of *Life* magazine in January 1951, the future lay analyst was a nineteen-year-old ingenue being groomed for stardom. The *Life* spread, promoting her screen acting debut in *Goodbye, My Fancy* with Joan Crawford, burbled about Rule's "girl-next-door wholesomeness," but noted, too, that she possessed a quality that "promises the audience something more than they usually associate with any next-door neighbor." In fashioning an image for the young actress, publicists repeatedly emphasized her independence and intelligence, attributes not generally assigned to up-and-coming starlets. One typical press release concluded that "her brief whirl in show business, which has vaulted her from night club dancing to stage success, and thence to a term contract with MGM, has taught her that Janice Rule does a better job of looking after Janice Rule than anybody else does."

Indeed, from the time she was fifteen, Rule was looking after herself. She danced as a chorine at the Chez Paree nightclub in Chicago, where, according to one studio flack, she claimed "as her adopted uncles a mob of characters whose mugs decorated post office bulletin boards all over America." That may have been hyperbolic, but it is certainly true that she grew up fast, and early on developed a knack for enticing older men into taking her under wing.

"Whenever I finished a performance, I was hustled into one of the vacant rooms in the gambling casino, where some big bruiser stood over me while I did my school homework," she said of her stint at Chez Paree. "However, as tough as the boys appeared to me, there were few of them who failed to soften up at the proper approach. If I talked long and hard enough, they would bring me ice cream from the kitchen as a bribe to get me to finish my homework."

Despite the encouragement of the Capone crowd, Rule never did finish high school; she dropped out at seventeen and moved to New York to study ballet with George Balanchine. To make ends meet, she danced at the Copacabana and as a Broadway gypsy. While appearing in *Miss Liberty* in 1949, she was spotted by a talent scout, who signed her to the contract with MGM that brought her to Hollywood.

The young actress was quickly disillusioned. She bristled at playing the role of nubile siren, off-screen as well as on. "They wanted me to go to Ciro's and the Mocambo with men I didn't know," she told an interviewer years later. She returned to New York and eventually enrolled at the Actors Studio, where she became one of Lee Strasberg's star pupils. In 1953 she landed the leading role in William Inge's Pulitzer Prize–winning play, *Picnic*. Her portrayal of (in her words) "the prettiest, but also the dumbest, girl in town" won critical plaudits and marked her first real breakthrough as a dramatic actress.

It also marked a significant turning point in her life, for it allowed her to explore all the psychological dimensions of acting. Inge's script had contained a reference to the girl's father, who disappeared several years before the action of the play began. According to Rule, she drew upon that allusion to imagine that "the father was the only person ever to take the girl seriously, that as a child she was his favorite. He talked to her a great deal, taught her many things, felt that she was bright and, in general, treated her as a person." The actress expanded upon this fantasy in performing the love scenes later in the story. "The author's view of love was limited to sex," Rule observed, "but I was able to use the early relationship with the father to justify playing the love affair on a deeper, more complex level." Even at that early stage in her career, she was intent on psychoanalyzing her characters.

On reflection Rule decided that she had constructed this image of a "dream father" out of resentment toward her own father, whom she felt had "abandoned" her by allowing her to leave home at fifteen and work as a dancer. Not long after *Picnic* closed on Broadway, Rule married playwright N. Richard Nash, eighteen years her senior, whom she described as "a fatherly man."

"Eighteen months of living with a dream father [on stage] left me with a hunger for such an experience in real life," she declared.

The marriage to Nash lasted less than two months. She was briefly engaged to actor Farley Granger, then married screenwriter Robert Thom. That union also ended in divorce. In 1961 she married the swaggering actor Ben Gazzara, with whom she had starred in *Night Circus* on Broadway. The couple shuttled between New York and California, trying to sustain two careers, but the pressures were explosive. "I was in a manic state, and a little too much boozing went on," Gazzara later confessed. "There were slam-bang fights in public places. I have to give Janice four stars for hanging in there." When Gazzara took on the role of the doomed lawyer in the television series *Run for Your Life* in 1965, they settled in Los Angeles, and Rule scaled back her stage and screen work to concentrate on raising her two daughters.

"I knew I had to stay home with the children—somebody did," Rule says of that period in her life. "And my husband's career was so flamboyant." She did manage to act occasionally, in such films as *Invitation to a Gunfighter*, *The Chase*, and *The Swimmer*. For the most part, however, she devoted herself to being a wife and mother. Through the social circle that developed around her daughters' schools, she became friendly with other movie people as well as some prominent psychiatrists. Among them were Dr. Joshua Hoffs, analyst to a number of top Hollywood players, and his wife, Tamar, an artist and filmmaker.

"There was this whole shrink-art connection," recalls Tamar Hoffs. "You would meet a young couple and you were immediately thrown into that whole gang—Leonard Nimoy and his wife, Paul

Mazursky and his wife, Ben and Janice. Mostly we would meet through our mutual little family-baby thing. We were all still products of the late fifties, when you were supposed to get married and have children, which we all did. Our kids either played in the same parks together or went to the same schools."

The Hoffses' daughter, Susanna (who grew up to achieve a certain celebrity of her own, as lead singer of the rock group the Bangles), attended nursery school with Rule's younger daughter. "My kid was playing with Liz Gazzara one day," Tamar Hoffs remembers, "and they decided they were both the same religion—they were both atheists. Ben and Janice invited us over and that's how we became friends." With the Hoffses' encouragement, Rule's interest in psychoanalysis intensified.

As a young actress in New York she had—like most members of the Actors Studio—entered psychoanalysis as an almost obligatory rite of initiation. But that early analysis was not congenial to her creative temperament; she describes it as "very 'hair shirt'—rather cruel actually." A lapsed Catholic, Rule believes that the experience did little more than reactivate her suppressed feelings of guilt about leaving her family and going to work at such an early age. "I thought you're supposed to suffer this way," she says. "I had superego problems to begin with and I thought, well, you deserve it."

Nevertheless, as she became more intimately acquainted with the Los Angeles analytic crowd, Rule decided to give psychoanalysis another go, this time with the eminent Ralph Greenson. "It was like the sky opening up," Rule says of her two-and-a-half-year analysis with Greenson. "Certainly he was able to undo a lot of the damage of the first analysis. I became much more of a full human being—more playful, more silly again." Greenson liberated her imagination, Rule says, by finally convincing her that her feelings were not "sick, terrible things to be hidden from anybody."

Although he urged her to vent her emotions, Rule remembers how the analyst winced at the earthy four-letter words she would sometimes utter. Like most Freudians, Greenson had certain preconceptions about what constituted appropriate female behavior, and a woman's use of foul language upset his sense of decorum. "I learned a lot of street verbiage from my husband," Rule recalls, "and it served me very well when I was angry, which of course happened quite frequently in the analytic situation. I was very fey, a kind of dancer-like creature, and Greenson once said to me, 'I just have to tell you that it's hard for me to put that face together with what comes out of your mouth!' Then when he became ill and had to have his third pacemaker put in, he got aphasia and became enraged when he found that he couldn't express himself. He later told me, 'You taught me that *fuck* is a very good word. When I could finally speak, that is the first word I said.'"

As she felt herself personally transformed by psychoanalysis, Rule became an eager disciple. She began reading psychoanalytic theory and pored over Greenson's published writings, developing a special interest in his theory of the "working alliance." Greenson had defined that relationship between analyst and patient as a bond based on the "nonsexual, nonromantic, mild forms of love." The feelings to which he was referring, Greenson wrote, were those "akin to liking, trust, and respect in particular." Of course no one knows the extent to which such affection can ever be wholly purged of its erotic overtones, and Greenson's own controversial relationship with his most famous patient, Marilyn Monroe, points up the difficulty in drawing the line at "liking, trust, and respect" when treating a seductive patient of the opposite sex. If these "mild forms of love" exist on both sides, a mysterious chemistry develops between analyst and patient. Certainly for Janice Rule, it was not just the hard work of analysis but the opportunity to create a "working alliance" with the dynamic Ralph Greenson that turned the therapeutic process into a life-altering experience.

The bond she established with Greenson extended well beyond the period of her treatment. He became her friend and mentor, and she also struck up friendships with Greenson's colleagues, David Rubinfine and Milton Wexler.

"I think I was terribly lucky," Rule observes. "These men were all the aces of the field." They were also analysts well known for their infatuation with celebrities. One day Rule was having dinner with Wexler, who mentioned that he had just participated in a colloquium with several actors, all of whom denied that they suffered real-life identity problems as a result of the diverse roles they played on stage or screen.

"I said, 'Oh, Milton, that's crazy. Of course we do,'" Rule recalls. "That got me to sit down and write about it."

She began rummaging through libraries to research published material about the identity problems of actors. She also collected pointers from her friends Hoffs, Greenson, Rubinfine, and Wexler. Then she began putting together a monograph on the subject. Quoting extensively from the analytic literature and citing examples from her own experience as well as that of her actor friends, she attempted to demonstrate how an actor's identification with the characters he portrays can impel him to give up or alter his own personality. After composing several drafts, she mustered the courage to show her paper to Greenson.

His reaction stunned her. Greenson was so impressed that he sent the essay to Karl Menninger, who promptly invited Rule to come to Topeka to discuss her ideas with him personally. Dr. Karl had a reputation for shining up to movie stars, many of whom were patients at his clinic or patrons of his foundation. He huddled with Rule and helped her to edit her paper. At his prodding, the Chicago Psychoanalytic Institute arranged for her to present it at a symposium there, with Menninger himself leading the panel of discussants. "For a novice," Rule once remarked, "that was like debuting straight onto Broadway."

The article that subsequently appeared in the *International Journal of Psychoanalytic Psychotherapy* was based on that presentation to the members of the Chicago Institute. It was peppered with analytic rhetoric applied to the relationships between actor and director, actor and audience, actor and self. Rule talked about the good director forming "a working alliance with the actor and hopefully a kind of positive transference," so that the actor would be willing "to dive down as far as possible for the unconscious inner life of the character." She suggested that the actor must "free associate along with the writer and, like both a good analyst and a good analytic patient, not be afraid of what it will bring up in himself." And she observed that many of the actor's traits "resemble the characteristics ascribed to adolescents by Anna Freud"—idealism, loyalty to one's peers, and a certain fickleness.

To illustrate her theories about the actor's protean identity, Rule provided several case histories, including that of someone whom she described as "one of the great dramatic actresses of her day." (The portrait appears to be a thinly-veiled sketch of Rule's *Picnic* co-star, Kim Stanley.) To achieve her trademark emotional intensity on stage, this brilliant actress would habitually, if subconsciously, create a climate of real chaos in her personal life—which explained why she had divorced two husbands and driven several lovers to abandon her in the course of performing in five plays. But while portraying "a sweet, dumb, rather sexy nightclub dancer" (like the role that Stanley played in *Bus Stop*), she broke that pattern and suddenly became "optimistic, bright, cheery, and adorable," qualities that mirrored the traits of her character in the play.

Like the other serious actors whom Rule analyzed, this performer had altered her own personality to comport with her stage persona. "The role the actor is playing replaces the real self to the outside world," Rule noted. The case studies Rule presented were intriguing, and while the application of psychoanalytic insights to the craft of acting was hardly novel, her respectful synthesis of Freudian ideas—delivered by a movie star no less—was bound to tickle the analytic elders.

Especially ingratiating was Rule's concluding recommendation that all actors reap the benefits of psychoanalysis as early as possible. That suggestion, she wrote, "is limited to actors because I feel qualified to discuss actors' needs, though generally I would like to see analysis an accepted part of all higher education."

Toward the end of her paper Rule criticized the actor who feels secure "only when some 'Big Daddy'—producer or director—allows him to live by giving him a role, an identity, someone to be." Of course such a dependence on the patronage of "Big Daddy" is not restricted to the acting profession. Psychoanalysis, too, has its share of paternalistic mentors, inclined to reward those protegées who, like Marie Bonaparte or Janice Rule, display an appealing blend of aptitude and reverence.

Rule's "debut" presentation was such a hit with the leaders of the Chicago Psychoanalytic Institute that they invited her to train there to become a lay analyst. Considering that she had never completed high school, the invitation was, to say the least, irregular. "I knew I lacked the scholarly credentials," Rule recalls, "but they said, 'With all the reading you've done, you're up to the level of our third-year candidates.'"

The offer came at a time when Rule was eager for a new vocation. Having forged a successful career for herself outside the home, she was dissatisfied with the idea of confining herself to the role of dutiful housewife. "I thought I'd like to have something that kept me alive while I stayed home with my children," she says. Gazzara and she maintained a bicoastal marriage while she took an apartment in New York and completed the required undergraduate courses at Manhattan Marymount College. She then applied to the doctoral programs at the Chicago and Southern California Psychoanalytic Institutes and was accepted at both. For her first year's training she commuted to Chicago, then completed the last two years in Los Angeles, earning her doctorate in psychoanalysis from the Southern California Institute in 1975.

It was a time when the Southern California Institute was opening its doors to other aspiring lay analysts, including several professors of history and literature from UCLA. But those academicians already held advanced degrees, and Rule's rather extraordinary entry into the inner sanctum was a source of some dismay to other prospective candidates, especially the psychologists and clinical social workers (most of them other women) who had long been denied admission to the institute's highly selective analytic training program. In the mid-1980s a group of clinical psychologists became so vexed about their systematic rejection from such programs all across the country that they filed a class-action lawsuit against the American Psychoanalytic Association, claiming that their exclusion amounted to restraint of trade. Dr. Toni Bernay, a plaintiff in that suit and one of the first clinical psychologists to be admitted to the Southern California Institute, notes that she had to wage her legal battle at "great cost in terms of time, energy, and money." Dr. Samoan Barish, the first licensed clinical social worker to be accepted into the institute's training program, remembers her own two-year struggle for admission as "an extremely arduous, inequitable procedure." Although both Bernay and Barish held doctorates and were already recognized authorities in their fields, they and others like them faced forbidding barriers that Janice Rule, with her influential connections, managed to avoid.

Once she completed her doctorate and set up a psychoanalytic practice, Rule discovered that her movie-star status could be both beneficial and problematic. She remarks that several patients sought her out because they thought she would "collude with their neuroses" rather than challenge them. Others came because they believed she would be "someone neat to talk to."

"There was a lot of instant intimacy," Rule says, and she found herself having to refer a number of star-struck patients to other analysts. In coming to terms with the consequences of her public persona, she learned much from the example of Ralph Greenson, who was himself something of a star performer on the local lecture circuit. "He made me see that my acting background was not necessarily a drawback," Rule says. Indeed it could even prove useful in dealing with particular neuroses. "I find myself primarily drawn to hysterical patients," she comments. "You need a greater proportion of hysteria—in a good way—to become a performing artist than you need, say, obsessive compulsiveness." Besides, Rule believes, there is "a *flair* to hysterical characters. They're more fun, except when they're really ill."

During the 1970s Rule virtually relinquished her acting career to concentrate on her analytic training and practice. She knew that if she did accept an acting role, she might be separated from her patients for extended periods, and that could wreak havoc with the analysis. "What would I say to my patients?" she asks rhetorically. " 'I can't see you for two weeks because I have to fly out to the Coast and do some television nonsense'? I made only two films during that whole time—on my vacations." One of them was Costa-Gavras's *Missing*, which did compel her to leave her patients for eight weeks because of delays in filming. "It was a great blow to some of them," she says.

The other movie was Robert Altman's *3 Women*, which was made in 1977 and turned out to be among the most psychologically penetrating films of the decade, examining many of the motifs of role-playing and fluctuating identity that Rule had written about in her monograph. Altman's dreamlike fable centers on a pair of young employees (Shelley Duvall and Sissy Spacek) at a desert geriatric clinic. At first Spacek's character is a blank page; like an actor with no clearly defined persona, she studies the behavior of her more flamboyant friend and begins to imitate all her quirks and mannerisms. Eventually both women lose their bearings as their separate identities merge. Rule, cast as a silent painter of sadoerotic murals, is the earth mother who ultimately emancipates them from the male dominance that has been their common curse.

Three years after the release of *3 Women*, Rule charted a more independent course for herself, personally as well as professionally, when her nineteen-year marriage to Ben Gazzara ended in divorce. In her paper on the identity crises of the actor, Rule gave some insight into the problems that plagued their relationship. One of the case histories she discussed had to do with a man she called Edward, who bears a striking resemblance to Ben Gazzara. She described Edward's bachelor days as a period when "he had spent a great deal of his leisure time in bars, having what he later romanticized as a kind of artist-café life—a life he had denigrated during his courtship as boring and wasteful, indulged in only because he had no home to go to." Several years after he got married, Edward returned to that neurotic pattern in real life while he was starring in a film about a group of bar-hopping pals who "indulge in a desperate bender." Playing that role is what triggered the regression on Edward's part, according to Rule, and he subsequently credited "his wife's perception, sensitivity, and psychoanalytic insights for saving their home."

In 1970 Gazzara starred with John Cassavetes and Peter Falk in *Husbands,* written and directed by Cassavetes. The film, about a trio of friends on a wild binge, is suggestively close to the movie Rule describes in her case history of "Edward." In an interview promoting *Husbands,* Gazzara observed, "Women can't understand why most men prefer the company of other men to women. They hate that and usually try—unsuccessfully—to combat it." Explaining why his marriage to Rule survived, he pointed out that she was willing to pamper him, "and women *have* to do that for their men."

A decade later Rule decided that such a self-abasing arrangement was no longer tolerable. Over the years Gazzara's career frustrations had made him increasingly irascible and difficult to live with. *Run for Your Life* had turned him into a well-paid TV star, but for a serious actor once hailed as the successor to Brando, the mediocrity of episodic television was a definite comedown. "When you've been spoiled by playing in works by top authors," Gazzara remarked, "it's punishing to do inferior material."

Rule arrived at much the same conclusion when, following her divorce from Gazzara, she decided to pick up the strands of her own acting career. She had always viewed psychoanalysis as a temporary occupation. "When my children were grown, I intended to go back to the theater, which is what I love most," she says. "I knew that while I could still walk around, I wanted to walk the boards again." Also, the death of her father and her mentors Greenson and Rubinfine, all coming within a few years of her divorce from Gazzara, prompted her to reevaluate her life once more. The practice of psychoanalysis, which had once so entranced her, was losing some of its allure.

Having removed herself from the limelight for more than a decade, however, she discovered a paucity of roles upon her return. She was consigned to acting in B movies (like the 1985 potboiler *Rainy Day Friends*) or making guest appearances in routine television fare such as *Murder, She Wrote.* Like her ex-husband, she found television a depressing medium for the well-trained actor. More often than not she was performing parts in which, she says, "motivation is out of the question—you just have to deliver the information." She returned to the Actors Studio, a haven for introspective actors, but found few opportunities to practice her craft outside the Studio's classes.

Rule's fate was not unique. Many actresses discovered that good roles were harder to come by as they approached middle age, and they had to make difficult life choices as their professional options narrowed. In the 1950 film *All About Eve*, the archetypal story of the plight of the middle-aged actress, Margo Channing finally accepts that her deepest fulfillment as a woman will come in surrendering her career (which offered fewer and fewer opportunities anyway) and embracing the role of loving wife and helpmate. That conclusion was perfectly consistent with society's biases at the time, biases reinforced by Freudian assumptions about the subordinate nature of women.

With the rise of the women's liberation movement in the late 1960s and early 1970s, such gender stereotyping was attacked on many fronts, although Hollywood remained a bastion of masculine mores. That period was the heyday of "buddy movies," when male camaraderie was celebrated in such pictures as *Husbands, Midnight Cowboy, Easy Rider, Butch Cassidy and the Sundance Kid, M*A*S*H, The Sting,* and *Scarecrow*. Women in these films were either invisible or relegated to weak supporting roles.

When Alan Ladd, Jr., took over as president of Twentieth Century-Fox in 1976, he cannily decided to provide some counterprogramming and sponsored a slate of films with strong female characters. The first was *3 Women*, and it was followed by four pictures that had an even stronger impact. *Julia*, about the friendship between playwright Lillian Hellman and a fiery anti-Nazi activist, and *The Turning Point*, which endorsed family and career as equally valid choices for women, were both films that earned rave reviews, prestigious awards, and healthy box-office returns. *Alien*, which featured Sigourney Weaver as a brilliant, gun-toting scientist, was a novel variation on a timeworn genre—a feminist sci-fi adventure; it, too, succeeded in capturing a huge audience.

Another Fox film in the cycle, Paul Mazursky's *An Unmarried Woman,* was the one that most explicitly dramatized the challenges women faced as they tried to strike out on their own. It focused on a thirtyish New York housewife who is initially devastated when her husband leaves her for a younger woman. But with the help of a compassionate female therapist (played by real-life psychologist Dr. Penelope Russianoff), she finds a new career, a new lover, and the serenity to glory in her independence.

Soon after *An Unmarried Woman* was released in 1978, Judy Klemesrud of *The New York Times* interviewed Dr. Russianoff and asked her to sum up the film's most important statement. "That a woman doesn't have to be married in order to live a life," the therapist replied. "Most women have felt for years that they're worthless if they're not attached to a man."

Four years later Dr. Russianoff parlayed that theme into a popular self-help manual entitled *Why Do I Think I Am Nothing Without a Man?* In a question-and-answer spread for *People* magazine (adorned with a medley of photos—one of the six-foot-tall Russianoff seated on a couch with her diminutive husband plopped in her lap; another showing a daisy chain of her friends cavorting at her country home; and a still from *An Unmarried Woman*), Russianoff rattled off several of the book's homilies. She described the cycle of "desperate dependency" to which most women fall victim, the "helpless little girl role" they play, and the dangerous syndrome of "wanting a man for protection." The *People* interviewer concluded by asking whether Russianoff usually follows her own advice. "Absolutely," she declared. "A lot of Freudian therapists attacked my direct approach in *An Unmarried Woman*, but the older I grow, the more secure I get from listening to my own philosophy. So when I wake up in the morning I say, as I would like my patients to do, 'Whoopee! Another day to me!' "

Pop feminism had replaced pop Freudianism as the latest tonic for self-improvement, and riding her prominence as a quasi-movie star, Russianoff was an ideal spokesperson for the cause. When her publisher sent her on a tour to plug *Why Do I Think I Am Nothing Without a Man?*, she was billed as "the second most famous female therapist in the United States"—after Dr. Joyce Brothers. In fact Dr. Brothers was the nation's most famous therapist, male *or* female. (Mel Brooks's 1977 spoof, *High Anxiety,* contained a memorable sight gag that made just that point. When Brooks—playing the Nobel Prize-winning director of the "Psycho-Neurotic Institute for the Very, Very Nervous"—steps to the podium to address a convention of his peers, he is dwarfed by a set of towering portraits honoring the five "giants" of the field: Freud, Rank, Jung, Adler, and Brothers.)

Penelope Russianoff's claim to fame was a single film role, but Dr. Brothers—with her widely syndicated newspaper column, her frequent movie cameos, and her ubiquitous TV appearances on everything from earnest talk shows to *Hollywood Squares*—had made a career out of blurring the line between therapist and performer. In the process she turned herself into an American icon, a bridge between the advice-to-the-lovelorn columnists of an earlier day and the so-called "media shrinks" who blossomed in the 1980s.

Back in 1968 May Romm, one of the first female analysts with a large show-business following, addressed the American Psychiatric Association on what was suddenly becoming a hot topic: "Women and Psychiatry." In explaining why she felt women were particularly well suited to practice psychotherapy, Romm said, "Women, through their very uniqueness of being females—mothers, or potential mothers—are natural healers who are endowed with a good deal of patience, and who are by nature empathic, intuitive creatures." It would not be long before a whole platoon of female therapists would capitalize on those maternal qualities to redefine the talking cure.

Through their radio call-in programs and best-selling primers, women such as Dr. Irene Kassorla (*Nice Girls Do*), Dr. Sonya Friedman (*Smart Cookies Don't Crumble*), Dr. Toni Grant (*Being a Woman*), and Dr. Beverly DeAngelis (*Secrets About Men Every Woman Should Know*) brought therapy directly to the masses. To the commonsense counsel of Ann Landers and Dear Abby, they added the authority of a doctorate in psychology. But rather than mimicking the imperious, impenetrable "blank screen" of the Freudian model, these effervescent pop psychologists took a user-friendly approach to the task of psychic problem solving.

One of the most successful practitioners of this new therapeutic format, Dr. Susan Forward, is also a leader of the anti-Freudian feminism popularized by movies like *An Unmarried Woman*. Dr. Forward, who calls her own four-year analysis "one of the most destructive influences in my life," had been treated by a classical Freudian while she was in her twenties. "He terminated me when I met my ex-husband because he felt I now had everything I wanted," she says. In her 1986 best-seller *Men Who Hate Women & the Women Who Love Them*, Forward mounted a frontal assault on the misogyny she believed was inherent in conventional psychoanalysis, admonishing her readers to avoid woman-hating analysts like the one who treated her. (She even provided a list of telltale words to listen for, such as *castrating, overbearing,* and *ball-breaker.*)

Tapping into women's resentment over Freudian notions of male superiority and making full use of her own gifts as a self-confident performer, Forward epitomized the sass and savvy of the new media sisterhood. She had studied acting before turning to psychology, and she was perfectly comfortable playing to an audience. Like Janice Rule, Forward had given up her performing career to raise a family. But when her children were grown, she started volunteering at the UCLA Neuro-Psychiatric Institute, where she developed a special interest in the therapeutic uses of psychodrama.

Her mentor there was another ex-thespian, Betsy Drake, who had starred in a few forgettable films of the 1940s, but who was best known for her real-life role as the third Mrs. Cary Grant. When her marriage to Grant fell apart in the late 1950s, Drake began volunteering at the Neuro-Psychiatric Institute and eventually rose to become its director of psychodrama therapy.

Drake, too, had given up acting in favor of marriage. Expressing the conventional wisdom of the time, she told Hedda Hopper in 1965, "I couldn't be an actress and a housewife too." But she chafed at the constraints of domesticity and searched for ways to satisfy her growing interest in human psychology. She experimented with hypnotism and LSD, both of which she introduced to Grant. And—in order to cope with her husband's moodiness and indifference, she would later claim—she entered psychoanalysis. Following her divorce from Grant in 1961, Drake tried a comeback in movies, but the parts she found, in such films as the kiddie comedy *Clarence the Cross-Eyed Lion,* were uninspired. Though she had never earned a high school diploma, she began taking classes in psychotherapy and went on to run workshops at the Neuro-Psychiatric Institute, where Susan Forward served as her assistant.

Using the techniques of psychodrama—in which patients play different roles in order to probe their problems—Drake and Forward were able to draw on their acting experience to help treat disturbed individuals. Forward developed a special expertise dealing with victims of incest and child abuse, and she sees a correlation between abused children and the actors she has known. "Both are constantly looking for the magic key to love and affection," she says. An acting career can be wildly unpredictable, Forward notes, oscillating between exhilarating triumphs and cruel disappointments. Most people could not tolerate a life spent teetering between such extremes, but actors, she suggests, often had parents who dispensed love and approval in the same capricious manner. "Show business takes the place of the parent who gives and withholds," she says. "Most actors hang in there so long because the rejection is so familiar. It's not that they're masochists, it's just that they manage to get enough positive reinforcement to keep them going until the next rejection. That kind of intermittent reinforcement can be very potent. It's like an addiction."

Forward also discerns a number of resemblances between actors and therapists. For one thing, she remarks, actors are often shameless narcissists, and so are many shrinks, especially those who are drawn to the media. "Maybe people who get into the media have a lot of narcissism to begin with," she suggests, and their fame rapidly inflates their already swollen egos. "It's scary how much adulation you get," Forward says. "I remember a woman who asked me if she could walk behind me—just to be in my aura! Women come up to me all the time, and I think, if they only knew how fucked up I am!"

The applause showered on any pop star can be intoxicating, and according to Forward, most media psychologists are fiercely protective of their privileged positions. They can also be brutally competitive with one another—taking potshots at their rivals on the air, bad-mouthing each other in print. "Some interesting things happen to healers when the siren song of the media calls," Forward says acerbically. "You expect backstabbing from a Donald Trump, but not from someone in a profession supposed to be sensitive to people's feelings."

Forward herself has been involved in a long feud with Dr. David Viscott, one of the few male shrinks to hit pay dirt as a media pundit. In addition to writing a series of best-selling books and hosting syndicated shows on radio and TV, Dr. Viscott presides over a commercial empire that has marketed self-help audiotapes, a collection of "In Touch" greeting cards, a series of "discovery weekends" at various resorts, and even a therapeutic Mexican cruise known as the "Coming from Love Boat" excursion. To Susan Forward he exemplifies the cocky, paternalistic psychiatrists whom she detests. Blunt and frequently confrontational, Dr. Viscott is far more interactive than the Freudian fathers of an earlier decade—an occupational necessity in the age of catchy sound bites—but he can be every bit as self-assured and peremptory in his judgments.

Susan Forward and her colleagues in the media sisterhood project a different image: intuitive, probing, but considerably more soothing than the brusque Dr. Viscott. All of these media maestros, however, are in the business of providing one-note answers to complicated problems. Susan Forward acknowledges the constraint, but she proudly defends her calling. "There is great value in media psychology," she insists. "It has demystified and destigmatized getting help. I'm very proud of the work I did in radio. You can make a special connection in that short time."

She also candidly admits that her vocation feeds her vanity. "I love the media—I'm honest about that," she says. Her work has provided "a wonderful way to get national recognition, a wonderful opportunity to do therapy and perform at the same time." Indeed she still harbors the dream of returning to the stage and emoting before an audience. "Part of me is dying to act again," Forward confides. "I've had the applause, and I know applause is transitory." But her experience communicating with radio audiences together with her psychological insight would, she thinks, make her a powerful dramatic actress. "People worry about my undermining my credibility—like Joyce Brothers doing all those crappy TV shows," Forward says. Her own aspirations are far loftier: "I believe in the *art* of acting, and I would like to exercise it more. Now, with my psychological smarts, the creation of a character would be much deeper."

Like Janice Rule, Susan Forward remains a trouper at heart, holding on to the fantasy that first propelled her beyond hearth and home. Her desire to capture a popular audience may be disdained by traditional psychoanalysts, but even Freud had a hankering to connect with the hoi polloi. Seventy-five years before Susan Forward penned her anti-Freudian best-seller, *Men Who Hate Women & the Women Who Love Them,* the Viennese seer was sailing to America to deliver the seminal Clark lectures. When he happened upon his cabin steward perusing *The Psychopathology of Everyday Life,* a book that he earnestly hoped would find a lay readership, Freud was openly delighted.

Today pop psychologists such as Susan Forward have managed to reach an audience far wider than any that Freud could have imagined. They did so not simply by "demystifying" his science but, to a considerable extent, by challenging the feminine mystique that he was instrumental in perpetuating. Casting aside the supporting roles to which they were once consigned, these winsome performers have shrewdly upstaged their Freudian masters.

12. THE MIRACLE WORKERS

Dozens of pithy self-help manuals continue to roll off the presses and vie for the attention of the psychologically distressed. But in the battle of the books, none is likely to surpass the work of a husband-and-wife team named Mildred Newman and Bernard Berkowitz. Their 1973 opus, *How to Be Your Own Best Friend*, sold an amazing three million copies in hardcover before going on to become a paperback perennial.

The fifty-six-page volume was not exactly a monumental contribution to psychoanalytic theory. As one reviewer commented, "What *Love Story* is to *The Brothers Karamazov*, *How to Be Your Own Best Friend* is to *The Interpretation of Dreams*." But the popularity of the Berkowitzes' tiny tome was no fluke. Their book heralded the dawning of a new psychotherapeutic age, a time when aggressive self-love replaced rigorous self-scrutiny as the cure of choice for neurotics in the know.

It was also the first pop-psychology primer to be flogged by the authors' famous patients, part of a nervy publicity campaign that was as controversial as it was successful. Mildred Newman—whose stable of celebrity analysands included actors Anthony Perkins, George Segal, Joel Grey, Paula Prentiss, and Richard Benjamin, playwrights Neil Simon and Terrence McNally, director Frank Perry, and columnists Rex Reed and Liz Smith—was not just America's most talked-about therapist-to-the-stars during the 1970s; with the publication of *How to Be Your Own Best Friend*, she emerged as a star in her own right.

Mildred Newman, née Rubenstein, had studied modern dance and worked as an artists' model before deciding to become a psychologist. Her analytic training was done at the National Psychological Institute for Psychoanalysis, the institute founded by the maverick Theodor Reik following his departure from the orthodox New York Psychoanalytic Institute. After divorcing her first husband, a postal worker named Philip Newman, she married Bernard Berkowitz, another analyst. Mildred and Bernie liked to tell patients that they first met when they were teenagers waiting in line for a free concert at Carnegie Hall; years later they renewed their acquaintance, and when Mildred suffered a near-fatal heart attack in 1960, Bernie nursed her back to health. Their romance blossomed, and they tied the knot two years later. The balding, roly-poly Berkowitz and the earthy Newman both exuded an air of affable unpretentiousness.

In *Heartburn*, the 1986 film based on Nora Ephron's witty autobiographical novel, Maureen Stapleton captured that gemütlich quality on screen when she played a fictionalized version of the analyst. Newman had been Ephron's analyst for several years, and in both her novel and screenplay for *Heartburn*, the author created a thinly veiled portrait of the robust Greenwich Village therapist, depicting her as a genial den mother in a muumuu.

Much as May Romm's good humor had warmed the cockles of the Hollywood crowd two decades earlier, Mildred Newman's maternal manner earned her the affection of New York–based writers and actors. Her first star patient was Paula Prentiss, the lanky, Texas-born comedienne whose chirpy image in the movies belied her private torment. Prentiss had always been subject to wild mood swings; her sudden success only exacerbated her sense of unworthiness, and she frequently felt suicidal. "I tried to do myself in about a thousand times," she once hyperbolized to *The New York Times*. In 1965, while she was filming *What's New, Pussycat?*—written by Woody Allen and starring Peter Sellers as a lecherous shrink—Prentiss lapsed into another of her psychotic interludes. In the middle of shooting she climbed onto a catwalk, started walking the beams, and announced that she intended to jump. A member of the crew managed to rescue her as she dangled from a girder by one arm.

The actress was flown back to New York and spent the next seven months confined to the Payne Whitney psychiatric clinic. "I didn't know anything about psychiatry," said her husband, Richard Benjamin. "They told me, in effect, that she had found fame too soon, before she was prepared to deal with being a celebrity, and all the pressures had brought on a nervous breakdown. They treated her with tranquilizers and I'd pretend everything was all right. I'd take her out to lunch when I visited her, but it was like taking a carrot out to lunch."

After she was released from Payne Whitney, Prentiss entered intensive therapy with Mildred Newman. A few years later she gushed about the transformation in her outlook that Newman had managed to effect: "I could not enjoy myself, did not love myself. And now! Wow! *I am me!* I am happy, beautiful, funny—people love me! I am my own best friend!"

Prentiss's husband was equally wowed by the results of his wife's therapy. "I was amazed at the way it helped her," Richard Benjamin declared. Not long after Prentiss began seeing Newman, Benjamin decided that he, too, needed a lift. He was starring in Neil Simon's *The Star-Spangled Girl* on Broadway and found himself racked with anxiety before many performances. "I wasn't too crazy about myself, and that was very hard for Paula to take," Benjamin explained. "She liked me, and the person she liked didn't like himself—which made her feel bad." After several sessions with his wife's therapist Benjamin was rejuvenated—and thoroughly versed in the distinctive language of Newmanspeak. "Now I like myself," he stated. "It's a process that's almost intangible, really. Everything changes. Your day changes. Everything's more awake and alive." (Another book by Newman and Berkowitz was titled *How to Be Awake and Alive.*)

Benjamin encouraged Neil Simon to visit Mildred, and he, too, got hooked. "Her philosophy seemed to me the most unique thing in the world," Simon told Dick Stelzer, author of a book called *The Star Treatment,* "because I didn't know it was OK to like yourself." (Evidently the playwright's celebrated wit had evaporated along with his hang-ups.) "I had been brought up thinking that liking yourself was a selfish thing," he reported soberly. "I discovered that the more you deny yourself, the more you start to put yourself down and not like yourself, the less chance you have of getting better."

Newman's patients were so thrilled with this "unique" philosophy that they could hardly contain their enthusiasm. In 1969 the set of Mike Nichols's lavish film version of *Catch 22* turned into a veritable recruiting office for Mildred's minions. Prentiss and Benjamin, who had featured roles in the film, sang the praises of their analyst to everyone within earshot. Two journalists covering the shoot were Nora Ephron and Dan Greenburg, who were then married to each other. As the author of the best-selling book of comic aphorisms *How to Be a Jewish Mother,* Greenburg was already something of an expert on psychological chicken soup. Listening to the vivid descriptions of Mildred Newman's recipe for success, his mouth began to water for more. Later, both he and Ephron landed on Newman's couch.

But the most immediate convert was Anthony Perkins, the actor who was playing the ineffectual Chaplain Tappman in *Catch 22.* In the late 1950s, when Hollywood was churning out a spate of psychiatric melodramas and films about mental illness, Perkins had achieved major stardom, most often cast as a timid, quavering neurotic. In *Fear Strikes Out,* the 1957 movie based on the life of baseball player Jimmy Piersall, Perkins gave a memorable performance as the volatile outfielder whose career was nearly destroyed by a nervous breakdown.

Three years later he starred as Norman Bates in Alfred Hitchcock's classic *Psycho,* a far more macabre dissection of mental illness; his role in that movie sealed the young actor's image as a shy, creepy loner. The film ends with a long scene, typical of the period, in which a psychiatrist blames Norman Bates's homicidal behavior on his twisted oedipal fixation and laboriously expounds on "the mother-half of Norman's mind." It is a tribute to Perkins's performance that the shrink's glib explanation seems utterly inadequate to define the brilliantly nuanced character he brought to life.

Perkins's tremulous screen persona was not so different from his real-life personality. Fearful and isolated, he was plagued by insecurities. His father, the actor Osgood Perkins, died when he was a child, and young Tony developed a relationship with his ferociously overprotective mother that bore some eerie parallels to the twisted mother-son dynamic of *Psycho.* "She was constantly touching me and caressing me," Perkins once revealed. "Not realizing what effect she was having, she would touch me all over, even stroking the inside of her thighs right up to my crotch." The theater promised to rescue him from this incestuous atmosphere, but his success as an actor could not erase his persistent loneliness and his almost pathological fear of women. He shared the screen with such voluptuous actresses as Sophia Loren, Ingrid Bergman, Melina Mercouri, and Jane Fonda, and while a number of his nubile costars tried to lure him into bed, he invariably fled in terror.

In the late 1950s Perkins entered psychoanalysis with the popular Hollywood psychiatrist, Gerald Aronson. Although he liked

Aronson, Perkins felt his analysis was a failure. His personal anxieties intensified in the mid-1960s, when his once-thriving movie career hit a dry spell. He decided to move back to New York, where he did seem to function more happily. Still Perkins found himself isolated much of the time. He had furtive homosexual contacts but felt incapable of developing long-lasting relationships. When he arrived at the remote corner of Mexico where *Catch 22* was filming in 1969, he began to question the self-imposed solitude to which he had grown habituated.

"I was stranded for a long time on location," Perkins said in an interview with the authors before he died of AIDS in 1992. "It was like going to an encounter weekend. There was no place to go, nothing to do except interrelate and coexist with others. And I just couldn't manage it. I didn't have any skills at intimacy. In New York a single person with a few bucks can devise a way of living that is tolerable. I would pretend I was living a life that was working for me—and in a sense it was—but it was a life of enormous limitations. When I was on that movie location, I realized I wanted to be more available to share my thoughts and feelings with others."

He was particularly impressed by the relaxed conviviality of Paula Prentiss. "I had known Paula in times of turmoil," Perkins said, "and I was astonished at the peacefulness she exuded. I said to her one day, 'What happened to you?' She told me about Mildred Newman." As soon as he returned to New York, Perkins called Newman and immediately began intensive therapy, seeing her four times a week in individual as well as group sessions. (The group was run jointly by Newman and Berkowitz.)

Perkins's analysis with Newman spanned nine years, and in the course of it he underwent several remarkable metamorphoses. On the professional side his acting grew less mannered and more natural. "After therapy I felt much freer and easier as a performer," Perkins said. "In some of my early movie roles I was so frigid in my own narrow smallness." He cited as an example *Green Mansions,* the 1959 drama in which he portrayed an explorer who falls in love with a jungle maiden played by Audrey Hepburn. "I gave a performance so austere, so monotonous, so fearful and remote that it still hurts to watch," Perkins said.

Perkins's therapy with Newman revitalized his attitude toward acting. "I was able to walk onto the set or into rehearsal and feel unfettered by any fears or anxieties," he declared. Newman also encouraged him to extend himself as an artist. With Stephen Sondheim, he cowrote the screenplay for the ingenious murder mystery *The Last of Sheila;* he also directed *Psycho III.* "Without therapy," Perkins said, "I would never have done writing or directing—not to mention being a husband and the father of two sons."

Indeed, it was in his personal relations that Perkins experienced the most astonishing sea change. When he went to see Mildred Newman in 1969, the thirty-seven-year-old actor had never had sex with a woman; his erotic experience was occasionally homosexual but, in his words, "mostly solitary." That was no deterrent to the plucky therapist, however, who was intent on introducing him to the joys of a heterosexual union. "She was constantly provoking me about women," Perkins said, "asking why I was repressed in that area. We had heated disagreements, knockdown arguments. I would say, 'I don't want to talk about this again today,' and she said, 'I *do* want to talk about it.' We kicked it to pieces."

Like psychoanalysts of an earlier era, Newman was an unabashed cheerleader for matrimony. Nora Ephron tweaked her shrink for this fixation in the screenplay for *Heartburn.* On the heroine's wedding day, the analyst, played by Maureen Stapleton, weeps tears of joy. "All you therapists ever want is for us to get married and have babies," the new bride says at one point. "It's the closest you ever get to a cure."

With a reclusive introvert like Tony Perkins, the "cure" was harder to come by. According to Perkins, Newman never advocated heterosexuality as the only course to follow. "She is a crusader for a wider road, for choice and limitlessness," Perkins said. "She was never *against* anything. She was for *more* rather than *less,* and that's very difficult to refute. She would say to me, 'It's not that I want you to spend less time by yourself in monosexual isolation. But wouldn't you want to make the choice to do that rather than have it be the only thing you *can* do?' It's like someone who only does water-skiing and refuses to try snow-skiing. I would say, 'I know I don't like it,' and she would say, 'How do you know unless you've tried it?' "

Newman kept harping on his relationships with women, and Perkins kept resisting. But over a two-year period of almost daily therapy sessions, she began to win him over. In 1971, while he was filming *The Life and Times of Judge Roy Bean,* the thirty-nine-year-old actor had his first heterosexual fling—with starlet Victoria Principal. Soon after that, at a party in New York, Perkins was introduced to twenty-three-year-old Berry Berenson, the socialite granddaughter of art historian Bernard Berenson and the sister of actress Marisa Berenson. Perkins and Berry Berenson started dating. When she got pregnant in 1973, they decided to marry.

"I owe the second half of my life to the years I spent in Mildred's office," Perkins stated flatly. "It would be errant dishonesty to put it any other way. Most analysts are content to fix what's there. They won't go the distance as Mildred did." At the same time, Perkins never claimed that his sexual orientation had been changed. "The second part of my life is different on a behavior level," he said, "but it's still me."

Just as Moss Hart's marriage to Kitty Carlisle had boosted the stock of Hart's analyst, Dr. Lawrence Kubie, the nuptials of Tony Perkins and Berry Berenson some three decades later gave Mildred Newman a similar reputation as a miracle worker. Perkins was not just his analyst's best advertisement but her chief pitchman as well. When Rex Reed came to interview Perkins for a *New York Times* article, he left with Mildred Newman's telephone number. Soon Reed, too, was a devoted patient. "What she did was just help me to say 'Fuck you' to the world," he later remarked.

In 1972 Perkins was cast as a gay producer in *Play It As It Lays*, the movie based on Joan Didion's existential meditation on Los Angeles anomie. That set turned into another spawning ground for Newman converts. Joel Schumacher, the film's costume designer, was a recovering drug addict. When he mentioned that he was frustrated by his lack of progress in Freudian analysis, Perkins recommended that he consult Newman. Schumacher did, and before long he had joined the ranks of her enthusiasts. "I left the Freudian after a short time," Schumacher recalls. "I didn't have time for that kind of analysis. I'm from the instant-gratification school."

Perkins also circulated copies of Newman and Berkowitz's *How to Be Your Own Best Friend*, which at that time had been privately printed in pamphlet form, to other members of the cast and crew. Frank Perry, the director of *Play It As It Lays*, started browsing through the little book one night and couldn't put it down. Soon afterward he phoned Mildred Newman in New York and set up an appointment.

A high proportion of Berkowitz and Newman's show-business patients were homosexual, and the analysts encouraged them to follow Tony Perkins's example and expand their horizons. "Analysts once thought they had little chance of changing homosexuals' preferences," Berkowitz and Newman declared in *How to Be Your Own Best Friend*. "But some refused to accept that and kept working with them, and we've found that a homosexual who really wants to change has a very good chance of doing so. Now we're hearing all kinds of success stories."

Several of their patients, however, were adamantly opposed to being turned into "success stories." Says playwright and gay activist Larry Kramer, who admits that he was thrown out of their therapy group for his obstreperousness, "I didn't feel any love from either Mildred or Bernie." Writer James Kirkwood was also put off by Newman's insistent harping on the subject of marriage. Kirkwood described himself as bisexual, and though he had no interest in settling down with a woman, Newman kept prodding him toward the altar. "She proselytized with me about getting married," Kirkwood told the authors shortly before his death in 1989. "I think Mildred proselytizes because she feels it's easier to live a heterosexual life, and she *has* had success with various people in helping them achieve that. She doesn't say, 'You must change.' But she'll keep questioning you: 'Wouldn't you like to?' "

Some of her patients view Newman's enthusiasm for marriage as simply a reflection of her Jewish mothering. "Most doctors treat homosexuality as aberrant behavior, and Mildred does fall into that category," says Joel Schumacher. "But she is also very generous and loving, with a profoundly maternal and Talmudic side. She really wants you to be a better you." James Kirkwood, too, described her as "a Mother Earth figure." In her Greenwich Village office a refrigerator stands next to the shrink's couch, and it is always filled with goodies. "It's like going to somebody's apartment," Rex Reed said of therapy with Newman. "I mean, Mildred makes tea for you and you raid the icebox. I eat and talk at the same time." Reed once took a cruise aboard the *France* with Mildred and Bernie, and they were frequent dinner guests at his apartment.

Like Yenta the matchmaker, Newman loved to make a good *shiddach*. She would call agents to help her patients get jobs, and once she introduced a singer she was treating to a patient of Bernie's, a voice coach. "Mildred believes that success is everyone's birthright," says Joel Schumacher, who, like his friend Tony Perkins, eventually stretched himself to become a writer and director. Other patients, too, were urged to act on their dreams. Gael Greene was toiling as a restaurant critic when she started with Newman, but after treatment she wrote a best-selling novel. Nora Ephron graduated from journalism to write novels and screenplays and eventually became a film director as well. Liz Smith went from writing movie reviews for *Cosmopolitan* to being the most powerful gossip columnist in the country.

If Newman gave her patients the self-confidence to pursue their secret ambitions, she and her husband also derived something from the bargain. For starters they got a charge out of mingling with famous people at premieres and A-list galas. "They show up at every party, every bar mitzvah, every opening night," says Larry Kramer. "I guess they see themselves as participants in their patients' lives." Veteran writer Arthur Laurents remembers seeing them at an early preview of their patient Terrence McNally's *Frankie and Johnny in the Clair de Lune,* after which the therapists held forth with deep-dish interpretations of the play. "They're at all the parties, beating the bushes for business," Laurents says.

"Mildred is the mother of the world," Laurents adds. "I guess she's made that whole *mishpuchah* happier." Indeed Newman's patients did seem like a tight-knit family, with a strong sense of loyalty to one another. Liz Smith often highlighted other patients of Newman's in her columns. She called Joel Schumacher "one of my all-time favorite persons" and regularly plugged his films. Once she conducted a lengthy tête-à-tête with Schumacher for *Interview* magazine in which they both rhapsodized about analysis in general and Mildred Newman in particular. "I think the world is divided between people who have had analysis and people who haven't," Schumacher opined. "Honestly, Lizzie, I don't know how people live without it." He went on to eulogize Newman: "Just like in show business, or any other business, there are stars and she's definitely a star."

"Well, you know I agree with you about that," Smith responded.

Petty rivalries did occasionally threaten the harmony of Mildred's *mishpuchah.* James Kirkwood was miffed when he learned that he hadn't been invited to a party given by Liz Smith. During a therapy session with Newman he mentioned how upset he felt. To his surprise she told him that she hadn't been invited either. "How do *you* feel about it?" Kirkwood asked.

"Not so bad now that I know you weren't invited," the therapist replied.

Although the Berkowitzes' fondness for socializing with their patients raised eyebrows among orthodox analysts, most of their famous clients staunchly defended them. "They may be outrageous," Liz Smith said of Berkowitz and Newman, "but in my opinion they could put on sandwich boards and walk around saying,

'Try us. Let us shrink your head.' I don't think that would change what they did for me and what I've seen them do for other people .... They just don't draw the line between the people they loved and worked with in therapy and the people they want to see socially."

"I couldn't see how Mildred's enjoyment of going out and being pointed out and talked to and photographed could negatively affect her ability to treat her patients," said Tony Perkins. "Why shouldn't she have some fun? If she wanted to go out and dance with Neil Simon, what's the big deal?" Nevertheless, Perkins admitted that after an astringent profile of Newman and Berkowitz by Susan Edmiston appeared in *Esquire* in 1977, skewering the couple for party-hopping with their patients, they did pull back from the social swirl. "They were very chastened by that article," Perkins said. "After that, Mildred didn't go out and dance at Studio 54 anymore."

In the canon of ethical dos and don'ts, dancing with patients was a relatively minor transgression. Far naughtier was the Berkowitzes' shameless enlistment of their celebrity patients to sell their great labor of self-love, *How to Be Your Own Best Friend*. The book grew out of an interview that Jean Owen, a free-lance magazine writer, conducted with the twosome in 1971. After she transcribed the interview, Owen convinced Newman and Berkowitz that their pithy comments were far too precious to waste on a single ephemeral article. The analysts spent twenty thousand dollars to have the interview privately printed in book format. It was being distributed out of a friend's garage in Connecticut at the time Rex Reed invited them to appear on a talk show he was hosting in Boston. Reed raved about the book and gave the Connecticut address where viewers could write to order a copy. Liz Smith, who was not yet a Newman patient but would soon sign on, was also a guest on that program. She told the Berkowitzes that they were foolish to rely on a mail-order operation and advised them to find a publisher in New York.

Newman and Berkowitz passed out copies of the book to other well-connected patients, soliciting their advice. Several thought it was indeed worthy of a major publisher, and Nora Ephron decided to give it an all-out push. She sent the manuscript to a number of editors, including Nancy Hardin at Bantam. Hardin remembers Ephron telling her, "Either this is the best book you've ever read or the worst book you've ever read, I can't decide which. Take a look at it." Bantam did make a bid, but it was topped by Random House, which offered $60,000. The paperback rights later sold for an astronomical $885,000.

But that was after something remarkable occurred. When the book came out in the spring of 1973, initial sales were anemic. Random House was having trouble marketing the slim volume—until someone came up with the bright idea of capitalizing on the authors' connections. A full-page ad was devised to run in *The New York Times Book Review* on June 17, 1973. In the center of the page was a photograph of the smiling authors. Surrounding the pair were pictures of their celebrity patients, spouting exuberant endorsements for the book. Rex Reed declared, "It will change your life." Dan Greenburg said it "should be read and reread at least once a week." There were also photos of two cuddling couples—Richard Benjamin and Paula Prentiss, and Anthony Perkins and Berry Berenson. In her boldface blurb Prentiss proclaimed, "This book demands that you give up responsibility to anyone but yourself." Referring to *Play It As It Lays,* Perkins said, "On a recent movie location the cast and crew who passed around a simple mimeographed copy of this manuscript called it simply THE BOOK. Appropriate title, I'd say." Finally a beaming Neil Simon gushed, "If I'm gloomy, I read it twice a day with a glass of water. It has never failed to uplift me."

Sales zoomed in the wake of that ad, and soon the Berkowitzes were turning up on all the talk shows, usually with one or another of their famous patients seated right beside them and puffing the book. "I think it was nice that people went on TV," Tony Perkins observed. "People loved Mildred and Bernie very much and didn't worry about being exploited."

Although *How to Be Your Own Best Friend* clearly benefited from all the celebrity hype, it also struck a chord with the public. Its message was perfectly suited to the Me generation. "The Bible says, 'Love thy neighbor *as* thyself,' not 'better than' or 'instead of' thyself," the Berkowitzes reminded their flock. "If we cannot love ourselves, where will we draw our love for anyone else?" Using a telling medley of mixed metaphors, Newman and Berkowitz concluded that learning to love oneself "is like drilling a well to an untapped energy reserve, like finding a bank account we haven't used. It's the cheapest form of entertainment there is."

As the years passed, a few of Newman's patients did develop a bit more irony toward such banalities. In Neil Simon's 1992 play *Jake's Women,* the protagonist lashes out at his bromide-spouting therapist, telling her, "You're not an analyst. You're a mother with a diploma." Then he mocks her best-selling self-help manual, the title of which he deliberately twists to *Love Yourself, Fuck Them.*

For the most part, however, Berkowitz and Newman's grateful patients have remained fiercely loyal, and they are capable of matching their mentors platitude for platitude. Analysis with Mildred Newman, Rex Reed said, "really taught me to be on my own team." Dan Greenburg, who had once burlesqued the smothering solicitude of the Jewish mother, dropped the sarcasm when he talked about his own maternal shrink. To illustrate the rewards of his therapy, Greenburg described meeting a movie producer who later told a mutual friend what he thought of Greenburg: "I'd say Dan has a crush on himself." Greenburg accepted the gibe as a high compliment. "I think *everybody* should have a crush on himself," he exclaimed.

While the New York cognoscenti were gathering pearls of wisdom from Mother Mildred, Hollywood was gravitating to a considerably more glamorous version of the therapist as materfamilias. With her designer gowns and luminous complexion, onetime beauty queen Evelyn Silvers projected a very different image from the down-to-earth Mildred Newman. But Silvers, too, was a Jewish mother at heart, whose celebrity *mishpuchah* included such Hollywood luminaries as Dudley Moore, Mary Steenburgen, and Malcolm McDowell.

Psychotherapy was not the career path that Evelyn Silvers first envisioned for herself. After graduating from the University of Florida, she set out for New York to become a fashion model. "I was the first Toni girl, the first Revlon girl," Silvers says nostalgically. "Eventually I became the highest paid spokeswoman on TV, although Betty Furness claimed that she was." The svelte widow of comedian Phil Silvers, she is probably best remembered as Hal March's attractive handmaiden on *The $64,000 Question.*

Silvers met her future husband in 1955, when he tagged along on a date she had with Freddie Fields, the comedian's agent. The three of them attended the opening night of *Desk Set* on Broadway. Young Evelyn was horrified when a tweedy fellow seated in front of her scurried out before the final curtain. Later that evening at Sardi's, Phil introduced her to the gentleman, whom she roundly scolded for his bad manners at the theater. She had no idea that the target of her tongue-lashing, a certain "Mr. Atkinson," was the redoubtable drama critic of *The New York Times*.

"Of course," she says, "Phil fell in love on the spot."

That ability to cut to the quick stayed with her. The ex-model's striking good looks, combined with her maternal sensitivities, made her a popular figure in Beverly Hills society. After raising the five daughters she had with Silvers (from whom she was divorced at the time of his death in 1985), Evelyn decided to parlay her skills as a confidante and "listener" into a full-time career as a therapist.

"I wanted to be a psychiatrist, but I didn't have the education, so it was more instinctual, more learn-as-you-go," Silvers reports. Eventually she did pick up a degree in counseling and began seeing clients, a number of whom were referred by the show-business friends she and her husband had made over the years. She quickly developed a loyal following, and the therapy group that she formed was second only to Milton Wexler's in star power. In fact, several former members of Wexler's group, including Dudley Moore and writer-director David Seltzer, joined up with Silvers after defecting from Wexler. Moore contrasts Silvers's comforting approach to Wexler's more critical posture. "She offered a sense of *laissez-faire* that was very liberating to me. I felt at ease, more unrestrained, and able to breathe in Evelyn's group," says Moore, who implies that Silvers was right in step with the how-to-be-your-own-best-friend school of therapy. "I progressed more with her than with any of the analysts I'd been to. I didn't feel any disapproval; I felt allowed to exist as I was." Moore also believes that Silvers was more responsive to his irrepressible sense of humor than his earlier therapists had been. "I think her marriage to Phil was a symptom of her desire to be around funny people," Moore says.

One longtime member of Silvers's group, agent Jeff Melnick, indicates that the presence of so many "industry" types may have skewed the group's perspective, although it did provide some unusual benefits. "I used to joke with Evelyn that the group was so heavily 'industry' that I should deduct it as a business expense rather than medical," Melnick says. "Once a year there would be a group marathon for twenty-four hours at Evelyn's house. You'd eat off Meissen china and Georgian silver. A caterer would come with midnight supper, which was usually bouillabaisse. In a strange way it was very Hollywood—but totally appropriate for everybody's lifestyle. It's very nice to have your therapist in a Galanos dress designed especially for her. Better than a suit from Kmart!"

Melnick also appreciated the advantages of his therapist's insider connections. Not long after he joined the group, he was fired from his post as an executive with Metromedia. "It was a rough period," Melnick recalls, "but Evelyn understood what I was going through. She'd been in the business, and she knew all the ins and outs." Like Mildred Newman, Silvers was always eager to arrange a *shiddach* for her show-biz patients. "She did some wonderful things—like set me up on interviews, which is so nontraditional," says Melnick. "We had career-counseling sessions, and she'd call clients or friends with a recommendation."

Silvers makes no apologies for such bold interventions in her patients' lives. "I have done it from the beginning and I will continue to do it," she declares. "If I can recommend someone who's out of work to someone else who's looking for that person's skills, it could end up saving the person and his family a lot of heartache. He may even need less psychotherapy as a result."

Although some of her patients have likened her group-therapy sessions to celebrity soirees, Silvers herself resents that characterization, as well as the suggestion that she has a fondness for attaching herself to the rich and famous. "If I were looking for major personalities and interesting people, my own husband and our friends would have sufficed," she insists. "Leonard Bernstein played my piano; Judy Garland worked on her songs at that Steinway. I played poker with Milton Berle. Those people have cooked in my kitchen. I don't get excited by stars. What I do get excited over is talent."

More recently, Silvers has also become excited about the study of "psycho-neuro-immunology," or, as she puts it, "the way man 'bodifies' disease." Her mother had died after a long bout with rheumatoid arthritis, and Silvers was herself diagnosed with the crippling illness. "I went to the library and researched the disease," she reports. "It took about three months for me to figure out how to put it in remission. Now I am working with cancer and AIDS patients, teaching them how to stimulate and release the neuropeptides in their bodies to put their diseases in remission."

In addition, she claims to have achieved remarkable success treating drug addicts. "They learn to release the morphine-like chemicals in the brain, using their own neurochemicals instead of street drugs," she explains. "I can teach anybody who hasn't burned too much brain tissue how to do it in fifteen minutes. It's a matter of putting the mind and the emotions in harmony."

*   *   *

Evelyn Silvers's foray into the new frontier of holistic psychotherapy is certainly the most surprising adventure in her extraordinary life's journey: A woman once famous for modeling lipstick and escorting contestants into the "isolation booth" is now dispensing mind-body cures to the afflicted and addicted. But her "laissez-faire" approach to therapy, as well as her new vocation as a psychosomatic healer, reflect the more pervasive disaffection with traditional psychoanalysis that swept America in the 1970s. It was a decade that witnessed an unprecedented explosion of alternative therapeutic systems and consciousness-raising techniques—"the biggest introspective binge any society in history has undergone," according to historian Theodore Roszak. All in all, this giddy spree encompassed an astonishing array of psychic remedies. Bioenergetics, a mode pioneered by the Reichian psychiatrist Alexander Lowen, promoted deep breathing and strenuous physical exercise as a means of releasing the blocked sexual energy that bred neurosis. Rolfing, developed by the matronly Dr. Ida Rolf, used excruciatingly painful muscle massages to expel destructive emotional memories. Psychosynthesis, the brainchild of Italian psychoanalyst Roberto Assagioli, employed meditation and guided daydreams to realign "subpersonalities" with an individual's "true self." Biofeedback used elaborate medical machinery to tell a meditating patient precisely which organs in his body were generating psychic tension. The Feldenkrais method, developed by Israeli physicist Moshe Feldenkrais, was an amalgam of yoga, jujitsu, and Sufi dancing that encouraged subjects to alter their body movements and thereby enhance their thought patterns; it promised relief from neurologic disease and even from the symptoms of aging. Silva Mind Control, a program in self-hypnosis created by Texas mesmerist José Silva, was a regimen for everything from smoking cessation to "effective sensory perception" (the ability to apprehend the essence of inanimate objects). Primal-scream therapy, inaugurated by Arthur Janov, encouraged regression to the womb as participants released the forces of repression with bloodcurdling howls and shrieks. And Arica, founded in 1971 by Bolivian mystic Oscar Ichazo, offered workshops in chanting mantras and meditating on multi-hued pictographs called yantras to access the "divine life" within.

Every one of these therapies had its celebrity champions. Candice Bergen and her then-boyfriend, producer Bert Schneider, were devotees of Arica. Dyan Cannon and Theresa Russell were primal-screamers. Sean Young once confided to an interviewer that she had been "seriously Rolfed." Of course Hollywood had always been hospitable to therapeutic experimenters and oddball swamis, from Aimee Semple MacPherson to Anton LaVey (founder of the First Church of Satan, whose cadre of supporters included Jayne Mansfield and Sammy Davis, Jr.). But with the dawning of the Me Decade, these quasi-religious movements and self-help programs gained unprecedented popularity. As the once-modish pastime of Freudian analysis became passé, the restless trendsetters of Tinseltown cast about for more exhilarating paths to enlightenment.

The consciousness revolution of the 1970s produced dozens of new gurus who wooed Hollywood, but none was more enthusiastically embraced than a failed used-car dealer named Werner Erhard, whose brash showmanship and formula for self-aggrandizement were tailor-made for the movie metropolis. Like Mildred Newman's prescription for self-love, Erhard's strategy for personal empowerment proved especially intoxicating to show-business personalities.

The son of a Jewish restaurateur who had converted to Episcopalianism, Erhard began life in Philadelphia as John Paul Rosenberg. He got married straight out of high school, opened an auto dealership (under the name Jack Frost), then took a job as a "motivator" of encyclopedia salesmen. At the age of twenty-five, Rosenberg abandoned his wife and three young children and resolved to reinvent himself. His new moniker was derived from a couple of magazine articles, one about the physicist Werner Heisenberg and the other about German Chancellor of the Exchequer Ludwig Erhard.

The idea for est (Erhard Seminars Training) had an equally bizarre origin. Driving along a California freeway one day in 1971, Erhard experienced a burst of inexplicable insight. All of a sudden he "got it"—and his course was set. He embarked on a mission to teach others how they, too, could experience this life-altering epiphany. Because the self is the source of all understanding, Erhard proclaimed, the only limits are those that are self-imposed. His followers were trained to "get rid of old baggage" and pursue their impossible dreams.

A slickly packaged blend of Zen, Gestalt, Scientology, and Dale Carnegie's positive thinking, Erhard's two-weekend marathons—with their now legendary drill-sergeant trainers, no-bathroom rules, and "I'm an asshole" mea culpas—became, for a few dizzying years, Hollywood's hottest ticket to self-discovery.

In March 1972 Erhard made his first incursion into the movie capital by hosting a much-ballyhooed luncheon at the Polo Lounge. Unfortunately, the only stars to show up for the affair were tired old-timers like Ann Miller and Glenn Ford. "They didn't get it," Erhard later groused.

Realizing that he needed a hipper corps of converts, Erhard concentrated on courting the movers and shakers of the New Hollywood. The game plan was remarkably successful. In the executive suites of certain studios, "getting your head straight" soon became as much a part of the workaday routine as doing lunch or taking a meeting. Warner Bros. chief Ted Ashley, one of the first to take the plunge, made est training mandatory for his minions. (So fervently was the new religion embraced out in Burbank that wags took to calling the studio Werner Brothers.) The head of one talent agency gave each of his employees two weekends of est in lieu of their Christmas bonuses. Major power brokers, such as David Geffen and Peter Guber, proselytized loud and hard, and soon a klatsch of celebrities—Yoko Ono, John Denver, Cloris Leachman, Joe Namath, and even Yippie-turned-Yuppie Jerry Rubin (who took the training three times)—climbed aboard the bandwagon.

Not everyone was so enthralled. Writer-director Tom Mankiewicz remembers the obnoxious enthusiasm of some of his colleagues: "Most people who went into est came back saying, 'This is the greatest thing in the world, and I'll kill you if you don't try it!' A friend of mine went to est and said, 'It changed my life. I'm a totally new person.' I said, 'I just spent two evenings with you, and you're exactly the same person you were before you left for est—only a little more argumentative.' "

Cajoled by several of his celebrity patients into attending one of Erhard's "VIP Seminars," Dr. Milton Wexler came away awed by Erhard's gift for gab, but appalled by his sophistries. "At one point Werner made the statement that since energy never dissipates, everything that has happened is out there in the universe to be recaptured," Wexler recalls. "Therefore if a murder was committed on a Sicilian farm back in 1850, we could travel out to space and capture the energy and the light that emanated from that murder and find out who the murderer was. This was a madman! There was a physicist in the audience who took him on. The physicist was enormously intellectual. Werner Erhard was enormously simple and talked in very primitive terms. But Werner actually convinced most of the audience that he was right and the physicist was wrong. He could talk his way around anything."

It wasn't simply the evangelism of a few zealots that accounted for est's popularity. The buzz was that Erhard's design for living had yielded some amazing results, and this produced hordes of new recruits among Hollywood go-getters. Screenwriter Colin Higgins's first film, *Harold and Maude,* was about the improbable romance between a suicidal young man (Bud Cort) and an octogenarian hippie (Ruth Gordon). As Higgins himself interpreted the story during an interview in 1979—eight years after it was filmed, and five years after he absorbed the rhetoric of est— it was "a metaphor for individual growth and transformation. Harold is introverted and afraid; all his life he's been repressing his feelings. Maude is an extrovert always embarking on some new experience. She knows that the essence of life is relationships with others, and she's trying to bring Harold out of his shell." After the movie came out in 1971, it slowly turned into a cult favorite, but Higgins had trouble capitalizing on its underground success. His screenwriting career was limping along in 1974 when he decided to attend an est marathon. Energized by the experience and determined to create a commercial script that could "transform" his own life, he holed up for six weeks cranking out the screenplay for a lighthearted romp called *Silver Streak,* about a mild-mannered doofus caught up in some murderous intrigue aboard a transcontinental train. It immediately sold for $400,000, turned its author into the most sought-after scribe in Hollywood, and spurred thousands of other aspiring screenwriters to "take the training."

Writer-director Joel Schumacher was another walking advertisement for the wonders of est. A self-described "poor boy from Queens who became a stoned lounge lizard in the sixties," Schumacher had managed to kick his drug habit with the help of his New York analyst, Mildred Newman. He became a successful costume designer, on films such as *Play It As It Lays, The Last of Sheila, Blume in Love,* and *Sleeper.* But what he really wanted to do—like almost everyone else in Hollywood—was direct. For an ex-window dresser at Macy's, that was a decidedly quixotic ambition. "I went to est for two weekends in 1974," Schumacher remembers. "I was trying to grow as a person. The trainer said, 'You are totally responsible for everything that happens in your own life—there are no victims.' I was struck down like Paul on the road to Damascus. It hit me like the sword from *Star Wars*. If I wanted to be a director, it was up to me."

While it was unheard-of for a costume designer to break into the directing ranks, lots of young screenwriters were successfully making the transition. With that in mind, Schumacher sat down at the typewriter. He concocted the scripts for two 1976 films— *Sparkle*, a musical about a Supremes-like singing group, and *Car Wash*, an ensemble comedy that turned into a modest hit. In her review of *Car Wash*, which she dismissed as "the movie equivalent of junk food," Pauline Kael noted, "This is the second 'black' script . . . by Joel Schumacher, the talented costume designer of *Sleeper*, who appears to have convinced somebody again that he's a writer." Actually he managed to convince a lot of people. In 1978 Schumacher was hired to write the screenplay for the thirty-million-dollar extravaganza *The Wiz*, starring another Erhard acolyte, Diana Ross.

The Wiz was not just another "black" script. Based on the Tony-winning Broadway musical, this spirited retelling of *The Wizard of Oz* was among the most highly touted projects in Hollywood, and Schumacher won the plum assignment that dozens of rivals had coveted. John Badham, who had just scored a smash success with *Saturday Night Fever*, was signed to direct, but he dropped out when Diana Ross was cast as Dorothy. (The character of Dorothy was preadolescent; Ross was thirty-two, going on thirty-three.) Abetted by Schumacher, Ross hoped to turn L. Frank Baum's charming fantasy into an advertisement for black self-esteem and self-actualization, a message suspiciously close to the credo of est. When the Good Witch, played by Lena Horne (the mother-in-law of Sidney Lumet, who replaced Badham as director), appears at the end to present the movie's crowning statement, her speech is a litany of est-like platitudes. Her big song, which sends Dorothy home in a glow, is a gospel number called "Believe in Yourself."

Producer Rob Cohen later told Ross's biographer, J. Randy Taraborrelli, that the movie became fatally flawed when Schumacher and Ross decided to turn the character of Dorothy into a "scared adult" who is miraculously transformed into a self-confident woman on her journey to Oz. "It was nothing like what John Badham and I had first envisioned," Cohen said. "But Joel and Diana were involved in est and Diana was very enamored of Werner Erhard, and before I knew it, the movie was becoming an est-ian fable full of est buzzwords about knowing who you are and sharing and all that. I hated the script a lot. But it was hard to argue with Diana because she was recognizing in this script all of this stuff she had worked out in est seminars."

(Ross was in such a dither over est that she made all the members of her household staff take the training. Unfortunately, they became such wholehearted converts to the dogma of aggressive individualism that they began to ignore their mistress's commands and had to be fired for insubordination.)

The Wiz turned out to be one of Hollywood's historic catastrophes. It had gone some twenty million dollars over budget during filming and, greeted by savage reviews, entered theaters dead on arrival. The picture finished off Diana Ross's screen career. She never starred in another movie, but Joel Schumacher—whom his old critical nemesis Pauline Kael branded "one of the most maladroit screenwriters of all time"—went on to achieve his dreams of glory. Not only did he cop other screenwriting assignments, he became a highly successful (though never very highly praised) director, with such films as *St. Elmo's Fire, The Lost Boys, Flatliners, Dying Young,* and *Falling Down* to his credit. Today he evinces more skepticism toward est. "It offered instant results," Schumacher says. "Everybody stayed exactly the way they were and ran around spouting all this bullshit. That's what really happened. But I will be eternally grateful for learning that I was responsible for my life."

A year before *The Wiz* delivered the gospel of est to the movie-going masses, one cheeky film poked fun at the craze—and a few of the other human-potential fads that were then tearing through Hollywood. *Semi-Tough,* written by Walter Bernstein and directed by Michael Ritchie, was based on Dan Jenkins's raunchy best-seller about the locker-room antics and off-the-field womanizing of professional football players. Bernstein and Ritchie embellished Jenkins's story with satiric jabs at the new religion of self-improvement. Lotte Lenya is a Rolf-like masseuse named Clara Pelf, and Robert Preston, playing the bumptious team owner, crawls around on all fours practicing "creep" therapy.

But the movie reserves most of its barbs for a fictional consciousness-raising seminar called BEAT, whose unctuous founder, Friedrich Bismarck, was played by TV quizmaster and Werner Erhard–lookalike Bert Convy. As the story opens, the team owner's daughter, Barbara Jane Bookman (Jill Clayburgh), is involved in a sexless ménage à trois with the team's two star players, Billy Clyde Puckett (Burt Reynolds) and Shake Tiller (Kris Kristofferson). Once Shake is converted to BEAT, he and Barbara Jane start sleeping together, but one obstacle to their relationship remains. Barbara Jane is not a devotee of BEAT, and as Bismarck warns, "Mixed marriages don't work."

So Barbara Jane does her darndest to "get it." She agrees to take the training, but finds herself incapable of surrendering to Bismarck's mixture of sadistic abuse, pious drivel, and sheer double talk. At the end of the session she walks out feeling bedraggled rather than blissful. She also feels slightly guilty, and the movie is especially perceptive in suggesting how creeds like est put nonbelievers on the defensive.

The film captures the peculiar mixture of spirituality and pragmatism that surrounded est. Like the Hollywood screenwriters who were boasting that est helped them to make their big sale, *Semi-Tough*'s Shake Tiller proudly reports that he hasn't missed a pass since attending BEAT. Perhaps the film's most sardonic touch is in the climactic scene, when the minister who is about to marry Shake and Barbara Jane turns to Bismarck and offers some pointers on how to avoid paying capital-gains tax.

Shortly after the movie was released, Bert Convy told an interviewer that he had received a number of communications from Erhard's followers, as well as one from the master himself. Erhard's letter, suggesting that "it would be great for us to get together," arrived after Convy appeared on the *Tonight Show* and joked about his experiences attending an est seminar to research the role of Bismarck. Convy recalled that when a fellow initiate complained of a headache, the group leader replied, "Experience it." When another participant said that he had wet his pants, the leader advised, "Experience the warmth."

During the filming, Convy got a late-night phone call from Valerie Harper, one of Erhard's most devoted Hollywood apostles. She wished him success with the role and indicated that Erhard was "pleased" about the movie, but Convy suspected that he was being subtly pressured to go easy on the guru.

That was not the first time Harper had risen to the defense of her pontiff. She made numerous pronouncements, both public and private, ballyhooing est and praising its mastermind. Her most memorable endorsement came at the 1975 Emmy Awards ceremony. Clutching the trophy she had just won for *Rhoda*, she expressed her gratitude to the customary list of professional associates. Then she added "personal thanks to someone who's profoundly influenced my life, Werner Erhard."

Asked if she still looks back on est as a positive experience, Harper responds, "Oh yes. Daily!" When she became embroiled in a nasty twenty-million-dollar lawsuit against Lorimar over the studio's decision to fire her from the TV series *Valerie* in 1987, Harper sought solace in the catechism of est: "I kept saying, 'What is the opportunity here?' In this disaster, in this horrible, painful pit, I kept looking for the opportunity. I didn't know what it was, but I just kept looking for where this could be serving to myself, a growing thing for others. I do feel it came from est."

Like other celebrity acolytes of Erhard, Harper became a champion of his multifarious post-est causes, including something called the Forum, a streamlined, Yuppified course in self-improvement that takes a single day to complete, rather than two entire weekends. "It's very different from est training," Harper explains. "There's been a breakthrough in terms of consciousness, so you don't have to do all those hours and not go to the bathroom and beat people with sticks. What Werner was really doing, I think, was getting Eastern philosophy to Western minds, and Western minds as a society have shifted." Harper, along with John Denver, is also active in the Hunger Project, which advocates the eradication of world hunger by "imagining" that it will end. As for Erhard himself, Harper describes him simply as "a class-A human being, a real wonderful person on the planet doing brilliant work."

Lately, however, that has come to be a minority opinion. In 1977 Erhard found himself on the defensive when the *American Journal of Psychiatry* reported a number of cases of est-induced psychoses. One businessman who had imbibed Erhard's anything-is-possible philosophy during two weekends of est training decided to try breathing underwater in his backyard swimming pool. After his wife resuscitated him, she promptly had him committed to a mental hospital. A few years later the whole movement was decimated by shocking charges against Erhard himself. Accusations of physical abuse were leveled by his ex-wife and two of his daughters, and he has been slapped with a variety of lawsuits alleging wrongful discharge, wrongful death, and fraud. Erhard has denied the charges, but his once-thriving financial empire has crumbled, as has his once formidable reputation.

If Werner Erhard has been toppled as kingpin of Hollywood's therapeutic gurus, there is no shortage of pretenders to his throne. John-

Roger Hinkins (J-R to his more intimate disciples) is a cherubic ex-schoolteacher from Rosemead, California, who bills himself as "the physical embodiment of the Mystical Traveler Consciousness." His Santa Monica-based John-Roger Foundation is a multimillion-dollar, tax-exempt enterprise that gained prominence for handing out the so-called International Integrity Awards, designed to promote "the transformational work of groups and individuals around the planet." Along with ten-thousand-dollar checks payable to their favorite charities, such honorees as Mother Teresa, Lech Walesa, Ralph Nader, Bishop Desmond Tutu, Stevie Wonder, and Oliver Stone have had their crystal pyramid awards bestowed at J-R's star-studded galas.

The money to bankroll these good works—and J-R's lavish lifestyle, which includes an opulent parsonage in one of Los Angeles's most exclusive neighborhoods and a "wellness" ranch in the Santa Ynez Mountains near Ronald and Nancy Reagan's Rancho del Cielo—is largely generated by the mahatma's series of "Insight" seminars. The six-evening course, "conveniently structured so that you can maintain your regular work week," is priced at $450. A tasteful publicity brochure describes the intense therapy marathon as consisting of "small group exercises, creative visualization, sharing, individual and group interactions." An Insight graduate describes it more succinctly as "est with bathroom privileges."

Those who have already attained the state of Insight are invited to join J-R's Movement of Spiritual Inner Awareness (MSIA, pronounced "messiah"), whose celebrity ministers include Carl Wilson of the Beach Boys and actresses Sally Kirkland and Leigh Taylor-Young. Arianna Stassinopoulos, the Greek-born socialite who authored a book called *The Female Woman* as well as a mud-slinging biography of Picasso, has served as another of John-Roger's main conduits to the rich and famous. In 1985 Stassinopoulos wrote a glowing profile of J-R for *Interview* magazine in which she recapitulated a long conversation they once had about "energy medicine," sex, karma, and hugging while the two soul mates "rode in a car to the Bronx to see Mother Teresa."

In 1988, after a couple of more skeptical articles appeared alleging sexual transgressions and financial hanky-panky on J-R's part, the annual Integrity Awards dinner (whose honoree that year was to be Jihan Sadat, widow of assassinated Egyptian president Anwar Sadat) was abruptly canceled. A story in *People* magazine charged that the Mystical Traveler had been intimidating MSIA members, using brainwashing techniques, and seducing young male staff members. ("He always had someone sleeping in his bedroom at night, supposedly to protect his body while he was out of it," said one disaffected disciple.) As the controversy swirled around him, J-R denied all charges and tried to remain beatifically aloof. His foundation continued to do a land-office business in tapes, videocassettes, and John-Roger T-shirts; his seminars still drew big crowds; and in 1991 he published a compilation of other people's witticisms called *Do It! Let's Get Off Our Buts!* that promptly rose to the top of the best-seller list.

If the images of est and Insight were blemished by their progenitors' notoriety, another self-actualization curriculum called Lifespring was extolled for *not* becoming a cult of personality. Like the competition, Lifespring holds intensive seminars where participants are steeped in Eastern philosophy, share their most tremulous emotions, and learn to "take responsibility" for their own lives. But unlike Werner Erhard and John-Roger, Lifespring's creator, an ex-Esalen trainer named John Hanley, has kept a scrupulously low profile. Producer Howard Rosenman found his second calling as a group leader for Lifespring, and he notes approvingly that Hanley "is very anonymous; he's a paradigm of 'principles before personality.' "

Hanley's program involves a series of increasingly complex exercises that mix scientific neurology and pseudo-scientific folklore. In the final training sessions, novitiates, who have been puffed up with ferocious self-confidence, learn how to become "leaders" and recruit others to the cause. "Lifespring is all about the mind and how it operates," Howard Rosenman explains. "It's the single most valuable communications tool and one of the most powerful experiences that I ever had, because I began to see just how powerful the mind is. I did the basic seminar, the advanced, and the leadership—which is ninety days. It's very rigorous. I was able to break through the shell that I had built up. From the advanced training I got to experience the child within me as very, very powerful. And then in the leadership, that child, that very powerful child, took his rightful place in the social order at the time and led the group. I learned about service. I learned about the spiritual component of things. Lifespring was the single most important thing I ever did."

And Rosenman, a therapy buff of long duration, has just about done it all. He dropped out of medical school in the late 1960s and plunged into analysis with various New York shrinks. He tried est, had a session or two with Mildred Newman ("I love her as a friend"), and in 1983, a few years after moving to Los Angeles, landed on the couch of Dr. Michael Franzblau. "He handles a lot of CAA agents," Rosenman notes. (He is also the son of Dr. Rose Franzblau, the psychologist-columnist for the *New York Post* who was an early forerunner of Dr. Joyce Brothers.)

Rosenman contends that analysis—and all the other "transformational" delicacies available in today's mind-bending smorgasbord—provide essential nourishment for Hollywood yuppies, or, as Rosenman calls them, YAVIS ("young, attractive, verbal, intelligent, success-oriented"). "In this day and age, with all its multilayered complexities, you can't get through it unless you resolve some of the 'stuff' of your childhood," Rosenman declares. "Any yuppie in good standing is going to do this, especially if they're in the communications business. Movies are about transformation, and analysis *is* transformation. People must want to transform themselves. If they don't, they're either in denial, or they're demented."

Far from being an alternative to analysis, Rosenman views Lifespring as an enhancement to it. "After I did Lifespring, my analysis zoomed. It opened up a door so I could see what I had to work on," he says. "It was like a super-duper AA seminar, using the most powerful communications technology known to man in the transformation area. A lot of people go to AA and do service to self-correct. You have to keep on correcting yourself."

"Service" is a key ingredient here, though it's hard to say whose interests are primarily being served. "I used the leadership program to learn how to run a company," Rosenman says. "There were about seventy-five people in the group, and I was able to assess what they were good at. I was the pope, as it were. On a Thursday night we were told we had to feed five thousand homeless people on Saturday morning. We couldn't use our own money, and we had to arrange for the food, the entertainment, the cleanup, everything."

Rosenman adroitly masterminded the operation. In the process he so impressed one of his trainees, Sandy Gallin, the personal manager of such superstars as Dolly Parton and Michael Jackson, that Gallin later hired Rosenman to run his Sandollar film production company.

The movies he has sponsored at Gallin's company were mostly flops, but the output has been prodigious. Many of his films grew directly out of Rosenman's own most solipsistic concerns. His eons of therapy have taught him not only to value himself personally, but to "transform" his private obsessions into screen fables that could edify others. It was Rosenman who spearheaded the production of Disney's *Gross Anatomy*, a drama about a group of medical students that was inspired by his own disillusioning experiences in med school. Two years later he convinced the same studio to finance *A Stranger Among Us*, a muddled murder mystery set in New York's Hasidic community. Rosenman, whose great-grandparents were Hasidim, told an interviewer that his passion for that particular project stemmed from the discovery of his spiritual roots during a period of intense soul-searching. *Straight Talk*, a paean to common-sense psychotherapy starring Dolly Parton as a self-taught radio shrink, reflected the producer's longtime enthusiasm for the talking cure. All of these personal testaments were panned by critics and ignored by audiences, but Rosenman's dazzling productivity does at least illustrate the power of his boundless self-confidence and relentless determination.

Howard Rosenman's reputation as a seasoned veteran of so many self-help programs, along with his willingness to talk about them with the fourth estate, made him a popular media maven. His pithy comments frequently popped up in press reports about Hollywood's various psychotherapy fads. In 1991 *Vanity Fair* had Leslie Bennetts write a lengthy piece about the newest New Age sensation, an ex-lounge singer turned mind-awareness minister named Marianne Williamson. Rosenman supplied Bennetts with a number of piquant quotes. "The first time I went to see her, it was like the Liberty Bell fell on my head," he said of the comely preacher. "The community she's addressing is a group that partied and drugged and sexualized through the sixties and seventies, and here comes this woman who looks like one of us, who you know could have been at Studio 54 or dancing at Fire Island Pines with a tambourine on her hip—and yet she's talking like Jesus Christ. She's talking about the most fundamental precepts. She's talking about the Golden Rule."

Then Rosenman made the mistake of adding that Williamson also wanted to be famous.

That remark didn't sit well with the strong-willed priestess, who purged Rosenman from the board of her nonprofit Los Angeles Center for Living, one of several programs she had created to help AIDS patients and other victims of "life-challenging" illness. Of course, what Rosenman indicated about Williamson's lust for the limelight only confirmed the obvious. She was playing to packed houses in New York and West Hollywood; she had pronounced the benediction at Sandy Gallin's glitzy birthday bash for David Geffen; and she even officiated at the star-spangled wedding of Elizabeth Taylor and blue-collar beau Larry Fortensky. But Williamson was trying hard to cultivate an image of unpretentiousness rather than star charisma. ("Charisma was originally a religious term; it means 'of the spirit,'" she explained. "I exist to empower other people. I'm a teacher; teachers love to teach. This is a privilege and an honor and a blessing, and it's my high.") Williamson liked to point out that she was a single mother, driving a beat-up Peugeot and residing in a modest two-bedroom apartment. If she wore designer dresses, they were picked off the rack at discount stores. By hinting that this self-effacing do-gooder from Houston might indeed have more grandiose ambitions, Rosenman had punctured that humble pose.

Williamson discovered her vocation in 1977 when she found a book called *A Course in Miracles* lying on a friend's coffee table. A few years before, she had dropped out of Pomona College and proceeded to experiment with sex, drugs, and rock 'n' roll, while supporting herself as a waitress, nightclub singer, and office temp. *A Course in Miracles*, she says, was her "personal path out of hell." The 1,200-page psycho-spiritual opus, composed in 1965 by a Columbia University psychologist named Helen Schucman, had developed a vast underground readership and gave rise to hundreds of informal study groups around the country. Williamson started teaching the catechism (which Schucman claimed was dictated to her directly by the Holy Spirit) at a place called the Philosophical Research Society in Los Angeles. Although she, like Schucman, was Jewish, Williamson's snappy sermons were infused with "Christic" imagery, and her upbeat, vivacious style won her a wide audience. Eventually her bicoastal lectures, public-access television shows, and 1992 best-seller *A Return to Love* made her the most celebrated popularizer of Schucman's arcane text.

In contrast to the introspective rationalism of Freudian psychoanalysis that prodded patients to be painfully self-critical, Helen Schucman's self-study course in "spiritual psychotherapy" preached a transcendent self-forgiveness. *A Course in Miracles* "teaches us to relinquish a thought system based on fear and accept instead a thought system based on love," Williamson wrote. "For me the Course was a breakthrough experience, intellectually, emotionally, and psychologically. It freed me from a terrible emotional pain."

Like Lifespring, the Course tempered its appeal for self-adoration with a call for service to others. It was in this spirit that Williamson created her Center for Living, as well as Project Angel Food, which delivers meals to housebound AIDS patients. Those charitable ventures, combined with her message of Christian love and cosmic forgiveness, have earned her a special following among gay men, including some of the most powerful behind-the-scenes players in Hollywood. A certain synergy has developed between them and this Avon Lady of miracles. To a group scorned by mainstream religion and ravaged by the scourge of AIDS, she offers the hope of holy redemption; to the ambitious psycho-evangelist, they offer big bucks for her worthy causes and a pipeline to celebrity endorsements.

Williamson's popularity ultimately extended well beyond the gay community. Shrewdly mastering the art of self-promotion, she has turned herself into a cultural icon. But she is only the latest of Hollywood's postanalytic pundits to peddle the same elixir for bliss. Nurturing therapists such as Mildred Newman and Evelyn Silvers, along with the prophets of the Me Decade such as Werner Erhard and the feel-good metaphysicians like J-R and Marianne Williamson, caught on because they filled a void. In many cases they restored a sense of belonging to individuals whose cutthroat ambition or inexplicable success had caused them to feel insecure and isolated. At the same time, these gurus scratched the itch for spiritualism that traditional psychoanalysis had denigrated. They promised a speedy trip to self-awareness, rather than the interminably arduous trek of Freudian analysis. And perhaps most important of all, instead of trying to "cure" narcissism, they actively encouraged it. Freud had warned that the narcissistic neuroses were all but impossible to treat, and Hollywood analysts were continually frustrated when they chose to disregard his admonition. But the new breed of healers who turned self-love from a "neurosis" into a virtue succeeded in winning an army of grateful followers.

13. THE FUTURE OF AN ILLUSION

At a time when most of Hollywood had moved on to trendier modes of psychic rejuvenation, a few diehards still celebrated the analytic mystique. Ironically, one of the most indelible testimonials to the wonders of conventional psychotherapy came from a reluctant convert to the cause. Robert Redford, whose 1980 film of *Ordinary People* won the plaudits of audiences, critics, and psychiatrists alike, had never been one of those angst-ridden actors who worshiped at the altar of Freud.

Redford grew up in a working-class family in Los Angeles; his father was a milkman. His background was Scots-Irish, and there was not a lot of emotional ventilation at home. "The Scots ethic says you suffer stoically," Redford notes. When he moved to New York to pursue an acting career, he encountered therapy enthusiasts for the first time, and over the next two decades he heard incessant chatter about psychoanalysis in the inner circles of theater and film. "It was socially chic in New York, and that turned me off," Redford says. "There was something old-fashioned in my upbringing that said you worked out your problems yourself."

Redford's own emotionally constricted upbringing, rather than any fondness for psychiatry, is what drew him to *Ordinary People*, Judith Guest's surprise best-seller about the teenage scion of an uncommunicative WASP family, whose life is saved through the intercession of a humane psychiatrist. Shortly after the novel was published in 1976, Redford bought the movie rights and decided to use the story as a vehicle for his directing debut.

The film is a canny update of the Freudian melodramas that first enthralled audiences in the 1940s. Unlike the magisterial psychiatrists in *Now, Voyager, Lady in the Dark,* and *The Snake Pit,* however, *Ordinary People*'s Dr. Berger (Judd Hirsch) is a rumpled, self-effacing, warmly accessible fellow. Nonetheless, beneath his unprepossessing exterior Berger is the same wise healer extolled in those earlier movies. He is the emotional anchor for the suicidal young protagonist, Conrad (Timothy Hutton), whose parents are unable to reach out to their son in a time of crisis.

Like its antecedents from the 1940s, *Ordinary People* is structured as a kind of detective story, with a series of flashbacks providing telltale clues that build toward the revelation of a buried psychological secret. In the climactic therapy scene, as he relives the boating accident in which he watched his brother drown, young Conrad finally confronts the terrible truth: He feels guilty for "hanging on" to the capsized boat, for having survived while his adored older brother perished. This denouement was fairly obvious from the start, so the film lacks the explosive surprise ending of the psychoanalytic whodunits of an earlier era. Despite its lackluster plotting, the movie appealed to audiences because of its fine acting and its simple prescription for curing acute psychological pain. Once Conrad breaks down and weeps like a baby, he snaps out of his paralyzing depression; and when his father also lets down his guard and blubbers, they fall into each other's arms in a fervent hug.

The one character who refuses to vent her feelings emerges as the villain of the piece. Conrad's mother (played with icy realism by Mary Tyler Moore) will neither visit the psychiatrist nor participate in the crying jags, and so she is damned as absolutely as the unrepentant atheist in films of an earlier era. Because she refuses to take communion with the shrink, Mom is finally banished from the family circle.

If Redford himself had once harbored a similar skepticism toward psychotherapeutic rituals and naked emotional "sharing," he had a change of heart while making the film. The adulation he received certainly helped to seal his conversion. Not only was he honored by his peers with Academy Awards for best picture and best direction, he also received a flood of testimonials from the psychiatric community. Writing in the *American Journal of Psychiatry,* Dr. Irving Schneider commented gratefully, "The pessimism and sarcasm so prominent in recent portrayals of the profession are more than balanced by the enormously successful and inspiring *Ordinary People.*" Indeed, as Dr. Schneider suggested, *Ordinary People* may be the only Hollywood movie about the talking cure that real-life psychiatrists were virtually unanimous in endorsing. A few persnickety Freudians objected to the fact that Dr. Berger hugs his patient in the climactic scene, but most analysts condoned Berger's paternal embrace as a legitimate indication of his compassion for the boy.

Following the heady success he enjoyed with *Ordinary People*, Redford experienced a number of personal and professional letdowns. A couple of his later movies fizzled at the box office, and his twenty-five-year marriage fell apart. In his late forties, he finally decided to seek therapy himself. "I did it when I was at a crossroads in my life," Redford says. Unfortunately, his psychiatrist turned out to be a glib publicity hound, and Redford was quickly disillusioned. "He kept appearing on television whenever a national figure got murdered," Redford recalls. "He wouldn't show up on a local channel. It had to be the network news, where he'd rattle on about Mark David Chapman." Redford left the media pundit in favor of another therapist—closer in spirit to the unassuming Dr. Berger—who did help him through his immediate crises. But Redford's time on the couch was relatively brief. "I don't have the patience for extended psychoanalysis," he says. "I'm the antithesis of Woody Allen."

On the other hand, Redford's onetime costar, Barbra Streisand, was in for the long haul. In their 1973 hit, *The Way We Were*, Streisand's characterization of a wired New York neurotic had created a memorable counterpoint to Redford's laid-back blond Adonis. That was a contrast they sustained offscreen as well. Unlike Redford, Streisand is a veteran analysand very much in the Woody Allen mold. When Mike Wallace interviewed her on *60 Minutes* and asked in some astonishment how anyone could remain in psychotherapy for twenty-five or thirty years, Streisand responded testily, "I'm a slow learner."

That interview was conducted in 1991, while Streisand was hawking *The Prince of Tides*, a picture that outdid *Ordinary People* in its glorification of the analyst as savior. It was not the first time that Streisand had made a film about psychiatry. In the 1987 drama *Nuts*, which she also produced, she played a shrill, defiant prostitute unjustly institutionalized by a cabal of male chauvinist doctors. In *The Prince of Tides*, which she directed as well as produced, she did a turnabout and cast herself as the shrink, providing a shrewd variation on traditional gender roles but keeping her own heroic persona intact.

In bringing Pat Conroy's overripe novel to the screen, Streisand turned the secondary character of Dr. Susan Lowenstein into the charismatic star of the show. As the impeccably manicured analyst, Streisand literally charms the pants off the guilt-ridden football coach played by Nick Nolte. The movie is something of a cross between *The Way We Were* and *Ordinary People*. Like the former, it chronicles the romance of a Jewish egghead and a Gentile jock; like the latter, it eulogizes a Jewish psychiatrist assuaging a dysfunctional WASP family. But it possesses neither the schmaltzy wallop of *The Way We Were* nor the subtle naturalistic acting that made *Ordinary People* appear more sophisticated than the shopworn melodramas that inspired it.

The Prince of Tides is yet another psychoanalytic detective yarn, with Dr. Lowenstein acting as both brilliant sleuth and beneficent healer. Once again flashbacks fill in the past of the troubled protagonist, Tom Wingo (Nolte). Wingo meets with Dr. Lowenstein to recount the childhood of his catatonic twin sister, whom Lowenstein is treating; in the process of remembering, he begins to plumb his own psyche as well. The flashbacks culminate with a scene that exposes the source of Tom's recurring depressions—the horrific night when he, his sister, and his mother were all raped by a gang of escaped convicts. None of the Freudian melodramas of the 1940s hinged on such a lurid secret (or such a ridiculous device as jailbirds *ex machina*), but *The Prince of Tides* needed some sort of eye-popping climax to get a rise out of jaded audiences. The plot may have been fashioned of porny pulp, but it was meant to celebrate a chic new gospel—the burning need to confront shameful family secrets and rescue the battered, whimpering "inner child."

The guiding light behind this new evangelism, a psychologist named John Bradshaw, had trained for the Roman Catholic priesthood before donning his more secular mantle. In the late 1980s this graybeard with a Texas twang became the darling of demi-intellectual taste makers, lecturing to the fold on public television, writing a column in *Lear's,* and holding private audiences with influential members of the Hollywood community like Streisand and Steven Spielberg (who reciprocated by casting Bradshaw's daughter, an aspiring actress, in his 1991 production of *Hook*). In addition, Bradshaw operated a nationwide string of recovery centers and wrote best-selling tomes about the dysfunctional family—"the ways in which toxic shame is passed from generation to generation," to quote one of his press releases. John Bradshaw, Pat Conroy, and Barbra Streisand were a triumvirate tailor-made for each other.

At a time when celebrities everywhere, from Roseanne Arnold and Gloria Steinem to Streisand herself, were spilling their guts about the abuses of their miserable childhoods, *The Prince of Tides* gave dramatic voice to the popular ethos of victimization.

The story was a pure Bradshavian parable—and a throwback to the most simplistic Freudian theories of repression and neurosis. Once Tom Wingo and his sister, Savannah, retrieve their memories and acknowledge the hurt of their youth, their problems dissolve. Savannah rebounds miraculously from her suicidal stupor. And Tom recovers a sense of purpose and passion. His awakening comes after he breaks into uncontrollable sobs while Dr. Lowenstein cradles him in her arms. Like *Ordinary People*, the movie proclaims that nothing is as cathartic as a cry and hug.

In addition to its soothing bromides, *The Prince of Tides* offered one of the most rapturous idealizations of the psychiatrist ever to appear on screen. But then, never before had a film's producer-director also cast herself as the saintly analyst. Dr. Lowenstein does have a few human foibles; she has stayed in a bad marriage with a loutish husband, a world-renowned concert violinist, and she cannot connect with her surly son (played by Streisand's own son, Jason Gould). Streisand's avowed intention was to show that the healer is also wounded, but the effect is quite the opposite. Both husband and son are such spoiled brats that audience sympathy never veers from the long-suffering Dr. Lowenstein. Moreover, the noble doctor is as much of a virtuoso with her patients as her spouse is with his fiddle. Not only does she relieve Tom Wingo's deep-seated neurosis with her skillful psychic probing, she also brings the hunk to ecstasy as she runs her lacquered talons across his back. In the final scene, although his gentlemanly sense of responsibility compels Tom to return to his wife and children in South Carolina, he recites the analyst's name in a worshipful incantation. "Lowenstein! Lowenstein!" he cries as the music on the soundtrack soars.

Because Streisand's character sleeps with a man who is at least a quasi-client, *The Prince of Tides* failed to garner the same unqualified raves from the psychiatric community that *Ordinary People* received. Several shrinks criticized the movie for Lowenstein's sexual lapse and for her other extracurricular relationships with Tom Wingo. (In addition to hearing his confession in her office, she enlists him to coach her nerdy son on the gridiron.) A few psychiatrists zeroed in on the movie's more significant defect—its ludicrous simplifications. Dr. Harvey Greenberg, the author of one of the first psychoanalytic studies of popular films, *The Movies on Your Mind,* aptly described Lowenstein as a perpetuation of the "unrealistic Dr. Wonderful stereotype." The movie rests, he noted, on the absurdly facile premise that "unburdening yourself about the past will cure everything from neurotic alienation to schizophrenia."

Both *Ordinary People* and *The Prince of Tides* were unabashed valentines to psychotherapy, but they were essentially anachronisms. From the 1940s to the 1960s, Hollywood had regularly served up the Dr. Wonderful stereotype that Greenberg cites. That was the Golden Age of psychiatry on screen, when the talking cure was depicted as a panacea for personal and societal ills. But the godlike image of the analyst soon tarnished, and most movies of the 1970s and 1980s were far more likely to mock the Freudian science than to exalt it. In the late 1960s a couple of seminal European films set the tone by exploding conventional pieties about mental illness. Karel Reisz's *Morgan,* ironically subtitled *A Suitable Case for Treatment,* focused on a disturbed dreamer who imagines himself as King Kong; the 1966 film saw him not as a neurotic misfit but as a free spirit thumbing his nose at the stuffy psychiatric establishment. A year later Philippe De Broca's whimsical comedy, *King of Hearts,* set during World War I, presented the inmates of a mental hospital as far more sane than the bloodthirsty soldiers all around them. Both movies developed cult followings in America and paved the way for more mainstream antipsychiatry films that followed.

Most notable of these was the Oscar-winning 1975 hit *One Flew Over the Cuckoo's Nest.* Ken Kesey's novel, upon which the movie was based, had been published thirteen years earlier but caught on very slowly. A Broadway adaptation starring Kirk Douglas had eked out a disappointing six-month run in 1963. Unable to find studio financing for a film version, Douglas, who owned the rights to the novel, finally turned the property over to his son, Michael, who convinced record magnate Saul Zaentz to fund the picture. It ended up grossing more than $200 million and sweeping all the major Academy Award categories, including best actor for Jack Nicholson as the irrepressible Randle McMurphy, leader of the motley group of mental patients who joust with their high-handed psychiatrists and the tyrannical Nurse Ratched. By that time Kesey's irreverent novel had sold eleven million copies and was a perennial favorite on college campuses.

In the decade since the book was first published, Kesey's iconoclastic view of psychiatry and mental illness had gone from outlandish heresy to accepted wisdom. Radical psychiatrists R. D. Laing in England and Thomas Szasz in America attracted a wide following by challenging rigid distinctions between sanity and insanity, and their ideas were eagerly adopted by popular artists. Laing's theories were dramatized on stage in Peter Shaffer's *Equus*, a play that created an immediate sensation when it opened in London in 1973. Shaffer's story revolves around the relationship between an earnest psychiatrist and a tormented stable boy. In the course of their sessions together, the doctor discovers that the young man is in thrall to a private pagan religion, which has dictated the ritual blinding of several horses. The psychiatrist methodically exorcises his patient's demons, but in the process, the playwright implies, he also purges the boy of his glorious mysticism and innate passion.

Shaffer's drama evinced a skepticism toward psychiatry that had rarely surfaced in the 1940s or 1950s. Sidney Lumet, who directed the movie version of *Equus* in 1977, suggests that Shaffer's homosexuality may have intensified that skepticism; Lumet points out that the play reflected not just Shaffer's Laingian belief in the sanctity of the visionary spirit but "the legitimate questioning of analysis in the homosexual community." The debunking of psychoanalytic dogma that accompanied the gay liberation and women's liberation movements of the 1970s accelerated the toppling of old idols. Feminist dramas like the 1982 *Frances*, which exposed the psychiatric persecution of the lobotomized Frances Farmer, cast a cold eye on Freudian paternalism. Even earlier, in 1966, *A Fine Madness* sounded a similar note with its portrayal of a lusty poet (Sean Connery) hobbled by a claque of lobotomizing shrinks.

It was not just the antipathy of women, gays, and "creative" geniuses that accounts for the analyst's fall from grace. Arthur Penn speaks of the dramatic change in attitude over the course of the turbulent decade of the 1960s. "In the 1950s, people were all proud of their analysis," he recalls. "Then in the sixties, they divested themselves of all authoritarian figures. Analysts were considered part of the establishment—and much to be loathed."

Like the absentminded professor, the bumbling psychiatrist had sometimes been used as a figure of fun in movies. But after the iconoclastic 1960s, the celluloid shrink was most often presented as a lecher, a killer, or a pathetic wimp considerably sicker than the patients he was treating. Brian De Palma's 1980 thriller *Dressed to Kill* presented Michael Caine as a suave psychiatrist by day who becomes a crazed transvestite by night, slipping into a pair of high heels and slicing women to pieces. De Palma offered a variation on the theme twelve years later with the far less successful *Raising Cain*, about a maniacal child psychologist who preys on innocent tots. In Nicolas Roeg's *Bad Timing* (1980), the analyst, played by Art Garfunkel, appears to be a closet necrophiliac, ravishing his comatose mistress after she has overdosed on sedatives. In the low-budget horror hit *The Howling* (1981), an august psychiatrist metamorphoses into a werewolf. In *The Terminator* (1984) the shrink is such a noodle-brain that he completely underestimates the threat posed by super-robot Arnold Schwarzenegger. In 1991 Alvin Sargent, the screenwriter who had adapted *Ordinary People*, supplied the story for the far less reverent *What About Bob?*, a farce about a pompous analyst who ends up in a straitjacket himself after being hounded by a particularly needy patient. A year later, *Whispers in the Dark, Final Analysis, Basic Instinct,* and *Used People* all portrayed shrinks who get involved in untoward sexual liaisons. In the most popular of the four, *Basic Instinct*, the tough cop played by Michael Douglas hurls his sex-starved therapist across the room in a bout of sadomasochistic lovemaking that has her panting for more.

But the coup de grace came with the critical and commercial success of *The Silence of the Lambs*, the first film since *One Flew Over the Cuckoo's Nest* to capture every major Academy Award. In making the sweep, it roundly defeated *The Prince of Tides*, symbolically as well as literally. Two more diametrically opposed visions of psychiatry could hardly be imagined. In contrast to Streisand's divine Dr. Lowenstein, the shrink in *The Silence of the Lambs*, Dr. Hannibal Lecter, is known as "Hannibal the Cannibal" because of his propensity for devouring human flesh, tearing his victims limb from limb with his teeth. Anthony Hopkins plays Dr. Lecter as a brilliant criminal mind, and in his conversations with the FBI agent Clarice Starling (Jodie Foster), he still acts like a shrewd psychoanalyst, methodically extracting the dark secrets of her childhood. His intellect is keen, but his own psyche is horribly twisted. A practitioner once lionized as the savior of troubled souls is now presented as a monster who eats his patients alive.

No doubt the deteriorating image of psychiatry on screen reflects the disenchantment of society as a whole. In his 1961 book *The Psychoanalytic Situation* the eminent analyst Leo Stone warned against the spurious assumption—quite prevalent at the time—that "there was scarcely any human problem" that psychoanalysis could not solve. Critics like Stone were troubled by the widespread belief, aided and abetted by Hollywood's idealization of analysis, that "hopeless or grave reality situations, lack of talent or ability (usually regarded as 'inhibition'), lack of an adequate philosophy of life, and almost any chronic physical illness may be brought to psychoanalysis for cure."

As Stone predicted, psychoanalysis proved incapable of meeting those inflated expectations, leading inevitably to disillusionment and resentment. As writer-director Tom Mankiewicz says, "The bloom is off the rose now with analysis, especially in Hollywood. It just hasn't been the saving solution that everybody anticipated." Mankiewicz wryly suggests that the preoccupation with mind cures may have finally run its course, only to be supplanted by a new craze. "People used to ask about your analysis," he says. "Now the questions I hear most often are, 'How is my halibut being prepared? Not with salt or butter, is it?' The new religion is taking care of your body. The personal trainer used to be the guy who got the actor in shape for a movie. Victor Mature would say, 'I gotta take my shirt off again, and I've been drinking since the last picture,' and the personal trainer would be brought in to whip him into shape. Now you can't be a junior-level executive at a studio unless you have a personal trainer. An awful lot of people have traded in analysts for trainers."

Tom Mankiewicz has observed the decline of analysis from a unique perspective. His father, the venerable Joseph L. Mankiewicz, was one of the movie capital's earliest apostles for the cult of Freud. Joseph underwent a rigorous analysis, steeped himself in psychoanalytic literature, ballyhooed his favorite shrinks to family, friends, and lovers, and at one point even wrote a letter to Karl Menninger volunteering to serve as the industry's watchdog in safeguarding the new science from ridicule. But the vaunted power of analysis was belied by Joseph Mankiewicz's personal life. He was a notorious womanizer whose wife of nineteen years, embittered by her husband's philandering and by his insistence that she give up her own career to raise their children, eventually committed suicide. In addition, he was long estranged from his older son, Chris, who still resents his father's smug egotism and the analysts who encouraged it. "When you see how unsuccessfully the shrinks treated your parents, it's not a great confidence builder in the art form," Chris Mankiewicz comments astringently.

Joseph Mankiewicz's devotion to analysis may have served him better professionally. His psychoanalytic understanding of human behavior helped him to write incisive stories and to draw astute performances from the actors he directed. That could be said of many filmmakers who were intellectually stimulated by analysis but who failed to resolve their personal issues even after decades of therapy. Indeed, for directors like Joseph Mankiewicz, Woody Allen, or Barbra Streisand, the protracted process of analysis seems largely to have reinforced their tendencies toward solipsism and megalomania. In one of his last papers, "Analysis Terminable and Interminable," Freud himself pessimistically pointed out that psychoanalysis was a therapeutic tool of limited utility; it is simply ineffective at mending deep-seated character flaws. That is a fact that both the star-struck analysts of Hollywood and their narcissistic patients have generally preferred to ignore.

As Chris Mankiewicz suggests, the daily dose of self-absorption that so exhilarates Hollywood analysands may actually make life far more difficult for their families and colleagues. That is also the view of Frances Lear, who was once married to another of the town's legendary devotees of therapy. (Norman Lear even married a psychotherapist after divorcing Frances.) "Long-term supportive therapy is parasitic—financially rewarding to the analyst and probably of little good to the patient," Frances Lear declares. "This one-on-one, two-hundred-dollar-an-hour, twenty-five-year therapy is outrageous. The patient thinks, 'I don't have to be any better than I am because I am in therapy and therefore I'm mixed up or sick.' And the feeling of the people around him is, 'Well, the patient is sick, so I as wife, husband, child, partner must give the patient his due and allow him to be difficult, neurotic, a pain in the ass.' If the patient simply indulges himself or herself, I don't care. He's entitled. But that rarely happens. Usually there are other people around him who are also affected."

Robert Walker, Jr., comes from another Hollywood family with a long involvement in psychiatry. His mother, Jennifer Jones, has been a devout analysand for more than fifty years, the favored protegée of half a dozen psychoanalytic gurus. His father, Robert Walker, was one of the first movie stars to be shipped off to the Menninger Clinic for psychological rehabilitation, and he died at the age of thirty-two when his own psychiatrist injected him with a fatal shot of sodium amytal. Personalities like Jennifer Jones and Robert Walker, Sr., spent most of their adult lives searching for a psychic trainer who could whip them into shape emotionally. But, as Walker Jr. suggests, it is not only the filmland royalty who yearn for a make-over. He chuckles when recalling what happened to the nanny he hired to take care of his newborn son. "She was seventeen years old when she came to work for us," Walker says. "She was fresh out of Mexico and couldn't speak a word of English. Within one year of coming to L.A. she was taking acting lessons and seeing a shrink."

Some dreams die hard in Hollywood. Freudian analysis may no longer have the special cachet it once enjoyed, but newcomers who migrate to the movie mecca in search of regeneration will always find obliging mentors to guide them in their quest, or simply to escort them down the garden path.

SOURCE NOTES

In some cases no source is noted because information was provided confidentially by an individual or individuals who requested anonymity.

PROLOGUE: UNDER THE BIG TOP

Page

13–15 Information on Dr. Wexler's birthday party is drawn primarily from firsthand observation. See also Sean Mitchell, "Off the Wall on Madison Avenue," *Los Angeles Times Magazine,* September 18, 1988; and Marylouise Oates, "Star Analyst Gets the Star Treatment," *Los Angeles Times,* September 26, 1988.

15–16 Freud and Rank: Peter Gay, *Freud: A Life for Our Time* (New York: W. W. Norton & Company, 1988); Paul Roazen, *Freud and His Followers* (New York: Alfred A. Knopf, 1975).

16 George Pollock case: News stories from Associated Press, May 9, 1988, May 13, 1988, and November 2, 1988; *Chicago Tribune,* September 4, 1988, and November 15, 1988.

16–17 Robert Willis case: Mary Billard, "Careful How You Couch It," *Worth,* June/July 1992.

17 Anne Sexton and Dr. Martin T. Orne: Alessandra Stanley, "Poet Tells All; Therapist Provides the Record," *The New York Times,* July 15, 1991; Leonore Tiefer, "The Neurotic Need of Psychotherapists to Exploit Their Patients," *Los Angeles Times,* July 21, 1991; Martin T. Orne, "The Sexton Tapes," *The New York Times,* July 23, 1991; Shari Roan, "Uncovering Secrets of a Very Public Poet," *Los Angeles Times,* August 19, 1991.

18 "were more like friends than doctors . . . ": Dr. Charles Wahl, "Analysis of the Rich, the Famous and the Influential," unpublished paper in the collection of the Simmel-Fenichel Library, Los Angeles Psychoanalytic Society and Institute.

CHAPTER 1: O PIONEERS!

19–20 Hall and Freud: Saul Rosenzweig, *Freud, Jung, and Hall the King-Maker* (Seattle: Hogrefe and Huber, 1992); Peter Gay, *Freud: A Life for Our Time* (New York: W. W. Norton & Company, 1988). Gay's book, the definitive biography, is used throughout as a principal source of information about Freud.

21 Goldwyn's efforts to woo Wells and Shaw: A. Scott Berg, *Goldwyn: A Biography* (New York: Alfred A. Knopf, 1989).

21 Freud and Goldwyn: Ernest Jones, *Sigmund Freud, Life and Work*, Vol. 3 (London: The Hogarth Press, 1957).

22 Ad Schulberg: Sonya Schulberg O'Sullivan and Budd Schulberg, interviewed by the authors. Budd Schulberg, *Moving Pictures: Memories of a Hollywood Prince* (New York: Stein and Day, 1981).

23 PSYCHOANALYSIS, READINGS: David Brunswick, "The Psychoanalytic Movement in Southern California," unpublished paper in the collection of the Simmel-Fenichel Library, Los Angeles Psychoanalytic Institute.

23 "Nowhere else . . . " and "Here is the world's prize collection . . . ": quoted by Carey McWilliams, "Don't Shoot Los Angeles," *Unknown California*, ed. Jonathan Eisen and David Fine (New York: Macmillan, 1985).

23–24 Beginnings of psychoanalysis in Los Angeles: Dr. Norman Levy, Dr. Leonard Rosengarten, Dr. Alexander Rogawski, Dr. Lee Shershow, interviewed by the authors. Also, unpublished oral histories in the Simmel-Fenichel Library, Los Angeles Psychoanalytic Institute: Dr. Ralph Greenson, interviewed by Dr. Robert J. Stoller, December 12, 1962; Mrs. Frances Deri, interviewed by Dr. Albert Kandelin, February 3, 1963; Mrs. Margrit Munk, interviewed by Dr. Arthur Ourieff, January 5, 1963. *Los Angeles Psychoanalytic Bulletin*, "10/40 Celebration—Special Anniversary Issue," December 1986; *Southern California Psychoanalytic Institute and Society Bulletin*, "25th Anniversary Issue," April 1975, and "35th Anniversary Issue," November 1985; Bernice B. Ennis, M.D., "Backgrounds of Psychiatry in Southern California," *Los Angeles County Medical Association Bulletin*, February 15 and March 1, 1973; Albert Kandelin, M.D., "California's First Psychoanalytic Society," *Bulletin of the Menninger Clinic*, November 1966.

24 Freud on David Brunswick: Paul Roazen, *Freud and His Followers* (New York: Alfred A. Knopf, 1975).

25–26 Ernst Simmel: Authors' interviews with Dr. Martin Grotjahn. Also, Lee W. Shershow, "10/40 Celebration: The Founders," *Los Angeles Psychoanalytic Bulletin*, December 1986; John S. Peck, "Ernst Simmel," *Psychoanalytic Pioneers*, ed. Franz Alexander, Samuel Eisenstein, and Martin Grotjahn (New York: Basic Books, 1966); Dr. Ralph Greenson, interviewed by Dr. Robert J. Stoller.

26 Screenwriters and analysis: Walt Odets, Budd Schulberg, Tom Mankiewicz, interviewed by the authors.

27–28   Herman and Joseph Mankiewicz: Authors' interview with Tom Mankiewicz. Richard Meryman, *Mank: The Wit, World, and Life of Herman Mankiewicz* (New York: William Morrow and Company, 1978); Kenneth L. Geist, *Pictures Will Talk: The Life and Films of Joseph L. Mankiewicz* (New York: Charles Scribner's Sons, 1978); Pauline Kael, "Raising Kane," *The Citizen Kane Book* (Boston: Atlantic-Little Brown, 1971).

28–29   Simmel and Gershwin: Gottfried Reinhardt, interviewed by the authors. Edward Jablonsky, *Gershwin* (New York: Doubleday, 1987).

30   Menninger on Kansans and Californians: Karl Menninger, *Sparks,* ed. Lucy Freeman (New York: Crowell, 1973). The letter to his father on the Vendôme, written February 27, 1937, was printed in *The Selected Correspondence of Karl Menninger,* ed. Howard J. Faulkner and Virginia D. Pruitt (New Haven: Yale University Press, 1988).

31   "Otto Fenichel, the famous psychoanalyst . . . ": Ralph Greenson, "Otto Fenichel," *Psychoanalytic Pioneers.*

31   "My God, I thought . . . ": Dr. Martin Grotjahn to the authors.

32   "If anything killed him . . . " Dr. Ralph Greenson, interviewed by Dr. Robert J. Stoller.

32–33   "I wanted to go to the United States . . . ": Mrs. Frances Deri, interviewed by Dr. Albert Kandelin.

33   "She looked just like a Buddha . . . ": Celeste Holm to the authors.

33–34   Deri-Romm rivalry: Authors' interviews with Dr. Leonard Rosengarten, Dr. Norman Levy, and Dr. Martin Grotjahn. *Los Angeles Psychoanalytic Bulletin,* "10/40 Celebration—Special Anniversary Issue," December 1986. Audiotape of "Interview with Dr. Norman Levy on the Occasion of the 35th Anniversary of the Southern California Psychoanalytic Institute," in Franz Alexander Library, Southern California Psychoanalytic Institute.

33   "They were both . . . ": Budd Schulberg to the authors.

33   "I have the clearest impression . . . ": Sonya Schulberg O'Sullivan to the authors.

34   "I kept delaying . . . ": Dr. Alexander Rogawski to the authors.

CHAPTER 2: THE QUEEN OF COUCH CANYON

37–39   Background of May Romm: Reminiscences of Dr. Judd Marmor, George Slaff, and Dr. Viola Bernard in the *Bulletin of the Southern California Psychoanalytic Institute and Society,* January 1978, as well as the authors' interview with Dorothy Colodny. All other quotes from Colodny in this chapter, unless otherwise noted, come from that same interview.

38   Sandor Rado: Roazen, *Freud and His Followers* (New York: Alfred A. Knopf, 1975).

39   Romm's reminiscence of A. A. Brill: *Psychoanalytic Pioneers* (New York: Basic Books, 1966).

39 Fenichel quote, "If you had paid attention . . . ": Dr. Ralph R. Greenson, interviewed by Dr. Robert J. Stoller, December 12, 1962.

39–40 May Romm and Karl Menninger: Dr. Leonard Rosengarten to the authors.

40 Romm's friendships: Dorothy Colodny, interviewed by the authors.

40–42 Romm and the Selznick family: Edith Goetz, Arthur Laurents, Daniel Selznick, and Dorothy Colodny, interviewed by the authors; Irene Mayer Selznick, *A Private View* (New York: Alfred A. Knopf, 1983); David Thomson, *Showman: The Life of David O. Selznick* (New York: Alfred A. Knopf, 1992).

42 "My grandmother liked to drop names . . . ": Julie Kurlander to the authors.

42–43 Romm and Louis B. Mayer: Dorothy Colodny; David Thomson, *Showman.*

43 Romm and Samuel Goldwyn; A. Scott Berg, *Goldwyn: A Biography* (New York: Alfred A. Knopf, 1989).

43–44 Romm and Leland Hayward: Brooke Hayward, *Haywire* (New York: Alfred A. Knopf, 1977); Bill Hayward, interviewed by the authors.

44 "She was the greatest Band-Aid psychiatrist . . . ": Joseph L. Mankiewicz to the authors.

44 "Don't have an hour end unpleasantly . . . ": Ralph R. Greenson, interviewed by Dr. Robert J. Stoller.

44 "She was looked on with disdain . . . ": Dr. Judd Marmor to the authors.

44–46 Romm's lifestyle and her relationship with her daughter: Dorothy Colodny, Julie Kurlander, and Artie Shaw, interviewed by the authors.

46–49 Romm and Artie Shaw: Artie Shaw, interviewed by the authors; Ava Gardner, *Ava: My Story* (New York: Bantam, 1990).

49 Bosley Crowther's review of *Spellbound: The New York Times,* November 2, 1945.

49–51 Romm's involvement with *Spellbound:* David Thomson, *Showman;* Leonard J. Leff, *Hitchcock and Selznick* (New York: Weidenfeld & Nicholson, 1987); authors' interviews with Dorothy Colodny and Dr. Judd Marmor. The letter to Karl Menninger, September 25, 1944, was reprinted in *The Selected Correspondence of Karl A. Menninger, 1919–1945* (New Haven: Yale University Press, 1988).

51 "If we had done that . . . ": Dr. Martin Grotjahn, to the authors.

52 Romm's move to New York: Dorothy Colodny and Mart Crowley, interviewed by the authors.

52–53 Romm's talk on "Neurosis: Yesterday, Today, and Tomorrow": Audiotape in the Franz Alexander Library, Southern California Psychoanalytic Institute.

53–54 Romm's old age and death: Dorothy Colodny, Julie Kurlander.

CHAPTER 3: THE BELIEVERS

55–56 Description of stage production: Moss Hart, *Lady in the Dark* (Cleveland: The World Publishing Company, 1944); Harry Horner, interviewed by the authors.

56 Paramount buys film rights: News stories in *The New York Times*, February 16, 1941, and January 23, 1944.

56–58 Moss Hart: Mona Gardner, "Byron from Brooklyn," *Saturday Evening Post*, November 25, 1944; Ann Rabinowitz, interviewed by the authors; Celeste Holm, interviewed by the authors; Alan Jay Lerner, *The New York Times*, December 24, 1961; Kitty Carlisle Hart, *Kitty: An Autobiography* (New York: Doubleday, 1988); Arthur Laurents, Gottfried Reinhardt, and Harry Horner, interviewed by the authors.

58 "the dean of psychiatrists . . . ": Joshua Logan, *Josh: My Up and Down, In and Out Life* (New York: Delacorte Press, 1976).

58–59 Lawrence Kubie background: Ann Rabinowitz, interviewed by the authors; Sandor Rado interview, Columbia University Oral History Project; Dr. Louis Jolyon West, interviewed by the authors.

59 Kubie and the European analysts: Dr. Arnold Richards, interviewed by the authors; Sandor Rado oral history.

59–60 Kubie as literary critic: Lawrence S. Kubie, *Neurotic Distortion of the Creative Process* (University of Kansas Press, 1958); Jeffrey Meyers, *Hemingway* (New York: Harper & Row, 1985).

60 Kubie's personal life: Authors' interviews with Ann Rabinowitz, Dr. Louis Jolyon West, and Celeste Holm.

60–61 Sid Caesar and Kubie: Sid Caesar with Bill Davidson, *Where Have I Been?* (New York: Crown, 1982).

61–62 Kubie and homosexuality: Glenn Paskin, *Horowitz* (New York: William Morrow and Company, 1983); Tennessee Williams, *Memoirs* (Garden City, N.Y.: Doubleday, 1975); Dr. Erika Freeman, Ann Rabinowitz, and Arthur Laurents, interviewed by the authors.

62–64 Gregory Zilboorg: Columbia University oral histories with Sandor Rado, Lawrence C. Kolb, and Abram Kardiner; authors' interviews with Dr. Leo Rangell and Dr. Louis Jolyon West; Gerold Frank, *Judy* (New York: Harper & Row, 1975); Charles Schwartz, *Gershwin: His Life and Music* (Indianapolis: Bobbs-Merrill Company, 1973); Edward Jablonski, *Gershwin* (New York: Doubleday, 1987); William Wright, *Lillian Hellman; The Image, the Woman* (New York: Simon and Schuster, 1986). Letters from Karl Menninger and Gregory Zilboorg were reprinted in *The Selected Correspondence of Karl A. Menninger, 1919–1945* (New Haven: Yale University Press, 1988).

64 Zilboorg and Lillian Hellman: Peter Feibleman and Arthur Penn, interviewed by the authors; Lillian Hellman, *An Unfinished Woman* (Boston: Little, Brown and Company, 1969).

64 Zilboorg's conversion: Dr. Theodore Rubin, interviewed by the authors.

65–66 Joseph L. Mankiewicz: Joseph L. Mankiewicz, Tom Mankiewicz, and Christopher Mankiewicz, interviewed by the authors; Kenneth L. Geist, *Pictures Will Talk: The Life and Films of Joseph L. Mankiewicz* (New York: Charles Scribner's Sons, 1978); *The Selected Correspondence of Karl A. Menninger.*

66–68 Judy Garland's analysis: Gerold Frank, *Judy;* Anne Edwards, *Judy Garland* (New York: Simon and Schuster, 1974); Vincente Minnelli with Hector Arce, *I Remember It Well* (Garden City, N.Y.: Doubleday, 1974); Dr. Margaret Brenman Gibson, Artie Shaw, Saul Chaplin, and Peter Feibleman, interviewed by the authors.

68–69 Rage for analysis: Artie Shaw, interviewed by the authors; Jill Schary Zimmer, *With a Cast of Thousands* (New York: Stein and Day, 1963); Vincente Minnelli, *I Remember It Well;* Frank, *Judy.*

69–70 Psychiatry during World War II: Dr. Louis Jolyon West and Dr. Peter Loewenberg, interviewed by the authors; William C. Menninger, *Psychiatry in a Troubled World: Yesterday's War and Today's Challenge* (New York: Macmillan Co., 1948).

70–71 *Let There Be Light:* Clarissa K. Wittenberg, "Let There Be Light," *Psychiatric News*, July 3, 1981; John Huston, *An Open Book* (New York: Alfred A. Knopf, 1980).

71–72 *The Snake Pit:* Arthur Laurents, Celeste Holm, and Dr. Theodore Rubin, interviewed by the authors.

73–74 Joseph L. Mankiewicz and *All About Eve:* Gary Carey, *More About All About Eve* (New York: Random House, 1972).

74–76 Joseph L. Mankiewicz and his family: Joseph L. Mankiewicz and Christopher Mankiewicz, interviewed by the authors; Kenneth Geist, *Pictures Will Talk.*

77–80 Bill Hayward incarceration: Bill Hayward and Brooke Hayward, interviewed by the authors; Brooke Hayward, *Haywire* (New York: Alfred A. Knopf, 1977); Slim Keith with Annette Tapert, *Slim: Memories of a Rich and Imperfect Life* (New York: Simon and Schuster, 1990).

79–80 "My father felt there were cases . . . ": Ann Rabinowitz to the authors.

80–81 Studios and psychoanalysis: Arthur Laurents and Saul Chaplin, interviewed by the authors; Gerold Frank, *Judy.*

81–82 Frances Farmer: Frances Farmer, *Will There Really Be a Morning?* (New York: G. P. Putnam's Sons, 1972); William Arnold, *Shadowland* (New York: McGraw-Hill, 1978); news stories in *Los Angeles Times*, January 14, 16, and 21, 1943, *Los Angeles Herald-Examiner*, January 16, 1943, and *Hollywood Citizen-News*, January 15, 1943.

CHAPTER 4: ROMEO AND MARILYN

83 Marilyn Monroe–Don Murray exchange during the filming of *Bus Stop:* Joshua Logan, interviewed for Columbia University Oral History Collection

84 Huston on Monroe's reasons for declining part in *Freud* and his statement, "What [audiences] wanted . . . ": John Huston, *An Open Book* (New York: Alfred A. Knopf, 1980).

84–85 Background on *Captain Newman, M.D.* and Greenson-Rosten relationship: Leo Rosten and Hildi Greenson, interviewed by the authors.

85 "He was a very dramatic guy . . . ": Julian Blaustein to the authors.

85–86 "He was always 'on' . . . ": Charles Kaufman to the authors.

86–87 Greenson childhood, family background: Hildi Greenson, Dr. Marvin Mandel, and William Fadiman, interviewed by the authors.

87 Peter Gay on Stekel: *Freud: A Life for Our Times* (New York: W. W. Norton & Company, 1988).

87–88 Greenson on coming to Los Angeles: Dr. Ralph R. Greenson, interviewed by Dr. Robert J. Stoller.

88 "People got hooked . . . ": Hildi Greenson to the authors.

88 "He gave full vent . . . ": Hildi Greenson, introduction to Ralph Greenson's papers, Simmel-Fenichel Library of the Los Angeles Psychoanlytic Institute.

88–89 "He talked democracy . . . ": Anita Rangell to the authors.

89 "Greenson wanted me to be a disciple . . . ": Dr. Leo Rangell to the authors.

89 Dr. Leonard Rosengarten's description of Greenson: "The Early Years," *Los Angeles Psychoanalytic Bulletin,* December 1986; also personal interview with the authors.

89 "Some of us were wary . . . ": Dr. Norman Levy to the authors.

89–90 Greenson's parties: Hildi Greenson, Tamar Simon Hoffs, Henry Weinstein, and William Fadiman, interviewed by the authors.

90–91 Tony Berlant on Greenson: Interview with the authors.

91 "She put him in charge . . . " Leo Rosten to the authors.

91 "People came to our house . . . ": Hildi Greenson to the authors.

92 Monroe and Arthur Miller's diary: Susan Strasberg, *Marilyn and Me* (New York: Warner Books, 1992).

92 Monroe and Dr. Hohenberg: Donald Spoto, *Marilyn Monroe: The Biography* (New York: HarperCollins, 1993).

93 Vivien Leigh's black-tie dinner: Celeste Holm to the authors.

93–94 Greenson's treatment of Monroe during the filming of *Let's Make Love* and *The Misfits*: Anthony Summers, *Goddess: The Secret Lives of Marilyn Monroe* (New York: Macmillan, 1985).

94 "She was like a hurricane unleashed . . . ": Ralph Roberts, quoted in Strasberg, *Marilyn and Me.*

95 Monroe telegram to Greenson: Summers, *Goddess.*

95–97 Monroe relationship to Greenson family: Hildi Greenson, interviewed by the authors.

96 Monroe at Joan Greenson's birthday party: Norman Rosten, *Marilyn: An Untold Story* (New York: NAL/Signet, 1973).

97–98 "I was jealous . . . ": Celeste Holm to the authors.

98 "You knew I love music . . . ": Janice Rule to the authors.

98 "You *knew* Romi was treating Marilyn . . .": Tamar Hoffs to the authors.

98 "Romi was furious with me . . .": Leo Rosten to the authors.

98 "You couldn't help but like her . . .": Hildi Greenson to the authors.

99 Greenson's diagnosis and treatment of Monroe: Summers, *Goddess;* Lucy Freeman, *Why Norma Jean Killed Marilyn Monroe* (Chicago: Global Rights Ltd., 1992).

100 "It's like my doctor's house . . .": Strasberg, *Marilyn and Me.*

100 "Marilyn would have been called upon . . .": Gloria Steinem, *Marilyn* (New York: Henry Holt, 1986).

100–101 Turmoil at Twentieth Century-Fox: Stephen Farber and Marc Green, *Hollywood Dynasties* (New York: Putnam/Delilah, 1984); Mel Gussow, *Don't Say Yes Until I Finish Talking: A Biography of Darryl F. Zanuck* (Garden City, N.Y.: Doubleday, 1971); Peter Harry Brown and Patte B. Barham, *Marilyn: The Last Take* (New York: Dutton, 1992).

101 Henry Weinstein on the making of *Something's Got to Give:* Interview with the authors.

101 " . . . if you needed to get in touch with Marilyn . . .": Gottfried Reinhardt to the authors.

102 Monroe's call to Weinstein: Henry Weinstein to the authors.

102 Monroe's fantasy of seducing her father: Gloria Steinem, *Marilyn.*

103 "He was furious . . .": Hildi Greenson to the authors.

103 "He might have been able . . .": Henry Weinstein to the authors.

103 "Henry, of course, felt Greenson's strength . . .": Celeste Holm to the authors.

104–105 Clemons on "murder": Sandra Shevey, *The Marilyn Scandal* (New York: William Morrow and Company, 1988).

105 Conspiracy theories: Frank A. Capell, *The Strange Death of Marilyn Monroe* (Zerephath, N. J.: The Herald of Freedom, 1964); Anthony Scaduto, "Who Killed Marilyn?" *Oui,* October 1975; Sam and Chuck Giancana, *Double Cross* (New York: Warner Books, 1992); Robert F. Slatzer, *The Marilyn Files* (New York: S.P.I. Books, 1992); Tim Powell, "Some Like to Plot," *Entertainment Weekly,* August 7, 1992.

105–106 The "fatal enema" theory: Spoto, *Marilyn Monroe: The Biography.*

106–107 Janice Rule and Hildi Greenson on Greenson's reaction to Monroe's death: Interviews with the authors.

107 "It was awful . . .": Audiotape of Dr. Ralph Greenson, "Mistakes and Beginnings in Psychoanalysis and Psychotherapy" (Ann Arbor, Mich.: Clinical Training and Education Associates, 1969).

107 On neurotic gamblers: Ralph R. Greenson, "On Gambling," *Explorations in Psychoanalysis* (New York: International Universities Press, 1978).

108 "I knew it was a difficult case . . .": Ralph Greenson, quoted by Hildi Greenson in interview with the authors.

108 Comprehensive textbook: Ralph R. Greenson, *The Technique and*

Practice of Psychoanalysis, Vol. I (New York: International Universities Press, 1967).

108 "You can't sit there like a computer . . . ": Greenson, "Mistakes and Beginnings in Psychoanalysis and Psychotherapy."

108–109 Assessments by Dr. Leo Rangell, Dr. Melvin Mandel, and Dr. Lorraine Kaufman regarding Greenson's treatment of Monroe are from personal interviews with the authors.

110 "I wanted to be . . . ": Quoted by Julian Blaustein to the authors.

110–111 Greenson on *The Exorcist:* Ralph R. Greenson, M.D., "A Psychoanalyst's Indictment of 'The Exorcist,'" *Saturday Review/World,* June 15, 1974.

112 "I will not discuss psychoanalysis . . . ": Quoted in Steinem, *Marilyn.*

112–113 Greenson's case study of "an emotionally immature young woman patient": "On Transitional Objects and Transference," *Explorations in Psychoanalysis.*

114 "Romi would often come to me . . . ": Leo Rosten to the authors.

CHAPTER 5: THE CONFIDENCE GAME

115–117 The death of Robert Walker: Robert Walker, Jr., interviewed by the authors; news coverage in *Los Angeles Times,* August 29, 1951; Dore Schary, *Heyday: An Autobiography* (Boston: Little, Brown and Company, 1979); Beverly Linet, *Star-Crossed: The Story of Robert Walker and Jennifer Jones* (New York: G. P. Putnam's Sons, 1986).

117 "Hacker killed Robert Walker . . . ": Dr. Alex Rogawski to the authors.

117 "That case didn't do Hacker any harm . . . " Dr. Leo Rangell to the authors.

117–119 Background of Dr. Frederick Hacker: Gottfried Reinhardt, Dr. Alex Rogawski, and Dr. Martin Grotjahn, interviewed by the authors; Kenneth Geist, *Pictures Will Talk* (New York: Charles Scribner's Sons, 1978); obituaries in *The New York Times,* June 30, 1989, and *Los Angeles Times,* June 30, 1989.

119 Hacker and Robert Mitchum: George Eells, *Robert Mitchum* (New York: Franklin Watts, 1984). Mitchum's affidavit to the court was printed in *Los Angeles Daily News,* February 20, 1949.

119–20 Hacker and the Mankiewicz family: Tom Mankiewicz and Christopher Mankiewicz, interviewed by the authors; Geist, *Pictures Will Talk.*

120 Hacker on the social circuit: Budd Schulberg and John Kohn, interviewed by the authors.

120 "Fred was once arrested . . . " Tom Mankiewicz to the authors.

121 "Those who are publicized in the magazines . . . " Dr. Leo Rangell to the authors.

121–122 Grotjahn and Merv Griffin: Merv Griffin with Peter Barsocchini, *Merv: An Autobiography* (New York: Simon and Schuster, 1980).

122–124 *Elephant Walk:* Dr. Martin Grotjahn, interviewed by the authors; Laurence Olivier, *Confessions of an Actor* (New York: Simon and Schuster, 1982); Anne Edwards, *Vivien Leigh* (New York: Simon and Schuster, 1977); Hugo Vickers, *Vivien Leigh* (Boston: Little, Brown and Co., 1988); Donald Spoto, *Laurence Olivier: A Biography* (New York: HarperCollins, 1992); newspaper articles in *Los Angeles Times*, March 14, 1953, and March 18, 1953, and *Hollywood Citizen-News*, March 20, 1953. The Louella Parsons column is from *Los Angeles Herald-Examiner*, March 25, 1953.

124–125 Background of Dr. Martin Grotjahn: Dr. Grotjahn, interviewed by the authors; Martin Grotjahn, *My Favorite Patient: The Memoirs of a Psychoanalyst* (New York: Peter Lang, 1987); Robert Rodman, "Interview With Martin Grotjahn," *Los Angeles Psychoanalytic Bulletin*, January 1984; Martin Grotjahn, "On Being Born Twice: An Attempt to Analyze the Immigration Experience," *British Journal of Psychotherapy*, Vol. 4, No. 4, 1988; Martin Grotjahn, "On Motherliness in the Therapist," *Journal of the American Academy of Psychotherapists*, Summer 1988; videotaped interviews with Grotjahn in the Franz Alexander Library, Southern California Psychoanalytic Institute.

125–126 Ingrid Bergman and Hedy Lamarr: Authors' interviews with Dr. Martin Grotjahn and Dr. Philip Solomon; Grotjahn, *My Favorite Patient*.

126–127 Grotjahn on movie stars: Authors' interviews with Dr. Grotjahn.

127–128 Grotjahn and group therapy: Martin Grotjahn, "The Treatment of the Famous and the 'Beautiful People' in Groups," in *Group Therapy 1975: An Overview*, ed. Louis Wolberg and Marvin Aronson (New York: Stratton, 1975); Dr. Grotjahn, interviewed by the authors.

128–129 Grotjahn and comedy: Dr. Grotjahn, Dr. Milton Wexler, and Dr. Louis Jolyon West, interviewed by the authors; Martin Grotjahn, *Beyond Laughter* (New York: Blakeston, 1957); Edie Adams and Robert Windeler, *Sing a Pretty Song . . . : The "Offbeat" Life of Edie Adams, Including the Ernie Kovacs Years* (New York: William Morrow and Company, 1990).

129 "The only person who entertained me . . . ": Dr. Grotjahn to the authors.

129 "Danny had his miseries . . . ": Dr. Louis Jolyon West to the authors.

130–131 Dr. Grotjahn's last years: Martin Grotjahn and Gail Parent, interviewed by the authors; Martin Grotjahn, "The Day I Got Old," *Los Angeles Times*, March 30, 1982.

132 Elia Kazan and Dr. Bela Mittelman: Elia Kazan, *A Life* (New York: Alfred A. Knopf, 1988).

132–134 Ernest Philip Cohen: Abraham Polonsky and Arthur Laurents, interviewed by the authors; Sterling Hayden, *Wanderer* (New York: Alfred A. Knopf, 1963); Victor S. Navasky, *Naming Names* (New York: The Viking Press, 1980).

134–135 Judd Marmor and the blacklist era: Dr. Judd Marmor, interviewed by the authors.

135 Marmor's essay: Dr. Judd Marmor, "The Feeling of Superiority:

An Occupational Hazard in the Practice of Psychotherapy," *American Journal of Psychiatry,* November 1953.

136 Marmor's background: Dr. Judd Marmor, interviewed by the authors; videotaped interview with Dr. Marmor, conducted December 11, 1984, by the Southern California Psychoanalytic Institute.

136 "In the New York Psychoanalytic Institute . . . " Dr. Arnold Richards to the authors.

136–137 Marmor's early years in Los Angeles: Julian Blaustein and Dr. Judd Marmor, interviewed by the authors.

137–138 Arthur Laurents's analysis: Arthur Laurents, interviewed by the authors; Irene Mayer Selznick, *A Private View* (New York: Alfred A. Knopf, 1983).

138 Shelley Winters: Shelley Winters, *Shelley: Also Known as Shirley* (New York: William Morrow and Company, 1980); Dick Stelzer, *The Star Treatment* (Indianapolis: The Bobbs-Merrill Company, 1977).

138–139 Marmor and the battles within the APA over homosexuality: Dr. Judd Marmor, interviewed by the authors; Kenneth Lewes, *The Psychoanalytic Theory of Male Homosexuality* (New York: Simon and Schuster, 1988).

139 Samuel Goldwyn and "Dr. Murmur": A. Scott Berg, *Goldwyn: A Biography* (New York: Alfred A. Knopf, 1989).

139 Abe Burrows and Stanley Praeger: Dr. Judd Marmor to the authors.

139–143 David Begelman case: Dr. Judd Marmor and Arthur Laurents, interviewed by the authors; David McClintick, *Indecent Exposure: A True Story of Hollywood and Wall Street* (New York: William Morrow and Company, 1982); Jeanie Kasindorf, "The Incredible Past of David Begelman," *New West,* February 13, 1978.

140 "temporary emotional problems": *The Wall Street Journal,* January 30, 1978.

142 "Ordinarily Judd is very discreet . . . ": Dr. Alex Rogawski to the authors.

143 "I don't know whether he was gullible . . . ": Dr. Dorothy Colodny to the authors.

CHAPTER 6: ACTING OUT

144 Stella Adler anecdote: Elia Kazan, *A Life* (New York: Alfred A. Knopf, 1988).

144–145 Background of the Actors Studio: Lee Strasberg, *A Dream of Passion: The Development of the Method* (Boston: Little, Brown and Company, 1987); Kazan, *A Life;* Christine Hradesky, "Creativity, the Actor and the Analyst," lecture to Southern California Psychoanalytic Institute, May 28, 1989.

145–146 Personal reminiscences of the Actors Studio: Authors' interviews with Frank Corsaro, Bruce Dern, Sidney Lumet, and Susan Strasberg; Joanne Kaufman, "Studio System," *Vanity Fair,* November 1992; Susan Strasberg, *Bittersweet* (New York, G. P. Putnam's Sons, 1980).

146–147 Anne Bancroft: Dr. Margaret Brenman Gibson, interviewed by the authors; Gilbert Millstein, "Seesaw Saga of an Actress," *New York Times Magazine,* February 9, 1958; "Who Is Stanislavsky?," *Time,* December 21, 1959; Joe Alex Morris, "Second-Chance Actress," *Saturday Evening Post,* December 9, 1961; Earl Wilson, "Star Analyzes Own 'Miracle,' " *Los Angeles Times,* May 19, 1962.

147 Mel Brooks's analysis: Dick Stelzer, *The Star Treatment* (Indianapolis: The Bobbs-Merrill Company, 1977).

147–148 William and Margaret Gibson: Dr. Margaret Brenman Gibson and Arthur Penn, interviewed by the authors.

148 Oscar Levant and *The Cobweb:* Susan Strasberg, *Bittersweet.*

148 Problems with *Two for the Seesaw:* Margaret Gibson and Arthur Penn, interviewed by the authors; William Gibson, *The Seesaw Log: A Chronicle of the Stage Production* (New York: Alfred A. Knopf, 1959).

148–149 *Golden Boy:* Authors' interviews with Arthur Penn and Margaret Gibson.

149–152 The career of Elia Kazan: Kazan, *A Life;* Budd Schulberg and Bruce Dern, interviewed by the authors.

152–153 Marlon Brando and analysis: Kazan, *A Life;* Bob Thomas, *Marlon: Portrait of the Rebel as an Artist* (New York: Random House, 1973); Charles Higham: *Brando, The Unauthorized Biography* (New York: New American Library, 1987); Jay Presson Allen, interviewed by the authors.

154–155 Natalie Wood and Dr. John Lindon: Lana Wood, *Natalie: A Memoir by Her Sister* (New York: G. P. Putnam's Sons, 1984); Warren G. Harris, *Natalie and R.J.* (New York: Doubleday, 1988); Edith Goetz, interviewed by the authors.

155–156 Evaluations of Method acting: Jay Presson Allen, interviewed by the authors; Kazan, *A Life.*

156 Montgomery Clift and *I Confess:* Bruce Dern, interviewed by the authors; Robert La Guardia, *Monty* (New York: Arbor House, 1977); Patricia Bosworth, *Montgomery Clift: A Biography* (New York: Harcourt Brace Jovanovich, 1978).

157 Montgomery Clift and Dr. William Silverberg: Patricia Bosworth, *Montgomery Clift.*

157–158 The making of *Freud:* Julian Blaustein and Charles Kaufman, interviewed by the authors; John Huston, "Focus on 'Freud,' " *The New York Times,* December 9, 1962.

158–159 Reviews of *Freud:* Bosley Crowther, *The New York Times,* December 13, 1962; Philip K. Scheuer, *Los Angeles Times,* December 13, 1962.

159–160 Background on *Tender Is the Night:* Authors' interviews with Jason Robards, Gottfried Reinhardt, and Daniel Selznick; David Thomson, *Showman* (New York: Alfred A. Knopf, 1992); Eugene Archer, " 'Tender Is the Night' on the Cote D'Azur," *The New York Times,* June 18, 1961.

160–161 Jason Robards and Dr. Ferruccio Di Cari: Jason Robards, interviewed by the authors.

161–163 On *David and Lisa:* Authors' interviews with Janet Margolin, Frank Perry, Dr. Theodore Rubin, and Ann Bayer. Articles on the making of the film appeared in *The New York Times,* May 6, 1962, and *Time,* December 28, 1962. Stanley Kauffmann's review: *The New Republic,* January 5, 1963.

163 Patty Duke's psychotherapy: Patty Duke and Kenneth Turan, *Call Me Anna: The Autobiography of Patty Duke* (New York: Bantam, 1987); Patty Duke and Gloria Hochman, *A Brilliant Madness: Living with Manic-Depressive Illness* (New York: Bantam, 1992).

163 Background of Dr. Rudolph Loewenstein: Obituary in *The Newsletter of the New York Psychoanalytic Society and Institute,* July 1976; Arthur Miller, *Timebends: A Life* (New York, Grove Press, 1987); Stephen Sondheim, interviewed by the authors.

163–168 Arthur Penn: Arthur Penn, interviewed by the authors; Dr. Margaret Gibson, interviewed by the authors.

169 Sidney Lumet's early involvement in analysis: Sidney Lumet, interviewed by the authors.

169–170 Other celebrities using LSD: W. A. Swanberg, *Luce and His Empire* (New York: Charles Scribner's Sons, 1972); Warren G. Harris, *Cary Grant: A Touch of Elegance* (New York: Doubleday, 1987); Charles Higham and Roy Moseley, *Cary Grant: The Lonely Heart* (San Diego: Harcourt Brace Jovanovich, 1989); Judith Balaban Quine, interviewed by the authors.

170–172 Sidney Lumet's later analysis: Sidney Lumet and Dr. Christopher Zois, interviewed by the authors.

172–174 Nicholas Meyer: Nicholas Meyer, interviewed by the authors; Nicholas Meyer, "Lost Boys Wandering Around the Peter Pantheon," *Annals of the American Society for Adolescent Psychiatry,* Volume 12, 1985.

CHAPTER 7: COMIC RELIEF

175–176 "You see Natalie Wood . . . " Leo Rangell to the authors.

177 Paul Mazursky's background, early film career: Paul Mazursky, interviewed by the authors.

179 "the best and most realistic therapy session . . . ": Irving Schneider, "Images of the Mind: Psychiatry in the Commercial Film," *American Journal of Psychiatry,* June 1977.

179–181 Mazursky and Donald Muhich: Paul Mazursky, interviewed by the authors. Muhich's experiences in television were reported by Krin Gabbard and Glen O. Gabbard in *Psychiatry and the Cinema* (Chicago: The University of Chicago Press, 1987).

181 "We can only wonder . . . ": Irving Schneider, "The Theory and Practice of Movie Psychiatry," *American Journal of Psychiatry,* August 1987.

182 Mazursky meeting Penelope Russianoff: Paul Mazursky and Penelope Russianoff, interviewed by the authors.

182–184 Russianoff's background: Dr. Penelope Russianoff, interviewed by the authors.

184 "One of my hidden goals ... " Quoted in Judy Klemesrud, "Film Role Sends Therapist to Therapy," *The New York Times*, July 31, 1978. Russianoff's comments on negative reviews were also reported in this interview.

184–185 Russianoff's experiences on *An Unmarried Woman:* Dr. Russianoff, interviewed by the authors.

185–186 Russianoff's desire to resume her acting career: Dr. Russianoff to the authors; Elaine Warren, "The Celebrity Shrink Who Became a Celebrity Herself," *Los Angeles Herald Examiner*, May 13, 1982.

186 "Because of Woody Allen ... ": Gail Parent to the authors.

186–187 Woody Allen's custody battle with Mia Farrow: Peter Marks, "Therapy Is Theme of Allen Hearing," *The New York Times*, April 4, 1993.

187 "It's worth it if you can see an end to it ... " Quoted in Eric Lax, *Woody Allen: A Biography* (New York: Alfred A. Knopf, 1991).

187 Woody Allen beginning analysis: Eric Lax, *Woody Allen.*

187–188 Allen on his Freudian regimen: Woody Allen, interviewed by the authors.

189 "It's very slow ... " Allen to Natalie Gittelson, "The Maturing of Woody Allen," *The New York Times Magazine*, April 22, 1979.

189 Joan Didion rejoinder: Joan Didion, "Letter from 'Manhattan,' " *The New York Review of Books*, August 16, 1979.

189 "Creative people have got to spend ... " Woody Allen to the authors.

190 Woody Allen's review of Ingmar Bergman's autobiography, *The Magic Lantern: The New York Times Book Review*, September 18, 1988.

191 "I would feel incomplete ... ": Woody Allen to the authors.

192 "In their works ... ": Irving Schneider, "The Theory and Practice of Movie Psychiatry."

192 "Unfortunately, what most people think about therapy ... ": Dr. Christopher Zois to the authors.

192–194 Allen's romance with Soon-Yi Previn: "Unhappily Ever After," *Newsweek*, August 31, 1992; Richard Corliss, "Scenes from a Breakup," *Time*, August 31, 1992; Phoebe Hoban, "Everything You Always Wanted to Know About Woody and Mia (But Were Afraid to Ask)," *New York*, September 21, 1992.

194 "That's a real common problem that people have ... ": Woody Allen to the authors.

195 "The amount of deference ... ": David Mamet, "I Lost It at the Movies," *American Film*, June 1987.

195–196 Allen's apologia: "The Heart Wants What It Wants," interview by Walter Isaacson, *Time*, August 31, 1992.

CHAPTER 8: THE HEARTBREAK KIDS

198   "It can be argued . . . " Krin Gabbard and Glen O. Gabbard, *Psychiatry and the Cinema* (Chicago: The University of Chicago Press, 1987).

199–200   Reactions to *Lovesick:* Authors' interviews with Marshall Brickman, Dudley Moore, Dr. Jacqueline Bouhoutsos, and Frances Lear; Richard Johnson, "A Review of *Lovesick,*" *Bulletin of the Southern California Psychoanalytic Institute and Society,* Summer 1984. Frances Lear's letter to the *Los Angeles Times* appeared February 27, 1983.

200–201   Other cases of doctor-patient sex: Dr. Jacqueline Bouhoutsos, interviewed by the authors; Susan K. Golant, "Therapists Admit Sex Lure," *Los Angeles Times,* June 24, 1986; Ann Landers, "Woman Issues Warning About Her Psychiatrist," *Los Angeles Times,* September 14, 1992; Lucy Freeman and Julie Roy, *Betrayal* (New York: Stein and Day, 1976); Evelyn Walker and Perry Deane Young, *A Killing Cure* (New York: Henry Holt and Company, 1986); Jeffrey Moussaieff Masson, *Against Therapy* (New York: Atheneum, 1988).

201–202   Background on Mike Nichols and Elaine May: Michael Braun, "Mike and Elaine: Veracity-Cum-Boffs," *Esquire,* October 1960; Robert Rice, "Profiles," *The New Yorker,* April 15, 1961; *The Best of Mike Nichols and Elaine May,* Mercury Records; *An Evening with Mike Nichols and Elaine May* (Highlights from the Broadway Production), Mercury Records.

202–204   Background of Dr. David Rubinfine: Dr. Milton Wexler, Dr. Margaret Gibson, Nicholas Meyer, Michael Pressman, Stephen Sondheim, and Marty Gwinn Townsend, interviewed by the authors.

204–205   Romance of Elaine May and David Rubinfine: Marshall Brickman, Dr. Milton Wexler, and Dr. Margaret Gibson, interviewed by the authors; Thomas Thompson, "Whatever Happened to Elaine May?" *Life,* July 28, 1967.

205   Rosa Rubinfine's death: Death certificate #5981, recorded at the New York Public Library; Dr. Milton Wexler, Jay Presson Allen, Arthur Penn, and Dr. Erika Freeman, interviewed by the authors.

206–208   Dr. Victor Rosen: Winifred Rosen, interviewed by the authors. Janet Malcolm's veiled discussion of the two cases is contained in her book *Psychoanalysis: The Impossible Profession* (New York: Alfred A. Knopf, 1981).

209–210   Elaine May and David Rubinfine after their marriage: Authors' interviews with Dr. Margaret Gibson, Dr. Milton Wexler, Janet Margolin, Arthur Penn, Janice Rule, and Hildi Greenson; Joyce Haber, *Los Angeles Times,* July 7, 1968.

211   *Mikey and Nicky:* News stories in *Variety,* October 22, 1975, and September 15, 1976; Andrew Tobias, "For Elaine May, a New Film—but Not a New Leaf," *New West,* December 6, 1976.

211–213   Rubinfine's later years: Authors' interviews with Arthur Penn, Julian Schlossberg, Robert Benton, Judy Walker, Robert Walker, Jr., Marty Gwinn Townsend, and Kim Townsend.

213–214 Victor Rosen's death: Winifred Rosen to the authors.
214 David Rubinfine's death: Judy Walker, Marty Gwinn Townsend, and Dr. Milton Wexler, interviewed by the authors.
214 "People make the assumption . . . ": Nicholas Meyer to the authors.
214 "In a way that is the very same discrepancy . . . ": Winifred Rosen to the authors.

CHAPTER 9: BREAKING THE RULES

216–217 Eugene Landy: Steven Gaines, *Heroes and Villains: The True Story of the Beach Boys* (New York: New American Library, 1986); Nancy Spiller, "Bad Vibrations," *Los Angeles Times Magazine,* June 26, 1988; Timothy White, "Beach Boy Brian Wilson Back from the Bottom," *The New York Times Magazine,* June 26, 1988; Tracy Wilkinson, "Beach Boy Brian Wilson's Psychologist Loses License," *Los Angeles Times,* April 1, 1989.
217–218 Milton Wexler's background: Dr. Milton Wexler, Jane Attias, and Peter Feibleman, interviewed by the authors; Nancy Wexler, "Life in the Lab," *Los Angeles Times Magazine,* February 10, 1991.
218 Wexler's approach to schizophrenia: Dr. Milton Wexler, interviewed by the authors; Milton Wexler, "The Structural Problem in Schizophrenia: Therapeutic Implications," first presented to the Topeka Psychoanalytic Society, June 1950, published in *International Journal of Psychoanalysis,* Vol. 32, 1951; Milton Wexler, "Working Through in the Therapy of Schizophrenia," *International Journal of Psychoanalysis,* Vol. 46, 1965.
219 Huntington's disease: Nancy Wexler, "Life in the Lab"; Marion Steinman, "In the Shadow of Huntington's Disease: Nancy Wexler's Quest for a Cure," *Columbia* (The Magazine of Columbia University), November 1987.
219 "What a lovely, charming . . . ": Milton Wexler to the authors.
219 Wexler and Ralph Greenson: Authors' interviews with Hildi Greenson and Milton Wexler.
219–220 Wexler, John Altoon, and other artists: Tony Berlant, Blake Edwards, and Dr. Milton Wexler, interviewed by the authors.
220 Frank Gehry and Wexler: Dr. Wexler to the authors; Leon Whiteson, "Frank Gehry: The Evolution of a Master," *Los Angeles Times,* October 30, 1989; Barbara Isenberg, "Frank Gehry's Creative Journey," *Los Angeles Times,* April 7, 1991; Cathleen McGuigan, "A Maverick Master," *Newsweek,* June 17, 1991.
220 Wexler's divorce, Leonore Wexler's illness: Nancy Wexler, "Life in the Lab."
220–221 Sigmund Freud and Horace Frink: Daniel Goleman, "As a Therapist, Freud Fell Short, Scholars Find," *The New York Times,* March 6, 1990.
221–222 Jennifer Jones's background: Robert Walker, Jr., and Jason Robards, interviewed by the authors; interview with Jones in *Los Angeles Herald-Examiner,* June 25, 1980; David Thomson, *Showman* (New York: Alfred A. Knopf, 1992); Beverly Linet, *Star-Crossed: The Story of Robert Walker and*

Jennifer Jones (New York: G. P. Putnam's Sons, 1986). Vincente Minnelli with Hector Arce, *I Remember It Well* (Garden City, N.Y.: Doubleday, 1974).

222 Jones's suicide attempt: News stories in *Los Angeles Times* and *Los Angeles Herald-Examiner*, November 10, 1967; Jones interview with *Los Angeles Herald-Examiner*, June 25, 1980.

222 "She came to me . . . ": Milton Wexler to the authors.

223 Jennifer Jones and Norton Simon: Phyllis Battelle, "Love at First Analysis Turns to Charity," *Los Angeles Herald-Examiner*, June 25, 1980; Suzanne Muchnic, "Simon Finally Breaks the Silence," *Los Angeles Times*, June 24, 1990.

223 Karl Menninger's letter to Ruth Mack Brunswick, February 17, 1945: *The Selected Correspondence of Karl A. Menninger 1919–1945* (New Haven: Yale University Press, 1988).

224 Jones lobbying for the Hereditary Disease Foundation: "Jennifer Jones Seeks to Work Real-Life Miracles," *Los Angeles Times* October 19, 1977.

224 "In many ways . . . ": Dr. Milton Wexler to the authors.

224 "In the first few weeks . . . ": Nancy Hardin to the authors.

224–225 "Knowing Milton . . . ": Blake Edwards to the authors.

225 The "Shower of Stars": Jody Jacobs, "Showers and Stars at Gala Benefits," *Los Angeles Times*, April 6, 1976; Camilla Snyder, "Jennifer Jones Simon on the Benefit Circuit," *Los Angeles Herald-Examiner*, March 22, 1976.

225–226 Ann Landers: "Charitable Group Says Thank You," *Los Angeles Times*, March 15, 1992; "Woman Issues Warning About Her Psychiatrist," *Los Angeles Times*, September 14, 1992.

226 "Maybe they do . . . ": Dr. Milton Wexler to the authors.

226 "I admire Milton as a smart man . . . " David Seltzer to the authors.

227 "I do feel that rich people . . . ": Nancy Hardin to the authors.

227 Socializing and vacationing with patients: Dr. Milton Wexler and Nancy Hardin, interviewed by the authors; William Wright, *Lillian Hellman* (New York: Simon and Schuster, 1986).

227–228 "Let's assume that a patient becomes very angry . . . ": Dr. Samuel Klagsbrun to the authors.

228 "You can be very effective . . . ": Dr. Melvin Mandel to the authors.

228 "I think a famous person corrupts . . . ": David Seltzer to the authors.

228–229 Nancy Hardin's experiences: Nancy Hardin to the authors.

229–230 The robbery: Nancy Hardin and Jonathan Krane, interviewed by the authors.

230 Wexler's group and *10:* Blake Edwards and Dudley Moore, interviewed by the authors; news report in *Variety*, October 3, 1978.

230–231 Jonathan Krane and Sally Kellerman: Jonathan Krane, interviewed by the authors; Judy Klemesrud, "Sally Kellerman Comes Back," *The New York Times*, May 11, 1980.

231 "I'm thrilled to have met him there . . . ": Sally Kellerman in *Beverly Hills [213]*, August 7, 1985.

231 Dudley Moore and the two therapy groups: Dudley Moore and Hunter Murtaugh, interviewed by the authors.
232 Wexler's screenwriting aspirations: Dr. Milton Wexler, Nancy Hardin, Jonathan Krane, and Linda Palmer, interviewed by the authors.
232–234 Background on Blake Edwards: Blake Edwards and Julie Andrews, interviewed by the authors; *Playboy* interview with Julie Andrews and Blake Edwards, December 1982; Paul Rosenfield, "Reconcilable Differences," *Los Angeles Times*, July 12, 1987; Kirk Honeycutt, "His Pain, His Gain," *Los Angeles Times*, May 5, 1991; Dick Stelzer, *The Star Treatment* (Indianapolis: The Bobbs-Merrill Company, 1977).
234–236 Screenwriting collaboration of Wexler and Edwards: Dr. Milton Wexler, Blake Edwards, and Julie Andrews, interviewed by the authors; Chris Chase, "Real Life Buoys 'That's Life!' " *The New York Times*, September 21, 1986. Stanley Kauffmann's review of *That's Life!* appeared in *The New Republic*, October 20, 1986. Wexler interviewed by Lawrence Van Gelder in *The New York Times*, September 26, 1986.
236–237 "to the enhancement of the analyst . . . ": Dr. Leo Rangell to the authors.
237 "I know there are canons of ethics . . . ": Dr. Milton Wexler to the authors.
238 Wexler's party: Marylouise Oates, "Star Analyst Gets the Star Treatment," *Los Angeles Times*, September 26, 1988.
238 "Milton has been with Mother forever . . . ": Robert Walker, Jr., to the authors.

CHAPTER 10: THE INTRUDERS

240 "The latest group of specialists . . . ": S. J. Perelman, "Physician, Steel Thyself," *The Most of S. J. Perelman* (New York: Simon and Schuster, 1958).
241 Kubie's proposal: Lawrence Kubie, "Psychiatry and the Films," *Hollywood Quarterly*, January 1947.
241 Irving Schneider on Kubie's plan: "Images of the Mind: Psychiatry in the Commercial Film," *American Journal of Psychiatry*, June 1977.
242 Sherry Lansing's analysis and her views on psychoanalysts as consultants: Lansing interviewed by the authors.
243–234 Daniel Melnick's use of consultants: Melnick interview by the authors.
243 "I told him I thought our film . . . ": Barry Sandler to the authors.
244–245 Dr. Martin Wasserman on role of consultants: Wasserman interviewed by the authors.
245–246 Bill Cosby and Dr. Pouissant: Edward Silver, "This Alter Ego Helps Scripts Be Psychologically Sound," *The New York Times*, July 1, 1990.
246–248 Dr. Melvin Heller: Interview with the authors.
246–247 "The editor is alerted . . . ": Melvin S. Heller, M.D., "Sexuality, Television and Broadcast Standards" (American Broadcasting Companies, Inc., 1984).

247 *The Execution of Raymond Graham:* David Rintels, interviewed by the authors; Heller memorandum to Alfred Schneider, March 14, 1985.

248–250 Dr. Carole Lieberman: Edward Silver, "This Alter Ego Helps Scripts Be Psychologically Sound"; Carole Lieberman, "A Psychological Approach to Rating Movies," *Los Angeles Times*, October 1, 1990.

250 "I will never again have a psychiatrist . . . ": Jack Valenti to the authors; other comments by Valenti are from the same interview.

251–254 The *Midnight Cowboy* controversy and Dr. Stern's activities as a consultant to the rating board: Stephen Farber, *The Movie Rating Game* (Washington: Public Affairs Press, 1972). (While serving as a student intern with the board, Farber was an eyewitness to events reported in that book.) Stephen Farber and Estelle Changas, "Putting the Hex on R and X," *The New York Times*, April 9, 1972.

253–254 Ernest Lehman, Sam Peckinpah, Don Siegel, and Clint Eastwood on Dr. Stern: "Did They Rate the Rating Board Unfairly?" (letters to the editor), *The New York Times*, May 7, 1972. Vincent Canby's response to these filmmakers appeared in his regular Sunday column, *The New York Times*, June 4, 1972.

254 "I am very happy that Aaron is in there . . . ": Quoted by Leonard Gross, "What's Blue at the Movies," *Los Angeles Times*, July 16, 1972.

254–255 The MGM censor: Jack Langguth, "Dr. X," *Saturday Review*, December 2, 1972.

255 "I said I wouldn't take the job . . . ": Quoted by Leonard Gross, "What's Blue at the Movies."

256 "It was kind of fun . . . ": Anita Rangell to the authors.

256 "Don't worry, Mike . . . " Linda Palmer to the authors.

257–258 Stern, Columbia, and Begelman: "Aaron Stern Joins Columbia," *Variety*, December 5, 1973; "Stern Suing Col for $20 Mil," *Variety*, September 4, 1974; "Aaron Stern, Col have a 3-Film 'Arrangement,' " *Variety*, January 8, 1976. Comments by Jack Valenti, Dr. Martin Wasserman, Arthur Penn, and Sidney Lumet are from interviews with the authors.

258–259 "By advancing far beyond his origins . . . ": Aaron Stern, *Me: The Narcissistic American* (New York: Ballantine Books, 1979).

259 " . . . only analyst with a three-picture deal": Thomas Baum to the authors.

259–260 Susan Rice on Stern: Rice interviewed by the authors.

260 "He was just a gust of wind . . . ": Dr. Leo Rangell to the authors.

260 "Any stone dropped into the huge ocean . . . ": Aaron Stern, *Me: The Narcissistic American*.

261 "The odds are overwhelming . . . ": Paul Mazursky to the authors.

261 "A psychiatrist suddenly pitchforked . . . ": S. J. Perelman, "Physician, Steel Thyself."

CHAPTER 11: THE FEMININE MYSTIQUE

262   "How wise our educators . . . ": Freud to Fluss, quoted in Peter Gay, *Freud: A Life for Our Time* (New York: W. W. Norton & Company, 1988).

262   Karen Horney on Freudian theory: "The Flight from Womanhood: The Masculinity Complex in Women as Viewed by Men and by Women," *International Journal of Psycho-Analysis,* VII, 1926.

262–263   Marie Bonaparte: Celia Bertin, *Marie Bonaparte: A Life* (San Diego: Harcourt Brace Javonovich, 1982).

263   "Freud encouraged the transference . . . ": Paul Roazen, *Freud and His Followers* (New York: Alfred A. Knopf, 1975).

263–264   Janice Rule's early career: "Starlet Janice Rule," *Life,* January 8, 1951; Janice Rule, interviewed by the authors.

263–264   "her brief whirl . . . ": Studio press release by Robert Birdwell, Library of the Academy of Motion Picture Arts and Sciences.

264   " . . . as her adopted uncles . . . ": United Artists studio bio, Library of the Academy of Motion Picture Arts and Sciences.

264   "They wanted me to go to Ciro's . . . ": Ann Guerin, "If Ben Gazzara Gets Hung Up, the Analyst Is Always In . . . " *People,* June 21, 1976.

264   " . . . the prettiest, but also the dumbest . . . ": Janice Rule, "The Actor's Identity Crises (Postanalytic Reflections of an Actress)," *International Journal of Psychoanalytic Psychotherapy,* II, 1973.

265   "There were slam-bang fights . . . ": Gazzara to Ann Guerin.

265   "I knew I had to stay home with the children . . . ": Janice Rule to the authors.

265–266   "There was this whole shrink-art connection . . . ": Tamar Hoffs to the authors.

266–270   Analysis with Greenson, relationship with Wexler and Rubinfine, the writing of her monograph: Rule, interviewed by the authors.

270   " . . . great cost in terms of time . . . ": Dr. Toni Bernay to the authors.

270   " . . . an extremely arduous, inequitable procedure": Dr. Samoan Barish to the authors.

270–272   Rule on her analytic practice, film commitments, and return to acting: Rule, interviewed by the authors.

272   "Women can't understand why most men . . . ": Quoted in Edith Keller, "3 Real Men Talk About Their Women," *Coronet,* November 1969.

272   "When you've been spoiled . . . ": Gazzara to Ann Guerin.

274   "That a woman doesn't have to be married . . . ": Penelope Russianoff, quoted in Judy Klemesrud, "Film Role Sends Therapist to Therapy," *The New York Times,* July 31, 1978.

274   "A lot of Freudian therapists attacked my direct approach . . . ": "What does a Woman Need? Not to Depend Upon a Man, Says Penelope Russianoff," *People,* September 17, 1982.

275   May Romm's address: "Women and Psychiatry," presented to the American Psychiatric Association, May 16, 1968.

275–278 Dr. Susan Forward on her career, actors, and media shrinks: Interview with the authors.

275–276 The telltale words: Dr. Susan Forward and Joan Torres, *Men Who Hate Women & the Women Who Love Them* (New York: Bantam, 1986).

276 "I couldn't be an actress . . . ": Betsy Drake, quoted in Hedda Hopper, "Betsy's Back and 'Lion's' Got Her," *Los Angeles Times*, January 3, 1965.

CHAPTER 12: THE MIRACLE WORKERS

279–280 Background on Newman, Berkowitz, and *How to Be Your Own Best Friend:* Susan Edmiston, "Celebrity Shrinks," *Esquire*, August 1977; Mildred Newman and Bernard Berkowitz with Jean Owen, *How to Be Your Own Best Friend* (New York: Random House, 1973).

280–281 Paula Prentiss's suicide attempt: Tom Burke, "Alexander Portnoy—This Is Your Wife!," *The New York Times*, December 5, 1971; Marshall Berges, "Interview with Paula Prentiss and Richard Benjamin," *Los Angeles Times*, May 20, 1979.

281 Richard Benjamin and Neil Simon: Dick Stelzer, *The Star Treatment* (Indianapolis: The Bobbs-Merrill Company, 1977.)

282–285 Anthony Perkins: Perkins, interviewed by the authors; Edmiston, "Celebrity Shrinks"; Brad Darrach, "Psycho II," *People*, June 13, 1983.

285 Rex Reed's therapy: Dick Stelzer, *The Star Treatment*.

285 Joel Schumacher: Schumacher, interviewed by the authors.

285–286 Mildred Newman's attitude toward homosexuality: Larry Kramer, James Kirkwood, and Joel Shumacher, interviewed by the authors; Newman and Berkowitz, *How to Be Your Own Best Friend*.

286 "It's like going to somebody's apartment . . . ": Rex Reed, quoted in Edmiston, "Celebrity Shrinks."

287 "They show up at every party . . . ": Larry Kramer to the authors.

287 "They're at all the parties . . . ": Arthur Laurents to the authors.

287 Liz Smith and Joel Schumacher: "Joel Schumacher, Showbiz Wiz by Liz (Smith of course)," *Andy Warhol's Interview*, September 1977.

287 Liz Smith's party: James Kirkwood, interviewed by the authors.

287–288 "They may be outrageous . . . ": Liz Smith to Susan Edmiston, "Celebrity Shrinks."

288 "I couldn't see how Mildred's enjoyment . . . ": Anthony Perkins to the authors.

288–289 Publication of *How to Be Your Own Best Friend:* Anthony Perkins and Nancy Hardin, interviewed by the authors; Edmiston, "Celebrity Shrinks."

290 Rex Reed and Dan Greenburg: Dick Stelzer, *The Star Treatment*.

290–291 Evelyn Silvers on her life and career: Interview with the authors.

291 "She offered a sense of laissez-faire . . . ": Dudley Moore to the authors.

291 "I used to joke with Evelyn . . . ": Jeff Melnick to the authors.

293 Theodore Roszak quoted in Kenneth L. Woodward, "Getting Your Head Together," *Newsweek*, September 6, 1976.

294–295 Background on Werner Erhard and est: Jesse Kornbluth, "Fuhrer over est," *New Times*, March 19, 1976; Leo Litwak, "Pay Attention, Turkeys!" *The New York Times Magazine*, May 2, 1976; Colin Campbell, "Salesmen of Serenity," *Psychology Today*, August 1976; Kenneth L. Woodward, "Super-Salesman of est," *Newsweek*, September 6, 1976.

295 "Most people who went into est . . . ": Tom Mankiewicz to the authors.

295–296 Milton Wexler on "VIP Seminar": Interview with the authors.

296 Colin Higgins on "a metaphor for individual growth . . . ": Quoted in John Stanley, "A New Happy Ending for a Wacky Comedy," *San Francisco Sunday Examiner and Chronicle*, February 18, 1979.

296–297 "I went to est for two weekends . . . ": Joel Schumacher to the authors.

297 Pauline Kael's review of *Car Wash: The New Yorker*, October 25, 1976.

297–298 Rob Cohen on *The Wiz*, Diana Ross's firing of her household staff: J. Randy Taraborrelli, *Call Her Miss Ross* (New York: Birch Lane Press; 1989).

298 Pauline Kael's review of *The Wiz: The New Yorker*, October 30, 1978.

298 "It offered instant results . . . ": Joel Schumacher to the authors.

299 Bert Convy on role in *Semi-Tough* and call from Valerie Harper: John M. Wilson, "Recollections of a Movie Guru," *Los Angeles Times*, January 25, 1978.

299–300 Valerie Harper on est and her relationship with Erhard: Harper, interviewed by the authors.

300 Man who attempted to breathe underwater: Leonard L. Glass, et al., "Psychiatric Disturbances Associated with Erhard Seminars Training," *American Journal of Psychiatry*, March 1977.

300 Erhard's troubles: David Gelman, "The Sorrows of Werner," *Newsweek*, February 18, 1991.

301–302 John-Roger and Insight: Bob Colacello, "The Social Rise of Insight," *Vanity Fair*, September 1986; Ariana Stassinopoulos, interview with John-Roger, *Interview*, April 1985; "Cult Leader John-Roger, Who Says He's Inhabited by a Divine Spirit, Stands Accused of a Campaign of Hate," *People*, September 26, 1988; Bob Sipchen, "Integrity Award Gala Is Canceled," *Los Angeles Times*, September 19, 1988.

302–304 Howard Rosenman on Hanley and Lifespring: Interview with the authors.

304–306 Marianne Williamson: Leslie Bennets, "Marianne's Faithful," *Vanity Fair*, June 1991; James Servin, "Bicoastal Guru Preaches Lots of Positive Thinking in the Pursuit of Miracles," *The New York Times*, February 19, 1992; Martha Smilgis, "Mother Teresa for the '90s?," *Time*, July 29, 1991; Terry Pristin, "The Power, the Glory, the Glitz," *Los Angeles Times*, February 16, 1992.

305 "For me the Course was a breakthrough experience . . . ": Marianne Williamson, *A Return to Love* (New York: HarperCollins, 1992.)

CHAPTER 13: THE FUTURE OF AN ILLUSION

307–309 Robert Redford and *Ordinary People:* Redford, interviewed by the authors; Philip Caputo, "Robert Redford Alone on the Range," *Esquire,* September 1992.

308 "The pessimism and sarcasm . . . ": Irving Schneider, "The Theory and Practice of Movie Psychiatry," *American Journal of Psychiatry,* August 1987.

310–311 John Bradshaw: Sally Ogle Davis, "Oh, Pablum!," *Los Angeles,* April 1992.

312 "unrealistic Dr. Wonderful stereotype . . . ": Dr. Harvey Greenberg, "Psychiatrists Analyze Dr. Lowenstein," *The New York Times,* January 19, 1992.

312–313 History of *One Flew Over the Cuckoo's Nest:* Stephen Farber and Marc Green, *Hollywood Dynasties* (New York: Putnam/Delilah, 1984).

313 "the legitimate questioning of analysis . . . ": Sidney Lumet to the authors.

313 "In the 1950s, people were all proud . . . ": Arthur Penn to the authors.

315 "there was scarcely any human problem . . . ": Leo Stone, *The Psychoanalytic Situation* (New York: International Universities Press, 1961).

315 "The bloom is off the rose now with analysis . . . ": Tom Mankiewicz to the authors.

316 "When you see how unsuccessfully the shrinks . . . ": Christopher Mankiewicz to the authors.

316 "Long-term supportive therapy is parasitic . . . ": Frances Lear to the authors.

317 "She was seventeen years old . . . ": Robert Walker, Jr., to the authors.

INDEX

Abraham, Karl, 32, 163
Academy Awards, 22, 43, 85, 138, 147, 159, 161, 163, 212, 219, 221, 251, 308, 312, 314
"Actor's Identity Crises, The" (Rule), 263, 268–269
Actors Studio, 96, 145–147, 149, 154, 156, 264, 266, 273
Adams, Edie, 129
Adler, Alfred, 22, 87, 274
Adler, Stella, 69, 144, 171
alcoholism, 61, 64, 68, 81, 93–94, 157, 177
Alexander, Franz, 25, 32, 63, 125
Alex in Wonderland, 191
Alice's Restaurant, 164–165
Alien, 273
All About Eve, 73–74, 97, 273
Allen, Jay Presson, 153, 155–156, 205
Allen, Woody, 176, 186–197, 280, 309, 316
Alpert, Hollis, 111
Alsop, Carleton, 62
Altman, Robert, 231, 271
Altoon, John, 219
America America (Kazan), 151–152
American Journal of Psychiatry, 181, 300, 308–309
American Psychiatric Association (APA), 16, 17, 65, 138–139, 200, 216, 225, 275
American Psychoanalytic Association, 30, 64, 65, 121, 128, 202, 205, 206, 236, 270
"Analysis of the Rich, the Famous and the Influential" (Wahl), 18

"Analysis Terminable and Interminable" (Freud), 316
"Analyst's Couch, The," 200
Andrews, Julie, 13, 15, 215, 232–236, 238
Annals of the American Society for Adolescent Psychiatry, 174
Annie Hall, 184, 189, 193, 197
Another Woman, 190, 191
Anspach, Susan, 180
Arica, 293
Arkoff, Samuel Z., 252
Aronson, Gerald, 232–233, 282–283
Arrangement, The (Kazan), 151–152
Art and Technique of Analytic Group Therapy, The (Grotjahn), 121
Ashley, Ted, 232, 256, 295
Asphalt Jungle, The, 84
Assagioli, Roberto, 293
Astaire, Fred, 36, 223
Atkinson, Brooks, 290
Attias, Jane, 217
Avildsen, John, 259

Bacall, Lauren, 148, 161
Badham, John, 297
Bad Timing, 314
Balanchine, George, 29, 264
Bananas, 190
Bancroft, Anne, 146–148, 163
Barish, Samoan, 270
Barrow, Clyde, 165–166
Bartemeier, Leo H., 59
Basic Instinct, 314
Baum, L. Frank, 297
Baum, Thomas, 259